# THE MIDDLE EAST AND BRAZIL

Public Cultures of the Middle East and North Africa
*Paul A. Silverstein, Susan Slyomovics, and Ted Swedenburg, editors*

# THE MIDDLE EAST AND BRAZIL

*Perspectives on the New Global South*

EDITED BY PAUL AMAR

Indiana University Press
*Bloomington & Indianapolis*

*This book is a publication of*

INDIANA UNIVERSITY PRESS
Office of Scholarly Publishing
Herman B Wells Library 350
1320 East 10th Street
Bloomington, Indiana 47405 USA

iupress.indiana.edu

*Telephone orders* 800-842-6796
*Fax orders* 812-855-7931

♾ The paper used in this publication meets the minimum requirements
of the American National Standard for Information Sciences—Permanence of Paper for Printed Library Materials, ANSI Z39.48–1992.

*Manufactured in the United States of America*

*Cataloging information is available from the Library of Congress*

The Middle East and Brazil : perspectives on the new global south / edited
by Paul Amar.
     pages cm. — (Public cultures of the Middle East and North Africa)
   ISBN 978-0-253-01223-4 (cl) — ISBN 978-0-253-01227-2 (pb) — ISBN 978-0-
253-01496-2 (eb) 1. Middle East—Relations—Brazil. 2. Brazil—Relations
—Middle East. 3. Muslims—Brazil—History. 4. Muslims—Brazil—Ethnic
identity. 5. Brazil—Ethnic relations—History. 6. Transnationalism—
Social aspects—Brazil. 7. Transnationalism—Political aspects—Brazil.
8. Transnationalism in literature. 9. Brazilian literature. I. Amar, Paul
(Paul Edouard), 1968- author, editor of compilation.
  DS63.2.B6M54 2014
  303.48'281056—dc23
                                                            2014017132

1  2  3  4  5    19  18  17   16  15  14

# Contents

## Part Three.  Literature and Transregional Media Cultures

# Acknowledgments

This collective, transregional, and transdisciplinary conversation began under the best of conditions thanks to the intelligence, vision, and hospitality of Paulo Gabriel Hilu da Rocha Pinto, professor of anthropology at the Federal University Fluminense in Rio de Janeiro, with whom I founded the Center for Middle East Studies in 2003. I thank him for his continued leadership in these areas, for his support to this team of scholars in the years since, and for his friendship. For the production of this ambitious volume itself, I would like to thank Paul A. Silverstein, Susan Slyomovics, and Ted Swedenburg, the editors of this special series at Indiana University Press, Public Cultures of the Middle East and North Africa, for moving beyond traditional approaches to the region, and embracing the new world of histories, cultures, politics, and methods we offer. Also, I would like to thank Indiana University Press Sponsoring Editor Rebecca Tolen for her enthusiasm and all her hard work that made this book a reality. And I would like to convey my gratitude to the anonymous reviewers and the members of the editorial board whose insights and suggestions improved each of these chapters, and refined the profile of this book.

Most of all, I would like to thank Silvia Ferreira, whose research and production assistance during the last two years has been truly incredible. Her intelligence, patience, language skills, and organizational capacity—not to mention her cutting-edge grasp of the scholarly issues and familiarity with the communities embraced by this project—have ensured the high quality of this volume.

# THE MIDDLE EAST
## AND BRAZIL

# Introduction

*Paul Amar*

What lies behind Brazil's new affiliations with the Middle East, and South America's attempts to unite, economically and politically, with the Arab League in order to counterbalance U.S. and Global North hegemony? How can we explain the sudden explosion of visibility and creativity among Brazil's approximately sixteen million citizens who are descendants of Syrio-Lebanese and other Arab migrants or who are practicing Muslims? From where erupted this wave of interest among Arab leaders and Middle Eastern social movements who are looking to Brazil as a model for democracy and a beacon for Global South leadership? Which histories, literatures, and cultures have provided the foundation for these new forms of transnational imagination and solidarity?

This book appears at a time in which shifting global orderings and ties between continental regions of the Global South and East are being reconfigured around newly visible, large-scale processes and shifting flows of power, imagination, and activism. This is an era in which Brazil is increasingly asserting itself on the world stage, hosting the World Cup (2014) and the Olympic Games (2016), serving as bridge builder between emergent regions of the Global South, and striving diplomatically to rival the old North Atlantic–centered geopolitical models. And Brazil is reaching out commercially and culturally to the Middle East, often through the initiatives of merchants, culture makers, and entrepreneurs descended from Arab migrants who have been integrated in the Americas for generations. This is also an era in which Middle Eastern leaders and peoples, with unprecedented enthusiasm, are reaching out to Brazil as a trade partner that can help counterbalance the old economic dominance of the West or provide alternatives to the intensifying presence of China. Also, the peoples of Turkey, Iran, and in particular the countries that have recently been

1

transformed by the uprisings of the "Arab Spring" are also turning their gaze toward South America. In this context, Brazil offers new models of democratization, demilitarization, and global solidarity that appeal (often in idealized forms) to changing polities in the Middle East that are striving to break free of an age of West-supported dictatorships, anti-terrorism campaigns, and devastating wars and occupations.

But when did this sudden wave of new connections appear on the international agenda and trigger the interest of scholars, social movements, and policymakers?

**Changing Worlds**

In December 2003, Brazil's then recently inaugurated president Luiz Inácio Lula da Silva found himself backed into a corner. He was facing the challenges of stabilizing his government in an atmosphere of domestic and international crisis: narcotrafficking and paramilitary violence exploding at home and in neighboring Colombia; revolutions sweeping through Venezuela and Bolivia; U.S. wars in Iraq and Afghanistan overturning diplomatic alliances and rocking Brazil's commercial prospects and investor contracts in the region; global security experts naming Brazil as a harbor for new kinds of terrorism; and international bankers attacking the credibility of Lula's government and Brazil's economy. Yet in the midst of these challenges, Lula made a surprising move: he flew to the Middle East.

During his visit to Libya, Lebanon, Egypt, and Dubai in 2003, President Lula launched a series of high-level negotiations that continued to evolve over the decade, aiming to economically, culturally, and geopolitically integrate the nations of the South American Common Market (Mercosur, which unites Brazil, Argentina, Uruguay, Paraguay, and now Venezuela) with the countries of the Arab League. These negotiations also aimed to establish new cultural, educational, and security cooperation between Brazil and the Middle East. Brazil went to the Middle East—as wars raged and U.S. legitimacy in the region crumbled—with the explicit aim of linking the Arab world directly with South America, offering both regions a way out of their troubling dependence on the U.S. and Europe. Lula opened up a new front in South-South relations that may eventually prove to mark the initiation of a historic shift in world power, as well as a dramatic rearrangement of economic, cultural, and security alliances. But very few could imagine why or how this process had been launched in the first place.

The international press did not know what to make of this set of visits and proposals. Was the Non-Aligned Movement being reborn as a protest against U.S. president George W. Bush's wars? What does Brazil have to do with the Middle East anyway? Why would Brazil want to plunge into such a troubled region when it has its own security and economic problems? And why did Brazil's masses as well as its political elites react so positively, applauding President Lula's courage for reaching out to the Middle East? Analysts of international relations, Latin American society, culture, and politics were surprised by this visit and could not grasp its context or motivations because they have long ignored Brazil's significant connections to the Middle East, the presence of Middle Eastern peoples and cultures in the country, and the existence of significant economic and strategic parallels between the two.

Further blocking understanding of Brazil-Mideast connections were the rigidities of much previous research on these kinds of relationships and misguided assumptions within the broader public sphere itself. In the field of international relations, scholarly interest on Brazil as the twenty-first century began was concerned first with the country's dependence on and interaction with dominant North American and European powers. Secondly, research had focused on the country's sometimes tense relationships with its neighbors within South America, including Argentina, Uruguay, and Paraguay. A third set of more interesting, interdisciplinary conversations had emerged among scholars interested in Brazil's relations with Lusophone Africa and insertion within the African diaspora. But "realist" scholars of geopolitics had largely overlooked the strategic, historic, and security interests that the Middle East and Brazil share. Similarly, and under the sway of their international relations colleagues, many journalists and social science scholars had largely ignored spaces of transregionalism. Migration specialists had only recently become interested in the huge Arab ethnic minority population in Brazil, thanks to the groundbreaking work of Jeffrey Lesser and John Tofik Karam, among others (Lesser 1999, 2013; Karam 2007). And students of transnational cultural politics, migration and diasporas, and Global South geopolitics had tended to focus on the legacies of colonialism and the dominance of transnational corporations; until the early 2000s, they had largely overlooked the emergence of alternative South-South ties that did not reflect the geographies of European colonial or U.S. corporate power.

But the Middle East is in Brazil, and Brazil is linking up with the Arab and Muslim worlds. These exciting and propitious developments merit thorough analysis.

## Mideast Peoples in Brazil

The Middle East is demographically and historically present in Brazil. The country includes a population of at least eight million descendants of Syrian-Lebanese migrants, who are widely dispersed throughout the country and represent one of the most politically and economically successful ethnic groups or immigrant communities. Gilberto Kassab and Fernando Haddad, the last two mayors of Brazil's largest and wealthiest city, São Paulo, are of Syrian-Lebanese origin, as were several members of President Dilma Rousseff's first cabinet. Brazil's population also includes a large group of Arabic-speaking Sephardic Jews, as well as significant migrant groups from Egypt, Morocco, and Muslim Africa. Brazil has a Muslim population topping one million, with conversion rates accelerating, especially among the country's white middle classes. One of Brazil's most significant revolts was led by the Malê Afro-Brazilian Muslim movement in Salvador de Bahia, in the nineteenth century. Another sociopolitical phenomenon that allows for comparison and connection between Brazil and the Middle East is that today many municipalities and state governments in Brazil are controlled by evangelical, conservative Christian popular religious movements which draw from social-class bases and operate through moralistic ideologies, "family protection" projects, pro-business politics, and community charity structures that, although not Islamic, seem remarkably similar to Muslim Brotherhood organizations in Egypt or Islamist "welfare and development" programs in Turkey.

In the diplomatic sphere, Brazil has established a bold diplomatic record of linking anti-racist and anti-colonial activism with expressions of solidarity with the Middle East, specifically in 1970s debates on Zionism, and in the United Nations World Conference against Racism in 2001. Brazilian diplomats have mediated East Timor peace diplomacy, achieving success in negotiations with the world's largest Muslim country, Indonesia. And Brazilian peacemaker Sérgio Vieira de Mello died at the helm of the UN Humanitarian Mission in Iraq. Closer to home, Brazil's border with Paraguay has been spotlighted by U.S. security "experts" who claim that the region has become a breeding ground for Lebanese "terrorists and pirates" selling counterfeit goods and training militants for violence. Economically, Brazil has an increasingly Mideastern profile. Its Syrian-Lebanese merchant and financial elites are well placed in São Paulo's and Rio de Janeiro's economies. Brazil's public-sector infrastructure companies and fossil fuel exploration firms have signed many billion-dollar contracts in Libya, Egypt, Saudi Arabia, the United Arab Emirates, and Iraq; Brazilian airplane and car manufacturers have established joint ventures with military companies and states in the Arab world; and Brazil has become a major exporter of essential food products to the Persian Gulf region and the Levant. In addition, Brazil is becoming a major oil producer on its own: it became a net exporter of petroleum in 2004, bringing it to the attention of the Organization of the Petroleum-Exporting Countries (OPEC).

In the realm of mass culture Brazil remains fascinated by, even enamored with, the Middle East. Brazil has linked its homegrown Tropicalism with a wave of pop Orientalism, portraying the Arab world as a land of rebels and passion, a kind of idealized and exoticized self-image. In Rio de Janeiro, Copacabana features "Árabe," a restaurant in an Alhambra-styled beach palace featuring Lebanese cuisine; a new gay dance club is called "Egypt" and features drag queen genies and Cleopatras; DJ Saddam runs a popular electronica parties for middle-class club kids; people lose weight learning a very Brazilian kind of belly-dancing aerobics; and the most popular prime-time television spectacle of the 2000s was a telenovela called *O Clone,* about conflict and romance between families, one in Morocco, the other in Rio de Janeiro. The historical foundations for the eruption of Orientalist popular culture in today's Brazil are explored in this volume in the chapter by Ella Shohat and Robert Stam; and the hugely popular telenovela is analyzed in detail in the chapter by Silvia Montenegro.

## New Generations of Networked Scholarship

In this rapidly changing twenty-first-century context, this groundbreaking collection represents the product of a global network of scholars who have been working over the last decade to challenge paradigms of area studies, advocate fresh methods for the analysis of transregional public cultures, and illuminate novel Global South–based perspectives on international relations. Many of the scholars included in this volume were first brought together in 2003, at a major conference at the Federal University Fluminense (UFF, in Niteroi, Rio de Janeiro), hosted by Paul Amar and Paulo Gabriel Pinto on the occasion of their founding of the Center for Middle East Studies at UFF. This conference coincided with the visit of President Lula to the Middle East and the Arab League in 2003, which would lead eventually to the signing of the Brasília Declaration (ASPA 2005) by a number of heads of state from the Middle East and the Americas on May 11, 2005. This declaration launched the South America–Arab States bloc (ASPA), dedicated to commercial, diplomatic, and cultural exchange, coordination, and solidarity between the two emergent world regions.

Participating in this 2003 conference hosted by Amar and Pinto were more than twenty-five scholars from Arab countries, the United States, Brazil, and Europe, coming from disciplines as diverse as anthropology, comparative literature, history, cultural studies, and political science; participants' primary languages included Arabic, Spanish, Portuguese, English, French, and Farsi. Despite its linguistic and disciplinary differences, this group managed to communicate with remarkable dynamism, and to come together around a collective objective: to launch a new commitment to transregional studies and to draw a new intellectual map of the changing world that could capture new strata of power and centers for innovation, tracking shifts from the Global North to the Global South. In the years that followed, we in this network kept apace of the exciting evolutions and controversies that marked the rapid maturation of cultural, geopolitical, migration, media, and commercial intersections in this transregional sphere of action. And we enhanced our network and deepened a set of institutional links.

UFF continued to serve as a key hub, as its Center for Middle East Studies there grew to be a high-profile site for public engagement and reflection in Brazil around transregional issues during the government of President Lula. Subsequently, Paul Amar hosted (at the American University in Cairo, at Cairo University, and at the Arab Council of the Social Sciences in Beirut) meetings with scholars based in the Arab region who were turning with great interest toward Latin America. These Arab, Berber, Nubian, Arab-American, and Arab-European scholars were breaking with the long tradition of researching mostly the cultures and politics of former colonial powers and were challenging the tendency to exclusively engage models of scholarship coming from the Global North when doing comparative, transnational, and international studies. Thanks to two members of this network, Camila Pastor and Ella Shohat, the University of California, Los Angeles, and New York University held meetings on Latin America–Middle East transregional studies, enriching these conversations. And John Tofik Karam at DePaul University, Jeffrey Lesser at Emory University, and María del Mar Logroño Narbona at Florida International University hosted productive workshops. In addition, Camila Pastor and Marta Tawil Kuri, at el Colégio de Mexico, welcomed many of this volume's contributors to that country during Mexico City's annual Semana Arabe, fostering vivid exchanges and deepening our network's breadth beyond the South American southern cone. Finally, the University of California, Santa Barbara's Center for Middle East Studies and Center for Global Studies generously hosted two international conferences, where the framework for this volume was finalized and where the latest developments in this transregional

sphere of inquiry were identified. As a product of these gatherings and collaborations, this volume thus represents three exciting phenomena: the maturation
of a new field of transregional study, the crystallization of a new generation
of transdiciplinary and transnational scholarship, and the boldness of a new
set of institutions and research centers that had the vision and courage to support this group and these processes.

**Engaging Conversations and Literatures**

The global scholarly network produced by this decade-long process has participated consistently in a particular set of debates and academic conversations,
although the full diversity of the literatures engaged by the contributors to
this volume is too vast and varied to detail fully here. Rather than doing an
extensive literature review here or a bibliographic essay—since individual
chapters will present their own intellectual antecedents and references—below I will focus on producing an overall map of key conversations, general
insights, and intervention trajectories. Among our most consistent commitments has been advocating new approaches to the fields of cultural studies
and American studies. The more critical and progressive branches of these
fields, with which many of us identify, have tended to focus productively on
U.S. imperialism and globalization as Americanization, often with racialized,
ethnicized, and sexualized "diasporas" situated as primary victims as well
as vehicles for contradictory processes of imperial consolidation, cultural
hegemony, and biopolitical violence. In order to push these debates forward,
we insist that critiques of imperialism and coloniality, historically as well as
in the current moment, can take account of ethnicity, sexuality, migration,
and power *without* overstating or rendering monolithic the U.S. state, without
giving undue centrality to the relatively privileged diaspora groups based in
North America, and without narrowing the space and subject of "America"
(often mis-synonymized with the United States). Imperialism, of course,
does persist, even in a world of Global South ascendance. Indeed, U.S. wars,
economic leveraging, and strategic interests impact the Middle East and
South America on every level. But other Global South players are becoming
increasingly relevant and influential in the Middle East and South America in
terms of shaping both reactionary and progressive trends. China is the largest
investor; Russia is a major arms and energy contractor; Korean, Indian, and
Greek labor union activists are linking up with their fellow workers in the
Middle East; Persian Gulf states Qatar and Saudi Arabia fund political parties
and media outlets from Iraq to Tunisia, and support religious charities and

invest in enterprises across South America. And in looking to the Americas, critical cultural studies work needs to also recognize that the United States is no longer the only assertive, multicultural, immigrant-rich "empire" in the Western Hemisphere. Uncle Sam now faces a rival emerging empire in the "tropics" in the form of Brazil.

Another set of conversations and literatures with which this collection engages is those around the political sociology and literary history of migration. Our work configures the subjects of migration and migrancy though distinct frames. We trace patterns of employment and economic insertion, tensions around ethnic identification, racialization, and assimilation within the nation, and the backflow of migrants and ideas to lands of origin. But our contributors also radically redefine the subject of migrancy. We see migration not just as a central, constitutive global public sphere that operates between cultures or between "minority" subgroups, but as a formation of public spheres and global imaginations that overarches and constitutes planetary power blocs and large-scale cultures, as described richly in the chapters here by Shohat and Stam, María del Mar Logroño Narbona, Armando Vargas, and John Tofik Karam.

Finally, our group challenges both the state-centric literature of the field of international relations, as well as the simplistic economic-market focus of some of the new global studies work on emerging powers and the "BRICS" (the bloc that links Brazil, Russia, India, China, and South Africa). Instead of compiling charts of foreign-investment patterns or monitoring economic growth rates in "emergent" polities, we focus on the production of new regimes of international identification at the level of the popular, and new imaginations of political action at the intergovernmental level. And we also provide vivid evidence to support recent shifts in transnational studies and globalization studies. Since the early 2000s, globalization studies has distanced itself from one of its founding hypotheses—that intensifying transnational communications and border-crossing flows of commerce and culture would diminish the sovereignty of nation-state governments. Instead, several of our contributors demonstrate here that new kinds of Global South geopolitical transregionalism, and the recent reactivation of transnational migration as well as cultural and commercial flows between the Middle East and Brazil, have provided opportunities for Brazil and for certain Arab states to assert new kinds of autonomy and to expand influence, although always in the fraught context of North Atlantic powers struggling to hold on to global hegemony as BRICS powers and others move into new positions of leverage.

**Insights for Readers**

This volume is designed to be read by students of globalization, teachers of world civilizations, area studies specialists of Latin America or the Middle East, analysts of the reconfiguration of U.S. geopolitics, and theorists of postcolonial regimes and identities. We also reach out to the general public spellbound by Brazil's Olympic ascendance or by the eruptions of the Arab Spring. For these publics, the rediscoveries we present here will render today's world more comprehensible, as well as raise critical questions for further inquiry. And for those who have become jaded or unconvinced by clichéd mentions of "emerging powers" or "BRICS," this book offers a much more satisfying and thorough intervention. We explore in depth one of the most crucial axes of emerging new South-South alliances, and witness the revival of forgotten histories and repressed identities that are now being reborn through the articulation of a kind of "alternative globalization."

This volume, and the network of scholars behind it, aim to convey a specific set of teachable insights and to propose a fresh set of intellectual interventions. The contributors gathered here develop three types of argument, around *origins, actors,* and *paradigms.*

1. *Origins.* We argue that transregional relations between the Middle East and Brazil began not with the twenty-first-century initiatives, not with President Lula's efforts to find a Global South counterbalance to U.S. hegemony, but more than two centuries ago, and have matured through a long history of transnational cultural struggles, migration histories, and battles around race/ethnicity, gender/sexuality, and the state.

2. *Actors.* We demonstrate that particular migration-based communities and transnationally embedded interest groups have driven the reshaping of modern cultural and political relations between these two Global South blocs. These actors have initiated experiments around Third Worldism and Global South assertion that have followed certain consistent ideological stances, animated certain genres of representation and narratives, and empowered certain public-cultural tropes and controversies.

3. *Paradigms.* And we prove that new scholarly methods and paradigms can be articulated in order to better appreciate these revived histories, social and cultural flows, and geostrategic alliances in their complexity and uniqueness.

As we examine the deeper history of Brazil-Mideast links, we reveal that connectivity between the Middle East and Brazil did not begin with President Lula's handshakes with Arab leaders in 2003, but represented the revitalization of long-standing processes of transnational public spheres built by migrants, assertions of Third World solidarity, patterns of commercial exchanges, and deeply affective globalizing literary and media imaginations. Giving historical context to these connections, in this volume we illuminate the long-term linkages between religious cultures and emancipation struggles that united Muslim Afro-Brazilians and the peoples of North and West Africa, dating back to the early 1800s, as José Cairus and Paulo Farah build on the work of João José Reis (1993). Looking to literary and ethnographic narratives, Alexandra Isfahani-Hammond and Silvia Ferreira in their chapters identify certain dominant social practices, imaginaries, and generic embodiments of race and sexuality that draw originally from the Arab and Moorish Middle East during the time of the *reconquista* and the Inquisition. These tropes animated the ruling ideologies and normalizing narratives that dominated plantation life in nineteenth-century Brazil and that continue to haunt Latin American racial and gender hierarchies in the contemporary period. And as Fernando Rabossi and Paulo Farah underline, these old plantation-era notions propel newly repressive forms of anti-terrorism attitudes and security strategies too. Silvia Ferreira's notion of a "genre triangle" structure for Brazilian literature, from "*Turco* peddlers, to Brazilian plantationists, to transnational Arabs," gives the reader a useful tool for understanding the broader patterns of evolving transregional identity. Ferreira argues that from Brazil's perspective, transregional identifications evolved through a three-stage process: these connections began as Ottoman-era migration patterns that subsisted, at first, on supporting petty commerce between the two regions and urban vendor networks within Brazil; Middle Eastern identities in Brazil then passed through a phase of intensive racialization as some Arab Brazilians became cleansed of their ethnic otherness and were "nationalized," reidentified as iconic plantation masters just as black Muslim Brazilians became the most successful and "menacing" anti-slavery organizers in the country's northeast; and then, as the twentieth century ended, a notion of a "Global Arab" identity reasserted itself, pushed from below by Arab-Brazilian communities and merchants lobbying for recognition and access to international markets, as well as from above by states and leaders that wanted to foster partnerships between South America and Middle East states on a variety of levels.

Our insights also include our identification of key actors and political conjunctures that have pushed or facilitated this new wave of transregional relations. In this vein, our contributors offer a profound rescripting of the story of how patterns of migration intersect with the dramas of international politics in the twentieth century. And our contributors identify the particular ethnicized communities, social roles, and political agendas that gave life to the Arab-Brazilian world during times of settlement, decolonization, empire, and modernization. Paulo Gabriel Pinto explores the complexity of religious and ethnic identities among Muslim Brazilians, particularly in Rio de Janeiro, revealing a diversity of practices of conversion, affiliation, and transnational connection. These migrant practices and cultures were brought together as well as separated by specific practices of imposed ethnic identification by the state as well as by cross-regional flows of cultural commodities and commercial relationships. In this volume, Neiva da Cunha and Pedro de Mello explore the contemporary Arab commercial community in the downtown market of the Saara (often pronounced in Brazil just like the word "Sahara" to maximize its Orientalist sense of mystery), where new ethnicized solidarities and rivalries have emerged between Arab-Brazilians and Chinese and Korean migrant groups, as well as in the context of urban social-cleansing operations and city modernization campaigns that seek both to discipline the area and to exploit its sense of exoticism. Paulo Farah brings us into the age of ASPA, mapping new Brazilian institutions that since 2005 have enabled unprecedented levels of cultural and scholarly exchange and educational partnership with, and artistic celebration of, the Arab world. And he profiles other institutions, like the Arab Chamber of Commerce in São Paulo, that have succeeded in revitalizing commercial exchanges between the regions. Farah's chapter also sets these exchange institutions into historical context, seeing them as the linear descendants of Afro-Muslim protagonism in Brazil's northeast during the anti-slavery era, as well as of the efforts of Syrian-Lebanese street-peddlers-turned-wealthy-businessmen in the megacity of São Paulo during the last century.

This volume also offers a number of insights that promise to reshape mainstream views on the political sociology of transregional solidarity and the international relations between regional blocs within the former Third World. Carlos Ribeiro Santana brings us back to the 1970s era of the OPEC "oil shock," when Brazil moved rapidly to strengthen its relations with Iraq and Saudi Arabia. These alliances led Brazil to develop a strong and broad-based trade pattern with the Gulf region, but also, after 2003, to come into conflict with U.S. neoconservative aims in the region. Monique Sochaczewski brings us into the debates in the United Nations in the 1970s and 1980s when Brazil adopted certain positions that put it on a collision course with Israel and the United States, and where it established the foundations for what it called more "pragmatic" and "non-aligned" stances, serving as the seed for today's transregional order and its distinction from the agenda of the North Atlantic community. Fernando Rabossi, working on very recent events that also reso-nate with North-South rivalry, brings us to the dynamic commercial hub and security "hot spot" of the Tri-Border Region in the Brazilian southern state of Paraná, at the border with Argentina and Paraguay. In the 2000s, this region became the world's largest hydroelectric power-generation hub and a key site of pipelines for natural gas. This region has served historically as the host for a well-established Syrian-Lebanese business community. But it is also a new home for thousands of recent migrants from Lebanon of Shi'a origin, whom the United States has accused of being at the center of "pirate networks" that ship and sell contraband and knock-off products across these borders; and the United States also accuses some of these merchant populations of including activists that are importing "terrorism" from their compatriots in the militant Lebanese movement Hezballah. This Tri-Border Region has thus become a window for the reassertion of U.S. security meddling in the heart of South America, and for the "Mideastification" of Brazil's border. Looking at the most recent period, from 2010 to 2013, Paul Amar brings us into the post-Lula era, and traces the bold stances of Lula's successor, President Dilma Rousseff. Rousseff has stood up firmly against U.S. war-mongering and sanctions in the Middle East as well as U.S. militarization in the Tri-Border Region in South America. Amar demonstrates how Rousseff backed away from some of the personalism that had brought Lula close to controversial figures such as Gad-dafi in Libya or Ahmadinejad in Iran; and President Rousseff launched a series of multilateral diplomatic initiatives as well as social-democratic agendas that better positioned Brazil to boost progressive elements in the Middle East facing counterrevolutionary backlash in Arab Spring countries.

In terms of our third set of insights around the assertion of new scholarly paradigms, this volume presents a model for academic collaboration and methodological innovation. We build on the best traditions of area studies and of disciplinary trainings; but we liberate ourselves from tendencies toward overspecialization in one region or fealty to any one methodology for produc-ing evidence. For example, each of us here has been fully trained in more than one area studies field. We are fluent in multiple languages; we have expertise as archival researchers; and we know the histories, terminologies, contexts, and literatures that are the hallmark of our profession. Yet we have all been enriched by the challenges and inspirations that come not just from taking on another area of specialization (Arabists understanding South America or Brazilianists probing the Levant, for example), but by our growing appreciation for how the categories and identities at the foundation of our research traditions have been formed within relations of power that flow between Global South regions, popular cultures, political diplomacies, and communities of socialization. We have discovered, for example, new ways for mapping the histories, narratives, embodiments, and politics of Orientalism. Orientalism, as vividly analyzed most notably in the work of Edward Said ([1979] 1994), is the set of discourses, practices, imaginaries, and structures dating back to the colonial period that deeply inform race, gender, sexuality, national and sectarian identities, and forms of authority over and among Middle Eastern peoples. In new ways, we illuminate here how Tropicalism in Brazil and throughout the Americas in its colonial, imperial, slavery-age, and samba-age forms, as well as its contemporary neoliberal and pop-cultural forms, has always traveled across what Ella Shohat and Robert Stam call the "Moorish Atlantic" to draw upon and influence the fears, desires, social norms, and regimes of rule that characterize Orientalism in the Middle East. These mutual co-constitutions of Orientalism and Tropicalism manifest themselves in literature, as described here by Daniela Birman and Armando Vargas, as well as in contemporary tourism marketing strategies, as analyzed by John Tofik Karam. Our interventions also reveal the utility of interdisciplinary work not just within social scientific disciplines, but between social sciences and humanities. Waïl Hassan's analysis of literary narratives of South-South dialogue, or Armando Vargas's cultural history of discourses of homeland and migrancy come to resonate with the geopolitical language of the Brazilian state as analyzed by political scientists within this volume. Silvia Montenegro's vivid account of the sexualization of Islam, and the "culture wars" that erupted around the telenovela *O Clone* (broadcast in 2001–2002 by the Globo network and depicting romances and struggles within and between two families, one in Rio, Brazil, and another in Fez and Marrakesh, Morocco) allows us to see the political sociology of ethnic migrant lobbying within Brazil differently, as well as serving as a new angle for Brazilian cultural critique of the ideologies and fetish-subjects that dominated the news during the time of the U.S. war on terror and subsequent war in Iraq. Similarly, the chapters by John Tofik Karam and María del Mar Logroño Narbona map out a new transnational geography, providing new starting points for transregional paradigms that reflect a sphere of intellectual and public-cultural consciousness and production that is always, already transcontinental, co-constituted by its vernacular cosmopolitan populations and markets, authors and readers, entrepreneurs and consumers.

In the end, our scholarly intervention does not just bring two fields to meet. We do not just encourage Middle Eastern and Latin American perspectives to migrate. We want to do more than integrate pan-American cultural studies and postcolonial studies. Instead, we generate new paradigms that are necessarily transdisciplinary and global, selecting distinct units of analysis and operating on other scales of vision inspired by the changing universe we engage.

## References

ASPA (Cúpula América do Sol–Países Arabes). 2005. Summit of South American–Arab Countries, 10–11 May. http://www.scribd.com/doc/51312638/DECLARACAO-DE -BRASILIA-ASPA, accessed 9 March 2013.

Karam, John Tofik. 2007. *Another Arabesque: Syrian-Lebanese Ethnicity in Neoliberal Brazil*. Philadelphia: Temple University Press.

Lesser, Jeffrey. 1999. *Negotiating National Identity: Immigrants Minorities, and the Struggle for Ethnicity in Brazil*. Durham, NC: Duke University Press.

———. 2013. *Immigration, Ethnicity, and National Identity in Brazil, 1808 to the Present*. Cambridge: Cambridge University Press.

Reis, João José. 1993. *The Muslim Uprising of 1835 in Bahia*. Translated by Arthur Brakel. Baltimore: Johns Hopkins University Press. Originally published in 1986 as *Rebelião escrava no Brasil: A história do levanter dos males, 1835*. São Paulo: Editora Brasiliense.

Said, Edward. (1979) 1994. *Orientalism*. New York: Vintage Books.

# Part One. South-South Relations, Security Politics, Diplomatic History

# 1

# The Middle East and Brazil
## Transregional Politics in the Dilma Rousseff Era

*Paul Amar*

This chapter traces the changes in transregional and geopolitical relationships between Brazil and the Middle East during the first two years of the government of Brazil's first woman president, Dilma Rousseff. Between the end of 2010 and the start of 2013, Rousseff's administration faced escalating tensions with the United States over relations with Iran, military intervention in Libya and Syria, and manufactured "crises" over Hezballah militants in Brazil's southern border regions. This period also witnessed the epochal transformations of the Arab Spring, and the emergence of new kinds of solidarity between state actors and social movements in the Arab region and Syrian-Lebanese diaspora groups within Brazil. In this study, Amar identifies some of the major causes of Brazil's shifts during this period, from politics of personalism to commercial and geopolitical pragmatism, and from "handshake politics" between Third Worldist leaders to a more liberal advocacy of human rights, gender justice, and democratization. He also analyzes some of the surprisingly counterhegemonic stances President Dilma took vis-à-vis the Middle East which challenged the U.S.-dominated global order during this period.

⁓

Dilma Rousseff, Brazil's first woman president, was elected to office on October 31, 2010, on the eve of the eruption of mass uprisings in Tunisia and Egypt that would captivate Brazil and the rest of the world, and that would demand radical transformations in relationships between emerging Global South countries and Arab governments. Would these surging movements and regime changes in the Arab region, combined with Rousseff's[1] commitment to promote women's empowerment and tackle cronyism and corruption, fundamentally alter the eight-year-old framework of South American–Arab solidarity that her predecessor, President Luiz Inácio Lula da Silva ("Lula"), had initiated? This transregional pact had been built as a top-down arrangement based on handshakes between Lula, who enjoyed a popular democratic mandate, and a few aging dictators who had long dominated the region. But now those Middle Eastern leaders were toppling, one after the other.

With her inauguration on January 1, 2011, Dilma immediately faced a vast array of challenges to her ambition to reframe, relegitimize, and deepen a set of transregional solidarities between her country and the Middle East region. Previously, during Lula's eight-year term, Brazil had been instrumental in forming a diplomatic bloc, ASPA (the Summit of South America–Arab States), that had become a key instrument of South-South economic and cultural cooperation and an incubator for cultivating geopolitical resistance to what Brazilians refer to as the "paternalistic mediation" of northern and western governments in the affairs of the Global South or the postcolonial East. In 2003, as part of the launching of the ASPA project, Brazil had even joined the Arab League, granted observer status (Ezzat 2003). Since 2003, trade between Brazil and the Arab region had boomed, especially with Saudi Arabia (Câmara Árabe TV) and other countries of the Arabian Peninsula. Also, the ASPA framework had fostered a myriad of cultural and educational exchange agreements. Under President Lula, Brazil had asserted itself as a leader of emerging Global South powers and an articulator of new forms of South-South cooperation. But while doing so, Brazil walked a fine line between two conflicting aspirations.

On the one hand, Brazil wanted to convince northern powers, particularly the United States and Europe, that South America's superpower was ready to provide "mature" world leadership and would act as a stabilizing force in global affairs. By impressing northern powers, Brazil aimed to prove itself worthy of being named the sixth permanent member of the United Nations Security Council (Amar 2013a; Nieto 2013). On the other hand, by reaching out to the Middle East in ways that deployed rival visions to Western geopolitical and policy approaches to the region, Brazil explicitly challenged the hegemony of those very powers with whom it was trying to win favor. With this more counterhegemonic project in mind, Lula revived the Third Worldist language of the Non-Aligned Movement of the 1950s and 1960s and of the Bandung Conference (Prashad 2007). Although in the mid-twentieth century Brazil had not been a member of those forums, by the dawn of the twenty-first, Brazil belatedly took up these banners and revived their claims and ideologies, in certain contexts. Lula's Brazil came to articulate in certain forums such as the

G20, a Third Worldist or Bandung[2]-type language of South-South solidarity. Lula demanded the articulation of a third path between capitalism and communism, integrating Brazilian nationalism and center-left populism with a new Global South–centered multilateralism aimed at ending northern dominance in world ordering. This southern multilateralist and counterhegemonic vision was launched at a moment when the United States' reputation as a global leader was at its lowest point in modern history, during the administration of George W. Bush. Brazil began reaching out to the Middle East in 2003 in the context of record-setting mass mobilizations (*Folha de S. Paulo* 2003) within Brazil (and across the Global South) against the U.S. war in Iraq, and in the context of the reemergence of millions of Brazilians of Syrian-Lebanese descent as a conscious identity group and collective lobbying force within Brazilian political society.

By the time Dilma Rousseff was inaugurated in January 2011, the events of the Arab Spring, debates at the UN about admission of the Palestinian Authority as a state, and controversy over Iran's nuclear program rendered it more difficult for Brazil to maneuver in this space of geopolitical contradiction where it strived to serve as the Global North's Security Council apprentice all the while acting as a neo–Third Worldist architect of counterhegemony. The uprisings, revolutions, and civil wars that swept through the Middle East, starting coincidentally at the moment of Dilma's election to the presidency, forced Brazil to put its cards on the table and to make hard choices. Also troubling Dilma immediately after her election, the United States had begun to assert a more aggressive and interventionist posture in South America, itself. U.S. president Obama did meet with Rousseff in the White House in 2012 and visited Brazil in 2011 and 2012, offering soaring progressive rhetoric and talk of partnership and solidarity. But behind the speechmaking, the United States under Obama had reestablished its dark ties to archconservative military and economic elites within Latin America and taken desperate measures to curb the spread of Latin America's "pink tide" of leftist and socialist governments. In this context, the United States had begun to target what it had identified as a growing menace of "terrorism" among Lebanese-Brazilian merchants in the southwest of Brazil, which the U.S. State Department claimed had been infiltrated by Hezballah elements.

Lula's summits and speeches had laid the groundwork for a new era of transregional collaboration between South America and the Middle East. But in the subsequent Rousseff era, whose side would Brazil take when significant strife split the Arab region or when Middle East conflict began to be identified as destabilizing the borders within South America itself? With whom would

Brazil stand when NATO and UN Security Council interventions unleashed military intervention in Libya and perhaps Syria? Whose side would Brazil take, when its public- and private-sector commercial and investor interests, tied to contracts signed by authoritarian rulers, were pitted against the interests of Arab democratic social movements?

In the chapter below I will explore Brazil–Middle East political relations and transregional solidarities during the first years of Dilma Rousseff's administration, covering the period from late 2010 through the beginning of 2013. During this incredibly challenging and dynamic time, the Brazilian government came to maintain an increasingly consistent and strong posture vis-à-vis the Middle East on the diplomatic front, augmenting Lula's personalistic approach with new substance and consistency. I argue that increased assertions of Arab-Brazilians as political actors on the domestic front, and an increasing awareness of Brazil's leverage in a multipolar world order where Russia, China, the African Union, and other powers were acting increasingly independently of Western agendas, gave Brazil a new set of incentives and opportunities. In this context, President Dilma realized that her country could not afford to kowtow to U.S. militarism and interventionism in the Middle East or abide U.S. meddling in affairs close to Brazil's own borders in South America. But in pursuing an agenda increasingly independent of that of the United States, Brazil had to make the painful decision to set aside what for more than a generation had been perhaps its number one foreign policy goal: that of winning a permanent seat on the UN Security Council and thereby being recognized officially as a first-tier world power. But after freeing itself from this goal, Brazil would strike out confidently, providing leadership on several geopolitical fronts in the post–Arab Spring era. This shift would mark Brazil–Middle East relations and transregional cooperation in ways that gravitated more toward a counterhegemonic stance, but one which would represent a pragmatically defined "BRICS alternative" more than a revival of the more visionary agenda of the Bandung Conference.

Below I will explore these transregional political debates and some of their social and cultural dimensions. First, I will focus on the Rousseff administration's stance on regime change and popular sovereignty during the Arab Spring events that erupted at the very moment the president took office. Second, I will examine Brazil's insistence on standing up as an alternative voice, articulating a UN-centered South-South dialogue modality for resolving tensions around Iran's nuclear program. Third, I will analyze the significant breaks with western powers that took place around Brazil's leading opposition to military-humanitarian interventions in Syria and Libya. And finally, I will explore Dilma's strong stance against U.S. meddling in South American affairs, particularly her evisceration of U.S. support for the "coup" against President Fernando Lugo of Paraguay, which she saw as preemptive U.S. aggression against groups the Obama administration had identified as "Lebanese terrorists" based in southwest Brazil.

## Democratic Insurgencies Challenge the "Crony Club" of ASPA

How did the Rousseff administration respond to the mass social movements that drove the first wave of Arab uprisings in Tunisia, Egypt, and Yemen? The popular uprisings and mass protests against dictators in the Arab world that began in late 2010 highlighted contradictions that had been latent within the ASPA transregional process from the beginning. The pairing of South American and Arab region blocs may have represented from the start a revolutionary shift in South-South relations, but it also embodied an essential paradox. Yes, many South American countries did have long histories of connection to the Middle East through immigrant populations, trade relationships, and some common experiences of European colonialism and repressive interference by northern powers during the Cold War. However, by the 2000s, the political profiles of the two regions could not have been more distinct.

In South America since the 1980s, a spectrum of strong social movements—including massive labor organizations, visible human-rights movements, land reform occupations, anti-militarization campaigns, participatory budgeting and governance reform movements, and mobilizations for women's empowerment, lesbian, gay, bisexual, and transgender (LGBT) rights, recognition of indigenous peoples, and racial justice—had managed to overthrow regimes of political repression and military rule. These movements had unseated authoritarian rulers and corrupt presidents and had pushed for the writing of new, thoroughly democratic constitutions. Then, starting in the late 1990s, these same social mobilizations and constitutional changes in South America brought to power, through free and fair elections, a series of progressive governments. These included center-left governments in Chile, Argentina, Uruguay, and Brazil; progressive populists in Peru and, for a time, Paraguay; and even several revolutionary socialist governments in Venezuela, Ecuador, and Bolivia. During the 2000s, these progressive administrations stabilized their rule and established durable popularity and legitimacy for the long term within their own countries, through inclusive policy programs that eventually managed to impress and win over business classes and certain military elites in their own societies.

But this trend toward leftist, populist, and social-democratic government, often called Latin America's "pink tide," was not reflected in any analogous processes in the Arab region during the years that immediately followed the signing, on May 11, 2005, of the Brasilia Declaration, which founded the South American–Arab bloc, ASPA. This meant that in the early years of the ASPA collaboration, popularly elected progressive heads of state from South America placed themselves in the difficult position of negotiating declarations of solidarity and shaping common visions with Arab counterparts who were military dictators, absolute monarchs, and intensely repressive and corrupt presidents. These Arab leaders resembled, all too clearly, the regime leaders that had arrested and tortured these very same South American presidents back in the 1970s when many of these leaders were engaged in brave struggles against dictatorship. Thus for the first years of the ASPA bloc, many social movement actors and human-rights groups throughout South America were enraged to see their leaders act to exclude clauses about democracy, human rights, gender and sexuality rights, and accountability from their accords with these Arab leaders. For example, in March 2004 Brazil withdrew its support for a UN Commission on Human Rights resolution on LGBT rights and protection against non-discrimination on the basis of sexual orientation (which Brazil itself had originally initiated) in response to the pressure from its Arab ASPA partners (Ontario Consultants 2009); and in May 2005, Brazil allowed for a clause about the importance of democracy and free elections to be stricken from the founding accord of ASPA (Ministério das Relações Exteriores 2005). For a time, geopolitical maneuvering—specifically the need to produce a transregional South-South alliance that could start to counterbalance the centrality of the United States and Europe, which was at war across the Middle East—overwhelmed, all too easily, the democratic and social-justice principles of the pink tide countries.

Some of the reasons for this tendency to sideline issues of democracy, rights, and social justice in this transregional process can be traced to very specific conjunctures and relations, such as the fact that during the George W. Bush administration, U.S. policies and wars had become so profoundly loathed by public opinion in the South American region that popular media outlets in countries like Brazil and Argentina portrayed Arab dictators as heroic resistance actors standing up against Uncle Sam. Also, many of the new leftist leaders of the pink tide countries had grown up feeling great admiration for the anti-colonial revolutions in the Arab world—the Algerian war of independence, Gaddafi's overthrow of the Italian-backed monarchy in Libya, Nasser's Arab Socialist movement in Egypt. These Arab regimes or their direct inheritors were still in power in the 2000s. So South American leaders' nostalgia for and old loyalties to these once-radical Arab governments made it difficult, at first, to recognize that these "revolutionary" regimes had been morphed into oligarchies of gross corruption, repressive atrocities, neoliberal authoritarianism, and political exclusion. But it was not just anti-Bush sentiment and misplaced nostalgia that shaped South America's, and particularly Brazil's, initial ability to discard human rights and social-justice agendas as it pursued transregional solidarity with the Arab world. There were other structural and political-cultural factors that rendered the regions more comfortable with each other's more repressive policy aims and power structures.

Indeed, elections and social movements in South America had dislodged military rulers and curbed some of the worst practices of neoliberal policy, challenging hasty and corrupt forms of privatization, job-killing austerity measures, and the growing gap between the super-rich and the poor. But many other political formations and structures of governance operating on other levels of rule did reveal closer resemblances and even deeper connections and overlaps between the persistent authoritarian governance practices in both regions of the Global South. In both the Middle East and South America, daily life in teeming slum communities as well as in the elite gated enclaves had become militarized in notably similar ways by the intensification of violent, unregulated policing practices. In both regions, these abusive and unaccountable practices had been empowered by emergency agendas attached to the launching of wars on narcotraffic and terrorism and shaped by private-sector and governmental "security experts" that circulated transnationally between South America and the Middle East. Also, the rise of conservative religious social organizations—linked to the Salafist movement or the Muslim Brotherhood in the Arab world, to the Pentecostal (evangelical) movement or Opus Dei (Catholic) in South America—had reconfigured civil societies in very similar ways in both regions at the grassroots level, supplanting left-progressive programs of empowerment, collective action, and social justice. In their place, moralistic religious mass movements in both regions worked to replace progressive mobilizations with programs advocating "family values" and individual piety in ways that wove communities into dependency-producing "charity" operations and preacher-centered clientelist networks. These apparatuses insisted on solving social problems not by political-economic means but by reinstituting gender hierarchies and sexual normativities, and by supporting privatization of public institutions in the interests of preserving the community.

And finally, both regions had witnessed increasingly "humanitarian" and "human security" approaches to intervention both in the international context and within conflict zones inside their own states. These human-security interventions, although seemingly well intentioned in their justifications, led to the intensification of militarism, police power, securitization, and armed occupation all while advocating for the "rescue" of vulnerable human subpopulations, women, children, and threatened cultural or ethnic minorities. For more on these three dimensions of overlap between the security regimes and social-control platforms, which I label the "human-security state," in South America and the Middle East, see Amar 2013b.

So on the surface, the ASPA process of transregional bloc formation proceeded under the dark shadow of contradiction—one remarkably progressive region (the pink tide countries of South America) was aiming to form a new South-South-centered world order by partnering with another region, the Arab world, still under the thrall of undemocratic, militarist, and repressive regimes. But, as described above, forms of militarization, moralization, and "humanitarianization" of rule below the level of elections and constitutions shaped the governance realities of daily life in both countries, particularly in the spreading campaigns of emergency intervention and governance moralization. However, when the uprisings of the Arab Spring began, the parameters shifted suddenly, recalibrating patterns of both the disjuncture and the overlap between the two world regions. As the Arab Spring spread, the politics of personalism, authoritarianism, and repressive moralism, on the local and geopolitical levels, came to be more exposed and questioned. Something like a pink tide of social-justice militance, center-left politics, and pressures for democratization began to sweep across the Arab world, at least in 2011-12. Into this moment of hope and contradiction stepped President Rousseff. She herself had been detained and tortured as a so-called "terrorist" by the Brazilian military dictatorship. By the time she took on the mandate of the presidency, she had come to represent a unique combination of feminism, progressivism, and technocratic social democracy, but she also displayed surprising deference to security experts, privatization advocates, and evangelical populists-moralists within her own political context.

As the protests in Tunisia and Egypt gained momentum, between December 2010 and February 2011, many Brazilian leaders were able to imagine a reconciliation between their social-justice policy aspirations and their country's geopolitical ambitions. On the day of Hosni Mubarak's downfall in February 2011, President Dilma's spokesperson for international relations, Marco Aurélio

Garcia, said, "We regard with much sympathy the strengthening of movements that have such a democratic character, from the political as well as social point of view, because this reveals that excluded populations in the Arab world want to change their lives and have hope . . . A government like that of the Federal Republic of Brazil, committed to democratic values in its foreign policy, desires a political transition that does not spill blood, that respects human rights, and that permits people to express themselves strongly as they have on the streets of Cairo and other cities where they have manifested popular sovereignty, popular will . . . We can only desire this for a country we cherish such as Egypt" (Borges 2011).

But within two months of the beginning of the Arab Spring, Brazil also witnessed the massing not just of pro-democracy elements but of reactionary forces—a counterattack by geopolitical powers seeking to reassert themselves during this time of global crisis and uprising. As NATO began organizing to intervene again in the Middle East, President Rousseff's attention would be diverted from celebrating democracy and popular victories over dictatorship in Egypt and Tunisia. She would confront contradictions between Brazil's democratic political goals and its global realpolitik aspirations, first with the "betrayal" by the United States of Brazil's good-faith efforts to negotiate an accord with Iran over the development of nuclear technology, and then more dramatically, as the United States, France, and NATO mobilized for armed intervention in the skies of Libya and then Syria.

## The Iran Betrayal

In May 2010, when Lula was still president and Rousseff was campaigning for election, Turkey and Brazil came together with Iran to develop a common declaration, a practical road map that would lead the international community out of the stalemate in negotiations over Iran's development of nuclear technology. In late 2009, Mohamed ElBaradei, the Egyptian Nobel laureate and then director general of the International Atomic Energy Agency, had supported the initiation of these three-party negotiations behind closed doors when he was still leading the IAEA. (Soon after, in February 2011, ElBaradei would emerge as a primary spokesperson for the democratic opposition in Egypt.) El Baradei hoped the talks between Turkey, Brazil, and Iran would provide an alternative track to that of the UN Security Council, which he perceived as too ready to go to war, and unable to countenance the lifting of sanctions against Iran—no matter what Iran did. On May 29, 2010, ElBaradei gave an in-depth interview to Brazil's newspaper *Jornal do Brasil:*

It would be madness to attack Iran right now . . . When you bomb a country and dissolve its dignity, you should not be surprised if a country comes back and develops the most powerful weapon they could have. We should learn from history that humiliating a country, isolating a country, is not a solution; in fact, you empower the hard-liners. Of course, the implication of this for the rest of the Middle East I shudder to think of in terms of oil and instability. . . . Turkey is part of the Middle East so it is legitimate that Turkey should be involved in a conflict in Iran, which is its neighbor. Brazil is a major player right now in the world and should be an economic powerhouse but also a political powerhouse and should be involved. One of the issues still debated is that the Security Council is not representing the world of 2010, it's still representative of the world of 1945; nonetheless, I very much welcome involvement by as many responsible players as possible, particularly countries from the South. If we want to have an international order that is based on equity and fairness, we have to take into account not only the Western approach but also the perception of the South, in countries like Brazil, South Africa, all these countries which are emerging economic powers, should also exert their soft power and their influence in making sure that we have a world that is balanced and at peace with itself. (Duarte 2010)

The negotiated declaration was thus shepherded by Egypt's ElBaradei and negotiated in Tehran by President Lula of Brazil, Prime Minister Recep Tayyip Erdoğan of Turkey, and President Mahmoud Ahmadinejad of Iran, and drafted on paper in an eighteen-hour marathon by Turkish foreign minister Ahmet Davutoğlu with his Brazilian and Iranian counterparts. The Tehran Joint Declaration (Mottabi et al. 2010) laid out a clear plan. Under the deal Iran would transfer 1,200 kilograms (2,645 pounds) of low-enriched uranium to Turkey. In exchange, as reported by the BBC, "Iran says it expects to receive 120kg of more highly enriched uranium (20%)—a purity well below that used in the manufacture of nuclear weapons—within a year" (BBC News 2010) for domestic energy production, scientific research purposes, and medical use of its isotopes. (This would of necessity come from one of the Security Council nuclear powers.) This plan would have placed rising Global South actors who didn't favor sanctions and were uninterested in an Iran war in a position to resolve this crisis and help ensure Iran did not build bombs (Preiss 2011). Russia spoke up in favor of the declaration. But the United States, which had supported Brazil's participation and co-leadership in this process, came out suddenly and strongly against the plan. Instead, the United States and France, with vocal outside support from Israel, moved in the opposite direction, mobilizing for harsher sanctions against Iran in the UN Security Council (UNSC). On May 27, U.S. secretary of state Hillary Clinton declared that the

Brazil-Turkey-Iran declaration "made the world more dangerous, not less" (Notícias R7 2010). The northern powers of the "world of 1945" seemed to have no interest in lowering its bellicose posture toward Iran or in admitting any new southern powers to the world's geostrategic inner circle.

Jacqueline Shire, of the Institute for Science and International Security in Washington D.C., said: "Turkey and Brazil clearly believed they were keeping the U.S. fully in the loop and negotiating on their behalf." And Henry Precht, formerly of the U.S. State Department, described Washington's response to the fuel swap deal as "irritated, blustering, threatening, captious and surly. . . . Iran offered compromise. When is the last time the US did so in negotiations?" (Reini 2010). And Brazilian foreign minister Celso Amorim said, "We got our fingers burned by doing things that everybody said were helpful, and in the end we found that some people could not take 'yes' for an answer" (*Today's Zaman* 2010).

After getting burned in this major attempt to become a substantive diplomatic player in the heart of Middle East conflicts, Brazil did pull back. After Dilma's inauguration, Brazil withdrew from its assertive stance as mediator between the West and Iran. For a while, on the economic front, Brazil continued to expand its cooperation with Tehran. Iran became the largest importer of Brazilian beef and other key food commodities as well as automobiles, and Petrobras, Brazil's semi-state-owned oil company, made substantial investments in Iran's energy sector. But then in 2012, there seemed to be an across-the-board effort to withdraw from commercial engagement with Tehran, as trade dropped, by some estimates, 73 percent (Oliveira 2012). On the diplomatic front, relations chilled, particularly as Dilma's administration became more vocal than Lula's in critiquing human-rights violations in Iran, particularly around issues of gender and sexuality. Dilma Rousseff was appalled by Iran's sentencing of Ms. Sakineh Ashtiani to death by stoning for adultery, calling this sentence "medieval behavior" (Gómez 2012). In April 2012, Rousseff's government ejected an Iranian diplomat, Hekmatollah Ghorbani, for allegedly fondling girls, aged nine through fifteen, at a Brasília country club (Petrossian 2012). Also, Dilma canceled her meetings with Ahmadinejad in Rio de Janeiro in June 2012, during the twentieth anniversary of the ecology-focused UN Earth Summit, after street protests mobilized against Iran's anti-Semitism and treatment of LGBT individuals (Covo 2012).

Even with the cooling of diplomatic relations between Iran and Brazil in 2011 and 2012, Brazilian leaders as well as social movements advocating new forms of South-South solidarity did not forget the betrayal by Washington around the Tehran Joint Declaration. This betrayal may have marked a turning point in Brazilian foreign policy, making it easier for Brasilia to stand apart from Washington in the subsequent crises in Libya and Syria.

## "BRICS Alternative" for Libya? Stalemate in Syria

U.S. president Barack Obama, while in Brazil during a diplomatic tour of South America, announced that the United States and NATO would enter the war in Libya, supporting a no-fly zone over the country and demanding that Libyan president Muammar Gaddafi implement a cease-fire and end hostilities against his own civilian populations. In Libya, armed uprisings and popular protests had erupted starting on February 17, 2011, particularly in the eastern provinces around Benghazi. Obama's announcement in Brazil of the launching of air-based military-humanitarian intervention came on March 17, 2011, two days after the UN Security Council had passed resolution 1973 authorizing the use of "all necessary measures." Brazil, then serving as one of the non-permanent rotating members of the council, had abstained from the vote on the resolution along with Germany, China, India, and the Russian Federation. For Brazil, for much of the pink tide bloc in Latin America, and for the loose alliance of emergent global southern and eastern powers referred to as the BRICS (for Brazil, Russia, India, China, South Africa), this bellicose move reflected an essential imbalance in the world security order: Wars driven by northern powers are too often endorsed by the Security Council before serious diplomatic efforts are pursued to their full extent. And sovereignties of Global South countries are not respected. Brazil resented that a BRICS-generated alternative—one that could move strongly against human-rights and humanitarian violations without unleashing war—was not engaged with full effect by institutions of global governance. Refusal by northern powers to consider implementing alternatives, such as the introduction into Libya of an African Union peace-keeping force which would have had broad support from both southern and many northern powers, reflected imbalance not just in the Security Council, but across the range of international structures. President Rousseff articulated this complaint during her meetings in Brazil that same week with President Obama, stating: "We are concerned by the slow pace of reforms of multilateral institutions that still reflect an old world order. We are working tirelessly to reform governance of the World Bank and the International Monetary Fund. We are also advocating fundamental reform in global governance, via the enhancement of the U.N. Security Council" (Ortiz 2011).

Former president Lula was even more critical in his appraisal, hinting that if Brazil had been a permanent member of the Security Council, it would have vetoed the Libya resolution: "These invasions only happen because the United Nations is weak . . . If we had twenty-first-century representation [in the UN Security Council], instead of sending a plane to drop bombs, the UN would send its secretary-general to negotiate." Fellow center-left leader President José Mujica of Uruguay followed, saying, "The remedy is much worse than the illness. The business of saving lives by bombing is an inexplicable contradiction." Historian Socorro Gomes, head of the Brazilian Centre for Solidarity with Peoples and the Struggle for Peace (Cebrapaz), said, "Obama failed to respect Brazil when he came to our country and declared war on another state from here" (Grandin 2011).

In addition to concerns about the northern bias of the international system, powerful economic interests may have also played a part in the Rousseff administration's divergence from the United States on Libya. Brazil's massive Odebrecht construction firm had signed a $1.7 billion contract to build airport facilities in Libya's capital, Tripoli; oil drilling and infrastructure contractors Quieros Galvão and Andrade Gutierrez also had hundreds of millions of dollars invested in joint projects in Libya; and Petrobras held majority stakes in certain oil and gas explorations there (Elizondo 2011). Hundreds of Brazilians lived in Libya, attached to such firms. After the UNSC-approved NATO action helped to topple Gaddafi and bring in a new transitional authority, it appeared at first that the United States, Europe, and the Persian Gulf states that had supported military intervention against Gaddafi (particularly the natural-gas-wealthy Emirate of Qatar) would be rewarded for their support by receiving the lion's share of new contracts to repair the damage to Libya's infrastructure and to develop oil and gas resources. The new prime minister of Libya, Abdurrahim al-Keib, said that the Libyan government would "explore whether the contracts signed [by Gaddafi] previously prioritized price or personal relationship with the Brazilian government" (Brazilian Bubble 2012), meaning that Lula's personalized support for the old regime would be sanctioned, post facto.

Following the overthrow of Gaddafi, the intensification of insurgency, civil strife, and eventually civil war in Bashar al-Assad's Syria came to dominate international security debates about the role of intervention in and around Arab Spring countries. The tensions over the Libya intervention—the sense among BRICS leaders that northern and western powers had moved too fast toward military action and that Global South powers had been economically punished for their diplomatic stance—directly impacted global response to violence in Syria. This time China and Russia vetoed UN Security Council resolutions (Weaver and Whitaker 2012) that would have led to armed military intervention directly in Syria or to a no-fly zone. And Brazil again stepped forward in an attempt to articulate Global South leadership, and to underline respect for diplomacy and sovereignty in international order. Global South representatives at the UN named the esteemed Brazilian academic and diplomat Paulo Sérgio Pinheiro as chair of the UN Human Rights Council's Independent Commission of Inquiry on Syria in 2011–2012. His report concluded in February 2012 that "widespread, systematic, and gross human rights violations amounting to crimes against humanity" had been committed by the Syrian government. His report also compiled a list of "particular individuals, including commanding officers and officials at the highest levels of government, responsible for crimes against humanity and other gross human rights violations . . . such as torture." But these names were not published as part of the report, since, as Pinheiro stated, "That would be irresponsible. It would consist of a de facto indictment and we don't have this juridical capacity, we are not an investigative body" (Hoge 2012). Yet despite its strong condemnation of the al-Assad regime, Pinheiro's report did not advocate armed intervention, but instead empowered a diplomatic and fact-finding mission by former UN secretary-general Kofi Annan, who would enter Syria as the joint representative of the Arab League and the UN.

Another factor driving Brazil's hesitation in 2011–2012 to back military action against the al-Assad regime was the mobilization of domestic lobbies within Brazil by its large, eight- to sixteen-million strong Arab–Brazilian community. Most of these individuals are descended from Christians who migrated from the Levant to Brazil between 1880 and 1930. Adding to these groups are more recent migrants from Lebanon who are of Shi'a origin. The "cousins" back in Syria of these two migrant groupings had been favored to an extent by the protections of the al-Assad government. And they feared repression, vengeance, or even ethnic cleansing by the Sunni-identified rebel militias that led the opposition to al-Assad. Christian Syrian leader Michel Khoury appealed to Brazilians from Damascus: "Advise Brazilians that the Christians of Syria support Al-Assad." Youseff Massad, a civic leader of the eastern Syrian city of Malloula, said that "radical Sunni Islamists . . . want to cleanse the region of Christians" (Estadão 2011).

In July 2012, President Rousseff, meeting with British prime minister David Cameron, again insisted that she "rejected any idea of the militarization of the Syrian conflict and of any intervention that could repeat the Iraq or Afghanistan scenarios" (Contextolivre 2012). Folding the Syria issue into a larger campaign for southern sovereignty over the former colonies of northern powers, she also underlined Brazil's support for Argentina's sovereignty over the British-occupied Falkland Islands, which Buenos Aires refers to as the Malvinas. Disappointing the U.S., it did not seem that Dilma would break with Lula's independent-minded foreign policy stances and be more submissive to northern powers.

## The Coup against Lugo and the "Mideasternization" of Brazil's Border Region

On June 21, 2012, the Paraguayan parliament voted 76 to 1 to impeach President Fernando Lugo. Lugo, a former Catholic bishop associated with progressive movements and liberation theology ideas, had been elected in 2008. At last, Paraguay had inaugurated a progressive, democratically elected leader, the first from outside the right-wing, U.S.-supported Colorado Party that had dominated the country for sixty-one years. But when a relatively small crisis struck, the old guard ousted Lugo. In early June 2012, a landless farmers' movement had occupied lands owned by a wealthy official of the Colorado Party in Canindeyú province. This land had been confiscated by farmers during the military dictatorship (also of the Colorado Party) a generation before. When 300 police moved in to remove the 150 members of the farmers' movement, a battle ensued, in which six policemen and eleven farmers were killed (Rulli and Sonderegger 2012). Members of the Colorado Party and some of Lugo's former allies used this "crisis" as a justification to move against him. Lugo was informed a mere two hours before that an impeachment vote had been scheduled, and obviously he had no time to mount a legal defense or mobilize political support.

Lugo himself and most governments in South America saw this explicitly as a "parliamentary coup" against a democratically elected president, and as a U.S.-backed overthrow of a pink tide leader (Merco Press 2012). At Brazil's insistence in particular, Paraguay was suspended from the Mercosur trade bloc. Also, the Inter-American Commission for Human Rights declared that the speed of the proceedings violated the rule of law. Driving a sense of shock and outrage, in addition to the obvious issue of the lack of respect for democratic legitimacy and rule of law, was a growing awareness that the United States was edging back to a 1960s-type policy of advocating right-wing coups and manipulating electoral processes in order to preserve its interests in the region. This process reminded many of the constitutional crisis and military coup in Honduras in June 2009, when an elected leftist president, Manuel Zelaya, was also removed by U.S.-allied conservative forces (Rosenberg 2009). Lula eventually granted Zelaya asylum in the Brazilian embassy in Tegucigalpa, the Honduran capital, from which the coup was contested and Brazil pushed for the president's reinstatement. But Zelaya was never reinstated; he went into exile in the Dominican Republic for a year.

Also troubling Rousseff's administration was the notion that the implicit U.S. support for the coup against Lugo in Paraguay was driven by an interest in setting up a military base on the Paraguayan side of the border with Brazil, particularly to confront what the United States perceived as the "terrorist" threat of Hezballah-linked communities in the Tri-Border Region, around Iguaçu, where Argentina, Brazil, and Paraguay meet. As revealed in a WikiLeaks cable from 2009, the U.S. embassy in Paraguay knew well in advance that conservative elites in Asunció were planning to launch a coup against Lugo as soon as they had any kind of justification (Kozloff 2012a). And the United States did nothing to turn back these plans or dissuade Paraguayan conservatives from acting. As the *Jornal do Brasil* stated after the coup, "It's no secret that Yankee hawks dream of controlling the Tri-Border region. There is no more strategically important point in the southern hemisphere than this place where Argentina, Brazil, and Paraguay meet. It is the center of the most populous and industrialized region of South America . . . and where are located the important Iguaçu falls, Guarani aquifer, and Itaipú Dam" (Santayana 2012). The Itaipu is the world's largest hydroelectric facility, powering many factories in the broader region. Influencing this key intersection of international borders, waterways, and power-production facilities could sway the balance of power in the region. For years, neoconservative U.S. academics and security "experts" had been condemning the lack of action by South American governments against what they perceived as Hezballah-linked immigrant populations in the Tri-Border Region, and particularly the refusal by President Lugo to police their activities or "root out the entrenched Hezballah infrastructure in the region that can potentially carry out directives by the Hezballah leadership or by serving as a proxy of Iran" (Costanza 2012).

With this crisis in the Tri-Border Region and Paraguay, three campaigns for Brazilian transregional leadership had converged on the heartland of South America itself—the struggle over resisting U.S. coup-mongering and militarism in the global order, the ambition to institute new relationships between South America and the Middle East and revive links between Arab migrants in Brazil and their homelands, and the battle against the "war on terror" practices that mock the sovereignty of Global South countries. Dilma Rousseff's strong response to the Paraguayan coup reflected her administration's insistence on standing firm against attempts to reinstitute the 1945-era world order, or to return to the 1960s era of U.S.-supported military coups in Latin America. The Brazil-Mideast transregional relationship, even under Rousseff's more human-rights-oriented and less personalistic agenda, would remain a laboratory for Global South assertion and for growing trajectories of Brazilian independence and leadership of counterhegemonic shifts within the international system.

## The Dilma Difference

On September 20, 2012, President Rousseff made history by being the first woman to give the opening speech of a session of the UN General Assembly. She took advantage of the spotlight to insist that the international community prioritize policies that would strengthen women's rights and leadership, promote social-solidarity responses to the global financial crisis, and recognize an independent Palestinian state. "Recognizing the legitimate right of the Palestinian people to sovereignty and self-determination increases the possibilities of [reaching] a lasting peace in the Middle East. Israel's legitimate concerns for peace with its neighbors, security on its borders, and regional political stability can only be achieved by creating a free and sovereign Palestine" (Margolis 2011). Brazil's delegation would also go on to support the Palestinian Authority's bid to be recognized as a member state by the UN General Assembly.

In the wake of these moves by her administration, the United States could not contain its frustration and disappointment in Rousseff's refusal to reintegrate Brazil into a North Atlantic–centered 1945-era world order. As Nikolas Kozloff reported, "Washington, which is used to calling the shots in South America, is wary of Brasília's intentions, and has been slow to accommodate the region's newest up and coming player. In Brazil, many commentators claimed that Obama snubbed Rousseff in Washington during her visit there earlier in 2012 by not granting [Brazil's] leader the honour of a full White House dinner. Such slights were not lost on the likes of Caio Blinder, a columnist for Brazilian magazine *Veja*, who declared that Obama had intentionally 'downgraded' Rousseff's visit. Going yet further, the *Veja* writer lamented the 'considerable lack of mutual respect' between the U.S. and Brazil" (Kozloff 2012b).

Rather than serving as a lackey or enforcer for U.S. policy in the South American region or in the Global South in general, Brazil was increasingly moving into a position to rival the United States, strategically and economically, in certain regions and fields of action. This rivalry between the United States and Brazil during the crisis over Paraguay and the Tri-Border Region, as well as in the fallout over the Iran negotiations and around questions of intervention in Libya and Syria, began to heat up during Dilma's first years in the presidency.

While maintaining to a large degree the Lula-era commitment to a BRICS philosophy of rebalancing in the global system, Rousseff did shift Brazil's priorities and profile significantly. The Rousseff administration has consistently provided leadership around human rights, participatory democratization, and gender empowerment in its dealings with the Middle East. And Brazil's stance on these issues during the Arab Spring did lead the country to more visibly support social movements and gender-justice campaigns in the Arab region. After the split between the BRICS countries and the NATO powers over intervention in Libya, Brazil distanced itself much more carefully from the man-to-man "handshake politics" of the Lula era which had been perceived as a highly personalist politics, centering on the figure of Lula himself, who some accused of cozying up to wealthy cronies and to human-rights abusers like Gaddafi and Ahmedinejad.

On November 7, 2012, Dilma Rousseff met in Brasilia with 2011 Nobel Peace Prize winner Tawakkol Karman, a Yemeni human-rights activist and social-movement leader. In this meeting Rousseff and Karman began to articulate what may be a more substantive advocacy role for Brazil, beyond the strategic level of Security Council bargaining, moving to the realm of social policy, to foster social democratic, participatory, and anti-neoliberal agendas. Karman praised Brazil and reached out to Dilma to explicitly push Arab Spring countries "to reconstruct social welfare protections, educate youth, and implant programs of food security . . . for which Brazil serves as a model for Yemen" (Damé 2012). President Rousseff agreed, celebrating Karman's leadership and the work of Arab women's social movements in general. Rousseff underlined that challenges to corruption in Arab Spring countries must not fall into anti-political or neoliberal traps, becoming justifications for rolling back crucial state action in the social sector and public sector. As Dilma stated, in Brazil and in the Arab world "the struggle against corruption should not ignore the role of the state in providing spaces for mobilization, nor block state regulatory actions to guarantee transparency" (Weber and Sassine 2012).

As the third year of Dilma's government began, her administration had shaped a relationship to the Middle East that was less personalistic, adopting a more principled and consistent stance supporting diplomatic and non-military efforts while protecting the sovereignty of developing countries, and even moving toward the elaboration of a social democratic agenda for public-oriented empowerment in post–Arab Spring countries. Her administration advocated a consensus-building approach that worked to include Global South and East powers in the decision-making processes of international institutions. She condemned atrocities and human-rights violations while advocating democratization, supporting anti-dictatorship movements, and championing gender justice. This reflected Brazil's increasing confidence in its transregional relationships with the Middle East as well as the increasing clarity and consistency of its articulation of alternative pink-tide-leaning social-democratic policies and BRICS-backed approaches to world order.

## Notes

1. In Brazil it is common for journalists and academic writers to refer to presidents by their nickname (as in the case of "Lula" for President Luiz Inácio Lula da Silva), or by their first name, as in Dilma Rousseff's case. This practice is supported as official practice, in particular, by leftist or populist presidents. So in this essay I will alternate between use of President Rousseff's first and last name.

2. The Bandung Conference, officially called the Asian-African Conference, was held in Indonesia in April 1955. It brought together large countries that had recently achieved independence and that promised to stand together against colonialism and neocolonialism of the United States, Europe, and the Soviet Union, and also to build a framework of non-alignment that would replace both colonial and Cold War North- and West-centered orders with a new multicentered economic, social, cultural, and political framework that was labeled "Third Worldist." In this context Third World was a very positive term, referring to a global third way or, as in the French Revolution, a Third Estate. This Third World rejected both imperialist forms of capitalism and communism and intended to realize the aspirations and social-justice claims of the majority of the world's peoples.

## References

Amar, Paul. 2013a. "Introduction." In *Global South to the Rescue: Emerging Humanitarian Superpowers and Globalizing Rescue Industries,* ed. Paul Amar. London: Routledge.

———. 2013b. *The Security Archipelago: Human-Security States, Sexuality Politics, and the End of Neoliberalism.* Durham, NC: Duke University Press.

BBC News. 2010. "Iran Signs Nuclear Fuel-Swap Deal with Turkey." 17 May. http://news .bbc.co.uk/2/hi/8685846.stm, accessed 6 March 2013.

Borges, Laryssa. 2011. "Garcia: Egito pós-Mubarak não pode confiscar vontade do povo." *Terra,* 11 February. http://deportesve.terra.com.ve/imprime/0,,OI4941952-EI17594,00 .html, accessed 6 March 2013.

Brazilian Bubble. 2012. "Business Contracts between Brazil and Libya from 'Lula-Kadafi Era' Could Be Terminated." 7 March. http://brazilianbubble.com/business-contracts -between-brazil-and-libia-from-lula-kadafi-era-could-be-terminated/, accessed 7 March 2013.

Câmara Árabe TV. 2010. "Economia e comércio exterior: Brasil e Arábia Saudita, Programa 14." http://www.ccab.org.br/arabe-brasil/br/home/camara-arabe-tv/camara

-arabe-tvprograma-14.fss?caderno=f6e37ebf-caed-438e-847b-6a5ffa59ce3e, accessed 6 March 2013.

ContextoLivre. 2012. " Dilma se opõe a intervenção military na Síria e no Irã." 26 July. http://contextolivre.blogspot.com/2012/07/dilma-se-opoe-intervencao-militar-na.html, accessed 7 March 2013. Blog.

Costanza, William. 2012. "Hizballah and Its Mission in Latin America." *Studies in Conflict and Terrorism* 35 (3): 193–210.

Covo, Valeria. 2012. "Jews, Gays Rally in Rio to Protest Ahmadinejad Visit." NTN24 News.com, 17 June. http://www.google.com/hostednews/afp/article/ALeqM5ggvQ8 _rW0B9W0XpzN7hUIy8ES88A?docId=CNG.58c14f67f250993f74e6b415fb20e657.201, accessed 9 August 2013.

Damé, Luiza. 2012. "Dima recebe ativista Tawakkol Karman, premiada com Nobel da Paz." *O Globo,* 7 November. http://oglobo.globo.com/pais/dima-recebe-ativista -tawakkol-karman-premiada-com-nobel-da-paz-6665569, accessed 7 March 2013.

Duarte, Joana. 2010. "Sanções vão polarizar hemisférios, diz o nobel Mohamed ElBaradei." *Jornal do Brasil,* 29 May.

Elizondo, Gabriel. 2011. "Brazil's Business in Libya." *Al Jazeera,* 21 February. http://blogs .aljazeera.com/blog/americas/brazils-business-libya, accessed 7 March 2013. Blog.

Estadão.com. 2011. "Comunidade crista síria apoia Assad." 9 October. http://www .estadao.com.br/noticias/impresso,comunidade-crista-siria-apoia- assad,782990,0. htm, accessed 7 March 2013.

Ezzat, Dina. 2003. "Latin Leanings: Closer Arab-Latin Ties Will Benefit All Involved." *Al-Ahram Weekly Online,* 18–24 December. http://weekly.ahram.org.eg/2003/669/re2 .htm, accessed 6 March 2013.

*Folha de S. Paulo.* 2003. "Milhares de pessoas planejam manifestação contra Bush em Londres," 17 November.

Gómez, Eduardo J. 2012. "Why Iran-Brazil Friendship Has Gone Cold." *CNN Opinion,* 5 April. http://www.cnn.com/2012/04/05/opinion/gomez-iran-brazil-chill, accessed 7 March 2013.

Grandin, Greg. 2011. "Brazil Stares Down the US on Libya." *Al Jazeera Opinion,* 30 March. http://www.aljazeera.com/indepth/opinion/2011/03/201133014435832732.html, accessed 7 March 2013.

Hoge, Warren. 2012. "Interview with Paulo Sergio Pinheiro, Chair of UN's Syria Human Rights Commission." *Global Observatory,* 22 March. http://www.theglobalobservatory .org/interviews/243-interview-with-paulo-sergio-pinheiro-chair-of-uns-syria-human -rights-commission-.html, accessed 7 March 2013.

Kozloff, Nikolas. 2012a. "WikiLeaks: Washington and Paraguay's 'Quasi-Coup.'" *Huffington Post,* 19 July. http://www.huffingtonpost.com/nikolas-kozloff/wikileaks -washington-and-_1_b_1683568.html, accessed 7 March 2013.

———. 2012b. "Is Obama Wary of Brazil and Dilma Rousseff?" *Al Jazeera,* 5 May. http:// www.aljazeera.com/indepth/opinion/2012/04/2012428134850333757.html, accessed 7 March 2013.

Margolis, Mac. 2011. "Dilma Thumps for Women." *The Daily Beast,* 21 September. http:// www.thedailybeast.com/articles/2011/09/21/dilma-rousseff-s-u-n-address-championing -women-s-rights.html, accessed 7 March 2013.

Merco Press. 2012. " 'Institutional Coup' Removes Paraguayan President Lugo from Office." 22 June. http://en.mercopress.com/2012/06/22/institutional-coup-removes -paraguayan-president-lugo-from-office, accessed 7 March 2013.

Ministério das Relações Exteriores. 2005. "ASPA: Cúpula América do Sul-Países Árabes." http://www.itamaraty.gov.br/temas/mecanismos-inter-regionais/cupula-america -do-sul-paises-arabes-aspa, accessed 6 March 2013.

Mottabi, M., A. Davutoğlu, and C. Amorim. 2010. "Nuclear Fuel Declaration by Iran, Turkey and Brazil." *BBC News,* 17 May. http://news.bbc.co.uk/2/hi/middle_east/ 8686728.stm, accessed 6 March 2013.

Nieto, W. Alejandro. 2013. "Brazil's Grand Design for Combining Global South Solidarity and National Interests." In *Global South to the Rescue: Emerging Humanitarian Superpowers and Globalizing Rescue Industries,* ed. Paul Amar. London: Routledge.

Notícias R7. 2010. "Hillary diz que acordo do Brasil com o Irã deixou o mundo mais peregoso." 17 May. http://noticias.r7.com/internacional/noticias/hillary-clinton -ve-serias-divergencias-com-brasil-sobre-o-ira-20100527.html, accessed 6 March 2013.

Oliveira, Eliane. 2012. "Brasil reduz en 73% o comércio com Irã durante o governo Dilma." *O Globo,* 9 January. http://oglobo.globo.com/mundo/brasil-reduz-em-73 -comercio-com-ira-Adurante-governo-dilma-3599441, accessed 7 March 2013.

Ontario Consultants for Religious Tolerance. 2009. "Early Attempts to Propose a UN Declaration on GLBT Rights." 13 February. http://www.religioustolerance.org/ homundec3.htm, accessed 7 March 2013.

Ortiz, Fabiola. 2011. "Brazil-US: Libya Attack Sours Obama-Rousseff Meeting." Inter Press Service (IPS) News Agency, 21 March. http://www.ipsnews.net/2011/03/brazil -us-libya-attack-sours-obama-rousseff-meeting/, accessed 7 March 2013.

Petrossian, Fred. 2012. "Accused of Molesting Children, Iranian Diplomat Leaves Brazil." Global Voices, 25 April. http://globalvoicesonline.org/2012/04/25/accused-of-molesting -children-iranian-diplomat-leaves-brazil/, accessed 7 March 2013.

Prashad, Vijay. 2007. *The Darker Nations: A People's History of the Third World.* New York: The New Press.

Preiss, José Luiz Silva. 2011. "As Relações Brasil-Irã: Dos antecedents aos desdobramentos noséculo XXI." *Fundación Centro de Estudios del Medio Oriente Contemporáneo-CEMOC* 1 (1): 45–60.

Reini, James. 2010. "US Rejects Iran Nuclear Deal Brokered by Turkey and Brazil and Sets Up New Sanctions." *The National,* 20 May. http://www.thenational.ae/news/ world/us-rejects-iran-nuclear-deal-brokered-by-turkey-and-brazil-and-sets-up-new -sanctions, accessed 6 March 2013.

Rosenberg, Mica. 2009. "Army Overthrows Honduras President in Vote Dispute." Reuters, 28 June. http://www.reuters.com/article/2009/06/28/us-honduras-president-idUSTRE 55RoUS20090628, accessed 7 March 2013.

Rulli, J. M., and R. Sonderegger. 2012. "A Tragic Week in Paraguay." Counterpunch, 26 June. http://www.counterpunch.org/2012/06/26/a-tragic-week-in-paraquay/, accessed 7 March 2013.

Santayana, Mauro. 2012. "O golpe em Assunção e a triplice fronteira." *Jornal do Brasil,* 26 June.

*Today's Zaman.* 2010. "Brazil Vents Frustration with West over Iran Deal." 22 June. http://www.todayszaman.com/newsDetail_getNewsById.action;jsessionid=6B8F 7338682%09C5F84802BD9F35B23882?newsId=213822, accessed 7 March 2013.
Weaver, Matthew, and Brian Whitaker. 2012. "Syria Crisis: Russia and China Veto UN Fesolution." *The Guardian,* 19 July.
Weber, D., and V. Sassine. 2012. "Dilma: discurso anticorrupção não deve ser confundido com anti-política." *O Globo,* 7 November. http://oglobo.globo.com/pais/dilma -discurso-anticorrupcao-nao-deve-ser-confundido-com-antipolitica-6657251, accessed 7 March 2013.

**2**

# The Summit of South America–Arab States
## Historical Contexts of South-South
## Solidarity and Exchange

*Paulo Daniel Elias Farah*
*Translated by Katia Costa-Santos*

This chapter traces the emergence of ASPA (the Summit of South America–Arab States) established by diplomatic concord in 2003 among the heads of state from the two world regions. ASPA constitutes a set of transregional diplomatic agreements and functioning institutions for educational, cultural, and commercial cooperation that have achieved broad success and visibility. Farah analyzes, in particular, the ASPA-related institutions that support cultural, educational, linguistic, and commercial exchanges and solidarity. Then this chapter does the important work of setting these new transregional connections into their historical context. He points out that the processes of integration with Muslim Africa and the Middle East are not new, but are part of the essential fabric of the Americas and date back more than two hundred years. A detailed social history is narrated here, of regional cultural, linguistic, and commercial integration. This history is animated by transnational circuits of forced and free migration, particularly to Bahia in the northeast (capital of anti-slavery unrest and Afro-Muslim cultural survival), and São Paulo in the southeast (capital of Levantine migration and commercial achievement).

∼

Since early 2003, a series of summits in the South American and Arab capitals were organized in order to establish initiatives for the development of cultural, educational, scientific, technological, economic, and financial cooperation based on the increasing sense of common interests between these two emergent world regions. This process of approximation was driven, in part, by the historical and sociopolitical influence of large populations of Arabs and Muslims in Brazil and throughout Latin America, as well as by the structural convergence of political and economic agendas that came to be embodied in this bi-regional vision.

During his official visit to Syria, Lebanon, Egypt, the United Arab Emirates, and Libya in December of 2003, Luiz Inácio Lula da Silva, then the president of Brazil, defended the strengthening of commercial relations with Arab countries and joint actions in international forums. Former president of Argentina Eduardo Duhalde, chairman of the Committee of Permanent Representatives of Mercosur, accompanied President Lula on his trip to show that the initiative had the support of other South American countries, despite some disagreements in the region. At that time, Lula urged the formation of an "Arab–South American bloc" so that developing countries could have a stronger voice in international forums. "The global vocation of Brazil is to work on the creation of an Arab–South American bloc in conjunction with Third World countries to deal on equal terms with countries of the North," said President Lula in Beirut.[1]

Although there are, according to the Ministry of Foreign Affairs, more than sixteen million Arabs and descendants of Arabs in Brazil, constituting the largest community of Arab descent outside the Middle East, none of the presidents of Brazil had ever visited the region. Lula's predecessor, Fernando Henrique Cardoso, had announced the trip at least twice, but never fulfilled the commitment. Therefore this was the first official visit of a head of state of Brazil to any Arab country since the emperor Dom Pedro II (1825–1891) visited the region in the nineteenth century, passing through Egypt in 1871, and then Lebanon, Palestine, and Syria in 1876.

Lula stated during his trip in 2003 that "few countries in the world have the privilege of having within its territory more than ten million Arabs or people of Arab descent. The number of Arabs we have in Brazil is the size of Sweden, is more than the population of Norway, it is the same population as in Cuba. This means that we have not only the political authority to do this but also that we have almost the obligation to do so. These Arabs, these men and women who are in Brazil, have helped to grow and to develop the country. We have to take advantage of it not only for the sake of Brazil, but also to make the integration much more effective and strong in all aspects, from political to commercial."[2]

In 2005, at the initiative of the Lula government, Brazil hosted the first Summit of South America—Arab States (América do Sul–Países Árabes, or

ASPA), whose institutionalization since then has served as a platform for the formulation and implementation of a common agenda between both regions. The final declaration of the summit consolidated positions and aspirations common to Arab and South American countries. ASPA held its second summit in 2009, in Doha, Qatar, a meeting which focused primarily on the promotion of cultural and educational exchanges and collaborations to stimulate "a better understanding" between the people of these regions. These were understood to be prerequisites for the strengthening of political, cultural, and economic relations in a consistent and durable way.

Since 2003, when leaders of the two regions began to negotiate the creation of the ASPA mechanism, the bi-regional pact has led to several significant achievements in education and culture, including especially the establishment of a flourishing ASPA Library and Research Center, called BibliASPA (www. bibliaspa.com.br). This institution promotes critical, cross-regional reflection through the publication of books in Portuguese, Arabic, Spanish, English, and French; by translating literary and social-science works from one region for the others; and by maintaining a website in four languages with over four hundred pages grouped in thirty thematic categories. BibliASPA also hosts the annual South American Festival of Arab Culture, the biggest festival of Arab culture on the continent. In March 2013 this vast, multi-city event took in Brasilia, São Paulo, Rio de Janeiro, Curitiba, Salvador, Porto Alegre, Buenos Aires, and Santiago de Chile. BibliASPA also organizes conferences, courses, debates, exhibitions, film shows, and theater performances, and publishes *Fikr: Journal of Arabic, African and South American Studies* (www.bibliaspa.com .br/EdicoesBibliASPA).

Held in Lima, Peru, in early October 2012, the third summit of heads of state and government of South American and Arab Countries (ASPA) built upon this educational and cultural collaboration to add important transregional political foundations to the pact. The Lima meeting was the scene of important debates on the relations between the two regions. In its Final Declaration, this third ASPA summit endorsed a set of actions that had been taken in the previous decade in the fields of education and culture and urged Arab and South American countries to support initiatives that contribute to the strengthening of these relations. The heads of state jointly passed a three-part motion in order to

(1) Congratulate BibliASPA for the offering of the Arabic Language and Culture Program in the premises of BibliASPA in Sao Paulo, and also in Curitiba, Rio de Janeiro and Buenos Aires, with the essential support of books in Portuguese, Spanish and Arabic especially developed for students of Arabic, such as *Writing in Arabic: Literacy, spelling and calligraphy* and *Arabic Grammar for South*

*American Students,* as part of a partnership with Qatar Foundation; (2) encourage the expansion of this Program to other cities in South America and recall the importance of teaching Portuguese, Spanish and Arabic, as mentioned in the Final Statement of the First Meeting of ASPA Ministers of Education, that lists, among its objectives, "to promote the learning of Arabic, Spanish and Portuguese for non-native speakers in the two regions"; and (3) recognize the importance of supporting the work developed by BibliASPA, which highlights the promotion of the Arab language and culture in South America, and call upon the ASPA member states to support its future initiatives.

The declaration emphasized the events that attest in particular to the interest of Brazilian society in Arab and/or Islamic culture, such as the 2010 exhibition "Islam: Art and Civilization," the world's largest thematic exhibition,[3] co-sponsored by BibliASPA and Banco do Brasil, with the fundamental support of the Ministry of Foreign Affairs and the Ministry of Culture. Likewise, the declaration emphasized the importance of expanding the teaching of Arabic, Portuguese, and Spanish in both regions; in line with the idea that no language should be taught out of context, they also emphasized the importance of teaching the cultural aspects of Arab society as well. The declaration commended "the signing of Memoranda of Understanding between BibliASPA and UNESCO, the National Library of Qatar, Qatar Foundation and the National Council for Culture, Arts and Letters of Kuwait" and "[e]xhort[ed] other countries to follow suit and sign similar agreements which could allow for the expansion of BibliASPA's bibliographic assets, language, culture and art courses, book and multimedia content translation, exhibitions and cultural events."[4]

Indeed, in the philosophy of the ASPA pact, exchanging proficiency and literary appreciation of regional languages, especially Arabic, Portuguese, and Spanish, across global borders paves the way for a new generation of cultural dialogue between Global South regions, and avoids the stereotypes and ignorance historically generated by the necessity of relying upon intermediation of a third language such as English or French, considering the possible imperial or geopolitical or cultural non-objectivity of these frames of understanding.

Arabic is spoken as the official language in over twenty countries, and it is a relevant language in more than fifty more countries with an Islamic majority. Arabic is also one of the official languages of the UN. The Arabic alphabet is the second most used in the world, after the Latin alphabet, and is used to write dozens of languages, including Urdu, Persian, Pashto, and Dari. Arabic is also a historically Brazilian language. Most of the documents written by the African anti-slavery activists and revolutionaries in nineteenth-century Brazil, who called themselves Malês or Malians,[5] also wrote and spoke Arabic, or wrote Portuguese in Arabic letters. "There were thousands of Muslim slaves in Brazil. Many knew the Arabic language and exchanged information on the uprisings against the slavery system in that language" (Farah 2001, 95) and in the local languages called Ajami, which were written with the Arabic alphabet.

But the importance of Arabic to Brazil and South America, historically as well as geopolitically and geoculturally, has been hard to establish for the public. One obstacle to implementing the recommendations of the third ASPA summit, and of the meeting of Arab and South American ministers of education in Kuwait in 2011, regarding the teaching of foreign languages is that the educational system in Brazil and in other South American countries does not reflect the contemporary reality in which languages such as Arabic and Chinese are widely used. The student in Brazil—and in South America in general—has no other option for foreign-language study in primary and secondary schools than English and, to a lesser extent, Spanish (for Brazil) or Portuguese (in Spanish-speaking South America). Unfortunately, in Brazil the student who wishes to learn any other language has to take extracurricular courses, which are often expensive, of very poor quality, and, in any case, extremely rare. ASPA's cultural and educational agenda, as well as the institutions it has fostered like BibliASPA, has insisted that it is essential that the Ministry of Education in Brazil allow students to choose among several globally and historically relevant languages in public schools, according to their interest and identification, and offer them the opportunity for transregional educational exchange. This would benefit individual careers, as well as Brazil's development, in such areas as commerce, culture, translation, and diplomacy. But the expansion of language teaching cannot proceed without processes and structures that support real, substantive, long-lasting forms of contact and knowledge exchange within and between respective cultures. Language proficiency is needed urgently to keep up with the expansion of Brazilian diplomatic relations, as evidenced by the opening of a vast array of new embassies in Asia and Africa. The teaching in Brazil of Middle Eastern languages needs also to be accompanied by the intensification of the teaching of the Portuguese language in the Middle East, which is still too rare.

Since its founding in 2003, BibliASPA has promoted the teaching of languages such as Arabic, Portuguese, and Spanish as a means of supporting researchers by making way for the study of non-Europhone sources and non-Eurocentric ways of reading and interpreting. In recent years, the Program of Arabic Language and Culture sponsored by BibliASPA in cities like São Paulo, Rio de Janeiro, Curitiba, and Buenos Aires has shown that South Americans' interest in these topics is strong. However, the bureaucratic and legal limitations of an educational system that does not provide plurality ultimately undermine the training of specialists. Among the challenges facing both education and Brazilian foreign policy, what stands out is exactly the need for training qualified experts in Arabic and Islamic themes. After years in which emigration rates exceeded immigration rates, Brazil has once again become a destination for waves of international migration. In this context, knowledge of a variety of cultures and languages has become increasingly essential in daily life as well as in diplomatic and commercial spheres. The process of integrating these immigrants as well as promoting multicultural vibrancy will enrich Brazil's future.

**Historical Presence**

In order to help create momentum for and interest in efforts to enhance language teaching, multicultural education, and research and literary production across these regions of the Global South, it is important to rewrite the histories of mutual contact and presence for these regions. New imaginaries based on forgotten histories can be invigorated. In fact, as the historical archive demonstrates, processes and institutions of educational and cultural exchange between Brazil and the Middle East did not begin in 2003, with the birth of ASPA. The historical presence of Arabs of different religions and Muslims of different origins in Brazil dates back to the nineteenth-century empire period.

The imam ʿAbdurrahman al-Baghdádi, who traveled to Brazil in a ship of the Ottoman Empire in 1866, reported that when they reached a port in Rio de Janeiro (which had been capital of the Empire of Brazil since 1808) and disembarked to explore the city, he encountered Muslims of African origin—the main community of followers of that religion on the American continent then—and they greeted him with the traditional Muslim greeting "*as-salamu ʿalaykum*"[6] (Farah 2007, 66). In attempting to communicate with the imam some of them told him, after welcoming him, "Ana Muslim,"[7] "I am Muslim" in Arabic. Despite failed attempts to converse in Arabic, Turkish, French, and English, the joint prayer in Arabic revealed their belonging to the *'umma*. Thus, after an initial doubt, the imam found that there was a significant Muslim community in the "magnificent city" (as he describes it). So al-Baghdádi remained in Rio de Janeiro, the government and military capital, for about a year and a half, at a time when the city was going through changes in infrastructure and when squares and parks were being reformulated and new buildings erected at an accelerated pace of urbanization. In 1872, shortly after the visit of Imam al-Baghdádi, as the census of that year indicates, there were 274,972 people living in the city, and 48,939 of them were enslaved. The imam describes the process of identity depersonalization and dehumanization to which the slaves were subjected.

The imam learned that the Africans had been forcibly taken from their homeland to the American continent, sometimes when they were still children; therefore often they did not receive sufficient instruction on Islamic doctrine and practices of worship. Those who had obtained their emancipation, al-Baghdádi saw, could practice their religion more freely.

Requests for al-Baghdádi to teach the Quran and the principles of Islam were made by Muslims of African origin in Rio de Janeiro and in the southeast of Brazil, where he preached religious sermons to "not less than five hundred people." He also traveled to Bahia, in the country's northeast region, where the largest Malian community in Brazil resided. The Malians had sent a delegation to Rio de Janeiro to ask the imam to visit and instruct them. He also received and fulfilled a request from communities in Pernambuco, also in the northeast. As we can see from the imam's report, the idea of *'umma* was very present in Brazil at that time. Muslim communities of faith were so well connected that the Muslims of Bahia knew about the presence of al-Baghdádi in Rio de Janeiro and invited him to a mission in the province where the Malian uprising occurred. The *'umma* unified the enslaved; Islam was a form of agglutination.

After Muslims sought the guidance of al-Baghdádi—believed to be the first-ever Arabic-speaking non-slave imam in Brazil—and as soon as he decided to stay in the country, the erudite man started studying Portuguese in order to communicate with the local Muslim community and avoid the need for an interpreter. Indeed, in the second half of the nineteenth century the number of Muslims in Brazil who knew Arabic decreased significantly, as the police continued to confiscate, especially in Bahia, manuscripts and books in that language, frequently seizing copies of the Quran. In 1869, three years after the arrival of al-Baghdádi in Rio de Janeiro, Count Joseph-Arthur de Gobineau (1816–1882), the French diplomatic representative in Brazil and the author of *Essai sur l'inégalité des races humaines* (a fundamental work for the establishment of what came to be called "scientific racism"), wrote that the French men Fauchon and Dupont, in their bookstore in Rio, then the capital of Brazil, annually sold about a hundred copies of the Quran to slaves and ex-slaves, as well as Arabic grammars with explanations in French (Raymond 1990, 143–144).

In his report, the imam reveals that while searching for a dictionary to help him communicate in Portuguese, he found in a bookstore of the city of Rio de Janeiro a Quran printed in France—which had been lying there for a considerable time apparently without arousing interest (Farah 2007, 84). In order to ensure access to the holy book and strengthen the knowledge of Muslims about this fundamental source, he ordered several copies of the Quran through the bookseller, making a down payment which was refunded to him later. After this acquisition, according to the imam, the knowledge about the Quran increased. Al-Baghdádi's stay reinvigorated Muslims' interest in the Arabic language and the Quran, which may explain in part the significant growth in the sale of copies of the holy book of Islam in Rio de Janeiro that Gobineau witnessed.

At the time, though many Muslims could not read Arabic, some could recite the Quran with a strong accent, according to al-Baghdádi, who also reports that the holy book they had was not used necessarily for reading or reciting from; it was viewed by the community more like a kind of talisman, "for blessings rather than instructions," as described by the imam. There was great similarity between the amulets used in Brazil, especially in Bahia, and those present in Africa. Quranic passages and other texts were often written in Arabic characters.[8]

In Brazil there are reports of significant Muslim presence from at least the early nineteenth century. African Muslims led many liberation movements of black slaves in the country. Consisting mostly of Malês (Malians), who were also labeled by Portuguese-speakers of the time as *muçulmis, muçulimi, muxurimim, mucuim,* or *muçurimi.* These Muslim rebels were responsible for black slave insurrections in 1807, 1809, 1813, 1816, 1826, 1827, 1828, 1830, and 1835; this last one, known as the Malians Revolt (Revolta dos Malês), was one of the main urban uprisings of slaves in the Americas during this historical period (see Farah 2007, 38–55).

After the several rebellions of the first half of the nineteenth century, especially the uprising of the Malians, the situation of Muslims worsened dramatically. The government and dominant classes severely repressed the practice of their religion and the organization of their communities. Many Malians decided to hide their religion and avoid public exposure during celebrations and prayers. In this context, al-Baghdádi narrates that, because of the fear of being identified as Muslims (Farah 2007, 346, citing p. 57 of the manuscript; and Farah 2007, 328), many practitioners went home during the day to pray secretly. Those who could not do the same used to make up midday and afternoon prayers at night, once at home.

The imam al-Baghdádi was told about the ban on the practice of Islam in the Empire of Brazil (as well as of any religion other than Catholicism, and the banning of any constructions or buildings "that looked like any kind of temple"[9]).

Catholicism, given the intrinsic relationship between religion and state, strengthened by the principles of Tridentine Christianity of the nineteenth century, was the main form of social integration of individuals in the impe-rial state. As al-Baghdádi demonstrates, Muslims were forced to baptize their children (unless they had been baptized at the port of departure in Africa) in order to receive a certificate proving that they had been baptized. In order to be buried they also had to submit this baptism certificate proving their bond with the church (Farah 2007, 328).

The lack of freedom, including the difficulty or impossibility of attending Muslim schools and the injunctions that were imposed on enslaved people, affected the Islam practiced in Brazil in the second half of the nineteenth century significantly.[10] But this did not end Brazil's relationship with the Arabic language, or with the religions of North Africa and the Middle East, although its racial and political-economic character did change dramatically. For by coincidence, at the end of the nineteenth century, shortly after this peak of repression against Afro-Brazilian Islam, an extensive migration of Levantine Arabs (and to a lesser extent, North Africans) began.

**From Malian Muslims to Levantine Arabs**

Arab immigration from the Levant (mostly from present-day Syria, Lebanon, and Palestine) to South America was driven by its own indigenous dynamics, not stimulated by incentives for workers or driven by offers of religious or political sanctuary of the kind that South American countries extended to population groups from Germany, England, and Italy, for example. Thus, from the beginning, the Arabs who came to the southern region of the Americas had to forge their own paths. Arabs traveled, settled, and integrated socially, commercially, and culturally through family networks, without the inter-vention of official state-based or industrial "mediators." In fact, when such mediators tried to intervene, Arab-Brazilian communities tended to respond with protests, uprisings, and other forms of insubordination (Farah 2011, 53).

Until 1892, the Arab immigrants were registered by the Brazilian authorities and other South American countries as "Turks" because of the fact that the Turkish Ottoman Empire dominated the region where the Arab countries are located today; thus most of them held a passport with that "nationality" when they went to Brazil. The vast majority of these immigrants came from locations that are currently in Lebanon and Syria, such as Zahle, Zgharta, Sib'il, Homs, Aleppo, and Damascus. The success of these migrants in occupying public spaces and achieving cultural and commercial visibility in both the cities of the coast and interior plantation regions of the country inspired Brazilian writers such as Jorge Amado (author of *A descoberta da América pelos turcos*

[The discovery of America by the Turks] and other works), Permínio Asfora (author of *Noite Grande*[11] [Big night]), and the Colombian writer Gabriel García Márquez, among other authors (Farah 2011).

Arab writers in South America also celebrated their new home countries in their literary writings and artistic communities in São Paulo (Brazil), Guayaquil (Ecuador), Lima (Peru), Buenos Aires (Argentina), Caracas (Venezuela), and Montevideo (Uruguay). Although these cities were distant from each other, and far from their home cities in the Arab region, they remained in close cultural contact, with journals, newspapers, and literary styles circulating intensively between them. Arab–South American literati founded cultural forums such as *Al-'Usba al-Andalusiyya* (Andalusian Association or League, in São Paulo, in January 1933), *Annadwa al-'adabiyya* (Literary Circle, in Buenos Aires, at the end of 1947) and *Annadwa al-'adabiyya* (Literary Circle, in Santiago, Chile, on June 29, 1955). Celebrating these creative circles in Brazil through poetry, Ilyas Farhat, a noted literary community fixture, wrote:

> If we cut all the cedars of Lebanon
> and cedars are sources of inspiration
> And with it erected here a temple
> Whose towers crossed the clouds,
> If we ravished from Baalbeck and Palmira
> Vestiges of our glorious past.
> If we snatched from Damascus
> The tomb of Saladin,
> And from Jerusalem, the sepulcher
> Of the Redeemer of mankind.
> If we donate all these treasures
> To the big independent nation
> And to its generous children,
> We would feel that even then
> We would not pay everything we owe
> To Brazil and to Brazilians. (Farah 2010, 15)

Endowed and enriched in these ways by such cultural communities, the history of the largest city in South America, São Paulo, is profoundly embricated within the stories of immigration. Starting from the late nineteenth century, the arrival of many immigration groups, which initially went to the rural areas, was a decisive factor in the expansion and growth of the country. Until the middle of the nineteenth century, São Paulo was a provincial town, confined to the central hill between the rivers Tamanduateí and Anhangabaú, whose center was the historical triangle composed of the streets São Bento,

XV de Novembro, and Direita and whose vertices were the St. Francis Church, the Monastery of St. Benedict, and the Church of the Third Order of Carmel (Emplasa 2001, 46).

When we analyze the commercial and cultural occupations of Syrians, Lebanese, and Palestinian migrants in São Paulo, we note that the settling of these immigrants in the state capital led to a change in the city's spatial configuration,with various ethnic groups concentrating themselves in particular areas. Specific neighborhoods formed a nucleus of solidarity that offered some protection and comfort during the language- and culture-learning period (Moura 2008, 129). When Syrians and Lebanese settled in São Paulo, most of them headed to the area around 25 de Março Street, following earlier Arab migrant groups that had established themselves in the area. The zone was transformed into a virtual Middle East city in the first half of the twentieth century due to the large concentration of immigrants who lived and worked there, imprinting their character on the street and adjacent areas. The zone around 25 de Março Street is framed by the now-dry course of the Tamanduateí River, whose name in the Brazilian indigenous language of Tupi Guarani means "river of many turns" and which sits in the basin of the Do Carmo Lowlands. The street was named in honor of the date of the enactment of the first Brazilian constitution, in March 1824.

Arab migrants became visible in the commercial profile of São Paulo very soon after the wave of migration began in 1880. By 1885 Lebanese and Syrian peddlers were a vibrant presence in the market square of São Paulo. These immigrants settled in the area of 25 de Março Street for several reasons. The rent was very cheap, and as most immigrants initially were single men who at first thought that eventually they would return to their country of origin, they tended to find accommodations in the tenements and pensions of the area. The train station through which they arrived was nearby, and most of them settled in houses in that neighborhood. The third reason was the commercially advantageous position: everyone going from the railway station to the town center would pass by 25 de Março Street. Another reason was the market itself, since immigrants, many of whom worked as peddlers, wanted to live near their businesses.

As stated by Knowlton, an important reason to have settled and formed a Syrian and Lebanese colony in the region was "the fact that the first Syrian and Lebanese who came were established there. Their relatives, friends and countrymen, upon arriving, settled near them" (Knowlton 1960). In the late nineteenth century, more than 90 percent of the city's peddlers were Syrians and Lebanese and most of the remaining 10 percent were Italian. Gradually, as they accumulated capital, they began to devote themselves to the retail trade at 25 de Março Street (Knowlton 1960). Usually, Syrian and Lebanese families owned their buildings, running their business downstairs and living on the second and third floors.

Over time, many Syrians and Lebanese moved to other areas of the city, such as the neighborhood of Paraíso, where they founded several cultural institutions. Throughout the late nineteenth century and the early twentieth, the city of São Paulo passed through an industrialization process, in which certain Arab families featured prominently. As cheaper land was needed for industry, they had to opt for property far from the downtown and the commercial area. Therefore, they settled in the neighborhood of Ipiranga, which became another center of Syrian and Lebanese occupation and eventually a thriving industrial-commercial center. As businesses continued to consolidate their growth around 25 de Março Street and its large Arab presence, new waves of immigration from Lebanon and Syria entered the country. And this area became increasingly expensive to live or open shops in. So these immigrants sought to settle in other neighborhoods such as Bras, a strategic location for commercial activities that was seen as extending the zone of the city's central market and of 25 de Março Street.

Until the late nineteenth century, Brazil's national political and economic life was not centered in São Paulo. Due to its isolation in its early periods, the city had a more inward-looking, community-oriented profile. From Brazil's independence on September 22, 1822, and especially with the establishment of the Law Academy in São Paulo in 1828, the isolation of the city began to rapidly diminish (Morse 1970, 48). The academy attracted students and teachers from around the country and outside it, providing a unifying hub for new ideas, nationalist identities, and activist communities. From the growth of this college there emerged in São Paulo other similar institutional sites for national identification, where immigrants played a strong role in building the national imagination (Setubal 2008, 16).

In Brazil, the decline of the age of sugarcane began after independence. The coffee business, which had been introduced in the state in mid-1790, began to generate profits higher than the cane business. Initially, coffee had been cultivated in the Paraíba Valley, which had a close political and economic relationship with Rio de Janeiro. But starting in 1860, the soil of this area started showing signs of exhaustion, making it necessary to expand westward into the state of São Paulo. This expansion was associated with a series of changes in the work organization and in the occupation of the interior, which would make the state's capital city, also called São Paulo, much more economically prosperous, and the commercial gateway for the coffee economy to the region and the world (Setubal 2008, 25). Between 1870 and 1880, the capital expanded explosively, building on this particular mix of the coffee boom, railroad construction, and immigration. For labor on these booming coffee plantations, an alternative was needed to the slave regime, since its extinction was imminent. The end of the slave trade was the first step of the abolitionist campaign and an incentive for immigration policies that would attract non-slave labor to the coffee plantations, enabling them to make the transition from the slave regime to paid labor (Osman 2000, 63). Between 1866 and 1873, Brazil received 304,796 immigrants; in 1887 that number increased to 549,990, and 34,710 of them went to São Paulo. In 1888, the year slavery was abolished, of the 131,268 new immigrants, 92,000 arrived in São Paulo at the ports of Santos and Rio de Janeiro (Emplasa 2001, 52). They came in crowded vessels, usually in third-class cabins, which departed from ports in the Mediterranean (Genoa, Marseille, and Malaga), Iberia (Lisbon and Vigo), the English Channel and the North Sea (Havre and Hamburg), and the Far East (Japan-Kobe). The trips took from fifteen days to two months. When landing in Santos, immigrants were referred to the Immigration Inspection Office, where health and luggage inspections were carried out (Moura 2008). The journey of Arab immigrants was usually accomplished in two parts: from the Levant to a port in Europe (often Marseille) and from there to the Americas. The state of São Paulo received about 2.5 million immigrants—more than half of the 4.8 million immigrants from seventy nationalities who arrived in Brazil between 1820 and 1949 (Porta 2004, 67).

Enriched with migration, the city of São Paulo became a central hub of the Brazilian labor market, even though only a portion of the newly arrived immigrants stayed there. Although the province was not the only site for bringing coffee to market, banking institutions did concentrate in the capital, a fact that would become decisive for the subsequent financing of the nation's industrialization. By the late nineteenth century, São Paulo had the conditions for the development of industry and business. It had become a hub for capital markets, labor markets, and currency circulations; it had established a consumer market of semi-durable consumer goods and foods and it had developed modern urban infrastructure (Setubal 2008, 48).

The expansion of the Syrians and Lebanese through this area was completed between 1915 and 1925. They dominated the areas around 25 de Março Street, from General Carneiro Street to Paula Souza Street, Porto Geral Slope as well, and other roads between the city's commercial center and 25 de Março Street. They also established themselves on new roads, such as Pagé (current Afonso Kherlakian) and Barão de Duprat, and began to move to the Anhangabaú (now

Carlos de Souza Nazaré) and Senador Queiroz Street. By 1925, they had occupied the entire region, with only few modifications in the perimeter of settlement that took place over the following years (Knowlton 1960).

Between 1920 and 1930, the areas surrounding these streets were monopolized by small manufacturing and wholesale trade of textiles, and commercial buildings replaced the two- or three-story houses. During World War II, many Syrians, Lebanese, and Armenians got rich and headed to other residential areas such as Vila Mariana and Ipiranga. After the war, the economic boom caused rent to increase sharply, so industries moved to cheaper areas of the city. The space abandoned by these factories was used for businesses focused on wholesale fabrics, haberdashery, farm goods, and ready-made clothing.

Later, in the 1980s, 25 de Março Street underwent a number of changes. From this period on, the "street of the Turks" began receiving other groups, especially migrants from Asia—Chinese and Koreans. By the early twenty-first century, various community cultural and social organizations continued to flourish in this area, such as the "Long Live the Centre" (Viva o Centro) Association and the 25 de Março Retailers Union. Its consumer potential became very attractive, and the street became home to the city's most expensive commercial square meters, according to the 25 de Março Tenants Union.[12]

The intensification of Arab–South American relations marked by the formation of ASPA and a new wave of transregional partnerships, for trade, education, culture, and geopolitical solidarity, described above, also strengthened the commercial relations of Brazil with the Arab countries, which created more influence and global access for these São Paulo Arab-Brazilian merchants. In Brazil, trade with the Middle East increased from $5.48 billion in 2003, the year in which the mechanism of ASPA was launched, to $19.54 billion in 2010, an increase of 260 percent. In August of that year, the first trade agreement was signed between Mercosur (Brazil, Argentina, Uruguay, and Paraguay) and an Arab country, Egypt (Ministério de Relações Exteriores 2010). Arab and South American states resumed their free trade agreement (FTA) talks in 2013, according to Michel Alaby, director general of the Arab-Brazilian Chamber of Commerce. "The GCC is discussing an FTA with Mercosur, the South American trade bloc," Alaby explains.[13] Brazil is a founding member of Mercosur.

The Arab-Brazilian Chamber of Commerce, headquartered in a skyscraper along the Avenida Paulista, in the heart of São Paulo's financial district, has been benefiting from ASPA since 2003. According to its website,[14] "The Arab-Brazilian Chamber of Commerce is the quickest and safest way for you to find new markets and to do business with the Arab countries." Since its founding over sixty years ago, the chamber has marketed itself as both an economic and cultural middleman for business transactions between Brazil and the Arab world. It issues certificates verifying the origin and authenticity of imports and exports that travel between these regions, as well as a number of other commercial documents. Besides offering economic services, the chamber also offers translation and consulting services to help those navigating unfamiliar markets in either Brazil or the Arab world.

During the last ASPA (Arab and South American) summit, in October 2012, the Peruvian Ministry of Foreign Affairs organized a business meeting on new opportunities in investments that both showed growth and included active and visible participation of the Arab chambers of commerce in South America. In a context in which the Arab countries are the largest net food importers in the world, food prices are rising considerably, and the Arab populations have suffered from the global increase in these prices, Brazil shared its experience with food security. In the agricultural sector, and in the food industry in general, great potential began to be realized for Brazil to receive Arab investment (particularly from Saudi Arabia and Persian Gulf investors) in order to secure food supplies. It is organizations formed by the nation's Syrio-Lebanese community that have stepped in to facilitate these encounters. Another significant example of the intensification of relations is the growing system of airline routes from the Middle East to Brazil and South America. In recent years, airlines from Doha (Qatar Airways), Dubai (Emirates), Turkey (Turkish Airlines), and, very recently, Abu Dhabi (Etihad Airways) have inaugurated direct flights to Brazil.

The era of "triangulating" South-South relations via the mediation of the United States or Europe is over. The history of relations between South American, African, and Arab countries is replete with catastrophic external interventions marked by the Global North's sense of superiority and arrogance (Farah 2011). Indeed, Brazil has features and is embedded in histories that are allowing it to develop a special direct relationship with the Arab and Muslim countries. The country has undergone a successful transition from dictatorship to a model of stable democracy whose experience it can share. Moreover, Brazil enjoys a very positive image in the Arab region, and the recognition of a Palestinian state at the UN by the Brazilian government in 2010, together with the criticisms of the failed "peace process" Quartet (formed by the United States, Russia, the European Union, and the UN secretary-general), has boosted Brazil's reputation in the region and strengthened its rapprochement with Arab countries.

As this rapprochement advances, Brazil should consolidate and expand its privileged relationship with the countries of the region through a respectful and non-invasive dialogue, but one that should never concede ground in key areas such as human rights, freedom of expression, social inclusion, and the environment. Fronts of broad cooperation require diverse forms of economic exchange, the rebuilding of the rule of law within and between both regions, the consolidation of democratic institutions, guarantees of freedom and social justice, and much more substantial investments in education and cultural creativity. The intensifying closeness between Arabs and South Americans has been, historically, a mutual process fueled by both regions. The ASPA movement of rediscovery and of cultural valorization will allow the construction of alternatives that benefit from mutual understanding and critical reflection upon the rich histories of linguistic, commercial, social, and development partnership and transregional exchange. The ASPA is an innovative initiative but one based in a history that has always been one of transregional integration, struggle, and cultural dialogue.

## Notes

1. Statement of President Luiz Inácio Lula da Silva to the author of this text during the president's trip.

2. Although aware of the possible political damage, during his visit to Lebanon, in the second stop on his tour in the Middle East, President Lula also declared that he was against the occupation of Iraq. In Beirut, the special adviser to the president for international affairs, Marco Aurélio Garcia, and the foreign minister, Celso Amorim, defended the use of the term "occupation" to describe the situation in Iraq. "It's an occupation. As there was war without UN authorization, obviously this is an occupation," said Amorim.

3. According to *The Art Newspaper* magazine, no. 223, April 2011, p. 24.

4. Taken from the Final Declaration of the third ASPA summit, signed by the heads of state and Government of South American and Arab countries in October 2012.

5. In nineteenth-century Brazil, Muslims organized the major urban uprising against slavery in America, the Malian Revolt in 1835 in Salvador (Bahia). *Deleite do estrangeiro em tudo o que é espantoso e maravilhoso: Estudo de um relato de viagem bagdali* (The Foreigner's Delight in Everything That Is Amazing and Wonderful: Study of a Travelogue of Baghdádi), by Paulo Farah (2007), on the first account by an Arab and Muslim ever recorded in Brazil, the erudite 'Abdurrahman bin Abdullah al-Baghdádi, demonstrates the level of organization that Muslims already had in the nineteenth century, during the empire, so much so that the idea of *'umma* was fairly present in cities like Rio de Janeiro, Salvador, and Recife, among others.

6. "Peace be with you!," traditional greeting among Muslims, to which the general reply is *"Wa'alaykum as-salam"* (And peace be upon you!) or, more thoroughly, *"Wa'alaykum as-salam wa rahmat Allah wa barakátuhu"* (May the peace, mercy and blessings of God be with you!).

7. Al-Baghdádi transliterates in Arabic the first-person personal pronoun in Portuguese, *eu*.

8. Over the last years we have translated Brazilian and African amulets written in Arabic characters (in languages such as Hausa and Soninke, and Arabic as well) in order to expand our knowledge about this Muslim community. One of the research lines of the research group registered at the National Council for Scientific and Technological Development (CNPq) in Brazil, "Arabic, African, Asian, South American and Diasporic themes, narratives, and representations," aims to promote reading, analysis, and translation of key texts and manuscripts directly from the original language without an intermediate language between the source language and the target language. Another research line of the same group conducts thematic oral history interviews with people of Lebanese, Syrian, and Palestinian origin in different cities of South America.

9. Muslims often tried to hide their religion in order not to be punished by the imperial laws, particularly the Criminal Code of 1830.

10. After abolition (1888) and the proclamation of the republic (1889), the persecution of Muslims was reduced considerably. And later, in the twentieth century, due to the Constitution of 1946, which guaranteed the freedom of religion, Arab Muslims founded mosques and study centers initially in São Paulo and later in other cities.

11. Permínio Asfora's *Noite Grande* is the first Brazilian novel to introduce a Palestinian as the main character. This work depicts the confrontation of a Palestinian Arab immigrant with the harsh reality of his new home in the inland of northeast Brazil. Palestine was going through a somber period. The author was praised by intellectuals such as Mário de Andrade and Ledo Ivo.

12. As stated during the "Árabes e muçulmanos no Brasil" (Arabs and Muslims in Brazil) conference, organized by BibliASPA in 2009.

13. See Gustavo Machado, "Brasil prepara acordos de livre comércio com países da Liga Árabe," *Brasil Econômico*, 14 March 2013. Online at http://economia.ig.com .br/2013-03-14/brasil-prepara-acordos-de-livre-comercio-com-paises-da-liga-arabe .html.

14. See http://www.ccab.org.br/arabe-brasil/br/quem-somos.fss.

## References

Almeida, Guilherme de. 2004. *Cosmópolis: São Paulo 1929.* 2nd ed. São Paulo: Companhia Editora Nacional.

Amado, Jorge. 2008. *A descoberta da América pelos turcos.* Rio de Janeiro: Companhia das Letras.

———. 1969. *Gabriela, Cravo e Canela.* São Paulo: Martins.

Asfora, Permínio. 2012. *Noite Grande.* 2nd ed. São Paulo: Edições BibliASPA.

Bosi, Ecléa. 1994. *Memória e sociedade: Lembrança dos velhos.* São Paulo: Companhia das Letras.

Castells, Manuel. 1999. *A Sociedade em Rede.* São Paulo: Paz e Terra.

———. 1999. *O poder da identidade.* São Paulo: Paz e Terra.

Emplasa. 2001. *Memória Urbana de São Paulo até 1940.* Vol. 1. São Paulo: Arquivo do Estado, Imprensa Oficial do Estado de São Paulo.

Farah, Paulo Daniel. 2001. *Islã.* São Paulo: Publifolha.

————. 2007. *Deleite do estrangeiro em tudo o que é espantoso e maravilhoso: Estudo de um relato de viagem bagdali*. Argel, Caracas, Rio de Janeiro: Edições BibliASPA, Fundação Biblioteca Nacional, Bibliothèque Nationale d'Algérie e Biblioteca Nacional de Caracas.

————. 2011. *Presença árabe na América do Sul*. São Paulo: Edições BibliASPA.

Hourani, Albert. 1981. *The Emergence of the Modern Middle East*. Berkeley: University of California Press.

————. 2006. *Uma história dos povos árabes*. São Paulo: Companhia das Letras.

Karam, John Tofik. 2007. *Another Arabesque: Syrian-Lebanese Ethnicity in Neoliberal Brazil*. Philadelphia: Temple University Press.

Knowlton, Clark. 1960. *Sírios e Libaneses: Mobilidade Social e Espacial*. São Paulo: Anhambi.

Macedo, Adilson. 2004. *Desenho urbano e bairros centrais de São Paulo: Um estudo sobre a formação e transformação do Brás, Bom Retiro e Pari*. FAU: Tese de Doutorado.

Ministério de Relações Exteriores. 2010. "Nota no. 491: Acordo de Livre Comércio Mercosul–Egito." http://www.itamaraty.gov.br/sala-de-imprensa/notas-a-imprensa/acordo-de-livre-comercio-mercosul-egito. Accessed 31 July 2013.

Morse, Richard. 1970. *Formação Histórica de São Paulo: De Comunidade à Metrópole*. São Paulo: Difusão Européia do Livro.

Moura, Soraya, ed. 2008. *Memorial do Imigrante: A imigração no estado de São Paulo*. São Paulo: Imprensa Oficial do Estado de São Paulo.

Osman, Samira Adel. 2000. *Guia Regional-Estado de São Paulo—Aspectos Históricos de Roteiros Turísticos*. São Paulo: Senac.

Ponciano, Levino. 2007. *Todos os Centros da Paulicéia*. São Paulo: Senac.

Porta, Paula, ed. 2004. *História da Cidade de São Paulo: a cidade na Primeira Metade do Século XX-Imigrantes na Cidade de São Paulo*. São Paulo: Paz e Terra.

Raymond, J.-F. de, ed. 1990. *Arthur de Gobineau et le Brésil: correspondance diplomatique du Ministre de France à Rio de Janeiro*. Grenoble: Presses Universitaires de Grenoble.

Said, Edward. 1979. *Orientalism*. New York: Routledge.

————. 1994. *Representations of the Intellectual*. Nova Iorque: Pantheon Books.

Setubal, Maria Alice, ed. 2008. *A formação do Estado de São Paulo, seus habitantes e os usos da terra*. São Paulo: Cenpec, Imprensa Oficial do Estado de São Paulo, 2008.

Truzzi, Oswaldo, 2009. *Patrícios: Sírios e libaneses em São Paulo*. São Paulo: Unesp.

Veras, Maura Pardini Bicudo. 2003. *DiverCidade: Territórios estrangeiros como topografia da alteridade em São Paulo*. São Paulo: Educ.

# 3

# Brazil's Relations with the Middle East in the "Oil Shock" Era
## Pragmatism, Universalism, and Developmentalism in the 1970s

*Carlos Ribeiro Santana*
*Translated by Bianca Brigidi*

Faced with the energy crises of the 1970s, Brazil pursued a model of economic development that led to strengthening its ties with the Middle East, particularly Iraq and Saudi Arabia, filling a diplomatic vacuum in its foreign policy. High oil prices made securing its supplies a crucial issue for Brazil. Brazil's foreign policy was thus geared to pragmatic ends, leading to the diversification of Brazil's relations with Middle Eastern states.

∼

The 1973 worldwide oil crisis, the result of geopolitical shifts beyond Brazil's control, produced an acute foreign policy crisis in the country. Brazil, during this developmentalist period when its military government was pushing both industrialization and export-oriented commerce, was a nation dependent on imported oil. In fact, Brazil was the main importer of oil in the developing world at the time. In response to the oil shock, Brazil ended a phase of diplomatic inactivity vis-à-vis the Middle East, and launched a new outward-looking economic development project. The high price of oil made it necessary to find a more balanced commercial exchange with Middle Eastern countries in order to guarantee a constant stream of oil, particularly because of ongoing international instability. Through this pragmatic process of diplomatic expansion, Brazil managed to diversify its bilateral agenda, establishing diplomatic relations with ten states from the region in the hopes of attracting new markets for its national exports.

Since the end of the 1960s, Brazilian diplomats had emphasized foreign commerce and searched for new markets for the country's incipient national industries. Brazil had also become increasingly concerned with securing access to oil; this resulted in a series of initiatives in the mid-1970s that were directed toward the Middle East. This chapter analyzes the practice of Brazilian foreign politics in relation to the Arab states during the 1970s, and focuses particularly on policy shifts articulated during the military presidencies of Emílio Garrastazu Médici (1969–1974), Ernesto Geisel (1974–1979), and João Baptista de Oliveira Figueiredo (1979–1985).

## The Médici Government

During the period 1969–1974, the Brazilian military regime launched a bilateral relations policy of "National Interest Diplomacy" (1969–1974), a doctrine developed and named by Foreign Minister Mário Gibson Barboza. This policy package called for changes to the "Prosperity Diplomacy" of President Costa e Silva, who preferred multilateralism and Brazil following global consensuses. According to Paulo Vizentini, with the new policy Brazil came to focus on articulating its self-interests in the global context, aiming for an "individual strategy of insertion, establishing essentially bilateral relations, especially with weaker countries" (1998, 142). Although Costa e Silva's multilateralism was not altogether abandoned, the direction of this new foreign policy emphasized bilateral relations with the specific aim of promoting economic development.

During the 1970s, Itamaraty (Brazil's Foreign Ministry, or Ministry of External Relations) emphasized two principles guiding foreign policy with the Middle East, taking into account both the nature of the oil crises and Brazil's understanding of its own geopolitical identity and interests. The first guideline, starting in 1973, was based on the condemnation of Israel's territorial expansion through armed conflict with its neighbors. The second guideline, based on the effects of the Yom Kippur War, related to support for the creation of a Palestinian state. These guidelines represented a move away from the rhetoric of equidistance. From 1947 to 1973, Brazil followed a policy of equidistance in relation to the Palestine question. This is not to be confused with neutrality. Neutrality implies a lack of interest, abstention, or absence. But equidistance is a unique and balanced position through which Brazil was able to contribute to attempts to resolve, albeit modestly, the Israel-Palestine conflict in accordance with its own values. The term "equidistance" was coined by Itamaraty (the ministry) itself, which supported maintaining commercial interests with both Israel and the Arab world. Furthermore, the presence of significant Jewish and Arab communities in Brazil also influenced the nation's balanced policy toward the region (Santana 2005, 101). According to Norma Breda dos Santos (2000, 20–21), Brazil's principles of equidistance and containment reflected a turn toward more realistic, nationalistic, and pragmatic strategies, and thus corresponded to the transformations in the foreign policy of many developing countries during the oil crises.

The initiative to strengthen relations with the Middle East occurred in both the political and commercial spheres. More than mere diplomatic rhetoric, it aimed for concrete results, such as guaranteeing access to oil in the face of the rising fuel prices, which was Brazil's main concern. Oil became the main preoccupation of Brazilian diplomacy, especially because of the accelerated industrial development the country was undergoing. This new bilateral policy was part of a larger strategy that sought to strengthen political and economic relations with the Middle East. The goal was to create new partnerships with Arab countries without affecting Brazil's relationship with Israel. The diplomatic strategy was also to continue to examine geopolitical alternatives that would lessen the centrality of Brazilian relations with the United States. The tactics aimed at creating partnerships with medium-sized world powers and with less-developed countries in order to increase Brazil's political autonomy in the international order.

## The First Oil Crisis

The Yom Kippur War began in October 1973 and caused the quadrupling of world oil prices. Importing oil thus became a strategic concern for Brazil, which subsequently sought to strengthen its relations with Middle Eastern states. Conflict in the Middle East led oil-producing countries to announce significantly higher prices of the product. The collective action of OPEC (Organization of the Petroleum-Exporting Countries) was an explicit attempt to raise the profile of their struggle with Israel in the face of United Nations inaction. In practice, the war created political conditions that led to the increase in the price of oil. It was in this context that Brazil's relations with Arab countries were reviewed on December 9, 1973. Brazil was the largest importer of oil among developing countries, and was the seventh-largest importer in the world. The rise in oil prices meant that by 1974, Brazil was spending nearly 40 percent of the income it earned on exports on importing oil. In comparison, in 1972, it had been spending only 15 percent of this income on oil (Breda dos Santos 2000, 56). This enormous increase in the average price of a barrel of oil also represented a major setback for the military regime's aim to promote major infrastructure projects and industrial development (while strongly repressing wages and labor activity and ruthlessly repressing political dissent). This military-led developmentalist model relied heavily on imported sources of energy. Thus, Brazil's trading profile was doubly affected by the oil crisis. On the one hand, the rising price of a product of which it was a major importer skewed its balance of payments and trade balance; on the other hand, its exports to the Middle East region were insignificant, leading to a huge increase in its trade deficit with oil-producing countries. According to Brazil's ambassador to Libya (2006–2009), Luciano Rosa:

> These realities led to a diplomatic offensive towards a region that not only represented the best option for supplying Brazil with oil, but also represented a market for non-traditional exports. Soon a more precise and well-defined position on the Middle East and particularly on Palestine became imperative, because without it the strengthening of relations with Arab states would have been compromised. (Rosa 1996, 443–444)

In the context of the Yom Kippur War and anti-colonial and national independence uprisings in Africa, states that supported Portugal, South Africa, or Israel risked having their oil supply suspended by boycotts. Indeed, on November 24, 1973, a resolution was passed by fifteen African states that they would impose a diplomatic boycott on six countries, including Brazil, if they did not cease supporting the white minority government in South Africa. The African threats were followed by similar ones from the Arab world, which targeted those states that supported Israeli expansion. It is important to remember that, at this time, Brazil imported approximately 80 percent of the oil it consumed, making it particularly vulnerable to the effects of a possible third Arab-Israeli war.

## Shifting toward "Pragmatism"

Before the outbreak of the Yom Kippur War, Foreign Minister Gibson Barboza traveled to the Middle East in an effort to increase Brazil's exports to the region and to guarantee its access to oil. The oil revenue pouring into Persian Gulf states gave them the dollars that made them suddenly into attractive consumer markets for Brazilian goods. Not coincidentally, in order to try to overcome the trade deficit and avoid reprisals in its bilateral relations with oil-producing states, Brazil assumed a pro-Arab position at multilateral forums after the oil crisis. The reality caused by the crisis created a new foreign policy orientation that was directly reflected in a wave of new missions and appointments by Brazilian diplomats to the Middle East during this time.

The oil crisis demanded a pragmatic response from the Brazilian government. The first step involved establishing diplomatic missions and exchanging plenipotentiary ambassadors between Brazil and Saudi Arabia. In May 1973, Saudi foreign minister Omar Sakkaf visited Brazil and met with the president, the foreign minister, and other political authorities. During his visit, it was agreed that full diplomatic relations between Brazil and Saudi Arabia would be established, and the first Brazilian representative in Saudi Arabia would be Ambassador Murilo Gurgel Valente. In 1974, Saudi Arabia sent Ambassador Mamoun K. Kabbani as its representative to Brazil.

The Saudi foreign minister returned to Brazil in September 1974 for the creation of the Brazil–Saudi Arabia Commission, which sought to create a "structure for the development of bilateral cooperation" (Ministério de Relações Exteriores 1974, 76). During this visit, the foreign minister met with various Brazilian authorities, including the ministers of foreign relations, industry and commerce, mining, and energy, and with the secretary of the planning of the republic. The visit led to the signing of the Joint Declaration, which highlighted the opportunity to reconsider bilateral relations and the international problems of the time, especially the question of Palestine. The Joint Declaration, imbued with the rhetoric common to this type of document, stated the need to act in solidarity for peace and development, and it emphasized the creation of a new international economic order that favored developing countries. The highlight of the visit, though, was the creation of the Joint Committee, which was to deal with Brazil's top priorities. Among these were securing Brazil's access to Saudi oil (as further embargos loomed), opening Saudi markets to Brazilian goods and services, promoting technological exchanges, launching technical assistance missions, and encouraging private and public joint ventures, financial cooperation, and cultural exchanges. In this contentious context, Brazil's economic agenda and the energy crisis of the time determined the political agenda for foreign relations with Saudi Arabia.

The Saudi foreign minister's visit also resulted in the signing of the Economic and Technical Cooperation Treaty, aimed at developing agricultural, manufacturing, and air and maritime transportation industries through the establishment of joint companies. While the signing of agreements between the two countries was important from a political point of view, in practice it produced few results. Although there was an increase in commercial exchanges between 1968 and 1978, the trade balance remained unfavorable for Brazil, with a gap of nearly US$900 million to US$1.3 billion. To try to compensate for this, Brazil greatly increased its export of footwear; other leather goods; veneer, plywood, and wood sheets; clothing; tiles; and household products to Saudi Arabia.

The increase in commerce with the region was meant to balance the uneven trade relationship and trade deficit with states in the region. Indeed, in 1971, after Petrobras (a semi-state-owned Brazilian energy corporation) and the then recently nationalized Iraq Petroleum Company established ties, it was decided that Iraq would acquire semi-manufactured and manufactured goods produced in Brazil that were of equal or greater value to the Iraqi oil already purchased by Petrobras. That same year, the first Iraqi ambassador in Brazil presented his credentials. Following this pattern throughout the 1970s, Brazil defied an international boycott of Iraq by authorizing Petrobras to buy oil from the country. This move strengthened relations with Iraq and began privileging Brazil as a commercial partner. Iraq became the largest importer for Brazilian services as well as for products such as automobiles, beef and poultry, and weapons (Flecha de Lima 1996, 226–227). Furthermore, Braspetro, a subsidiary of Petrobras, discovered the largest oil field in Iraq in 1977. The Majnoon field measured more than one billion cubic meters (Wang 2003, 123) and was valued at US$10 billion, and it had very low costs of extraction. Unfortunately, the Brazilian company had to abandon it in 1979 because of the war between Iraq and Iran, though Iraq had to pay Brazil US$300 million in indemnization for costs related to geological research. It also had to sign a supply contract for 150,000 barrels of oil per day for fifteen years, on terms that were highly favorable to Brazil (Bandeira 2004, 59).

As for Israel, in January 1972, Brazil signed an agreement that supplemented its Basic Agreement on Technical Cooperation of 1962. The supplement related to bilateral collaboration for irrigation and valorization of areas afflicted by drought in Brazil's northeast. In August 1972, Israeli's minister of finance, Pinhas Sapir, visited Brazil and met with the ministers of finance, foreign affairs, trade and industry, and planning. In March 1973, the two countries then agreed that Israel would send technicians to instruct Brazilian pilots and technicians in the use of sixteen Mirage fighter planes. The Brazilian Air Force hoped to learn from the Israeli experience of using these supersonic planes during its wars with its Arab neighbors. Brazilian officers attended training workshops in Israel and were given information about possible adaptations that could be made in order to enhance aircraft performance. The training also included maintenance of the aircraft (Vizentini 1998, 184).

## President Geisel's Foreign Policy

During the subsequent period, 1974–1979, the administration of another military president, Ernesto Geisel, took Brazil's foreign policy in the boldest direction of any of Brazil's military governments. Indeed, the emphasis placed on ideological identification with the Western military political bloc that had characterized Castelo Branco's government (1964–1967), and which became significantly more visible in Costa e Silva's government (1967–1969), gave way to a much less West-centric foreign policy orientation in Geisel's government (1974–1979). This move out of the Western orbit was referred to euphemistically as "pragmatism." Launching a new agenda that would persist into the twenty-first century, this new diplomatic agenda rejected automatic and a priori alignments with the West, while nevertheless declaring itself to be in line with its values. Multilateralism and globalization of foreign policy were reaffirmed again during the "ecumenical and responsible pragmatism" strategy of Geisel's government.

The term "pragmatism" was used often during the period, emerging for the first time on March 19, 1974, in Geisel's speech at his first presidential meeting in Brasilia, the capital of Brazil. It referred to a foreign policy that was pragmatic and "responsible in light of the Nation's Duties," with special attention to "our relationship with sister-nations on this side and the other side of the ocean" (Brazil/MRE 1974, 9). As Vizentini notes, the president's conception of "responsible pragmatism" was a foreign policy that repudiated ideological polarization or semantic discussions, as well as the bipolar East-versus-West logic of the Cold War (1998, 205).

As Foreign Minister Azeredo da Silveira himself explained in a class he taught on March 4, 1975, this approach to foreign policy was pragmatic because it opposed "apriorism and verbal idealism." It was based on the "search for the realistic facts and the careful evaluation of circumstances" that aimed for "material efficiency rather than formal coherence in the achievement of national objectives" (qtd in Brazil/MRE 1975, 39–40). The term "responsible" aimed at avoiding charges of opportunism while making the concept of pragmatism palatable to the military and to the most conservative sectors of society. The term "ecumenical" referred to the universal aspect of the foreign policy, which sought to look in all possible directions in order to expand Brazil's international relations. In this sense, the foreign policy showed Brazil's interest in reaching out, unhindered, to all countries.

The ecumenical aspect of Brazilian diplomacy was always highlighted in the political discourse of Geisel's government. The new direction did not fit with the a priori exclusion of certain countries from the scope of diplomatic work, so there was a concerted effort to fill the holes in Brazilian diplomacy without ideological prejudices and always in light of national interests. In this sense, the oil crisis brought attention to one of the clearest examples of such a diplomatic hole: the Middle East.

During the Cold War, Brazil lived under the hegemony of the United States and the USSR, and was thus limited in its diplomatic initiatives. One way to expand its autonomy was to distance itself from U.S. influence by universalizing its foreign politics, that is, by multiplying its international contacts. This independent foreign policy—what came to be known as this doctrine of ecumenical and responsible pragmatism—originated in an intellectual-political project conceived in an attempt to overcome policies begun in 1964, the year of a U.S.-supported military coup against an elected leftist government in Brazil. The pragmatist project aimed to take Brazil beyond the Cold War logics that had propelled that coup so that the country could pursue its own national interests independent of either superpower. This new consciousness of national interests demanded the revision of its diplomacy. As Foreign Minister Azeredo da Silveira said in 1974 at the Army Superior School:

> In a changing world, there are no permanent coincidences nor perennial differences. Under these conditions, there can be no automatic alignments, because the subjects of diplomatic action are not countries but situations. What we must seek at all times is to exploit the coincidences that we have in each country, while seeking to reduce the areas of conflict or confrontation. This pragmatic attitude is the very essence of diplomatic activity. (Fonseca 1998, 321)

The diplomacy of Foreign Minister Azeredo da Silveira sought the right to assert independent positions for Brazil without concern for pressure from the two superpowers. Brazil's expansion of its foreign policy toward other countries became indispensable, leading to important changes in relations with the Arab world. The inaugural speech of Foreign Minister Azeredo da Silveira on March 15, 1974, announced the guidelines of the universalism of foreign policy by affirming that "Brazil will not be able to alienate itself from what occurs in other areas, especially potential opportunities in Africa, the Near East, Asia, and Europe" (Brazil/MRE 1974, 21). According to Geisel, Brazil's diplomacy should always be looking for new opportunities and able to act in the service "of the interests of our foreign trade, ensuring the adequate supply of essential raw materials and products and access to the latest technology that we do not have yet, [and] it should be done with prudence and tact, but firmly, with options and necessary realignments" (9).

Regarding the Middle East, Geisel's pragmatism intensified his predecessor's "diplomacy of national interest" in order to boost Brazil's developmental aims and its policy of "equidistance" in the region. During Foreign Minister Azeredo da Silveira's administration, the main goal of any foreign policy toward Arab countries was to increase the export of Brazilian products, which was based on Minister of Finance Delfim Neto's belief that it was necessary to export in order to import. Itamaraty gave such importance to the issue that it disbanded the Department of Near East, Asia, and Oceania and replaced it with a Department of Trade Promotion, opening individual country offices that met the government's expectation to increase bilateral trade with Arab countries.

## Geisel's Government during the First Oil Crisis

Geisel's government, beginning in 1974, immediately faced the impact of the first oil embargo that OPEC had declared in 1973. Geisel, who aspired to lead Brazil in its economic development, had bet everything on a developmentalist agenda prepared by Minister of Planning Reis Velloso, which invested heavily in infrastructure and advanced industrial integration. This project, in turn, relied heavily on imported oil and foreign capital. In this urgent developmentalist context, "responsible pragmatism" became a critical instrument of policy, aiming to meet the demands of an economy that had substantially advanced industrially, but which featured many points of vulnerability, revealed acutely by the turmoil caused by the oil crisis. Thus, it was necessary to build priority relationships with certain countries and regions through political outreach, through large joint projects, or through commercial expansion. In this push, the vision of the Middle East as a strategic partner was born. It was in this vein that Brazil sought regional cooperation with countries such as Algeria, Libya, Iraq, and Saudi Arabia in the form of joint ventures for oil exploration through Braspetro and for a wide range of technological and industrial-military development efforts, including Brazilian arms sales and joint missile manufacturing projects.

According to the scholar Antônio Lessa, the Geisel government was guided by a clear objective, to "pursue the necessary elements for achieving their development aims sketched in the lines of the Second National Development Plan" launched in September 1974 (1995, 24). Far from adopting a defensive strategy, the plan called for more industrialization by substituting imports in order to make the country self-sufficient in its basic needs and, if possible, in energy as well. The Geisel government, therefore, aimed to review the agenda of bilateral relations through diversifying its external ties.

The move away from West-centric or pro-colonial attitudes that defined Geisel's foreign policy made it necessary to first review "exclusive relationships," defined by Lessa as bilateral relations and political dependencies that were "explicit or hidden, and that prevented the country from expanding its markets as well as denied it access to products important for its project of development" (2000, 162). Geisel thus immediately tried to free Brazil from the limitations imposed by its association with the dying Portuguese empire and to distance itself from South African apartheid, which had blocked Brazil's ability to establish diplomatic and economic access to newly independent African nations. Brazil also moved away from its policy of equidistance, which aimed at "balance" but in practice had been perceived as favoring Israel and thus had hindered relations with the Arab world. Brazil also moved away from nationalist China (Taiwan), which had hindered Brazil's efforts to build trade relations with mainland China (the People's Republic). According to Vizentini, the new policies were based on the "pragmatic analysis of the energetic conjuncture of the moment (1998, 12)." As interpreted by Araújo Castro, foreign minister and UN ambassador in the late 1960s, the ideological foundation of this policy of engagement with the Middle East derived from the economic necessities of the country's National Development Plan (246).

The Brazilian diplomatic discourse during Geisel's term began to prioritize the question of Palestine in relation to the conflict in the Middle East. Indeed, the impact of the new policy for the Middle East reached its apex on November 10, 1975, when Ambassador Sergio Corrêa da Costa, head of Brazil's delegation to the United Nations, voted in favor of the draft of the General Assembly resolution declaring Zionism to be a form of racism and racial discrimination. The repercussions of the Brazilian vote, however, were far more negative than could have been expected. At the time, many Brazilian diplomatic elites assumed that the vote would gain sympathy from the Arab states and would help promote the sale of Brazilian weapons to them, although this charge was denied by Geisel (Breda dos Santos 2003, 12).

Brazil's vote was criticized both domestically and internationally, and it demonstrated a break with the policy of equidistance, to Israel's detriment. It surprised the public, as well as diplomats and senior army officers. Nevertheless, according to Lessa, "voting anti-Zionist at the UN [was] the symbol of an important process in the construction of universalism in Brazil" in that it showed that the country's international relations were not attached to extreme Westernism or to U.S. foreign policy (2000, 168).

The oil crisis, the evolution of North-South relations (that is, dialogue between developed and developing countries), and the ongoing Cold War led Brazilian diplomacy to align itself in international forums with developing countries during a time when nearly all Middle Eastern states were identified as "developing." The Middle East became of great interest to Brazil. According to Vizentini, "it was not just to secure oil imports and to access a broad consumer market for agricultural products, manufactured goods, services and arms. . . . It was the outline of an axis of cooperation between emerging middle powers in the Third World" (1998, 12).

## Increase in Relations with the Region

By 1974, Brazil had considerably increased its presence in Arab countries, both politically and economically. Indeed, in June 1974, Brazilian embassies were opened in the United Arab Emirates and in Bahrain. In July of that year, diplomatic relations were established with the Sultanate of Oman and, soon after, with ten other states in the region. This marked the onset of a season of intense exchanges and high-level visits where Brazil aimed to create new markets for its national exports (Lessa 2000, 169). In 1978, a large contract for the construction of a railway connecting Baghdad and Akashat was signed by the Brazilian consortium of Mendes Junior (an engineering company) with Interbras (a construction contractor), and with Iraq's Ministry of Transports (Vizentini 1998, 249). Iraq also began importing large quantities of vehicles, frozen poultry, and sugar from Brazil (Ministério de Relações Exteriores 1978, 66). In addition, Braspetro continued the exploration and extraction of oil in the Iraqi region of Basra.

But trade deficits did not disappear, despite these efforts, as oil prices continued to soar. In 1973, the negative balance of trade with Arab countries was US$353 million. By 1974, the deficit increased to more than US$1.7 billion, and by 1978, to above US$3.3 billion (Silva 2003, 583). In order to mitigate the negative trade balance, throughout the 1970s Brazil attempted to increase its sales to the Middle East and to receive foreign investments in petrodollars. Brazil strengthened its diplomatic and trade ties with the region through several initiatives, signing agreements with Egypt, Libya, Kuwait, Saudi Arabia, Iran, and Iraq. In an attempt to balance this inequity, Brazil increased its exportation of manufactured goods to the region, mainly aircraft produced by Embraer and weapons manufactured by Imbel. Iraq, Saudi Arabia, Kuwait, and Iran all emerged as major suppliers of oil to Brazil. This allowed Petrobras to develop a broad program of oil research in these countries in 1974, in order to import oil on specific terms (Silva 2003, 583).

Iraq and Brazil maintained particularly close diplomatic ties starting in 1974, and Iraq was the largest exporter of oil to Brazil between 1974 and 1979. Indeed, in August 1975, Brazil was importing 930,000 barrels per day from the Iraq National Oil Company. To balance trade, Brazil exported manufactured goods such as cars, trucks, and appliances; minerals such as iron ore and aluminum oxide; products such as lumber and frozen meat; and services. It also encouraged the participation of Brazilian construction companies in infrastructure projects in Iraq.

In 1975, Itamaraty organized Brazil's participation in international trade fairs hosted in Tripoli, Tehran, Algiers, Baghdad, and Casablanca. Under the sponsorship of Brazil's foreign ministry, the second Brazilian Industrial Exhibition was held in Kuwait; it included representative samples of national industrial products (Ministério de Relações Exteriores 1975, 121). In 1976, Brazil once again participated in international fairs in Tripoli, Tehran, Algiers, and Baghdad, and held its first industrial exhibitions in Saudi Arabia and Damascus (Ministério de Relações Exteriores 1976, 83). In the same year, to boost trade relations with Arab countries, Interbras opened an office in the Middle East, while Petrobras technicians were sent to the region to negotiate an extension of payment deadlines with the main suppliers of oil. In 1977, Brazil participated in several fairs to promote exports in order to reduce the trade deficit, and maintained a presence in the international fairs of Tripoli, Tehran, Algiers, Baghdad, and Cairo. Also in 1977, another Brazilian industrial exhibition was organized in Kuwait, and a technology exhibition was organized in Saudi Arabia (Ministério de Relações Exteriores 1977, 78).

**General Figueiredo's Foreign Policy**

During the years 1979–1985, Brazil experienced unfavorable internal and external conditions, including a domestic economic crisis, with declining growth, external debt, and high inflation. Also, the United States' aggressive raising of interest rates worsened the situation of highly indebted countries like Brazil. In this period, the military president João Figueiredo's administration continued Geisel's "responsible pragmatism" foreign policy. The presence of Brazilian diplomacy worldwide was intensified under the "universalism" of Foreign Minister Ramiro Saraiva Guerreiro, who tried to maintain the international autonomy of previous Brazilian governments. Itamaraty aimed to increase cooperation with other Global South countries, in order to strengthen bargaining power for economic multilateral negotiations. The Middle East was seen as essential in this regard. They fit the model of South-South cooperation (that is, cooperation between developing or newly independent countries) sought by the Foreign Ministry.

The new government immediately faced yet another oil crisis in 1979, which forced Brazil to borrow from the International Monetary Fund (IMF) in order to pay off the debts it had acquired during the "economic miracle" (the period of booming growth Brazil experienced during the late 1960s and early '70s) and because of the increase in international interest rates. Debts were increasing, and none of the national policies alleviated the chronic trade deficit. Although the quantity of agricultural exports had increased, it was not yet sufficient to cover the deficit. National businesses were simply not prepared to become significant exporters to Arab countries, despite the federal government's incentives to encourage this. Inexperience was the main cause of the negligible increase in trade with the Middle Eastern countries during this period, including exporters' inexperience with the subtleties of the Arab market and all of its cultural dimensions, as well as the heavy bureaucratic obstacles both in Brazil and its targeted Middle East market countries. Indeed, exports to Asia and the Middle East only grew from 3.46 percent in 1971 to 9.86 percent in 1981 (Flecha de Lima 1996, 236).

Yet, regarding the oil crisis, Foreign Minister Saraiva Guerreiro noted that "few countries have done so much to reduce their dependence on oil than Brazil, either by increasing its domestic production or launching pro-alcohol [ethanol]" (1992, 176). The reduction of spending on oil imports, from US$28.3 billion in 1984 to US$12 billion in 1986, was due to the efforts that were made to install new drilling infrastructure and to increase domestic oil production, although many of these plans were implemented with foreign capital and the taking on of more debt. Even with these improvements, however, Itamaraty could do little to solve the looming oil crisis, as the negotiation of foreign debt, once part of the Foreign Ministry's responsibilities, had been moved to the Ministry of Finance. So as the neoliberal 1980s began, foreign policy issues came to be dominated by debt and finance agendas, so trade agreements and renegotiations of loan obligations quickly undermined other aims and alternatives that had been inserted into Brazil's foreign policy agenda.

Fortunately, for most countries, the oil shock of 1979 did not have the intensity and duration of the 1973 crisis. Several factors contributed to the moderating impact of the global crisis on Brazil in 1979, such as Brazil's accumulated surplus of oil, use of alternative energy sources, and its decrease of oil consumption (which was tied to the drop in economic activity). So as the neoliberal financial frame was imposed, Brazil's focus turned to grappling with the overwhelming foreign debt.

## The Figueiredo Government and the Second Oil Crisis

The global economic and political situation worsened with the revolution in Iran and the subsequent Iran-Iraq War (1980–1988). With the conflict between

Iraq and Iran, new political instability was created in the Middle East, which brought another global crisis and a consequent rise in international prices for barrels of oil. The new crisis produced immediate repercussions in Brazil, where oil reserves were in decline. For Brazil, the main fear brought by the outbreak of war was the interruption of supplies, since Iraq accounted for half of its imported oil. Thanks to its special relationship with Iraq, spearheaded by Ambassador Paulo Tarso Flecha, Brazil had survived both the oil crises of 1973 and 1979 without the need for rationing, even when the price of a barrel jumped from US$3 to US$12 in October 1973 and when it hovered around US$36 a barrel between 1981 and 1983. When the 1979 political crisis in Iran broke out, Iraqi ambassador Zaid Haidas announced that his country was ready to fill the supply gap left by Iran—which had been supplying 25 percent of Brazil's oil—in recognition of the fact that Brazil in 1971 had been the first state to break the boycott of Iraqi oil that had been imposed when that country nationalized its petroleum companies in 1961 (Wang 2003, 123).

The lack of diversification in oil suppliers was the fault of Petrobras, which pursued a policy of exclusively acquiring oil according to the lowest price, and did not consider maintaining a diversity of providers. However, the strategy cannot be fully criticized, as importing oil from other countries, such as Ecuador, Mexico, or Venezuela, would have been much more expensive and thus have caused a deeper deficit, which in turn could have jeopardized the industrial development aims of the military regime. Indeed, in 1979, Iraq, Saudi Arabia, and Iran were still responsible for providing approximately 80 percent of oil imported by the country (Wang 2003, 170).

Brazil was unable to balance trade with the Middle East. The data regarding the increase of exports from Brazil to the Middle East (Lessa 2000, 171–172) indicate that there was a jump of 1 percent of total exports between 1967 and 1972; another jump to 3 percent between 1973 and 1978, and a third to 6 percent between 1980 and 1985. In the opposite direction, the costs of imports increased to 6 percent of Brazil's total expenditures between 1967 and 1972; to 22 percent between 1973 and 1978; and went down to 14 percent between 1980 and 1985. The expectation of attracting direct investments from the Middle East was also frustrated, notwithstanding the fact that the OPEC countries were highly capitalized at the time due to the high oil prices. The figures indicate that between 1967 and 1994, only 8 percent of direct foreign investments recorded in Brazil came from the Middle East (Lessa 2000, 171–172). One of the few infusions of capital from petrodollars during this period was the loan Saudi Arabia granted to Brazil, valued at US$54 million, for the hydroelectric project of the São Francisco Valley (Ministério de Relações Exteriores 1977, 78). But on the whole, at this time the Saudis preferred the safe and quick return on the investment of petrodollars in Europe and the United States.

## The Failure of Increased Trade with the Region

Brazil's initial attempts during the 1970s to enter the Arab market were frustrated at first. Even Foreign Minister Saraiva Guerreiro recognized that the results of the Brazilian race to obtain investments and funding opportunities, and to increase trade in goods and services in the states that were accumulating reserves of petrodollars, were lackluster. This also reinforced the conclusion that the Western commercial powers were still coming out on top. Saraiva Guerreiro summed this up by saying that even with "some contracts for services with Brazilian companies, mainly of construction, little was concretized" (1992, 178). The failure to increase exports to the Middle East was, in Itamaraty's point of view at the time, due to the lack of aggressiveness on the part of Brazilian businessmen in competing with Western/developed countries in providing products and investment opportunities. Businesses, in turn, complained about Itamaraty's excessive bureaucracy and the lack of flexibility in government sectors. According to Silva (2003, 57–59), the effort to fill the markets of Arab countries with Brazilian goods came "late," preventing Brazil from broadening its economic participation in the Arab world. Silva points to the lack of Brazilian experts on the Middle East and to the slow responses of the Brazilian bureaucracy as the main reasons for the failure in the region. Silva also highlights the inexperience of the national business community, explaining that "they had no time to prepare to compete in an unknown market and with very peculiar characteristics, for example, the restriction of certain products for religious reasons." Lessa agrees with Silva, affirming that "Brazil's efforts to penetrate the Middle East were undoubtedly late and rushed, as they were largely determined by the oil crisis" (2000, 165).

However, if the economic results of the policies left something to be desired, the advances made on the diplomatic level were considerable. Political ties with nearly every country in the Middle East were strengthened. Although the results did not meet the government's expectations, Itamaraty played a key role in the national initiative of trying to increase and diversify trade with Arab countries after the first oil shock in 1973. In addition to promoting national products at major Arabic trade fairs—especially in Iraq, Libya, and Saudi Arabia—to enhance Brazilian industrial production, the ministry also underwent internal changes to accommodate the new demands that the foreign policy created. Although Foreign Minister Saraiva Guerreiro did not reach his goal of eliminating trade imparities with the oil producers of the Arab world, the effort made it possible to establish a wide range of both diplomatic and commercial relations that would prove useful and productive over the long term.

## Conclusion

This study has argued that political-economic processes drove shifts in Brazil's foreign policy orientation toward Arab countries, leading to the articulation of a "pragmatic" agenda through which diplomatic relationships were strengthened in order to increase the flow of hard currency and stabilize friendly relations with besieged Arab states, which in turn would enable the securing of oil imports. Although this political-economic and diplomatic pragmatism intended to make foreign policy lasting and meaningful through a more solid and permanent exchange with the Third World markets, foreign policy toward the Arab countries had as its immediate objective the lowering of the trade deficit. In this sense, President Geisel's policy of responsible pragmatism allowed for the provisional survival and consolidation of the military government's developmentalist import-substitution industrialization model by finding foreign markets for Brazilian manufacturing. And this pragmatism permitted the intensification of commercial contacts with Africa, China, and the Middle East. Regarding the Middle East, Itamaraty adopted an aggressive export policy focusing on industrial and agricultural products and services in exchange for oil supplies. Later, during Figueiredo's government, the Palestine Liberation Organization (PLO) was allowed to set up an office in Brasilia to help raise sympathy for Arab countries, even though the Israeli ambassador in Brasilia had requested that Brazil not recognize a "terrorist organization" (Santana 2006, 78).

Despite all these efforts, in the end, Brazil's efforts to equalize trade with the Middle East during the 1970s (and 1980s) was unsuccessful—no quantity of increased exports could counterbalance the skyrocketing price of oil. In 1974, Brazil exported nearly US$198 million to the region, and in 1979, it exported US$975 million. However, the deficit remained high throughout the 1970s because Brazil spent, for example, US$353 million in 1974 on oil, and nearly US$3.7 billion in 1979 (Silva 2003, 589). Then during the 1980s, Brazil supplied industrial products to the Middle East, especially military hardware. The trade with Arab countries, though small, was significant because it had been practically nonexistent previously.

The Geisel government's initiative to create alternative sources of energy production to help reduce dependence on oil was one of the most positive aspects of the unfavorable international situation at the time. Thus, one of the most beneficial effects of the energy crisis in the medium and long term was Brazil's ability to increase extraction and refinement of oil at home through Petrobras. Starting with the first oil shock of 1973, the military government encouraged domestic oil production. However, after the second crisis, in 1979, the exploration of new wells became more important due to the high price of a barrel of oil on the international market. The economic integration of logistical and operational knowledge of the Arab market was growing in the diplomatic sphere and this drove the reevaluation of priorities on the international agenda.

While Brazil's attempts to expand commercial relations with the Middle East ultimately did not meet expectations, the pragmatic international politics with the Middle East regarding the search for a solution to the energy crisis in the 1970s had many positive results. One such result was that the policy of moving Brazil out of the Western orbit and opening it to developing countries, particularly in the Mideast and Africa, contributed to the diversification of Brazil's foreign relations and laid the groundwork for Brazil's twenty-first century cosmopolitan identity as a pioneer of South-South solidarity.

## Note

Portions of this chapter were published in an earlier version in Portuguese as "O aprofundamento das relações do Brasil com os países do Oriente Médio durante os dois choques do petróleo da década de 1970: Um exemplo de ação pragmática" in *Revista Brasileira de Política Internacional* 49(2) (2006): 157–177.

## References

Bandeira, Muniz. 2004. *As Relações Perigosas: Brasil e Estados Unidos (de Collor a Lula)*. Rio de Janeiro: Editora Civilização Brasileira.

Brazil/MRE. 1974. *Resenha de política exterior do Brasil*. Vol. 1, no. 1. Brasília: Departamento de Comunicação e Documentação do MRE.

———. 1975. *Resenha de política exterior do Brasil*. Vol. 2, no. 4. Brasília: Departamento de Comunicação e Documentação do MRE.

Breda dos Santos, Norma. 2000. "O Brasil e a questão israelense nas Nações Unidas: da criação do Estado de Israel ao pós(?)-sionismo." In *Brasil e Israel: Diplomacia e sociedades,* ed. Norma Breda dos Santos. Brasília: Editora Universidade de Brasília.

———. 2003. "As posições brasileiras nas Nações Unidas com relação ao Oriente Médio." *Cena Internacional* 5(2) (December).

Flecha de Lima, Paulo Tarso. 1996. "Diplomacia e Comércio: Notas sobre a política externa brasileira nos anos 70." In *Sessenta anos de política externa 1930–1990,* ed. José Augusto Gilhon Albuquerque. São Paulo: Cultura Editores Associados / Núcleo de Pesquisa em Relações Internacionais–USP.

Fonseca, Gelson, Jr. 1998. *A legitimidade e outras questões internacionais*. São Paulo: Paz e Terra.

Lessa, Antônio Carlos. 1995. "A estratégia de diversificação das parcerias no contexto do nacional desenvolvimentismo (1974–1979)." *Revista Brasileira de Política Internacional* 38(1): 24–39.

———. 2000. "Israel e o Mundo Árabe no Cruzamento das Escolhas Internacionais Brasil." Chapter 4 in *Brasil e Israel: Diplomacia e Sociedades,* ed. Norma Breda dos Santos, 149–186. Brasília: Editora da Universidade de Brasília.

Ministério de Relações Exteriores (MRE). 1974. *Relatório do Ministério de Relações Exteriores.*

———. 1975. *Relatório do Ministério de Relações Exteriores.*

———. 1976. *Relatório do Ministério de Relações Exteriores.*

———. 1977. *Relatório do Ministério de Relações Exteriores.*

———. 1978. *Relatório do Ministério de Relações Exteriores.*

Rosa, Luciano Ozório. 1996. "O Brasil e o Oriente Médio (1930–1990)." In *Sessenta anos de política externa 1930–1990*, ed. José Augusto Gilhon Albuquerque. São Paulo: Cultura Editores Associados/ Núcleo de Pesquisa em Relações Internacionais–USP.

Santana, Carlos Ribeiro. 2005. "O Brasil e conflito árabe-israelense-palestino (1947–2005)." Master's thesis, International Relations: Universidade de Brasília.

———. 2006. "O Brasil e as tensões permanentes no Oriente Médio: A questão palestina." Master's thesis, International Relations: Instituto Rio Branco.

Saraiva Guerreiro, Ramiro. 1992. *Lembranças de um empregado do Itamaraty*. São Paulo: Siciliano.

Silva, Heloisa Conceição Machado. 2003. "Da substituição de importações a substituição de exportações: A política de comercio exterior brasileira de 1945–1979." PhD diss. Brasília: Universidade de Brasília.

Vizentini, Paulo Gilberto Fagundes. 1998. *A Política Externa do Regime Militar Brasileiro: Multilateralização, Desenvolvimento e a Construção de uma Potência Média (1964–1985)*. Porto Alegre: Editora da Universidade.

Wang, Ana Beatriz Gaertner Marabuto. 2003. "Dilema energético e política exterior (os)." Master's thesis, International Relations. Universidade de Brasília.

# 4

# Palestine-Israel Controversies in the 1970s and the Birth of Brazilian Transregionalism

*Monique Sochaczewski*
*Translated by Bianca Brigidi*

Sochaczewski discusses changes in Brazilian foreign policy toward the Middle East throughout the 1970s. She explores how Brazil's policy of "equidistance" was challenged by oil crises and Palestine-Israel controversies, and how it was gradually abandoned in favor of more economically productive relations with the region, thus charting the emergence of a doctrine of Brazilian transregionalism.

∾

Before the 1970s, Brazil's foreign policy toward the Middle East was referred to as "equidistant," oscillating between support for Israel, embodied in the important role Oswaldo Aranha, Brazil's UN ambassador, played in 1947–1948 when he served as president of the UN General Assembly and supported the partition of Palestine and recognition of Israel as an independent state, and support for Israel's critics, embodied in Brazil's support for UN Resolution 242, which in 1967 mandated the full withdrawal of Israel from all territories occupied during the Six-Day War. Implementing this "equidistant" tradition, in early 1973, Brazil's foreign minister, Mário Gibson Barboza, traveled to Egypt and Israel in order to serve as mediator and messenger between the two sides. He was convinced then of the possibility of peace between the two countries (Barboza 1992, 316). However, the war in October 1973 would force him to change this position.

When military president General Ernesto Geisel's government came to power in March 1974, his administration began to restructure foreign policy in general and toward the region in particular in hopes of making Brazil a more assertive power. This policy would be elaborated and implemented by the president and his foreign minister, Antônio Azeredo da Silveira. Their agendas converged on pursuing an international activism: "Geisel thought of foreign policy as an extension of the domestic political game. Whereas Silveira conceived of it as a lever to project Brazil upwards in the international hierarchy" (Spektor 2009, 64).

At the same time, the Middle East's oil was still very important for the developmental projects undertaken by the military regime. Geisel had a personal interest in oil issues because he had chaired Petrobras, Brazil's semi-government-owned petroleum company, from 1969 to 1973. This chapter aims to present significant changes in the foreign relations between Brazil and the Middle East between 1974 and 1979, and will focus particularly on the controversies involving Palestine and Israel and how they played out in the United Nations context.

The war in the Middle East in October 1973 had definitively affected the economy as well as world politics. It began as a personal project of the Egyptian president, Anwar el-Sadat, with the aims of recovering Arab self-esteem after the humiliating defeat of the 1967 war and of bringing Israel to negotiate (el-Sadat 1983, 261–302). However, it ended up becoming part of a movement of Arab nations that were gaining control over their own oil production and proclaiming a common pan-Arab agenda.

The repercussions were immediate in Brazil. By the end of Emílio Garrastazu Médici's governing term in 1973, Foreign Minister Gibson Barboza, worrying about the oil threat, had shifted his position, advocating closer relations with Arab nations. In the following government, led by Ernesto Geisel, these same initiatives led Brazil to diversify its international relations as much as possible.

Even before assuming the positions of president and foreign minister in March 1974, Ernesto Geisel and Azeredo da Silveira spoke of "correcting the direction" of relations with the Middle East. Taking advantage of relations already established by the previous administration and concurrently exploring new possibilities, the government became engaged in building relations with Arab nations from the very beginning—especially with those that produced oil. As discussed in the chapter by Carlos Ribeiro Santana in this volume, Saudi Arabia and Iraq were the primary targets of this strategy, since they were the major exporters of oil to Brazil and had the most petrodollars. Other Arab regions of interest were the Persian Gulf and North Africa. The Arab countries in the eastern Mediterranean also got some attention, although they had little oil, but cities like Beirut and Aleppo played important commercial or financial roles in the Arab world.

## The End of the Policy of Equidistance

In January 1973 Gibson Barboza stated to Brazilian newspapers that they should not assign arbitrary political value to his trip to Egypt and Israel. Brazil has remained "strictly equidistant between Israel and the Arab world and aspires not to exert any action in mediating conflict" (*O Estado de São Paulo* 1973). The correspondence he sent to Arab authorities at the end of his term as foreign minister, however, provides evidence that the policy of equidistance (which leaned toward Israel as it counterbalanced Arab nations diplomatically) was under review. Geisel's government would abolish it altogether. The term "equidistance" was used by the foreign ministry itself for several decades to portray its relations with Middle Eastern countries. It was avoided, however, during Geisel's administration, because it had come to be understood as, in practice, pro-Israel. Later on, Silveira would stress his opposition to such a concept:

> [Brazil's] position of equidistance in the Middle East [is] in reality a pro-Israel statement because an equidistant position does not exist in politics. . . . As everything is a matter of degree, there is always a degree that defines one's position. [Equidistance] does not exist. I tried to put an end to that invention Gibson created to defend himself. (FGV/CPDOC 1979a)[1]

In March 1974 Silveira wrote a document listing what was to be the general position of Brazil toward the Middle East. The first item spoke of the need to change the policy of equidistance practiced in previous governments. Such a policy was useless and distasteful to the involved parties. It also suggested Brazil was available for mediation, which did not really fall in its domain, for "besides having no real potential for success, it was a line of action that did not attend to national interests" (FGV/CPDOC 1974a). This was highlighted by Brazil's vote in favor of UN Resolution 242 (of 1967), which demanded the total withdrawal of Israel from territories occupied during the Six-Day War.

Silveira also wanted to demystify what he called the "false image" that Brazil played a major role in the creation of the state of Israel and that Oswaldo Aranha was the Jews' greatest defender (FGV/CPDOC 1975a). Silveira highlighted the fact that the Brazilian vote at the UN in 1947, at a special session presided over by Aranha, was presented by the delegate Artur de Sousa Costa and not solely meant for the creation of the state of Israel. Later, Silveira said, "That is the biggest joke in this world. The foreign ministry's archives have official circulars signed by Mr. Oswaldo Aranha that make the fiercest claims against the Jews" (FGV/CPDOC 1979a).

These documents, dated between 1938 and 1941, were sent to President Geisel in August 1978 (FGV/CPDOC 1978). The documents confirm that Oswaldo Aranha, when he was foreign minister, did sign several official memoranda—the majority of them top secret—imposing numerous barriers to the entry of Jewish immigrants to Brazil (Koifman 2002, 103–126). Apparently, even though Silveira had secured copies of these documents, he did not release them to the public. Instead, he used them to generate a new discourse regarding Aranha. He also searched the archive for Sousa Costa's original speech regarding his actions at the UN. In possession of the transcript that initially defended a bi-national state (a united Palestine that could have included Arabs and Jews in an integrated democracy), Silveira felt authorized to revise Oswaldo Aranha's image as well as Brazil's role in the partition of Palestine.

**Diplomatic Expansion**

A second shift in approach vis-à-vis the Middle East was that of cementing bilateral relations by ensuring that Brazil sent ambassadors to as many countries as possible in the region, thus increasing the chance of dialogue. In the beginning of April 1974, the president took Silveira's suggestion of making the Brazilian ambassador in Kuwait, Murilo Gurgel Valente, also responsible for relations with Bahrain, Qatar, the United Arab Emirates, and Oman, countries with which Brazil had just established diplomatic ties (FGV/CPDOC 1974b; FGV/CPDOC 1974c; Lessa 2002, 179). By the end of May, Hisham el-Shawa would receive the *agrément* to be the chief of the Jordanian diplomatic mission in both Chile and Brazil (FGV/CPDOC 1974d). In the first half of 1974, the Brazilian government was already either establishing or amplifying its diplomatic presence throughout a good part of the Middle East. It especially concentrated on embassies created during the previous government in Libya, Iraq, and Saudi Arabia, entrusting them with the responsibility of representing Brazilian interests in the region.

The government also searched for mechanisms through which to consolidate its economic relations with countries from the area. On April 30, Silveira pointed to the bilateral agreement signed between Spain and Saudi Arabia as a model to be emulated. In this agreement, Saudis pledged to grant Spain priority over its supply of crude oil. It also established the basis for ample financial, industrial, and agricultural cooperation between the nations. A mixed commission was constituted in order to support similar economic agreements. Although without any previous experience, Brazil was inspired by the Saudi-Spanish framework to consolidate its economic relations with Saudi Arabia.

It also became a model for similar negotiations with Iraq, Libya, Kuwait, and Algeria (FGV/CPDOC 1974e).

The Arab diplomatic movement to Brazil was also intense; by the end of this government's term Brasília was home to embassies from Saudi Arabia, Algeria, Kuwait, Egypt, Iraq, Lebanon, Libya, Morocco, and Syria, as well as representatives from Jordan and Qatar (*Revista da Liga* 1979, 64). Several agreements were signed between Brazil and the countries of the region, mainly about economic and technical cooperation, as well as air transport (Vizentini 1998, 245–256).

Another notable development could be seen in Brazil's participation in international fairs throughout the Arab world. Brazil sought prestige events, especially in oil-producing countries, and explored opportunities for Brazilian companies, especially contractors. At the International Technology Fair of Algiers, in 1974, for instance, the Brazilian interest was to ensure opportunities for Brazilian companies in building highways and dams. The Algerians, in turn, "saw in the Brazilian engineering a chance to escape, in this sector, the dependence of European technology, particularly French" (*O Estado* 1974a). Between 1974 and 1977, Brazil was represented at fairs in Algiers, Tripoli, Cairo, Casablanca, Tehran, Damascus, and Baghdad. In 1975 and 1977, the Second Brazilian Exhibition and the Brazilian Industrial Exhibition, respectively, took place in Kuwait. In 1976 and 1977, the Brazilian Industrial Exhibition and the Brazilian Technological Exhibition, respectively, took place in Saudi Arabia for the first time (Lessa 2002, 178–182).

Sending missions to the Middle East, which had already been initiated during the oil crisis by Médici's administration, became another front used by the government. They also received representatives from Arab countries with special honors. Silveira's strategy was to invite well-known figures from Arab countries to visit Brazil, and to organize a Brazilian delegation from the ministerial level to travel to the region in order to promote Brazil's potential and its interests.

The first Discussion Forum on Economic Relations between Brazil and the Arab world (the ancestor of today's South America–Arab States partnership) took place in Rio de Janeiro in the beginning of April 1974 (*O Estado* 1974b). The event was also frequented by Brazilian business people of Syrian or Lebanese descent. Three main points were discussed. First was trade—oil, coffee, phosphates, manufactured goods, and agricultural products were some of the main products analyzed. Next was investments, and Brazil's need for capital was analyzed sector by sector, as was the applicable legislation. And finally, services were discussed, as well as the conditions and prospects for developing relations in the sector (*Jornal do Brasil* 1974).

As for relations with Libya, these were developed along two trajectories. In June 1974, the Libyan oil minister, Ezzedin al-Mabrouk, visited Brazil and talked to various authorities, declaring himself in total favor of closer relations and of ensuring Brazil access to Libya's oil supply. At the end of July 1974, a Brazilian business mission visited Libya, and in 1975, a mission led by the secretary general of trade and industry visited Tripoli and signed the protocol that created the Joint Brazilian-Libyan Commission, whose goal was to enhance economic and trade cooperation. In 1978 the Technical, Scientific, and Technological Cooperation Agreement was signed by the two countries.

In July 1974, a trade mission formed by businessmen and bankers from Kuwait visited Brazil, and in November, the Brazilian trade mission that had gone to Saudi Arabia also went to Kuwait. In 1975, not only did the business minister of Kuwait visit Brazil and sign the Economic Cooperation Agreement that created a joint commission between the two countries, but the prime minister himself came to Brazil. A Brazilian business delegation also visited Kuwait in the same year. In 1976, the Interbras—a Petrobras subsidiary—established a central office for the Middle East that aimed to increase exports to the region. It also ended up decreasing the number of visits of Brazilian authorities to the Arab world (and vice versa), since the country now had a representative in residence full-time in many of the nations.

Relations with Saudi Arabia were more active during the term of Omar Sakkaf (FGV/CPDOC 1979b). Sakkaf visited Brazil in June 1973, as well as in September 1974, when the Joint Brazilian-Saudi Commission was created in order to develop bilateral cooperation. The Saudi minister passed away in New York a short time after the commission had its session at the UN General Assembly in 1974. According to Silveira, Omar Sakkaf's death "ended a very important opportunity for cooperation with an Arab country that seemed then to be the best one with which to start a major dialogue." In November 1974, a Brazilian trade mission visited Saudi Arabia, which resulted in the signing of the Agreement on Economic and Technical Cooperation the following year. In mid-1975, the new Saudi foreign minister, Prince Saud al-Faisal, told Silveira in New York that he expected a visit from him. The contacts of the minister of Iraq, Hammadi, advised the Brazilian foreign minister to send a technical mission to Baghdad and then visit the city himself. Silveira's much-anticipated trip to the Middle East never happened. However, the fact that it was discussed with the president himself shows how important this region was.

Iraq had already been visited by the foreign ministry's head of the Department of Africa, Asia, and Oceania. In 1975, still during Médici's administration, Ambassador Wladimir do Amaral Murtinho sent an economic mission to the country, whose task it was to assess possibility of supplying sugar refineries and establishing a Brazilian car factory. Two years later, Saddam Hussein's country was not only Brazil's number one oil supplier, but also a large-scale importer of vehicles, frozen chicken, and sugar. That same year, agreements on air transport and on economic and technical cooperation between the two countries were signed. In 1978, the contract between Mendes Junior–Interbras Consortium with the Iraqi Ministry of Transport was signed in order to build a railway connecting Baghdad to Akashat.

There were also visits from representatives of Arab countries that were not oil producers. However, these were more political in nature than economic. Right before the Geisel's inauguration in January 1974, during a special Arab League mission to South America, the Lebanese foreign minister, Fouad Naffah, sought to clarify different nations' positions on the Arab-Israeli conflict, including that of Brazil (*O Estado* 1974c). He said that "no developing country who supports the Arab cause, suffers shortage of oil, and can get it easily at low prices." During the transition period from Médici to Geisel, the Brazilian government still maintained the policy of "equidistance and support [for] UN resolution 242" (*O Estado* 1974d). In 1975 an "Egyptian mission of goodwill" came to Brazil to show the government Egypt's take on the Middle East situation (*Manchete* 1974).

Another important event in the development of closer ties between the Middle East and Brazil was the Second Arabic Pan-American Congress, which took place in São Paulo from November 9 to 15 in 1975. This event was sponsored by the Federation of Arab Brazilian Entities and aimed to become the vehicle for the intensification of relations between the Arab world and the Americas. The event was attended by the minister of public infrastructure of Syria, the plenipotentiary minister of the League of Arab States in Brazil, delegations from other South American countries, and all Arab ambassadors working in Brasilia. The event aimed to "inform Brazil and other American countries about the Arab reality, as well as to take back to the Arabs a better understanding of American characteristics" (*O Estado* 1975). The event also sought to create bi-national chambers of commerce as well as a Pan-American–Arab chamber of commerce, and to investigate the possibility of founding financial programs that could facilitate commercial exchanges between the regions.

**The Search for a Commercial Approach**

Foreign trade between 1974 and 1979 was part of the government discourse on national priorities and became the main focus of politicians. Exports to the Middle East were among the responsibilities of the Foreign Ministry's Department of Trade Promotion, which was led by adviser Paulo Tarso Flecha de Lima (Lima 1996, 219–237). A specific commercial policy toward the Middle East was only implemented very gradually. For this reason, Brazilian attitudes toward commerce with the Middle East tended initially to be reactive rather than active. The government responded to questions that were emerging rather than being proactive. An example of this was the possibility of suspension of vehicle exports to Israel by Volkswagen of Brazil, believing that it would be more harmful to alienate the Arabs than the Israelis (FGV/CPDOC 1974e).

Since the end of the Médici administration, the selling of weaponry has come to be a part of foreign relations. It appears in the information sent to Geisel in the index "Exportation of Weapons: News about the Engesa Operations" (FGV/CPDOC 1974f). This note informed him that the Brazilian media had divulged information published by a French periodical regarding a possible operation between Brazil and Qatar involving the supplying of military combat vehicles. It was said that Brazilian cars were to be equipped with French cannons. Even images of the Engesa facilities and the cars manufactured there were published. Silveira writes that the Foreign Ministry immediately questioned the company about "the improper disclosure of that information," and called its attention to the "need of total discretion in the matter due to its highly secret nature, as it does not exclusively deal with the company's interests but with matters of foreign policy and national security" (FGV/CPDOC 1974f).

At this point, the nation already had an incipient military industry. Engesa manufactured armored tanks and other vehicles for military use, such as the armored Cascavel and the amphibious Urutu; Embraer manufactured aircraft and aerospace instruments like the planes Bandeirantes, Xavante, Tucano, and Brasília, among others; and the Avibrás manufactured rockets and missiles of short and medium range, such as the Sonda I, the SBAT, and the Astros II. As Marcelo Luís Montenegro observes, the creation of these industries was not just the result of strictly situational or commercial factors, such as empty market niches ready to be filled with newcomers in the 1970s, but rather as a result of decisions adopted by sectors of the political, military, and business elite that understood that the nation should implement such industry for strategic reasons (Montenegro 1992, 7).

Brazilian diplomacy thus put effort into selling Arab countries products such as weapons, food, and engineering services. Builders like Andrade Gutierrez, Rabelo, Odebrecht, and Mendes Junior had an important role in the region, mainly in road construction.

## UN Votes and the Status of the PLO

During the Geneva talks regarding peace between Israel and the Arab world that occurred at the end of the Yom Kippur War (October 6–25, 1973), there was already talk of the Palestine Liberation Organization (PLO) being represented there. This sparked a controversy with the Israeli government, which declared it would not negotiate with the PLO under any circumstances, even if it became part of the Jordanian delegation (*Veja* 1974, 48, 50). However, things changed when the Arab League's 1974 meeting resulted in the decision to make Palestine a political issue in multilateral contexts rather than a humanitarian one, with the PLO as its only legitimate representative. According to the league's point of view, without the resolution of the question of Palestine, there would be no peace for the Middle East (*O Estado* 1974e). The league thus sought to compel Israel to change its attitude and to recognize the entity as representative of Palestine.

However, there were several internal differences in the Arab world concerning the PLO's role, especially in Jordan. In 1970, the Jordanian government massacred thousands of Palestinians who were seen as threatening to stage a coup against the king in Amman, in an event that became known as Black September. This violence, however, did not stop the PLO from claiming to be the legitimate representative of the Palestinian people in international forums. This claim appeared on the agenda of the twenty-ninth session of the United Nations General Assembly (UNGA) (FGV/CPDOC 1974i).

Brazil's take on this question became clear in September 1974. Although it emphasized its support for Resolution 242 during the oil crisis as well as its support for Palestinian claims, this seemed inadequate to the Arab countries. Arab countries' representatives in Brasilia, such as those of Syria and Algeria (FGV/CPDOC 1974g), expressed their hope for the Brazilian government's explicit support for the proposal to recognize the PLO made at the twenty-ninth session of the UN General Assembly. As soon as the UNGA was asked to include the proposal on its agenda, the Israeli government requested a meeting with the secretary general of the Foreign Ministry, Ramiro Saraiva Guerreiro. The Israeli ambassador emphasized that the PLO expressed literally in its founding charter its objective of annihilating Israel and establishing a Palestinian state in its place. He argued that Brazil should oppose the question of Palestine in the UNGA and that, if it was impossible to avoid its inclusion altogether, the Brazilian delegation should vote against any draft resolution of the kind (FGV/CPDOC 1974h).

Saraiva Guerreiro reminded the ambassador that Brazil had already declared on several occasions that the resolution of the Palestinian problem was essential for a just and durable solution to the Middle East situation. He added that Brazil did not have precise plans with which to attend to the legitimate rights of the Palestinians, since those plans should result mainly from the efforts of countries directly involved in the conflict. During several other conferences in 1974, the Brazilian government participated as an observer, recognizing movements for national liberation, in both the Organization of African Unity and the Arab League (FGV/CPDOC 1974h). In this context, Saraiva Guerreiro made it clear that Brazil would not be opposed to the Palestinian question being included on the UNGA's agenda.

Of the several resolutions on the Palestinian question that were adopted by the General Assembly in 1974, two are directly linked to the role of the PLO. Resolution 3210 stated that the General Assembly invited the PLO as a representative of the Palestinian people to participate in their deliberations on the question of Palestine (United Nations 1974a). Resolution 3236 showed concern over the lack of a just resolution of the Palestinian question, affirming that this problem threatened international peace and security and reaffirmed Palestinians' rights to self-determination without external interference and to national independence and sovereignty. Also, this resolution appealed to states and international organizations to understand its support for the Palestinian people and to restore their rights, and requested the secretary-general to establish contacts with the PLO in every matter regarding the Palestine question (United Nations 1974b).

Although Brazil did recognize the PLO within the UN, it hesitated at first to accept the establishment of a PLO office in Brasilia. Yasser Arafat chose Brazil as the location of the first PLO office in Latin America, hoping to build a network of supporters of the "Arab cause" there and in other nations of the continent (*O Estado* 1976). Yet the Brazilian Foreign Ministry studied such steps carefully for their legal and diplomatic implications. Their conclusion was that since the PLO did not represent a state, it could not have an embassy.

### "Zionism Is Racism" UN Resolution

Although the Palestinian question was discussed during the following year's session of the General Assembly, the real focus was on a controversial resolution, number 3379, that determined that "Zionism is a form of racism and racial discrimination" (United Nations 1975). Brazil's vote in favor of this resolution would become emblematic of its shift in position toward the Middle East at the multilateral level. The project that culminated in General Assembly Resolution 3379 was presented by the Arab working group at the UN in the beginning of 1975. The Brazilian delegation, led by diplomat Sérgio Corrêa da Costa, asked for urgent instructions on how to respond to the resolution, because the vote was to occur in the same week in which the resolution was presented.

The text presented by the Arab diplomats stated that the resolution was based on the declarations and commitments previously undertaken by the countries within the UN as well as in other conferences and meetings of 1975, like the World Conference of the UN International Women's Year, the Assembly of Heads of State and Government of the Organization of African Unity, and the Conference of Foreign Ministers of the Non-Aligned Movement. In all of these events there were direct critiques of Zionism that compared it to regimes such as apartheid South Africa. This series of meetings produced formal statements that condemned Zionism as a "form of racism and of racial discrimination." And this was exactly what the UN resolution was calling for.

Brazil had several options: it could be altogether absent when it came time to vote on the resolution; it could be present but abstain from voting; it could support a milder resolution; or it could vote for the Arab proposal, but endorse its vote with a declaration that would justify and reduce its probable impact. According to Silveira, the Foreign Ministry agreed with the president's original decision to abstain. However, for many reasons, President Ernesto Geisel's personal and final decision was to vote in the affirmative without any caveats. Brazil did just that in the drafting commission, even though it had the opportunity to change its mind before the plenary session of the General Assembly, which was to be held the second week of November 1975.

The Brazilian vote for the "Zionism is racism" UN resolution was accompanied by four other affirmative votes from Latin American countries: Cuba, Guyana, Chile, and Mexico. According to the press at the time, Cuba's vote could be understood automatically as that of a country aligned with the Soviet Union, Mexico's as that of a country interested in making Mexican president Luis Echeverria the UN secretary-general, and Chile's as a way to win Arab support against accusations that Chilean authorities had violated human rights during the Pinochet regime.

Due to their votes in the commission, most countries received a note of disapproval from the United States. The text said that if the vote was to be endorsed by the plenary session of the General Assembly, it would destroy the moral force of the UN's actions in the combat against racism and racial discrimination. It also stated that from the U.S. point of view, painting Zionism as racist was a misrepresentation of the movement and encouraged anti-Semitism, a well-known form of racism. Finally it expressed the hope that the resolution would not be endorsed in the General Assembly and that the Brazilian government would "instruct its delegation to vote against the approval of such resolution when it comes to vote" (FGV/CPDOC 1975b). This note, phrased as a direct order and warning from the United States to Brazil, profoundly irritated the Brazilian authorities and backfired, serving as a justification for Brazil to *not* change its vote in the General Assembly's plenary session.

During the plenary session on November 10, 1975, Brazil affirmed its position of condemning Zionism as a form of racism and racial discrimination, along with sixty-nine other countries. The repercussions of Brazil's support for Resolution 3379 suggests that the views and attitudes of Geisel and Silveira diverged more from each other than is commonly thought. The final decision for the favorable vote in the General Assembly was made by President Geisel, and it went against the Foreign Ministry's recommendation for an abstention. There seems to have been an active effort on the part of the bureaucracy to mitigate the damage of this divergence and provide justifications for the final decision. This creates the illusion of a joint decision-making process that apparently did not exist.

The telegram authorizing the Brazilian delegation to maintain its favorable vote at the UN's plenary session aimed to clarify that this vote did not alter the country's recognition of Israel and its right to exist as an independent state, nor did it legalize any aggression against the country. Rather, it sought to clarify that this recognition of Israel was not related to the "acceptance of Zionist theses": "Right now it is not the survival of Israel that is at stake, but its continued occupation of territory by force. Zionism is a philosophy that seeks to rationalize this occupation" (FGV/CPDOC 1975c).

The text was written by the secretary general of the Foreign Ministry, Ramiro Saraiva Guerreiro, and amended by Silveira. As the foreign minister was traveling in Europe, Guerreiro refined the instructions to be sent out to the Brazilian delegation at the UN and to all of the Brazilian diplomatic missions for guidance. Silveira added to the text an explanatory paragraph in which he highlighted the absence of racism in Brazil.

The search for justifications for the affirmative vote even led to the evoking of the myth of racial equality in Brazil. Silveira explicitly admitted in an interview that he feared that the vote would be misinterpreted because of Geisel's German background:

> I felt it was my duty to defend the President. . . . If I had not done that they would have called him German—which is unfair, because he is the son of Germans, but I never saw a Brazilian visit Germany in a more Brazilian fashion. . . . Also, truth be told, he is a man that, although he is of German background, does not like racial prejudice, and he has given many proofs of that. (FGV/CPDOC 1979c)

Many of those who came forward in the Brazilian press mentioned the "historical contradiction" between the Brazilian condemnation of Zionism and the efforts made at the UN in 1947 by Oswaldo Aranha, president of the General Assembly, who was regarded as being in favor of the creation of Israel. In the context of discussions around the passage of Resolution 3379, Israel was considered for expulsion from UNESCO in 1974, and Idi Amin Dada, president of Uganda and head of the Organization of African Unity, gave a speech to the General Assembly clearly suggesting the expulsion of the state of Israel from the UN and the extinction of Israel as a state (Manor 1996, 16). Some interpreted the vote as another step in this direction.

European countries, with the exception of Portugal, collectively voted against the resolution, and the European and U.S. press was very critical. The liberal West's pressure on countries like Brazil was strong, as China had also voted in favor of the resolution. The report sent by the Brazilian delegation stated that the Arab victory would have a very high price in terms of global repercussions and that notions of Nazism and anti-Semitism were constantly being evoked. The powerful performance of the U.S. delegate at the UN, Daniel Patrick Moynihan, was interpreted, on the one hand, as pandering to the Jewish community in the United States in order to obtain a U.S. Senate seat in the following year's elections, but which also exposed the contradictions of Brazil's position, as a military regime, on this issue.

When Moynihan gave his passionate reaction at the UN, he also raised another delicate topic in terms of Brazil–United States relations: the human-rights issue (*Veja* 1975, 40–41), and he proposed a draft General Assembly resolution (A/C.3/L.2175) demanding immediate amnesty for all political prisoners. Geisel's government, after all, was a military dictatorship at this time with a grim human-rights record of imprisoning and torturing political prisoners. In this context, Silveira submitted a request to Geisel creating a discourse specifically aimed at responding to questions related to human rights:

> Brazil regards humanity as the main goal of every attempt at development, and respect for his rights to be a fundamental issue in contemporary societies. Thus although we could initially have voted in favor of Resolution A/C.3/L.2175, there are no prisoners of public opinion in Brazil—only prisoners guilty of subversive crimes. Brazil voted against the project because it disagrees with its restriction on sovereignty, which allows other states to interpret what is correct and to secure the protection of their own citizens' human rights. Besides that, according to the United Nations Charter and the practice of the Economic and Social Council, the UN powers regarding human rights are general and normative and not investigative or specific. Nor could it be otherwise in light of the Charter's perspective on sovereignty. (FGV/CPDOC 1975d)

The above text is evidence that the vote caused real tension in Brazilian diplomacy. On one hand, Brazil had approved a resolution that aimed to restrict
Israel's sovereignty (and to critique Israel's human-rights record), but on the
other hand, it had declared itself against a project that was understood as re-
stricting its own sovereignty and critiquing Brazil's own human-rights history.

## Conclusion

The Geisel administration preoccupied itself with implementing a set of measures in order to bring Brazil closer to Arab nations. Brazil thus explicitly declared the end of the equidistance toward the region, tilting the country away
from Israel and toward the Palestinians, and invested in opening embassies as
well as signing agreements of the most diverse nature with Arab countries. It
also encouraged commercial strategies, especially through the sending of missions and official visits.

While Brazil was beginning to emphasize bilateral ties with Arab countries, it also took a new multilateral position by voting in favor of the 1974
resolution that declared the PLO to be the only and legitimate representative
of Palestine. However, Brazil backed itself up by not allowing the opening of a
Palestinian embassy in Brasilia, thus avoiding confrontation with those who
considered the PLO to be a terrorist group associated with leftist Brazilian
guerrilla organizations.

The year 1975 gave way to a larger polemic with its anti-Zionism vote, emblematic of the new Brazilian politics toward the Middle East. The foreign policy
decision that was vehemently supported by Geisel was evidence of Brazil's
strategy of developing deeper ties with Arab nations, a move that was seen as
potentially profitable.

In the second half of his term, Geisel sought to do business of all kinds
with countries in the Arab region. This policy was particularly successful with
Iraq until the Gulf War in 1991, even with disruptions to trade caused by the
war between Iraq and Iran (1980–1988) (Fares 2007). Generally, however, due
to internal difficulties and the international ones spurred by a new oil crisis
in 1979, Brazil's relations with Arab countries did not advance too far, leaving
behind many doubts. Brazil's position in the UN on the issue of Zionism was
reviewed during the term of President Fernando Collor de Mello. Brazil was
one of the 111 countries that approved Resolution 46/86, which revoked Resolution 3379 in December 1991. It was only in the administration of Fernando
Henrique Cardoso (1995–2002) that Brazil tried to normalize relations with
Israel. During Cardoso's term, Foreign Minister Luiz Felipe Lampreia visited

Israel and Yasser Arafat was received in Brasilia (Lampreia 1999, 248–59; FGV/CPDOC 1995).

Such attempts were suspended at the beginning of the 2000s decade, due to Brazilian discontent with U.S. policies in the Middle East and its "war on terror," the collapse of the Oslo peace process between Israel and the Palestinians, and the Palestinian uprising or intifada against Israeli rule in the occupied territories. What seems have been a brief return to the idea of "equidistance" under Cardoso's administration was thus quickly reversed in the Lula administration. A new proactive politics toward the region was established in 2003 with President Lula. The charismatic Brazilian president visited the Middle East in 2003, 2009, and 2010. This greatly increased political, commercial, and cultural relations with the region, building on the process of commercial transregionalism launched by the Geisel administration in the 1970s, but also building on the contradictions and tensions around Palestine-Israel policy that date back to that same period of struggle and debate.

## Note

1. The twenty-two-hour interview granted to CPDOC/FGV by Azeredo da Silveira between 1979 and 1982 has been published as a book. See Matias Spektor, ed., *Azeredo da Silveira: Um depoimento* (Rio de Janeiro: Editora FGV, 2010).

## References

Barboza, Mario Gibson. 1992. *Na diplomacia o traço todo da vida*. Rio de Janeiro: Record.
el-Sadat, Anwar. *Autobiografia*. 1983. São Paulo: Círculo do Livro.
*O Estado de São Paulo*. 1973. "Hora importante dos árabes." January 28.
———. 1974a. "Ampliada ação do Brasil na Argélia." October 24.
———. 1974b. "Árabes vão tentar mais intercâmbio." March 20.
———. 1974c. "Líbano falará de petróleo e feira." January 8.
———. 1974d. "Só Geisel responderá aos árabes." January 29.
———. 1974e. "Hussein não vai à genebra." October 30.
———. 1975. "Árabes querem conhecer a experiência brasileira." November 7.
———. 1976. "Governo veta a instalação da sede regional da OLP." April 7. 1).
Fares, Seme Taleb. 2007. "O Pragmatismo do Petróleo: As relações entre o Brasil e o Iraque, entre 1973 a 2007." Brasília: Universidade de Brasília. Master's thesis.
Fundação Getúlio Vargas / Centro de Pesquisa e Documentação (FGV/CPDOC). 1974a. "Posição em relação ao Oriente Médio e especificamente aos países árabes." FGV/CPDOC. Archive AAS. Brasília. March 12.
———. 1974b. "Silveira a Geisel. Informação para Senhor Presidente da República." FGV/CPDOC. Archive AAS. April 10.
———. 1974c. "Manchete." FGV/CPDOC. Archive AAS. July 20.

———. 1974d. "Silveira a Geisel. Informação para o Senhor Presidente da República."
FGV/CPDOC. No. 0114. Archive AAS. Brasília. May 28.

———. 1974e. "Silveira a Geisel. Informação para o Senhor Presidente da República."
FGV/CPDOC. No. 0191. Archive AAS. Brasília. August 8.

———. 1974f. "Silveira a Geisel. Informação para o Senhor Presidente da República."
FGV/CPDOC. No. 0068. Archive AAS. Brasília. April 30.

———. 1974g. "Embaixada da República Árabe da Síria. Aide Memoire." FGV/CPDOC.
Archive AAS. Brasília. September 13.

———. 1974h. "Silveira a Geisel. Informação para o Senhor Presidente da República."
FGV/CPDOC. No. 0051. Archive AAS. Brasília. April 22.

———. 1974i. "Sérgio Armando Frazão para MRE. Telegrama Confidencial Urgente."
No. 116177. Archive AAS. New York. September 17.

———. 1975a. "Silveira a Geisel." FGV/CPDOC. No. 8A12. Archive EG. Brasília. November 5.

———. 1975b. "MRE para BRASEMB Washington. Minuta de telegrama." FGV/CPDOC.
Bo. 1600. Archive AAS. Brasília. October 24.

———. 1975c. "Silveira para Guerreiro. Telegrama Secreto Urgentíssimo XXX Assem-
bléia Geral. Sionismo. Instruções." FGV/CPDOC. Archive AAS. Paris. October 25.

———. 1975d. "Projeto de declaração de voto." FGV/CPDOC. Archive EG. November.

———. 1978. "Silveira para Geisel." FGV/CPDOC. Archive AAS. Brasília. August 30.

———. 1979a. "Depoimento Antonio Azeredo da Silveira." Cassette tape recording. No. 6
Side A. CPDOC. Rio de Janeiro. May 18.

———. 1979b. "Depoimento Antonio Azeredo da Silveira." Cassette tape recording. No. 17
Side B. CPDOC. Rio de Janeiro. June 7.

———. 1979c. "Depoimento Antonio Azeredo da Silveira." Cassette tape recording. No 3.
Side B. CPDOC. Rio de Janeiro.

———. 1995. *LFL pi Cardoso*, FH, 1995. October 17. CPDOC/FGV.

———. 1995. *LFL mre1*. July 7. CPDOC/FGV.

*Jornal do Brasil.* 1974. "Árabes vêem como investir mais no mercado brasileiro." February 18.

Koifman, Fábio. 2002. *Quixote nas trevas: O embaixador Souza Dantas e os refugiados
donazismo.* Rio de Janeiro: Record.

Lampreia, Luiz Felipe. 1999. *Diplomacia brasileira: Palavras, contextos e razões.* Rio de
Janeiro: Lacerda Editores.

Lessa, Antônio Carlos. 2002. "Israel e o mundo árabe no cruzamento das escolhas internacionais do Brasil." In *Brasil e Israel: Diplomacia e sociedades,* ed. Norma Breda dos
Santos. Brasília: Editora Universidade de Brasília.

Lima, Paulo Tarso Flecha de. 1996. "Diplomacia e comércio: Notas sobre a política externa
brasileira nos anos 1970." In *Sessenta anos de política externa brasileira, 1930–1990,* ed.
José Augusto Guilhon Albuquerque. Vol. 2. São Paulo: Cultura Editores Associados/
NUPRI.

*Manchete.* 1974. "Posto de escuta." May 5.

Manor, Yohanan. 1996. *To Right a Wrong.* New York: Shengold Publishers.

Montenegro, Marcelo Luis. 1992. *Indústria Bélica e Diplomacia na Relação Brasil-Irak (1979–1989)*. Master's Thesis. International Relations. Pontifica Universidade Catolica do Rio de Janeiro.

*Revista da Liga dos Estados Árabes.* 1979. "Embaixadas árabes acreditadas em Brasília." May-June.

Spektor, Matias. 2009. *Kissinger e o Brasil.* Rio de Janeiro: Jorge Zahar Ed.

United Nations. 1974a. "Resolution 3210, October 14, 1974."

———. 1974b. "Resolution 3236, November 22, 1974."

———. 1975. "Resolution 3379, November 10, 1975."

*Veja.* 1974. "O lado palestino." July 24.

———. 1975. "O vendaval anti-sionista." November 19.

Vizentini, Paulo Gilberto Fagundes. 1998. *A Política Externa do Regime Militar Brasileiro: Multilateralização, Desenvolvimento e a Construção de uma Potência Média (1964–1985).* Porto Alegre: Editora da Universidade.

# 5

## Terrorist Frontier Cell or Cosmopolitan Commercial Hub?
The Arab and Muslim Presence at the Border
of Paraguay, Brazil, and Argentina

*Fernando Rabossi*

Rabossi calls for a reframing of the discourse surrounding South America's Tri-Border Region. He moves away from stereotypical discussions of terrorism to explore alternative narratives that are informed by migration trajectories, commercial engagements, and political complexities of the region's Arab and Muslim populations.

∽

Reading the international media, one would infer that the *Tríplice Fronteira* (in Portuguese) and *Triple Frontera* (in Spanish)—the region where the borders of Brazil, Argentina, and Paraguay meet, known as the Tri-Border Region in English—is a threat to international security. It condenses all aspects of a contemporary security agenda: terrorism and transnational mafias, piracy, smuggling, laundering of money and stolen goods, drug and arms trafficking. The region became (in)famous during the 1990s after being denounced as the logistical base for the attacks in Buenos Aires against the Israeli embassy in 1992 and against the Argentine-Israeli Mutual Association (AIMA) in 1994. The existence of an important Arab and Islamic business community actively involved in cross-border commercial activities was enough to lead to the conclusion that Islamic terrorism existed in the region. Once suggested, the connection that linked Muslim Arabs, terrorism, commerce, and all kind of illegalities across the borders became a vicious circle that reinforced the accusations and insecurities.

This chapter attempts to establish alternative narratives about the Arab and Muslim presence in the border region of Paraguay, Brazil, and Argentina. It is based on fieldwork and historical evidence.[1] Given the importance of this presence, these narratives are essential to open up a more nuanced understanding of the region.

The vast majority of newspaper articles and analysis produced about the region seek to demonstrate or to deny the presence of terrorism or the financial activities that sustain terrorist groups in faraway world regions. The affirmation of the absence of terrorism in the region articulated by some journalists and community members is called into question by evidence of ties between the region and the political dynamics of the Middle East and the Islamic world. Instead, I argue, we should push the discussion in a different direction and begin with different questions. What are the criteria that set the frame of terrorism around these populations and activities? Who set up these frames and in whose interests?[2]

The objective of this chapter is to create a space for other narratives to flourish, a space delineated by migration trajectories, commercial engagements, and political compromises. First, I will present the social geography of the border region. Next, I will describe the trajectories of the first Arab migrants in the region and compare them to similar trajectories of other Arab migrants in Brazil in order to identify the singularities of the Arab Muslim presence in the Tri-Border Region. I will explore the development of the Arab migration by following their commercial activities, institutions, and political engagements. Finally, I will problematize the portrait of the region as a haven for Islamic terrorists and other criminal activities, advocating for a historical and ethnographical analysis that challenges these stereotypes.

## The Scenario

The borders of Brazil, Paraguay, and Argentina meet at the confluence of the Parana and the Iguaçu rivers. On the banks of these rivers lie the cities of Ciudad del Este in Paraguay, Foz do Iguaçu in Brazil, and Puerto Iguazú in Argentina. Over the rivers, the Friendship Bridge connects Paraguay and Brazil and the Tancredo Neves Bridge connects Brazil and Argentina.

The cities are different in size, shape, and degree of importance to their own country. Ciudad del Este is the capital of the state of Alto Paraná—one of the seventeen states of Paraguay—and it is the second city of the country in demographic and economic importance; this is remarkable considering that it was founded in 1957. With a population of 320,000 inhabitants in 2008, the city has local newspapers, universities, an international airport, and an important urban infrastructure (which is still precarious and reflects urban social inequalities). Ciudad del Este is fundamental for contemporary Paraguay.[3] On the Brazilian side, Foz do Iguaçu has experienced significant development since the 1950s, as reflected in a modern urban infrastructure, media, universities, and an international airport. However, it is less significant than Ciudad del Este at both the national and the regional levels. With a population of 250,918 inhabitants in 2010, it was the fifth-largest city in the state of Paraná, one of the twenty-six states that make up Brazil. Compared with its neighbors, Puerto Iguazú in Argentina is a small city with little or no autonomy in terms of production or reproduction of a local public sphere. With 82,000 inhabitants in 2010 (INDEC 2010), it was the fourth city of Misiones province, one of Argentina's twenty-three provinces.[4]

The cities of Puerto Iguazú and Foz do Iguaçu are the destinations for those visiting the Iguazu Falls, one of the main tourist attractions of Latin America. The economy of Puerto Iguazú revolves around tourism, which also plays a fundamental role in the economy of Foz do Iguaçu. However, two other activities are central for the Brazilian city: the trade in Brazilian goods to neighboring countries (mostly Paraguay) and the production of electricity. If the importance of tourism for the Argentine and the Brazilian side derives from a natural attraction shared by both countries, Foz do Iguaçu and Ciudad del Este share these other activities, trade and energy, whose existence is the outcome of governmental policies, entrepreneurial ventures, and, crucially, the practices of thousands of people that make these activities possible.[5] The Arab presence at the border, like the presence of other immigrant groups, becomes comprehensible in the light of the commercial dynamism of the region. To address this dynamic, however, it is necessary to introduce some historical references that will help us to understand the constitution of that space.

Formally incorporated into the territorial domains of the Portuguese and the Spanish crowns and, later, into Brazil, Paraguay, and Argentina, the region at the confluence of the Iguaçu and the Parana rivers remained outside the spheres of governance and development until the end of the nineteenth century. Nevertheless, it was not an uninhabited area. Together with the indigenous population that occupied the subtropical forest that made up the region, there were individuals from different backgrounds on the banks of the rivers as well as groups that worked on the exploitation of yerba mate and wood, opening trails and passages into the forest.[6]

Since 1876, the lands located in Paraguay were granted in concession to a private company for the exploitation of wood and yerba mate. The seat of the company, Tacuru Pucu (current Hernandarias, twenty kilometers north of present Ciudad del Este), was the first regular settlement in the region. In 1889, to ensure the Brazilian presence at the border, the army founded the military colony of Foz do Iguaçu. Across the river Iguaçu, on the Argentine side, a village known as Puerto Aguirre began to take form (later Puerto Iguazú).

The first half of the twentieth century witnessed the slow but growing presence of state institutions, on both the Brazilian and the Argentinean side; farming colonists; and the incorporation of the region in regional flows of merchandise. These flows included not only the traditional yerba mate and wood but also products that followed contextual demands, as for example the flow of tires from Brazil to Argentina to escape the strict control over rubber and derived products that the United States established over Brazil during the Second World War. During the 1940s and the 1950s, several agreements opened the possibility for Paraguay to escape from its landlocked situation, via Brazil. These agreements included the construction of a corridor of roads from Asunción city—Paraguay's capital—to the Brazilian Atlantic coast, where Paraguay accessed harbor facilities that guaranteed a channel for its exports and imports.[7] The founding of Puerto Presidente Stroessner in 1957, on the right bank of the Paraná River where a bridge would be constructed, was part of that project.[8] The Friendship Bridge was inaugurated, in its finished version, in 1965.[9]

**From Peddlers to Merchants: Commercial Trajectories**

The possibilities envisaged in the future connection with Paraguay were what attracted many traders to the border. The early traders brought Brazilian goods to Paraguay, playing a key role in opening the route that channeled the flow of merchandise until that moment. In the stories I gathered in my interviews and from the local media, the arrival of the first Arab migrants is related to these flows. At the beginning, migrants focused on the development of Brazilian industrial production in the far west of Paraná State, where Foz do Iguaçu constituted just one among many boomtowns. Later, with the 1956 agreement to build the bridge that would link Brazil with Paraguay and the founding of Puerto Presidente Stroessner the following year, some of these traders settled in Foz do Iguaçu taking into account the prospect of trade with Paraguay, then a virgin market for Brazilian products. They were the first Arab migrants that settled in the region. They were following the same pattern that had characterized the Arab migration in Brazil since the late nineteenth century, using trade as general strategy of incorporation in the social and economic dynamics of the new country, and peddling as the particular practice of entering into commerce.[10] The following trajectories of early migrants reflect these patterns.

In an article about the trajectory of Hamad Ahmad Rahal, we read in a local newspaper that "like almost all Arabs who migrated to Brazil and other countries, Hamad Rahal left Lebanon with few or no resources, having to start again with virtually nothing—and with no other option than the stereotypical profession of peddler, equivalent to the well-known traveling salesmen who flood Brazilian cities nowadays."[11] Originally from Lebanon, Hamad was twenty years old when he arrived in Brazil in 1951. He arrived in São Paulo, where he started in the trade. Two years later, he decided to try the interior of Paraná State, selling goods carried in his luggage, especially clothes that he brought from São Paulo. His circuit included emerging cities like Guarapuava, Cascavel, Foz do Iguaçu, Rondon, Toledo, and Guaira. "In his wanderings as a peddler, Rahal arrived in Foz do Iguaçu in the early '50s, where he found three Arab families already established." He peddled in the villages between Foz do Iguaçu and Guaira, over the Parana River. Finally, he settled in Foz do Iguaçu, where he opened his own shop in the center of the city in 1958.

Abdul Rahal, a Lebanese, arrived in Brazil in 1959 when he was twenty-two years old. He followed the same itinerary as many of his countrymen: he arrived at the port of Santos, went to São Paulo, and circulated and peddled within the states of São Paulo and Paraná. In 1961, he established himself in Foz do Iguaçu and began to sell goods to Paraguay. Abdul Rahal is considered a pioneer of Brazilian goods into the Paraguayan market, which had been hitherto dominated by Argentinean products. Foz do Iguaçu was not chosen by chance: his cousin Hamad lived there. His brother, who had arrived in Brazil in 1954 and was living in Argentina with his wife when Abdul Rahal arrived, also settled in Foz do Iguaçu later.[12]

Another important businessman of Foz do Iguacu, Mohamed Osman, arrived in Brazil in 1952 from Lebanon. He went to the city of Jataizinho (Paraná State), where his brother was living. His first business was to peddle a suitcase filled with clothes given him by another countryman. "I sold in the farms and in the coffee plantations in the region,"[13] he said. He opened his first store in Assaí; later he moved to Ivatuva, where he had relatives, and went into the business of buying and selling coffee and cereals. In 1962, he settled in Foz do Iguaçu, where he made a successful career. He built Textile Osman and became the exclusive agent for Kraft Suchard, whose products were exported to Paraguay.

These trajectories share certain features that characterize the early Arab migration in Foz do Iguaçu. They came from southern Lebanon, particularly from the Bekaa Valley. Some of them had already circulated through the interior of Paraná and São Paulo states as itinerant merchants. They had even settled in other cities before moving to Foz do Iguaçu.

The growth of the neighborhoods around the Friendship Bridge—Vila Portes and Jardim Jupira—during the late 1960s and 1970s paralleled the strengthening of commercial ties with Paraguay. The Arab presence in these neighborhoods shows the importance that these migrants had in the consolidation of that trade. Another inscription of this presence in Foz do Iguaçu was the Clube União Árabe, the first community institution, which was founded in 1962. Attracted by the commercial movement or following relatives or acquaintances, new immigrants continued to arrive.

The trajectories of these Arab migrants who settled in Foz do Iguaçu are similar to those described for earlier periods in Brazil. However, we can compare them with the ones established in similar locations like Chui, a Brazilian city on the border with Uruguay. In her detailed research on the Palestinians of Chui, Denise Jardim identifies significant parallels with the trajectories of those who settled in Foz do Iguaçu. The chronology is similar: The migrants arrived during the 1950s and early 1960s. The route taken before settling down in Chui is the same. They arrived via the port of Santos, utilized São Paulo as their site for connecting with other countrymen (relatives, acquaintances, or just contacts), and, finally, proceeded to circulate widely through several Brazilian cities—generally peddling—before settling in Chui. The rationale behind this mobility and the eventual linking of both cities is also similar: it allows us to glimpse a spatial logic based on "personal contacts with fellow countrymen, relatives and informants that indicate the places where 'it is good' for trade" (Jardim 2000, 110).

As in the case of Chui, many of the traders in Foz do Iguaçu and Ciudad del Este had no previous commercial experience in their places of origin. The reasons for turning to commerce were many. On the one hand, on their arrival to Brazil, they joined the networks of relatives and acquaintances who had already assumed trade as their core business. Moreover, for those who arrived without capital, trade was an activity with rapid return, with the possibility of accumulation and the prospect of investment in new opportunities. The realization of these possibilities was linked to the form of trade in which they used to start in the business: peddling. By selling door by door, first in the cities and later in the villages and farms, they guaranteed an expansive market where they could establish themselves as regular traders.

The period during which many of these migrants arrived, the fifties and sixties, is essential to understanding the commercial success they achieved because this period also witnessed the expansion of Brazilian industrial production, chiefly in the textile sector. Peddlers became key actors in the process of distributing the products of these expanding industries into the interior of Brazil. Later, when they settled down at border cities, they played the same function for the neighboring countries. In the search for a place to settle down, it was important to identify the presence of fellow countrymen who could become commercial partners. Foz do Iguaçu and Chui had both characteristics.

In an interesting formulation regarding the place of these border cities in that movement, Jardim suggests that "in the trajectory of the migrants of Arab origin, Chui can be understood as the frontier of expansion for the peddlers" (Jardim 2000, 125). This description also applies to migrants of Arab origin who settled in Foz do Iguaçu. However, the differences between both cases illuminate the singularity that the border with Paraguay began to acquire and the consequences it had for the Arab migratory circuits.

Some of the Arabs who arrived in Latin America and established themselves as traders ended up in several border towns like Chui and Foz do Iguaçu in Brazil. We also find them at Encarnación and Ciudad del Este in Paraguay, or at Maicao, on the border between Colombia and Venezuela. At the Brazilian cities already mentioned, we find them selling Brazilian goods. In the other cases, we find them selling imported ones. The combination of both flows of merchandise and the possibilities of participating in both of them is, precisely, what distinguishes Foz de Iguaçu and Ciudad del Este, making the border region an attractive destination for the Arab migrants who continued to arrive in Latin America during the 1970s and 1980s.

After the founding of Puerto Presidente Stroessner in 1957 and the inauguration of the Friendship Bridge in 1965, the Paraguayan side of the Parana River experienced accelerated growth. At the exit of the bridge, the first stores were established by Paraguayan traders. Later, some traders who also had their stores on the Brazilian side started to work on the other side of the river. Thus, from the late '60s, some Arab traders who were already established in Foz do Iguaçu opened imported-product houses in Puerto Presidente Stroessner. In order to establish themselves on the Paraguayan side, they needed legal permission and commercial incentives to do so. The Stroessner regime encouraged the trade of imported goods in the border region and facilitated the granting of legal papers and permits to foreign traders wishing to establish there. The possibilities that opened up for these traders transformed the commercial and migratory trajectories of the Arab migrants in the region.

The trajectory of the brothers Mohamad Said and Atef Said Mannah illustrate the possibilities associated with the import business. They came from

Ba'aloul, in the Bekaa Valley, and arrived in Puerto Presidente Stroessner in 1972, where they opened the New York store, part restaurant and part grocery store. Over time, they turned to imported goods and expanded their businesses, operating three of the most important shops in the city that sell liquor, perfumes, electronics, and accessories: La Petisquera, Frontier, and Mannah. Since 2007, the group has been operating the duty-free shops of the international airport at Asunción and at Ciudad del Este. Mohamad Mannah—also known as Alejandro or Alex—became vice president of the Ciudad del Este Chamber of Commerce.[14]

Another example of this trajectory related to imported goods is represented by the Monalisa Group. Faisal Hammoud, from Lebanon, established his first store in Puerto Presidente Stroessner at the early 1970s. The group headed by Hammoud became one of the most important commercial groups of the city: Monalisa. The growth is impressive: offices in New York in the 1980s, offices in Miami and São Paulo in 1990, boutiques in Asunción's malls, and diversification beyond the marketing of imported commodities, into tourism, education, Internet, and even furniture for stores and commercial activities. The sons of Faisal Hammoud, Shariff and Sadek, were born in Lebanon but grew up in Paraguay. They will be key figures in the development of the group; the former has become the president of the Alto Parana Importers and Traders Center.[15]

When the war in Lebanon began, in 1975, the flow of migrants increased. Some of them settled down in Foz do Iguaçu, some in Puerto Presidente Stroessner and others operated on both sides of the border. The prospect of a place with relatives and acquaintances and with good economic opportunities turned that border region into an attractive location for many Lebanese, Palestinians, and other Middle Easterners escaping from the conflicts in their home regions. An illustrative case of this new phase is Samir Jebai, who in 2001 was president of one of the city's business chambers. He arrived from Lebanon in 1977, fleeing the civil war. He settled down in Puerto Presidente Stroessner, where he had relatives involved in commerce. Eager to continue his studies but with limited knowledge of local languages—Guarani, Spanish, and Portuguese—he started to sell with his relatives. He is still in business.

If by the mid-1970s the region had become an attractive destination for traders of Arab origin, from the second half of the decade the southern border between Brazil and Paraguay became a "safe haven" with good opportunities to work. These opportunities also attracted many people who simply left the Middle East in search of a better future.

Foz do Iguaçu consolidated as an export market of Brazilian products and Ciudad del Este became an emporium of imported goods from different parts of the world. The new immigrants were crucial in the making of both markets. To analyze the causes of this commercial growth—and its decline—is beyond the scope of this work. I am interested, however, in describing the flows that intersected in Ciudad del Este in order to understand the configuration of the region.

Until the late 1980s, American or European merchandise came from the places of production. Products from Asia—at the beginning from Japan, later from Taiwan and Korea, and afterwards from China—arrived via re-export markets. Miami was the main source of imported goods in Puerto Presidente Stroessner. Slowly, during the 1980s and clearly during the '90s, the commercial channels that supplied the city changed. Miami remained an important market for Ciudad del Este, but its place was eclipsed by direct links with Southeast Asia and alternative re-export markets such as Panama. As trade routes changed, so did the business partners and the contacts. These changes were reflected in the growing importance of Chinese merchants and migration in the city.

It is in this expansive commercial universe that the Arab migration of the 1980s and '90s can be understood. As with commercial activity, Arab migration has suffered a slowdown since the second half of the 1990s. It is difficult to have trustworthy numbers about the merchants of Arab origin in Ciudad del Este. In one of the few studies that make some estimates, the distribution of store owners was 28 percent Paraguayan, 27 percent East Asian, 24 percent Arab, 11 percent Brazilian-born, and 10 percent unspecified (Penner 1998, 27). Since the estimated number of stores in operation in 1998 was 7,000, almost 1,680 stores were in the hands of Arab traders or importers.[16]

## Numbers and Institutions: Trajectories of a Migration

Until the 1980s, both in local publications and in the writings of occasional travelers and journalists, the references to the Arabs of the border focused exclusively on trade. Some immigrants did begin to appear in the overall dynamics of Foz do Iguaçu. Fouad Fakih, an important businessman, became president of the Associação Comercial de Comércio de Foz do Iguaçu, the city's chamber of commerce, between 1974 and 1980.[17] Since then, other people of Arab origin have occupied relevant public positions. Some of them became candidates in local and regional elections. Others have become prominent members of communal councils and various local institutions.

Since the 1980s, the Arabs of the border have appeared with a new face in the local media. Particularly, the journal *Nosso Tempo*, a local newspaper of Foz do Iguaçu, started to cover the Arab presence through the lens of its community makeup, including its associations, traditions, and political align-ments.[18] In the early 1980s, the Arab population of the border seemed to have reached a considerable number considering its recent arrival in the region. In a 1982 article, the paper noted that "over a thousand people make up the Arab community living in Foz do Iguaçu and Puerto Presidente Stroessner. About 80 percent are from Lebanon and they are dedicated almost exclusively to trade" (*Nosso Tempo* 1982).

The Centro Cultural Beneficente Islâmico de Foz do Iguaçu (Islamic Mu-tual-Aid Cultural Center of Foz do Iguaçu), founded in 1981, has become an important institution in religious matters and in the educational efforts of the "Islamic family" at the border.[19] The center offers an Arabic course, targeting the children of migrants, and has created a mosque space in a building that also houses the Ali Bem Abi Taleb school, which is nowadays known as Escola Árabe-Brasileira. The foundation stone for this building was laid on March 20, 1983. The ceremony was attended by several ambassadors from Middle Eastern countries and representatives of the Islamic communities of different Brazilian cities.[20] According to the narratives gathered by John Tofik Karam, the Centro Cultural Beneficente Islâmico was composed of Sunni and Shi'a Muslims who worked together to build the mosque (Karam 2011). However, when the wealthy Sunnis managed to impose on the mosque the name of Omar ibn al-Khattab—a caliph considered by Shi'a Muslims to have usurped the true heir of the *'umma,* Ali—the Shi'as broke away from the center and founded the Islamic Society of Foz do Iguaçu. In 1985, they would construct the Husseiniyya al-Imam al-Khomeyni. The version of the story gathered by Paulo Gabriel Hilu da Rocha Pinto from the *shaykh* of the mosque pointed out that the Shi'as had chosen to have their own place for maintaining their rituals, which are considered unacceptable for Sunni Muslims (Pinto 2011, 193).[21]

Already in March 1987, an article on the ongoing works in the mosque commented that there were "about two thousand Muslims, many of them with over twenty years of residence in the region."[22] Even before construction was completed, the mosque housed the *jum'ah,* the Friday prayer service. In October 1988, after more than five years of hard work, the Omar ibn al-Khattab mosque was officially inaugurated.[23]

Over the years, several associations were created. Some of them were founded on religious grounds, others on more cultural or political ones. Among them were the Associação Cultural Sírio-Brasileira (Syrio-Brazilian Cultural As-sociation), the Centro Cultural Árabe-Brasileiro (Arab-Brazilian Cultural Center), the Sociedade Árabe Palestina-Brasileira (Arab Palestine-Brazilian Society), the Associação Cultural Sanaud (Sanaud Cultural Association), the

Associação dos Jovens Muçulmanos de Foz do Iguaçu (Young Muslims Association of Foz do Iguaçu).

In Ciudad del Este, the associative life has evolved along different lines. The overwhelming presence of Arab migrants in the leadership of the commercial chambers of the city demonstrates their prominence in business life. But these leaders and organizations are not necessarily united in their aims or efforts. At least until 2001, Ali Abou Saleh was president of the Cámara de Comercio de Ciudad del Este (Ciudad del Este Chamber of Commerce); Shariff Hammoud was president of the Centro de Importadores y Comerciantes del Alto Paraná (Center for Importers and Traders of Alto Paraná); and Samir Jebai was president of the Unión de Cámaras y Asociaciones de Ciudad del Este (Union of Chambers and Associations of Ciudad del Este). All of them were born in Lebanon. None of these associations provided overarching representativeness as did the Chamber of Commerce in Foz do Iguaçu. In Ciudad del Este associations often constitute themselves around particular persons or groups, instead of representing an entire business sector. This is true even of the chambers of commerce structured on nationalities, such as the Cámara de Comercio Paraguayo-Árabe (Paraguayan-Arab Chamber of Commerce). Civic associations that are not related to trade also tend to be identified with specific persons or groups. An example is the construction of the Prophet Mohammed mosque, the efforts for which were organized by a local merchant.[24] The same process was behind the construction of the prayer hall related to the Centro Árabe Islâmico Paraguayo (Paraguayan-Arab Islamic Center).

By the mid-1990s, the number of people of Arab origin living in the wider surrounding region reached an estimated 12,000, based on information provided by community spokesmen. Of them, 80 percent came from Lebanon (mostly from southern Lebanon and particularly from the Bekaa Valley), 15 percent were of Palestinian origin, and the remaining 5 percent came from Syria, Egypt, and other Middle Eastern countries. According to the same report, 95 percent were Muslims (40 percent Sunni and 50 percent Shi'a).[25]

The official data collected during my research provide just partial information. For example, according to the Federal Police of Brazil, the total number of foreigners living in just the town of Foz do Iguaçu in 1999 was 9,178. The Lebanese constituted the majority group with 2,939 people.[26] However, one should take into account that these figures include only foreigners with permanent, temporary, or interim residence status. It does not include naturalized citizens, tourists, or illegal immigrants. If we add to that figure the immigrants from other Arab countries and the population living in Ciudad del Este, 12,000 does not seem exaggerated. This figure was repeated again and again in the media and by community members.

What was true at the end of the 1990s is not necessarily true a decade later, especially considering the commercial decline of the region and the consequent dispersion of many traders. According to Mohamed Hassan, president of the Sociedade Árabe Palestina-Brasileira, there were about 50 Palestinian families on the border in 2001 (no more than 300 people). This number contrasted sharply with the 1,800 people of Palestinian origin reported in 1996.

According to many observers, after 9/11 thousands of people of Arab origin left the region. In 2003, the mayor of Cuidad del Este said that at least 20,000 Arabs had lived in the city, "but after the attacks of September 11th, that number decreases to a half" (Oz 2003). However, this figure seems to belong to the universe of vagueness that characterized statistics after 9/11.[27] The numbers highlighted in the media vary as much as the accusations. The numbers used by journalists for people of Arab origin range from 30,000 down to 10,000.[28] Sometimes the numbers vary that much even within the same report.[29] The inaccuracy is so great that it is not difficult to find figures that vary by 100 percent or more.[30]

## Stereotypes and Political Engagements:
## The Prospect of Other Narratives

If the data can be so unreliable and still keep circulating in serious discussion, we have to search elsewhere for the truth. Analyzing French stereotypes of the Lebanese of Ivory Coast, Didier Bigo notes that "the image of the Lebanese community in Abidjan was once that of an appendage to colonization, symbolized in the figures of the Maronite Christian, the good tradesman or the civil war refugee; in a short time this image changed into one of a supposed haven of anti-western terrorist lackeys of Hizbollah, usually Shi'a and Arabic speaking" (Bigo 2002, 509). In fact, this is the stereotype shift that Lebanese migrants have faced since the 1990s, particularly in places where the influx of migrants continued during the civil war.[31]

I quote Didier Bigo's characterization for two reasons. First, it reveals the globalization of a certain stereotype that we must take into account when speaking about terrorism. The Lebanese presence is sufficient evidence to presume the existence of terrorism in certain locales. Second, it can help us to illuminate the way this image has taken root in the Tri-Border Region and the consequences that it has had for the narratives of the Arab presence in the area. What we find in the current images about the Lebanese of the Tri-Border

Region is an absence of the past: their presence seems to have flourished together with the illegal activities that characterize that border region. From the material presented thus far, however, it is possible to trace a clear continuity between the migrants established in the border region and the Arab migration that arrived in Brazil at the end of the nineteenth century and the first half of the twentieth century. Their spatial mobility and economic activities reflect the same pattern as in other places in Brazil: they were key actors in the distribution channels of Brazilian industrial production, contributing to consolidate the internal market. When these traders met the borders, they became important actors for the provision of Brazilian goods to the neighboring countries.

The possibilities that they found on that particular border—that is, selling imported goods on the Paraguayan side and Brazilian goods in Foz do Iguaçu —laid the basis for the dynamism of the region, which in turn continued to attract new migrants. It was this dynamism that attracted those who escaped the conflicts in Lebanon and the Middle East from the 1970s onwards. If São Paulo was the city of arrival in Brazil until the 1960s, two decades later that place was occupied by Foz de Iguaçu, which had become the preferred city for arrival in the country.[32]

The flows of migrants into Foz do Iguaçu and the border region allow us to glimpse the continuity and the transformations of the patterns of migration among the Arabs that came into Brazil. Both elements are central to understanding why that place was important in the geography of traders and why it turned out to be so important in the reconfiguration of the Arab migration in Brazil and Latin America. This reconfiguration presents some elements that can be interpreted as substantiating the suspicions about terrorist presence in the region. The point is how to analyze the history and politics that give meaning to the Arab presence in the region without accepting the stereotypes so well portrayed by Didier Bigo—the good tradesman versus the anti-Western terrorist.

As in the case of other groups living outside their places of origin which are under conflict, the Lebanese and the Arabs that lived in the border region did not remain isolated from what happened at home. They were connected to the events in their countries not only through discussions but also through several actions. The civil war in Lebanon and the Israeli invasion demanded positioning and alignment; these generally took place within the debates of those years that revolved around socialism, Arabism, and Islam and all the possible combinations and resignifications in their local contexts. This is not unique to the region under study but is a dynamic that has characterized the

Lebanese throughout the world, as was well pointed by Michael Humphrey: "War in Lebanon over the last decade has had reverberations in Lebanese immigrant communities around the world. The political and ideological currents of contemporary Lebanon have often become part of the culture and politics of these immigrant communities" (Humphrey 1986, 445).

The streets of Foz do Iguaçu were the stage for rallies, protests, and celebrations, as in many cities around the world. Street demonstrations were carried out against the invasion of Lebanon and occupation of Palestine by Israel (1982) and denouncing the massacres of Sabra and Shatila (1982), for example. In 1987, there were solidarity acts with the people of Libya after the U.S. attacks. The same year, the tenth anniversary of the Libyan revolution was celebrated. In 1989, a public celebration was undertaken to celebrate the proclamation of a Palestinian state. During the 1980s, the Centro Cultural Árabe-Brasileiro was particularly active in organizing activities regarding the conflict in the Middle East and the Maghreb countries, particularly Libya.

As in many other places, the government of the new country received pleas and demands to take positions over the conflicts in the migrants' countries of origin. For example, in 1987, representatives of political parties and several Arab associations asked the Brazilian government to intercede with the government of Israel, asking that a presidential pardon be granted to the Brazilian Lamia Maruf Hassan, twenty-one years old, who had been sentenced to life imprisonment by an Israeli military court for her alleged complicity in the action that resulted in the death of an Israeli soldier.

If these activities show the involvement of the Arab migrants in events in their region of origin, their importance for the governments and political actors in those countries can be measured by the visits they made to the migrants' new country. Among many others, for example, in October 1986, the ambassador of the Palestine Liberation Organization (PLO) in Latin America visited the region for meetings with members of the Arab community. In March 1989, other representatives of the PLO were there. The president of the World Islamic Call Society—the Islamic society founded and funded by Libyan president Colonel Muammar Gaddafi—visited the region in December 1987. In May 2001, the deputy of Hezballah at the Lebanese parliament, Abdalla Kassir, was there. All these visits were public, reported in the media, and assisted by authorities, local representatives of the migrant association, and community members.

Far from confirming the suspicions over terrorism, to highlight these dynamics is to put Foz do Iguaçu and Ciudad del Este in the transnational space of the Arab diaspora. Although mainly coming from Lebanon, the migrants of the frontier are part of a population with competing definition criteria: in geographic terms (Middle East), in national terms, in ethnic terms (Arab), and in religious terms (between Islam and other religions as well as among the different Islamic groups). It is from these multiple dimensions that we need to construct alternative portraits of the migrants at the border.

## Back Again to the Tri-Border Region

The urgent need to question representations of the inhabitants of this region as terrorists arises from the inconsistencies of the reports denouncing terrorism's presence in the region and from the dependence of these denunciations on particular contexts.[33] This position led us to question whether terrorism is an issue which can be reduced to a discussion over its presence or absence. It demands that we engage in a broader discussion about the criteria behind the definitions that created such representations.[34]

The activities that underlie the reports about illicit activities and transregional connectivities that emerged in the late 1990s were present in the region before. However, before this period they never led to the depiction of the area as a hotbed of terrorism, even during times of crisis. For example, in May 1970, the secretary of the Israeli embassy in Asunción was killed. According to a confidential document of the Delegacia de Ordem Política e Social in Paraná, the attack was carried out by two men identified as members of al-Fatah, who entered Paraguay via Foz do Iguaçu and who had received the collaboration of "elements of the Arab colony" in that city, as the document said.[35] According to that report, the alleged local supporters and facilitators were interrogated, but they were released for lack of evidence. In many cases, the construction of the Tri-Border Region as a hotbed of terrorism is based on similar reports that are heavy on speculation but free of any credible evidence. The question, then, is why did that event in the 1970s *not* trigger a wave of terrorist representations and security panics? At this time, many governments in South America were reaching out to anti-colonial and anti-imperial movements, including through the Organization of Solidarity of the People of Africa, Asia, and Latin America (OSPAAAL, founded in Havana in 1966). For this organization at this time, Al-Fatah was less a Middle East problem than the expression of the universal legitimacy of national liberation struggles.[36] In the national liberation script, Al-Fatah and the revolutionary movements of Latin America were seen as brothers. So in the 1970s, the alleged participation of Palestinian guerrillas in an attack that had, apparently, some connection with Foz do Iguaçu did not transform the region into a new security problem. At that time in this region, national security crises were not defined in relation to transnational terrorism, but rather in relation to tensions between the armies of Brazil and Argentina.

In the 1960s and '70s the Tri-Border Region was the critical point of Latin American geopolitics because of the "concerted" decision of Brazil and Paraguay to build a hydroelectric dam over the Parana River without consulting Argentina, the downstream country. Between 1966, the year that Brazil and Paraguay signed the accord to use together the hydroelectric potential of the Parana River, and 1979, the year that Brazil, Argentina, and Paraguay agreed to use that potential among the three countries, the possibility of an armed conflict between Brazil and Argentina was considered serious by both countries. In this context, the border region under analysis was central because it was the place where the Itaipú Dam was constructed. Including regional geopolitics, national security, and development, the border region combined some elements of a twentieth-century modernization agenda. There was little space for alternative scripts.

On the other hand, in the late 1990s and 2000s, transnational terrorism concerns took the place of interstate rivalries in the security profile of the region. But violent events directly linked to the Middle East that occurred in other Latin American cities never transformed the urban locations of those actual attacks into security targets. Buenos Aires, after two bombings against Israeli targets there, would have been one candidate to be labeled a site for terror cells, rather than the Tri-Border Region. But it was not. Another candidate could have been São Paulo, with its huge Arab population. On March 7, 2002, Mikhael Youssef Nassar and his wife were murdered in São Paulo. He had been a member of the Lebanese forces, the Maronite Christian militia, during the civil war, and was intimately connected to the militia chief Elie Hobeika. But neither the murder of Nassar nor the al-Fatah attacks generated representations of this region as a site for Middle East terrorism or as a new target for geopolitical security agendas.[37]

But after the 1990s, the Tri-Border Region did become a target for such securitized representations and geopolitical concerns. Besides the Arab Muslim presence at the border, I think that the other reason that panic about "terrorism" emerged was the threat that the region's impressive commercial activity posed to other business interests—and the fact that tri-border business often took advantage of several illegalities, loose copyright and property regimes, and institutional complicities. Its reputation as a hotbed of illegality, however, is also dependent on contexts. It is interesting to read, for example, one of the first descriptions that appeared in the international media about Ciudad del Este, in the *Economist* in the early 1990s. "The city, founded 20 years ago, lies where Paraguay meets both Argentina and Brazil. The commodities it deals in are desk-top computers, Scotch whisky, authentic Levis, children's toys, even cars. The customers are Brazilians and Argentines who cannot buy such things at home because their governments have for decades 'protected' them from good cheap imports in favor of bad, expensive home products." Eight years later, analyzing the possibilities of the Mercosur to become a customs union, an article in the same magazine presented a very different region. "One worry is the lawless area around Ciudad del Este, where Paraguay borders both Argentina and Brazil. Its neighbors—and the United States—suspect this to be a haunt not only of drugs and arms-traffickers but Islamist terrorists." On the agenda of the free market, the border between Paraguay and Brazil was the forefront of the free and competitive market in the early 1990s. Eight years later, on the agenda of the fight against terror, the border region became one of the scenarios where alliances and alignments could be shown and where international goodwill could be expressed and tested.

Questioning terrorism as the structuring element of the narratives about the Arabs of the border, and over the border in general, does not mean considering that everything stated or denounced is a lie. The questioning tries to underline the relationship between certain assumptions, events, and situations and to realize the consequences that they have for the way we conceive of certain groups and histories. Rather than something that can be pronounced true or false, terrorism at the border is a "productive" discourse that produces subjects, power formations, and subjects. And its productivity can be assessed from the effects it has to define the elements of the agenda it imposes. First, it sets the parameters of the discussion by framing the region as one that must constantly prove the existence or absence of terrorism within it. Second, it establishes a temporality that produces a specific story: the one that starts with the terrorist acts that have focused attention on that area.

Just as the Latin American migrants and exiles living abroad were portrayed as communist or pro-guerrilla every time they engaged with the events in their home countries during the 1970s, nowadays the Arabs and Muslims around the world are vulnerable to portrayals of their activities as embedded in terrorism and fundamentalism. Today, as yesterday, these pictures obscure a reality full of nuances and differences, homogenizing a world in turmoil and radicalizing conflicts. Reintroducing the historical, political, and social dimensions that structure these worlds is essential in order to create alternative paths. The Arabs of the border between Brazil and Paraguay—their real histories, agency, and productive centrality—are essential to this project of re-imagining global as well as local security regimes and social identities.

**Notes**

1. The fieldwork research included eleven months between 1999 and 2001 and successive visits in 2006, 2008, and 2009. The historical material presented in the paper was gathered in interviews, local media, and historical records.

2. These are not new questions in research about the Middle East and particularly about Islam. Almost thirty years ago, in "Islam as News," the first section of the book *Covering Islam: How the Media and the Experts Determine How We See the Rest of the World,* Edward Said established a paradigm to deconstruct the images and representations of media coverage of the Middle East. In his words, "It is only a slight overstatement to say that Muslims and Arabs are essentially covered, discussed, apprehended, either as oil suppliers or as potential terrorists. Very little of the detail, the human density, the passion of Arab-Muslim life has entered the awareness of even those people whose profession it is to report the Islamic world" (Said 1981, 26). For an analysis of these issues after September 11, see Poole 2002 and Alatas 2005. For Brazil, see the analysis of Silvia Montenegro (2002).

3. The urban area of Ciudad del Este also includes the districts of Presidente Franco, Hernandarias, and Minga Guazú, totaling 386,354 people (331,592 if we exclude the rural population of those districts). For the data of the 2002 census, see DGEEC 2004. In November 2012, the 2012 census was still under way.

4. The preliminary results of the 2010 census in Argentina are not broken down. The population given for the department of Iguazú, 81,215, includes Puerto Esperanza—the head of the department—Puerto Iguazú, Wanda, and Puerto Libertad (INDEC 2010).

5. For an extended analysis of the commercial circuits and their history, see Rabossi 2012.

6. According to José Maria de Brito, a member of the expedition that founded the military colony of Foz do Iguaçu, "[I]n the occasion of discovering the mouth of the Iguassu river, the Brazilian territory was already inhabited. There were 324 souls, thus described: Brazilians, 9; French, 5; Spaniards, 2; Argentineans, 95; Paraguayans, 212; English one" (Brito [1937] 1995, 13). If we added the people that the expedition met on their way to their destination, we also have some Dutchmen, Germans, and Uruguayans.

7. The first harbor facilities were granted in the Brazilian city of Santos (São Paulo State) in 1941. In 1956, an accord was signed for the use of the port of Paranaguá (Paraná State).

8. The city was named after the president who ruled Paraguay from 1954 to 1989, General Alfredo Stroessner. An authoritarian and anti-communist regime, its thirty-five-year rule had a profound impact on Paraguayan society. After the coup d'état that deposed him in 1989, the name of the city was changed to Ciudad del Este. For simplicity's sake, I will use this name even when I discuss the city before 1989.

9. In 1961, the structure, still under construction but enabling the passage of vehicles over the river, was inaugurated by presidents Juscelino Kubistchek and Alfredo Stroessner.

10. See Knowlton 1960 and 2002; Safady 1966; Truzzi 1992; Lesser 2002; Karam 2007.

11. *Nosso Tempo* 1989a.

12. Interview with the author, October 2001. A public presentation of Abdul Rahal is in Lima 1996, 12–13.

13. Lima 1996, 12–13.

14. Interview with Larry Luxner (Luxner 2005).

15. The trajectory of the group can be consulted at the site of the group (http://www .monalisa.com.py). See also Lima 1996 and *Classe 10* 1996.

16. The study was undertaken by the Department of International Economy, Central Bank of Paraguay, in 1998. Although it is based on a small sample, it gives an idea of the distribution of traders by origin.

17. Fouad Fakih was born in Lebanon and arrived in Brazil at the end of the 1950s, when he was eight years old.

18. It is interesting to note that, although the journal gave more attention to the Arab community, it maintained a critical stance in relation to political developments in the Middle East, particularly regarding the Islamization of politics.

19. The "Islamic family" was the formula used by the center to describe the collectivity addressed for their wishes for Ramadan in 1989 (*Nosso Tempo* 1989b).

20. Kamal Osman, secretary of the Centro Cultural Beneficente Islâmico, introduced above, made the official greetings and presented the objectives of the center and the construction of the mosque. Also attending the ceremony were the ambassadors of Kuwait, Iraq, Saudi Arabia, Libya, Lebanon and the League of Arab States, as well as the *shaykhs* of São Paulo, Rio de Janeiro, Curitiba, and Paranaguá, the president of the Confederation of Islamic Societies of Brazil, and the president of the Centro Cultural Beneficente Islâmico (*Nosso Tempo* 1983).

21. For a comprehensive analysis of the relationships between Sunni and Shi'a Muslims at the border region, see Pinto 2011. For a general overview of the Arab migration in Paraguay that pays close attention to the relationships between the different denominations of Islam, see Montenegro 2009.

22. The previous year, during the visit of the ambassador of the Palestine Liberation Organization for Latin America, another local publication spoke of a population that "here in Foz do Iguaçu revolves around four to five thousand families." Although the reference is to people of Arab origin in general, not only Muslims, the number seems exaggerated even for Foz do Iguaçu and Ciudad del Este considered together (*Três Poderes* 1986).

23. Among those present at the inauguration of the mosque were several representatives of the Arab communities of Paraná State and of Brazil, the deputy secretary general of the Muslim World League, the ambassadors of Iraq, Saudi Arabia, and Lebanon, a representative of the Libyan embassy, and several Brazilian officials.

24. The building where the mosque of the Prophet Mohammed is located has nearly twenty floors. Its walls are painted green, and at the top there are small white domes crowned by a golden crescent moon. The mosque was linked to Shi'a religious leaders in Lebanon.

25. The article was written by Jackson Lima, a local journalist very well informed about the Arab community of the border. If we transform the percentages into numbers,

the figures would correspond to 9,600 Lebanese, 1,800 Palestinians, and 600 people arriving from Syria, Egypt, and other Middle East countries (Lima 1996).

26. Numbers collected by the author from the Sistema Nacional de Estrangeiros da Policia Federal do Brasil, a digital database of the Federal Police, August 1999. Other important groups registered at the database were the Paraguayans (1,770 persons) and the Chinese (1,709 persons).

27. The numbers problem predates September 11, 2001, and it is related to the increasing interest in the magnitude of the Islamic presence in the region. For example, in 1996, the number given by the journalist Mario Chimanovitch in a magazine article was 60,000 people of Lebanese and Palestinian in the region (Chimanovitch 1996).

28. For the first figure, see Lopes 2002; for the second one, CNN 2001.

29. Reuters 2001.

30. For example, see the numbers presented in the following report: "[E]stimates of the size of the Arab community of immigrants of the TBA (mainly in Ciudad del Este and Foz do Iguaçu) range from 20,000 to 30,000, with most residing in Foz do Iguaçu. Of these general figures, Foz do Iguaçu Arab population accounts for 10,000 to 21,000 Arabs of Palestinian and Lebanese descent" (Hudson 2003, 9).

31. This is related to the fact that the image of a "haven of anti-western terrorist lackeys of Hizbollah, usually Shi'a and Arabic speaking" mentioned by Bigo depends on the presence of Lebanese Muslims. The massive emigration of Lebanese Muslims—particularly, Shi'a ones—was driven by the Israeli invasions of south Lebanon in 1978 and 1982.

32. The new spatiality of the Arab migration in Brazil appears in the interviews conducted by Omar Nasser Filho in his research on the Muslim Arabs in Curitiba (Nasser Filho 2006) and in the interviews conducted by Denis Ricardo Carloto (2007). The youth of the new migrants—mostly between twenty and forty years of age—and their religious affiliation—mostly Muslim—are also highlighted by Nasser Filho and by Aline Arruda in her description of the Arab communities of the border region (2007).

33. The analysis of the portrait of the Tri-Border Region deserves an article of its own. For a specific analysis on how this portrait was constructed in the media, both in its hegemonic and in its contrahegemonic version—the so-called alternative media—see Montenegro and Béliveau 2006. For a genealogy of the portrait of the *Triple Frontera,* see Rabossi 2004, 21–24. For the discussion of alternative academic portraits of the region, see Rabossi 2010.

34. For an excellent analysis regarding the responses of the Arab community to the portrait drawn by the U.S. government and the media, see Karam 2011.

35. The Delegacia de Ordem Política e Social—which can be translated as the Bureau of Political and Social Order, commonly known by its acronym, DOPS—was the section of the Federal Police in charge of investigating activities against the social and political order, functioning as a "political police.." For an introductory overview, see Davis 1996. For the case of the secretary of the Israeli embassy in Asunción, see Müller 1998, 33 and the report at *Voz Árabe* 2001, 6.

36. OSPAAAL was founded at the Tri-Continental Conference at Havana in 1966, and combined the radical movements of Latin America and the anti-imperial and anti-colonial movements of Africa and Asia.

37. Nassar's uncle was Antoine Lahad, head of the pro-Israeli militia the South Lebanon Army, currently in exile in Israel. See *A Noticia* 2002, Fisk 2002, and Godoy 2003a and 2003b.

## References

Alatas, Syed Farid, ed. 2005. *Covering Islam: Challenges & Opportunities for Media in the Global Village*. Singapore: RIMA & KAF.

Arruda, Aline M. T. 2007. *A presença libanesa em Foz do Iguaçu (Brasil) e Ciudad del Este (Paraguai)* [Lebanese presence in Foz do Iguaçu (Brazil) and Ciudad del Este (Paraguay)]. Master's thesis, Social Sciences. Universidade de Brasília, Brasilia.

Barakat, Saad el Din. 1999. *Economia de Foz do Iguaçu—PR e balanço das importações clandestinas* [The Economy of Foz do Iguaçu: Parana and a Balance of Illegal Imports]. Monografia No. 498. Curitiba: Ciências Econômicas—UFPR.

Bigo, Didier. 2002. "The Lebanese Community in the Ivory Coast: A Non-native Network at the Heart of Power?" In *The Lebanese in the World: A Century of Emigration*, ed. Albert Hourani and Nadim Shehadi, 509–530. Oxford, UK: Centre for Lebanese Studies and I. B.Tauris.

Bojunga, Claudio, and Fernando Portela. 1978. *Fronteiras. Viagem ao Brasil desconhecido* [Borders: A journey to unknown Brazil]. São Paulo: Editora Alfa Omega.

Brito, José Maria de. (1937) 1995. *Descoberta da Foz do Iguaçu e Fundação da Colônia Militar* [The discovery of the Iguaçu River mouth and the foundation of the Military Colony]. Foz do Iguaçu: FOZTUR—Departamento de Pesquisa e Estatística.

Carloto, Denis R. 2007. *O espaço de representação da comunidade árabe-muçulmana de Foz do Iguaçu-PR e Londrina-PR: da diáspora à multiterritorialidade* [The Arab-Muslim community representational space in Foz do Iguaçu and Londrina: From diaspora to multi-territoriality]. Master's thesis, Geography. Universidade Federal do Paraná, Curitiba.

Chimanovitch, Mario. 1996. "O triângulo do terror" [The Terror Triangle] *Revista Isto É*, May 8. São Paulo.

*Classe 10*. 1996. "Ciudad del Este: O maior shopping da América Latina" [Ciudad del Este: The Major Shopping Center of Latin America]. No. 4: 11–15. Foz do Iguaçu.

CNN. 2001. "Arrestan a 14 árabes en Paraguay por los atentados en EE.UU." [Fourteen Arabs arrested in Paraguay for the attacks in the United States] (Reuters). http://www.cnnenespanol.com/2001/latin/09/21/paraguay.reut/index.html. September 21, 2001. Accessed October 25, 2005.

Davis, Darien J. 1996. "The Arquivos das Policias Politicais of the State of Rio de Janeiro." *Latin American Research Review* 31(1): 99–104.

DGEEC. 2004. *Atlas Censal del Paraguay 2002* [Paraguay 2002 Census Atlas]. Fernando de la Mora: DGEEC.

*Economist*, The. 1990. "The Gentlemen Go By." Vol. 316(7670): 42 ss. London.

———. 1998. "Back and Forth." Vol. 345(8048): 32–33. London.

Fisk, Robert. 2002. "Third Former Militiaman with Links to Sabra and Chatila Is Murdered." *The Independent*. March 11, 2002. London.

Godoy, Marcelo. 2003a. "Polícia faz nova perícia no caso do libanês morto" [Police make new investigation in the case of the Lebanese dead]. *O Estado de São Paulo.* June 26, 38.

———. 2003b. "Polícia busca no Líbano pista para a morte no Itaim" [Police Search in Lebanon for Clues to Itatim Dead]. *O Estado de São Paulo.* June 24, 28.

Hudson, Rex. 2003. *Terrorist and Organized Crime Groups in the Tri-Border Area (TBA) of South America.* Report prepared under an Interagency Agreement by the Federal Research Division, Library of Congress. Washington, D.C.: Federal Research Division—Library of Congress.

Humphrey, Michael. 1986. "The Lebanese War and Lebanese Immigrant Cultures: A Comparative Study of Lebanese in Australia and Uruguay." *Ethnic and Racial Studies* 9(4): 445–460.

INDEC. 2010. *Censo 2010,* http://www.censo2010.indec.gov.ar/.

Jardim, Denise Fagundes. 2000. *Palestinos no extremo sul do Brasil: Edentidade étnica e os mecanismos de produção da etnicidade. Chui/RS* [Palestinians in the Brazilian South: Ethnic identity and the production mechanisms of ethnicity]. PhD dissertation, Social Anthropology. Universidade Federal de Rio de Janeiro, Rio de Janeiro.

Karam, John Tofik. 2007. *Another Arabesque: Syrian-Lebanese Ethnicity in Neoliberal Brazil.* Philadelphia: Temple University Press.

———. 2011. "Atravessando as Américas: A 'guerra ao terror,' os árabes e as mobilizações Transfronteiriças desde Foz do Iguaçu e Ciudad del Este" [Crossing the Americas: The "War on Terror," the Arabs, and the Border Mobilizations from Foz do Iguaçu and Ciudad del Este]. In *A Tríplice Fronteira: Espaços e Dinâmicas Locais,* ed. Lorenzo Macagno, Silvia Montenegro, and Verónica Giménez Béliveau, 203–231. Curitiba: Editora UFPR.

———. 2011. "(Un)covering Islam and Its Fifty-Year History in a South American Frontier Region." http://www.islamamericas.com/index.php/academia/85-uncovering-islam-and-its-fifty-year-history-in-a-south-american-frontier-region. Accessed December 6, 2011.

Knowlton, Clark S. 1960. *Sírios e libaneses: Mobilidade social e espacial* [Syrians and Lebanese: Social and spatial mobility]. São Paulo: Anhambi, 1960.

———. 2002. "The Social and Spatial Mobility of the Syrian and Lebanese Community in São Paulo, Brazil." In *The Lebanese in the World: A Century of Emigration,* ed. Albert Hourani and Nadim Shehadi, 285–311. Oxford, UK: Centre for Lebanese Studies and I. B.Tauris.

Lesser, Jeff H. 2002. "From Pedlars to Proprietors: Lebanese, Syrian and Jewish Immigrants in Brazil." In *The Lebanese in the World: A Century of Emigration,* ed. Albert Hourani and Nadim Shehadi, 391–410. Oxford, UK: Centre for Lebanese Studies and I. B.Tauris.

Lima, Jackson. 1996. "Os árabes da fronteira" [The Arabs of the Border]. *Classe 10,* no. 3: 11–15. Foz do Iguaçu.

———. 1998. *Na Terra das Muitas Águas* [In the Land of the Several Waters]. Foz do Iguaçu: W.A.P. Impressos.

Lopes, Roberto. 2002. "Ciudad del Este pode virar alvo" [Ciudad del Este can become a target]. *Jornal do Brasil.* September 8. Rio de Janeiro.

Luxner, Larry. 2005. "Paraguay's Ciudad del Este Cleans Up Its Act." *Travel Markets Insider,* April 2005. http://www.luxner.com/cgi-bin/view_article.cgi?articleID=1343. Accessed May 12, 2005.

Montenegro, Silvia M. 2002. "Discursos e contradiscursos: O olhar da mídia sobre o Islã no Brasil" [Discourses and Counterdiscourses: Media Representations of Islam in Brazil]. *Mana* 8(1): 63–91.

———. 2009. "La Inmigración Árabe en Paraguay" [Arab Immigration in Paraguay]. In *Los Árabes en América Latina: Historia de una Emigración* [The Arabs in Latin America: History of an Emigration], ed. Adeluahed Akmir, 281–316. Madrid: Siglo XXI & Biblioteca da Casa Árabe.

Montenegro, Silvia, and Verónica G. Béliveau. 2006. *La Triple Frontera: Globalización y construcción del espacio* [The Tri-Border Region: Globalization and Construction of the Space]. Buenos Aires: Miño y Dávila Editores.

Müller, Adelmo. 1998. *Fronteira das emboscadas* [Border of Ambushes]. Foz do Iguaçu: Gráfica Rosanngela.

Nasser Filho, Omar. 2006. *O Crescente e a Estrela na terra dos pinheirais: Os árabes muçulmanos em Curitiba, 1945–1984* [The Crescent and the Star in the Land of the Pines: Arab Muslims in Curitiba, 1945–1984]. Master's thesis, History. Curitiba: Universidade Federal do Paraná.

*Nosso Tempo.* 1982. "Protestos dos Árabes ao terrorista Beguim" [Arab protests against terrorist Beguim]. June 15, 1982, 28. Foz do Iguaçu.

———. 1983. "Com embaixadores e sheiks é iniciada construção da mesquita" [Mosque Construction Starts with Ambassadors and Shaykhs]. March 30–April 6, 4. Foz do Iguaçu.

———. 1989a. "Rahal: De mascate a empresário" [Rahal: From peddler to entrepreneur]. February 17–March 2, 9. Foz do Iguaçu.

———. 1989b. "Muçulmanos comemoram o fim do mês de Ramadan (jejum)" [Muslims Celebrate the End of Ramadam (Fast)]. June 5–11, 4. Foz do Iguaçu.

*Noticia, A.* 2002. "Casal baleado quando trocava pneu em posto." March 10, 2002. Joinville.

Oz, Fernando. 2003. "Paraguay: Desde el 11 de septiembre, doce mil árabes abandonaron Ciudad del Este" [Paraguay: Since September 11 Twelve Thousand Have Left Ciudad del Este]. *Noticias del Mundo Islámico* no. 206, March 25.

Penner, Reinaldo. 1998. *Movimiento comercial y financiero de Ciudad del Este: Perspectivas dentro del proceso de integración* [Commercial and Financial Movement in Ciudad del Este: Perspectives from the Integration Process]. Asunción: Departamento de Economía Internacional—Gerencia de Estudios Económicos—Banco Central del Paraguay.

Pinto, Paulo Gabriel Hilu da Rocha. 2011. "As Comunidades Muçulmanas na Tríplice Fronteira: Significados Locais e Fluxos Transnacionais na Construção de Identidades Étnico-Religiosas" [Muslim Communities at the Tri-Border Region: Local Meanings and Transnational Fluxes in Ethno-Religious Identity Construction]. In *A Tríplice Fronteira: Espaços e Dinâmicas Locais,* ed, Lorenzo Macagno, Silvia Montenegro, and Verónica Giménez Béliveau, 183–202. Curitiba: Editora UFPR.

Poole, Elizabeth. 2002. *Reporting Islam: Media Representations and British Muslims.* London: I. B. Tauris.

Rabossi, Fernando. 2004. *Nas ruas de Ciudad del Este: Vidas e vendas num mercado de fronteira* [On Ciudad del Este's Streets: Lives and Sales in a Border Market]. PhD dissertation, Social Anthropology. Universidade Federal de Rio de Janeiro, Rio de Janeiro.

———. 2007. "Árabes e muçulmanos em Foz do Iguaçu e Ciudad del Este: Notas para uma re-interpretação." [Arabs and Muslims in Foz do Iguaçu and in Ciudad del Este: Notes for a re-interpretation]. In *Mundos em Movimento: Ensaios sobre migrações* [Worlds in Movement: Essays on Migrations], ed. Giralda Seyferth, Helion Povoa Neto, Maria Catarina Chitolina Zanini, and Miriam de Oliveira Santos, 287–312. Santa Maria: Editora da Universidade Federal de Santa Maria.

———. 2010. "Cómo pensamos la Triple Frontera?" [How do We Conceive the Tri-Border Region?]. In *La Triple Frontera: dinámicas culturales y procesos transnacionales.* [The Tri-Border Region: Cultural Dynamics and Transnational Processes], ed. Verónica Giménez Béliveau and Silvia Montenegro, 21–45. Buenos Aires: Espacio Editorial.

———. 2012. "Commodities and Circulation: Ciudad del Este and the Brazilian Circuits of Commercial Distribution." In *Globalization from Below: The Other Global Economy,* ed. Gustavo Lins Ribeiro, Gordon C. Mathew, and Carlos José Alba Vega, 55–68. London: Routledge.

Reuters. 2001. "Suposto financiador de terror tem prisão pedida no Paraguai" [Alleged Financier of Terror Sentenced to Prison in Paraguay]. http://br.yahoo.com/noticias/mundo/reuters/article.html?s=br/noticias/011023/m. undo/reuters/Suposto_financiador _de_terror_tem_prisao_pedida_no_Paraguai.html Asunción, October 23. Accessed October 25, 2001.

Safady, Jamil. 1966. *O Café e o Mascate* [The Coffee and the Peddler]. São Paulo: Ed. Comercial Safady.

Said, Edward W. 1981. *Covering Islam: How the Media and the Experts Determine How We See the Rest of the World.* New York: Pantheon.

*Três Poderes.* 1986. "Farid: Americanos massacram Palestinos" [Farid: Americans Slaughter Palestinians]. Vol. 26. November 10, 25. Foz do Iguaçu.

Truzzi, Oswaldo. 1992. *De Mascates a Doutores: Sírios e Libaneses em São Paulo* [From Peddlers to Doctors: Syrians and Lebanese in São Paulo]. São Paulo: IDESP/Ed. Sumaré.

*Voz Árabe.* 2001. "Tríplice fronteira sempre foi vítima de investigações" [Tri-Border Region Was Always under Investigation]. Vol. 5(82), 6. Londrina.

Ynsfran, Edgar L. 1990. *Un giro geopolítico: El milagro de una ciudad* [A Geopolitical Turn: The Miracle of a City]. Asunción: Ediciones y Arte SRL.

# Part Two.  Race, Nation, and Transregional Imaginations

# 6

# Tropical Orientalism
## Brazil's Race Debates and the Sephardi-Moorish Atlantic

*Ella Shohat and Robert Stam*

Shohat and Stam put forward the idea of a Tropical Orientalism in Brazil. They interpret the contemporary Brazilian imaginary of the Orient against the backdrop of a Moorish-Sephardi unconscious, thus highlighting not only the positive cross-Atlantic historical, discursive, and cultural links between "the Orient" and "the Occident," but also the anxieties that such links provoked.

∾

On Avenida Rio Branco in downtown Rio de Janeiro, at a busy juncture between the palm trees and the art deco buildings, stands an obelisk. Dating back to 1906 and the period of the world's fairs, this homage (by the Italian Society of Brazil) evokes not only a supposed Greco-Roman past of a tropical "Latin" country, but also an Egyptian civilizational origin. The obelisks, which grace the thoroughfares of many cities in the Americas such as São Paulo, Buenos Aires, and Washington, D.C., are partly a by-product of the Egyptomania that swept France, Britain, Germany, Italy, and the United States, a mania that was itself a by-product of a post-Enlightenment discourse that celebrated ancient Egypt. Ever since Napoleon set foot in Egypt, and especially during the heydays of imperial expansionism, modernity has been preoccupied with the display of "the ancient" in metropolitan centers. Museums and world's fairs exhibited archaeological artifacts extracted for popular consumption from the ruins of Luxor, resuscitating Ozymandias, as it were, to testify to the newly invigorated mastery of ancient times and spaces.

The display of a replica of an "ancient" monument in modern Rio de Janeiro touches on an underemphasized aspect of Brazilian identity: its palimpsestically complex relation to "the Orient." Apart from ancient obelisks, contemporary Brazilian culture, both erudite and popular, proliferates in references to Middle Eastern culture. In twentieth-century Brazilian literature, the figure of the *turco* (or immigrant-merchant coming from the former Ottoman Empire) appears in novels such as Mario de Andrade's *Macunaima* and Jorge Amado's *Gabriela, cravo e canela*. In culinary terms, Middle Eastern *quibe, esfiha*, and *tabule* have become Brazilian staples, found across the country partly thanks to the fast-food chain Habib. Carnival costumes of odalisques and belly dancers display a playful capacity to incorporate an eroticized image of "the Orient" into Carnival's own fantasy rituals. We find *turco*/Arab characters and "Oriental" references in the popular musical comedies (*chanchadas*) of the 1950s such as *Barnabé tu és meu* (1952) and *Nem Sansão Nem Dalila* (Neither Samson nor Delilah, 1954), a parody of the Orientalist excesses of Cecil B. DeMille's *Samson and Delilah*.

A number of scholars have usefully delved into the history and the ethnography of immigration in Latin America generally and Brazil more specifically.[1] Their work examines these issues largely in the context of immigration from the regions of the former Ottoman Empire to the Americas since the late nineteenth century, as well as in relation to more recent Muslim immigration to the Americas. This history is replete with stereotypical images of Jews and *turcos*/Arabs, but at the same time Arab-Brazilians have gained visibility within the public sphere: celebrated writers like Antonio Houaiss, Milton Hatoum, and Raduan Nassar; famous actresses like Dina Sfat, Claudia Ohana, and Malu Mader; and powerful politicians like Paulo Maluf and Geraldo Alckmin. *Turcos* have attained powerful positions within the economic, political, and cultural spheres. Contemporary telenovelas, meanwhile, incorporate the Middle East into the narrative, whether through providing the scenic backdrops against which romantic plots unfold (for example, *Viver a Vida*'s location shooting in the Middle East, especially in Jerusalem and Petra), or through major *turco* characters (*Belissima*), or even by placing Islam at the very center of the drama (*O Clone*). In this sense, within the ambivalent situation that we hope to explore in this chapter, the achievement of powerful positions by Middle Easterners exists simultaneously with a neo-Orientalist representation of the Middle East.

Our focus here, however, will be both on the question of the beginnings of Orientalism generally and on Brazil's ambivalent relation to "the Orient." Although Brazilian debates about national identity have usually centered on questions of race—especially the formulaic red, white, and black triad—they have also touched on broader geopolitical questions such as Global North versus Global South; pseudo-ethnic questions like the Latin versus the Anglo-Saxon; and demographic questions like the impact of *converso*/Jewish/Arab immigration. In this chapter, we will examine these issues through the prism of Orientalism/Occidentalism in order to "unveil" marginalized yet constitutive aspects of Brazilian identity. We will take a multifaceted and multidirectional approach to Brazil's complexly layered racial discourse. We will focus especially on two intellectuals whose writing sheds light on these issues: first, the anthropologist Gilberto Freyre, who engaged Indianness and blackness alongside Sephardiness and Moorishness; and second, the historian João Reis, who has illuminated the Muslim role in Bahia's anti-slavery rebellions. In distinct ways, both authors highlight the crucial role of Brazil's "Orient" and the place of the Arab/Muslim/Jew within Brazil's cultural history. We will be concerned with the early tropical imaginary of the Orient that prepared the ground for later ambivalent relations to a geography at once familiar and alien.

## Wrestling over the Iberian Legacy

To understand Brazil's "Orient" in its historical depth, we need to go at least as far back as Christopher Columbus, and even to the Christian crusades against the infidel. (Even before Columbus, the *conquista* was itself already informed by the "proto-Orientalism" and the persecution of Muslims and Jews during the *reconquista* of Iberia.) Columbus, in our view, can be seen as one of the first Orientalists, even in the sense of imagining himself, as his diaries indicate, to be actually *in* the Orient, in the "land of the Great Khan." By traveling west, Columbus intended to go east to convert the diverse heathens and infidels, including Muslims and Jews. Orientalism, in this sense, begins with the very arrival of the Iberian theological vision in the Americas. In the wake of the conquest, Orientalist discourse traveled to the Americas, generating the emergence of Western world order, which in turn created another base from which to disseminate colonial power and colonialist conceptions of the world. Infused and empowered by the Americas' material wealth, Europe subsequently colonized Egypt, Algeria, and the rest of the Middle East and North Africa, subjecting these regions to an old/new kind of Orientalism. Even before arriving in the Orient, then, the Orientalist imaginary had already arrived in the Americas, arguably becoming a constitutive element in the cultural mix.[2]

During the cataclysmic moment of the various "1492s," the beginning of the conquest of the "new" world converged with the expulsion of Sephardic Jews and Muslim Moors from Spain. In the long view, the ground for colonialist racism was prepared by the Inquisition's *limpieza de sangre* (cleansing of blood), by the Edicts of Expulsion against the Jews and Muslims, by Portuguese incursions along the west coast of Africa, and by the transatlantic slave trade. Forged in centuries of *reconquista*, fifteenth-century Spain provided a template for the creation of racial states and for ethno-religious cleansing. Although the *limpieza de sangre* was formulated in religious terms—the "problem" of Jewishness and Muslimness could be remedied by conversion—the metaphor of the "purity of blood" prepared the way for nineteenth-century biological/scientific racism; Christian demonology thus set the tone for colonialist racism.[3]

Examining the circulation of tropes and metaphors, as well as the discursive connections and links between the various 1492s, affords us a historically grounded way to begin the story of Orientalism in Latin America. In Brazil, more specifically, discourses about Muslims and Jews armed the conquistadores with a ready-made demonizing vision, transferable from the "old" to the "new" world. Discourses, along with languages such as Arabic and Hebrew, travelled together to the "New World." Columbus took the *converso* Luis de Torres as his interpreter, because his knowledge of Semitic languages was supposed to facilitate encounters in the "East." The linguistic heritage of the *conversos* and Moriscos who traveled to the Americas was not completely abandoned, despite the fact that the Inquisition continued in places like Mexico (including what is now the southwestern United States) and Brazil. Some Sephardic Jews, especially from Portugal, who had fled the Inquisition to Holland, ended up in the Dutch-dominated territories in the Americas; and in 1654, the Sephardis of Pernambuco in northern Brazil departed with the withdrawing Dutch for New Amsterdam, where they established the first (Portuguese) synagogue in what is now downtown Manhattan, where rituals and prayers persisted in Aramaic and Hebrew, alongside lessons in Portuguese). In Brazil, Spanish and Portuguese, which had already been influenced by centuries of Arabic, and to a lesser extent Hebrew, were not severed from their Moorish-Sephardi linguistic/cultural matrix. Indeed, in his 1943 book *Influências Orientais na Língua Portuguesa,* the Lebanese-Brazilian Miguel Nimer researched the Arabic and Arabized, along with the Persian and the Turkish, etymologies of Portuguese vocabulary (2005).

Although *reconquista* and Inquisition ideology justified the cleansing of the "Orientalized" Moorish-Sephardic past, Latin America, as a site of complex global cultural encounters and mixed feeling toward the colonial metropole, has also demonstrated a certain nostalgia for that "Oriental" past. The Latin American imaginary, in this sense, has been partly shaped by what could be called "the Moorish unconscious," in a situation where denial, longing, and repressed memory coexist. The mundane pride of some Latin American families in their Morisco or Sephardi *converso* lineage has been expressed in popular tales and registered in the work of various writers. From José Martí's exhortation "Seamos Moros!" (1938) to Carlos Fuentes's celebration of Mexico's "buried mirror" (1999), the question of the Moor has never stopped haunting the Latin American imaginary.[4] In his theorization of Brazilian identity, Gilberto Freyre, as we shall see, gives great weight to the Moorish-Sephardic cultural history of Portugal as actively shaping Brazilian customs and practices.[5] But the programmatic adoption of Occidental/European customs, institutionalized already with Brazil's independence in 1822, furthered by the various French cultural "missions," and later reinforced by Anglo-American economic domination, catalyzed a detachment from the Moorish-Sephardic heritage (Freyre 1963).[6] Once part of a shared cultural landscape, both Muslims and Jews came to be seen by some Ibero-American authorities as alien excrescences to be symbolically excised from a putatively coherent and pure body politic.

Most nations define themselves diacritically, with and against the other nations and civilizations with which they have been in contact. A long intellectual tradition has emphasized the Iberian origins of Brazilian nationality, alternatively seen as the putrid fount of Brazilian obscurantism, authoritarianism, and bureaucracy, or as the sacred spring of its easygoing social conviviality. As suggested by the aphorism "Europe begins at the Pyrenees," Iberia represents a southern, Orientalized Occident. In the negative view, the Iberian heritage forms an irrational, counter-Enlightenment force. In the positive view, that very same heritage makes Brazil tolerant and gregarious. The most euphoric proponent of the pro-Iberian view, ironically, was the American literary scholar Richard Morse, who in his book *Espelho do Prospero* (Prospero's Mirror, published in 1982 in Mexico and in 1988 in Brazil) saw the Iberian influence as infusing into Brazil a more humane and communitarian set of values. The Iberian heritage, far from corrupting Brazil, actually generated cultural superiority. The refusal of utilitarian individualism provided the key to a more generous ethos that transcended both communist and capitalist forms of productivism. Morse's idealizing view, as even Latin American critics pointed out, had little place for the horrors of the *reconquista*, the Inquisition, the *conquista*, colonialism, slavery, and predatory forms of Latin American–style capitalism.

As a country formed by indigenous peoples, enslaved Africans, European colonizers, and immigrants of every possible provenance, Brazil partially formulates issues of identity through cross-national comparisons. Comparisons with the United States, for example, have been unending, forming even, at times, an integral part of a specular and reciprocal process of self-definition.

Although cross-cultural comparisons often betray a penchant for narcissistic nationalism, in the case of Brazil they have just as often generated not self-satisfaction but insecurity, whether about Brazil's supposedly derivative culture or its inadequate political institutions or economic backwardness. In Brazil, cross-cultural comparison has often been wielded to the detriment of Brazil by Brazilians themselves. Indeed, playwright Nelson Rodrigues famously called Brazilians "upside down Narcissists" who spit on their own mirror image. In the wake of the Hegelian (and Weberian) dichotomy of dynamic Protestant North and indolent Catholic South, many Brazilian intellectuals have searched for culturalist explanations for Brazil's putative "failure," seen in comparison, usually, with an idealized United States or Western Europe. (This idea of "failure" is less current now that Brazil is emerging as a major economic power and the United States and Europe are beset by political and economic decline.) Some Brazilian intellectuals appealed to race as a cause for backwardness. Paulo Prado, in *Retrato do Brasil* (1928), spoke of Brazil as a melancholy mélange of "three sad races"—the Portuguese, the Indians, and the Africans—contrasting Brazil's libidinous languor with the United States's hygienic dynamism. The predatory nature of Portuguese colonialism, Prado argued, created a situation where manual labor was scorned, where culture was ornamental and derivative, and where *malandragem* (roughly, quick-witted hustling street smarts) was a cultural norm. Other modernists, such as the writers Mario de Andrade and Oswald de Andrade, meanwhile, saw these cultural contrasts in a more positive light. Decades later, José Guilherme Merquior argued in *Saudades do Carnaval* that Brazilian carnivalism inoculated the country against the deadening rationalization, Puritanism, and disenchantment typical of the relentlessly productivist Occident.[7]

As many Brazilian commentators have pointed out, the comparison to the United States is never far away whenever Brazilians talk about their own history or "national character." Many of the major theorists of Brazilian history and character—Gilberto Freyre, Sérgio Buarque de Holanda, Raimundo Faoro, Roberto da Matta, Dante Moreira Leite—invoke the comparison, often explicitly. Thus a fatalistic causality, rather like original sin, was supposed to mark the history of Brazil. What varies in the comparative accounts of "failure" is exactly who or what is being blamed for a supposed Brazilian insufficiency. For the Weber-influenced but non-essentialist Sérgio Buarque de Holanda in *Raizes do Brasil* (1956), the problem largely derives from Brazil's inheritance of authoritarian personalism from Portugal, a backward country where the Enlightenment, the Reformation, the French Revolution, and industrial capitalism had had little impact. For the lawyer, philosopher, and literary critic Raimundo Faoro, in his 1958 book *Os Donos do Poder: Formação do Patronato Político Brasileiro,* the villain is the patrimonial state, again derived from Portugal, where Faoro's ideal model is implicitly conceived on the basis of liberal North American norms, in contrast with the Iberian tradition that shaped Brazil. Whether explicitly stated or not, these texts are haunted by a submerged dimension of the "primal sin" of Iberia—the taint of the African-Moorish-Jewish influence. Our purpose here, in any case, is to suggest that the inferiority/superiority debates, the tradition/modernity debates, and the Latin versus Anglo-Saxon debates have all been intricately entangled with the less noted debates about the Moorish-Sephardic dimension of the Brazilian identity.

## Gilberto Freyre: A Study in Ambivalence

The work of Gilberto Freyre, who was to become one of the most influential theorists of Brazilian national identity, instantiated an intense dialogue with various currents of thought. The son of an Americanophile Brazilian, Freyre studied at Columbia University, where he worked with the anti-racist German-Jewish anthropologist Franz Boas, the advocate of an analysis based on culture rather than race.[8] Freyre's classic *The Masters and the Slaves* (1956), first written as a dissertation at Columbia University, was a social history of slaveholding Brazil. Freyre's method was partially comparative, in that Freyre thought that a knowledge of the U.S. "Deep South" facilitated understanding of the patriarchal economy of Brazil. Freyre analyzed the big house and the slave quarters (*Casa-Grande e Senzala* is the book's title in Portuguese) as a social microcosm incarnating, shaping, and revealing the intimate history of Brazil. Although somewhat serendipitous and unsystematic in his research method, Freyre's methodology nonetheless anticipated what would later be called "cultural studies" or, more accurately, "cultural history." In a sensuous Proustian style, he mobilized the most diverse social phenomena—clothing, cuisine, toys, games, rhymes, architecture, interior design, family photographs—to construct a portrait of the racialized social formation of Brazil. Turning scientific racism on its head, Freyre transformed what antecedent theory had seen as negative—the epidermically obvious presence of blacks and Indians, and the less obvious, more submerged presence of Moors and Sephardis—into a point of national pride.

Freyre's highly eroticized account of Brazil's origins highlights the "sexual exaltation" of the basic formative couple—the Portuguese man and the Indian woman—whose very possibility was facilitated, in Freyre's view, by a Moorish-Portuguese flexibility with regard to race. Freyre's account of European-indigene romance relays what Doris Sommer calls a key "foundational fiction," the romantic fable, developed in nineteenth-century Indianist novels like *Iracema*, of the origins of Brazil as a nation in the fecund heterosexual encounter of European male and indigenous woman, presented as the primal matrix of Brazil's identity. In a kind of genre/gender mistake, Freyre envisions the sexual politics of enslavement, first of Indians and then of Africans, through the steamy prism of erotic fantasy, transforming the base reality of sexual coercion into a myth of delicious hanky-panky in tropical hammocks.

At other times, however, Freyre emphasizes the violence and even sadism inherent in such relations, claiming that "there is no slavery without sexual depravation" (Benzaquen de Araujo 2005, 57). In *The Mansions and the Shanties: The Making of Modern Brazil*, Freyre emphasizes a sadistic dimension of the child rearing of colonial patriarchs, a sadism subsequently transmitted to other institutions like religious and state schools (1963, 64). For Freyre, the hierarchical structures of slavery filter down and spread outward into a general all-pervasive plantation patriarchalism that comes to characterize Brazil as a whole. But Freyre traces both characteristics—patriarchal authoritarianism and sexual-racial flexibility—to a Moorish lineage. The approach to gender, meanwhile, is conjunctural in Freyre's work; his thinking changes as a function of the ideological needs of the moment. Gendered in contradictory ways, the Moorish lineage simultaneously connotes both conquering masculinity and a stereotypically feminine passivity and softness. Updating and reconfiguring the European gendering of the land as female and "virgin," Freyre posits femaleness as characteristic of Brazil as a whole. So blithely masculinist in his view of Brazilian culture, Freyre contrasts Brazil as psychologically female and eager for "the equivalent of full sexual experience," in contrast with "male nations" like the United States (1959, 271). Indeed, as often occurs within colonial discourse, gendered tropes about "the East" and tropes about "the South" here become virtually interchangeable.[9]

Freyre's positive association of Moorish Portugal with flexibility is seemingly contradicted by the fact that Moorishness is also associated with its negative opposite—authoritarianism. While Freyre recuperates the Moorish cultural contribution, he also associates the Moor with Brazilian underdevelopment. The Portuguese, meanwhile, despite Freyre's praise for their Moorish "flexibility," do not escape his censure; often, they appear as villains, and not very bright ones at that. (Freyre in this sense prolongs a venerable Brazilian tradition of portraying the Portuguese as dim-witted, as evidenced in the popular expression *coisa de Português* to denote idiotically absent-minded behavior). Moorish Iberia, in this sense, occupies an ambivalent position in Brazilian discourses. Thus with

Freyre, the role of Portugal partially changes its valence, now becoming the positive fount of Brazil's penchant for mixture and compromise and seduction. This Portuguese "plasticity" is found, for Freyre, even in Brazilian modalities of slavery, which were influenced by the Arab-Moorish model, wherein the slave was a subaltern member of an extended patriarchal family. (Freyre acknowledges having gotten the idea of Muslim/Arab influence on Brazilian slavery from Boas, who suggested that "the Muslims, Arabs, and Moors had for many centuries been superior to the Europeans and Christians in their methods of assimilating African cultures into their civilization" [Freyre 1969, 180]).[10]

A key Freyrean concept was the "equilibrium of antagonisms," a kind of homeostatic balance mechanism regulating social relations between master and slave, African and European, elite and people. Although Freyre is often cited as the originator of the cognate concept of "racial democracy," the phrase, as many critics have pointed out, never actually appears in *Masters and Slaves*. In fact, many passages in the book contradict the very idea of "racial democracy." Numerous passages portray in excruciating detail the often gratuitous cruelty of Brazilian slave masters (and mistresses), reaching the extremes even of slaves and their children being deliberately burned alive in the furnaces of the sugar mills. Freyre notes a general Brazilian tendency toward sadism created by a habitual abuse of blacks and Indians. Given all this, as both Ricardo Benzaquen de Araújo and Hermano Vianna stress, it is difficult to see Freyre's work as portraying a tropical paradise of transracial cohabitation rooted in a Portuguese sensibility. Rather, he portrays colonial Brazil as a combination of paradise and hell, and he can be cited in support of either position.[11] The real problem in Freyre's work has less to do with his supposedly idyllic portrait of slavery than with the rather more fundamental issue of social evaluation and point of view. Heterosexual desire, and perhaps homosexual desire as well, overdetermine Freyre's tumescent account of sexuality under slavery, which Freyre recounts from the perspective of the master enjoying "access" to the body of the slave, without acknowledging the possible attitude of the enslaved toward that "access." The other problem is Freyre's view of an unchanging homeostatic society, seen as in perpetual equilibrium, with little room for cultural dissension or social heteroglossia, for historical mutation, or for any real intellectual and political agency beyond cultural "contributions" on the part of racialized others.[12] The dominant white Brazilians get all the economic and political power; the racialized masses get cuisine and folklore.

Rather than praise or demonize Freyre as the apostle of racial democracy, it is perhaps more helpful to see him as someone fascinating precisely in his contradictions. Freyre's relation to the racial question in the United States, for example, was extremely complex. There was nothing inevitable about Freyre opting for the exact positions that he ended up adopting. One of Freyre's intellectual biographers, Maria Lúcia Garcia Pallares-Burke, in her *Gilberto Freyre: Um Vitoriano dos Tropicos* (2005), speaks of the multifarious influences—Brazilian, North American, European—that shaped the Freyre of the 1930s. Pallares-Burke reveals some surprising sources for Freyre's turn from the dominant racist attitudes of the time toward a more affirmative attitude toward miscegenation and blackness. Apart from Boas, Freyre fell in love with the "romantic exoticism" of the novels of Patrick Lafcadio Hearn (1850–1904), a Greco-Irish immigrant to the United States and negrophile author of *Two Years in the French West Indies*. Fascinated by the Latin mestizo culture of New Orleans, which he called a "Southern Paradise," Hearn rejected what he saw as the cold, industrial North in favor of the warm life of the South, not for its colonial-style Big Houses but rather for its Africanized cultural vibrancy. Like Freyre later, Hearn lauded the positive values of blackness and miscegenation, within a cross-cultural comparative frame. Pallares-Burke notes that Freyre would often write "just like Brazil" in the margins of Hearn's books, and it is no accident that Freyre, in *Masters and Slaves,* says of Hearn that he was a thinker, who, simply as a writer, "discerned more than many sociologists" (qtd in Pallares-Burke 2005, 350). The irony, then, was that two "hyphenated Americans," the Greco-Irish Hearn and the Jewish-American Boas (whom Freyre describes, in quasi-Brazilian terminology, as a "Latinized Moreno") were key catalysts for the transvaluation of values that led to Freyre's affirmation of miscegenation and the black cultural contribution within Brazil itself.[13]

Prior to Freyre, the dominant racial orthodoxies had favored two views of miscegenation: (1) a downward-trending miscegenation that led to sterility and degeneration; and (2) a supposedly "upward"-trending miscegenation that led to the assumed-to-be-positive "whitening" of Brazil. Both views saw Indianness and blackness as negative, but one was more "optimistic" about their possible transcendence. Freyre credited Boas, especially, with alerting him to the true value of black culture. Freyre's voyage to North America catalyzed his revisionist view of South America. Going against the grain of hegemonic views of African and Indian cultures, one might argue, made it possible for Freyre to transcend negative discourses about Moorish and Sephardic cultures as well. While the latter may have been more submerged in the historical period in which Freyre was writing, one can nonetheless analyze the discourses both about the African-indigenous element and about the Sephardi-Moorish element, within a broader relationality dating back to the twin 1492s of the *reconquista* and the *conquista*.

The Iberian wariness about both an "Orient" associated with Africa and the South and an "Occident" associated with Europe and the North thus persisted in the Americas. The negative influence of the Jewish and the Muslim was seen as "Orientalizing," that is, as tainting Christian and European Latin identity and sense of self, whether in Europe or throughout its extensions in the Americas. The Iberian clash generated decrees (in 1501 and 1530) against Moors and Jews entering the Americas. (Arab Christians, especially when representing churches, in contrast, were welcomed, as evidenced in the seventeenth-century travel narrative of Elias al-Mūsili, a priest of the Chaldean Church, one of the early arrivals in the Americas from Baghdad [al-Mūsili 2003].) Orientalism, although conceptualized by Edward Said in relation to the post-Enlightenment era, and especially in relation to the 1798 Napoleonic invasion of Egypt, can thus be examined in a distinct earlier incarnation, in Iberia and in Ibero-America. The critique of Orientalism can help illuminate the hostility to what was viewed as the Moorish Muslim and Sephardi Jewish "Orientalization" of Iberia and consequently of its new territories in the Americas.[14] While in contemporary critical discourse "Orientalism" refers to the ways the Middle East has been constructed in anti-Semitic (Judeophobic) and Islamophobic discourse, "Orientalization" evoked the tainting of blood, religion, race, and/or culture. De-orientalization, in contrast with Saidian anti-Orientalist critique, which deconstructed colonialist assumptions about the Orient, was premised on those very same assumptions.

Within the new expansion of Atlantic space, the ritual memory of the struggle between Christians and infidels continued to be reenacted in choreographed equestrian combats between Spaniards and Moors, as well as in Easter Sunday street festivals. "The Christians," in the words of Gilberto Freyre, "were always victorious and the Moors routed and punished. And Easter Saturday ended or began with the effigy of Judas being carried through the streets and burned by the urchins in what was evidently a popular expression of religious hatred of the Catholic for the Jew" (Freyre 1963, 297). Jews were viewed, in Freyre's words, as the "secret agent of Orientalism" (ibid.). Thus, before the contemporary Eurocentric erasure, as it were, of the hyphen in "Judeo-Islamic" and its replacement by the hyphen in "Judeo-Christian," the "Jew" and "the Muslim," or "the Sephardi" and "the Moor," or "the Morisco" and "the converso" were articulated within the same conceptual space, as one allegorical unit; hence our usage of the hyphen in "the Sephardi-Moorish Atlantic."[15] As a form of Iberian anxiety about Arabization/Judaization, "Orientalism" was thus carried over to the Americas, where it participated in the foundational shaping of emerging regional and national identities.

## The Return of the Sephardi

Sephardi Jews have a long history in Brazil, going back to the very beginnings of Portuguese arrival. In 1502, a consortium of Jewish merchants, headed by the *converso* Fernão de Noronha, after obtaining a three-year lease from the Portuguese Crown for exploration and settlement, brought sugar cane from Madeira and São Tomé to the newly "discovered" land then called "Vera Cruz." For Noronha and his group Brazil offered both a business opportunity and a refuge from persecution. Some Jews maintained their Jewish customs in hiding, while others assimilated into the Catholic mainstream. New Christians (Jewish converts) investors scouted the coast and shared with the Crown their monopoly contracts to harvest Brazil-wood. While non-Jews called them (euphemistically) *cristãos novos* (New Christians) or *conversos* (converts), or pejoratively "Marranos" (pigs), the Jews called themselves "people of the nation," or *anusim* or *bnei ausim* (literally, the "raped ones" or "children of the raped ones"). But the Inquisition visited Brazil at the tail end of the sixteenth century, sending many Jews into hiding. Many Jewish customs, such as respect for the Sabbath, were maintained in the backlands, including in the Amazon. New Christians euphemistically commemorated Yom Kippur and Sukkot. Traveling from cities like Fez, Tangiers, Marrakesh, and Casablanca, Moroccan Jewish traders and tappers also arrived in the Amazon as early as 1810. Jews founded a synagogue, Essel Avraham, in Belém (Portuguese for Beit Lehem, or Bethlehem), as places were often named in the Americas in remembrance of the birthplace of Christ. Rabbi Shalom Imanu El-Muyal—referred to as *Santo Moisezinho*—came to be seen as healer and holy man by Jews and non-Jews alike. Jewish-Moroccan-Spanish surnames like Albaz, Assayag, Azulay, Benchimol, Benayon, Benguigi, Ohana, and Ovadia became common in Belém and Manaus.[16] Although often relegated to the margins of Latin American history, the Sephardi, in Freyre's remaking of Brazil, is recuperated for the narrative of Brazil's national formation. In *The Mansions and the Shanties*, Freyre discusses Brazil's transition over centuries from a rural, agricultural sugar-based patriarchal society to an urban industrial society. For Freyre, this transition coincided with the growth of cities as well as with the beginnings of the mining and coffee industries. Freyre devotes considerable attention to the Dutch colonization of northern Brazil, where the Dutch allowed many Sephardi Jews to settle and practice their faith without fear of persecution. Yet the Inquisition followed the Jews across the Atlantic after the Dutch defeat; Jews professed Catholicism publicly while practicing their own faith covertly.[17] Although in some ways a marginal chapter in Brazil's history, the

Dutch-Sephardi alliance, perhaps because of Freyre's Pernambuco origins, occupies a significant place in Freyre's account, allowing him to transform the Sephardi from a virtually mythical figure relegated to an Iberian Andalus into an agential subject of Brazilian history.

Freyre invokes the Iberian anti-Jewish discourse that persisted in Latin America, but in order, ultimately, to subvert it by undermining its mythical anti-Semitic underpinnings. Although Jews were regarded with suspicion by the agrarian and mining industrialists who accused Jewish moneylenders of cheating plantation owners and miners through markups of interest and goods, Freyre points out that markups were a widespread phenomenon, not the monopoly of a single ethnicity or religion. Freyre also stresses the multifaceted Sephardi contribution to the development of Brazil through providing capital for the founding of the sugar industry, distributing Brazilian goods internationally, introducing European goods to Brazil, and advancing medicine, science, and culture. Viewing Sephardis virtually as extensions of the Dutch, Freyre highlights their role as agents of modernization and progress.

Dutch Recife became the greatest center of what Freyre calls "differentiation" in the colony:

> Under Count Maurice of Nassau, in a grove of cashew trees, the first observatory of America was built; in what had been mangrove swamps, a botanical and a zoological garden. Piso and Marcgraf made their appearance, the first to study from a scientific approach the native, the trees, the animals of Brazil; Calvinist ministers preaching new forms of Christianity; the artists Franz Post and Zacarias Wagner painting plantation houses, Indians' huts, Negro cabins, cashew trees along the riverbanks, colored washerwomen with bundles of clothes on their heads, Indians, half-breed, Negroes; Peter Post drawing up the plans of a large city of tall houses and deep canals on which one could travel by canoe as in Holland. A wealth of intellectual, artistic, scientific, religious differentiation. The Portuguese and Catholic monopoly had been broken in Pernambuco, the monopoly on architecture, religion, way of life; and, for a time, even the monopoly on language. (Freyre 1963, 213–214)

Freyre's admiration for (his native) Pernambuco is thus linked to his admiration for both the North European or "Anglo-Saxon" currents and for the South European "Latin" currents. Freyre, in other words, deploys a Hegelian-Weberian dichotomy—of Northern Anglo-Saxon and Southern Latin—or what we prefer to see as an ideological binarism between two narcissistic and Eurocentric ideologies, what we call Anglo-Saxonism and Latinism.[18] At different moments, paradoxically, Freyre seems to embrace these apparently opposite poles. Although the Sephardi and the Moor are usually linked within an Iberian memory, with Freyre the Moor forms part of patriarchal Latinidad whereas the Sephardi forms part of the modernizing North European. In terms of modernization discourse, the Sephardi is seen as less proverbial "Latin" than industrious "Anglo-Saxon"; rather than the romantic figure of a Moorish-Iberian genealogy, the Sephardi in this context is assimilated into a productivist North European ethos.

Rather than view the Dutch period as a defeat for Luso-Brazil, Freyre recovers this period for an Iberian-inflected Brazilian syncretism. For Freyre, Recife differed from other Brazilian colonial cities due to its cosmopolitan culture and its multifarious inhabitants of diverse religious, national, and racial backgrounds, including Dutch, French, Germans, Africans, and Sephardic Jews. During a Dutch domination of thirty years, multiple European and African languages were spoken in Recife, while Hebrew was used and studied in the synagogues. With his gift for literary evocation, Freyre affectionately hails "the old and aristocratic Hebrew maintained in all its purity by the black-bearded, sad-eyed rabbis whom the Congregation of Amsterdam sent out to Pernambuco" (Freyre 1963, 213–214). While paying attention to the Sephardi linguistic presence, Freyre also details cuisine as a dimension of Pernambuco's cosmopolitanism and of Brazilian national syncretism:

> In the kitchens of many a home, with the liberty that the Jews enjoyed under the Count of Nassau, favorite Israelite dishes were undoubtedly prepared, and it is possible that the custom of cooking beans overnight, that is to say, food prepared on the eve of the Sabbath, may be a Jewish legacy. On country estates, lambs were raised, and chickens fattened to be slaughtered according to the Mosaic law, and eaten during the Passover with unleavened bread and bitter herbs. And in the rear of the shops, and even in public, the God of Israel was worshipped, Judaism was practiced. Perhaps even the Kabbala, which accorded so well with the lively imagination of the Sephardim. (1963, 214–215)

Freyre regards Dutch rule, in other words, as an epoch of transculturation, with the conquerors coming to terms with the conquered, ultimately resisting the Portuguese-Catholic metanarrative (ibid.). Freyre credits the Dutch/Sephardic period with infiltrating cosmopolitan forms of merchant culture into the coastal areas of northern Brazil, but he also insists that these forms benefited the landlocked interior zones not dominated by the Dutch as well. Minas Gerais, for example, sought out its own markets principally via the Dutch/Sephardi network.

Thus despite their different "geographical situation[s]" and the distinct "moral make-up of their settlers," Minas and Pernambuco were crucial for

Brazil's becoming "one of the countries of America which profited most from the best the Jews had to offer in cultural values and in stimuli to our own intellectual development" (Freyre 1963, 220). Freyre in this sense refuses to bracket the Dutch/Sephardi impact as merely regional in space (limited to Pernambuco) and merely temporary in time (limited to the period of Dutch occupation) in order to offer an influence thesis that imbues Pernambuco (his region) with national significance, giving it a major place within the broader Brazilian metanarrative. One can detect here a kind of regional pride for the Pernambucan intellectuals who felt excluded from the Rio–Minas–São Paulo axis of cultural prestige. (In another turn of the regional screw, the São Paulo sociologists of the 1950s would systematically discredit Freyre's theses about race.)

The Sephardis who arrived in Bahia were skilled not only in trade but also in medicine, turning Bahia into the first medicine center in Brazil as early as the seventeenth century. Freyre argues that Sephardi doctors and teachers, sent by the Jewish congregation of Amsterdam to Recife and Salvador, contributed to Brazil's scientific, intellectual, and technical progress. Freyre's emphasis on the Sephardic scientific contribution subverts the exclusive association of Jews with money and greed. Alluding to the continuous Catholic persecution in the Americas, he points out that some *converso* physicians prescribed pork as a decoy to outwit the Inquisition. Medicine, as a "Sephardi specialty," was a "way of competing with the confessors and chaplains in influencing the great families in Christian countries and the important figures in the government" (Freyre 1963, 213). Thus, while on the one hand Freyre argues that Sephardis brought more advanced forms that impacted the development of Bahia and Recife, he also recycles certain phobic discourses about secret Jewish power.

The variegated contribution of the Sephardis was at once economic, scientific, literary, and philosophical:

> The principal element of differentiation which the Jews brought to Brazil was their aptitude for international trade, which enriched us with a variety of contacts which would have been impossible had we been exclusively Portuguese. And also their scientific and literary inclination, which was stimulated in them by their multiplicity of contacts, in contrast to the rustic, Old Christian Portuguese. This inclination had been stimulated not only during exile, but in the Iberian Peninsula itself, when barred from politics and a military career, they found compensation for their repressed desires of glory and triumph, personal or of family or race, in an intellectual or scientific career: medicine, teaching, literature, and up to a point, mathematics, and philosophy . . . this was the process of their social ascent in Portugal. (Freyre 1963, 213)

Stressing the economic benefits brought by the Sephardi presence, Freyre deploys the same explanatory grid concerning powerful networks:

> Scattered through the north of Europe, the Italian republics, the Near East, Africa, wherever the Sephardim, whom the Inquisition had driven out of Spain, settled, they established business relations with one another, and thus developed a vast international network of trade. Brazil came to share in the benefits of this in the seventeenth and in the eighteenth centuries, developing contacts through the Jews with Holland and England, with the Near East and the Italian republics. (Freyre 1963, 222)

Here the notion of powerful Jewish networks links the Sephardi not merely to European but also to Muslim spaces. In this double-edged discourse, the anti-Semitic image of the Jew is simultaneously turned into a positive for the formation of Brazil; the Christians who were previously denied access to Muslim spaces now enjoyed access thanks to the Sephardis. Freyre can thus be said to have turned Sephardim, viewed as "secret agents of Orientalism," into "agents" of the Occidentalization of Brazil; yet both negative and positive discourses about the Sephardi figure assume a Sephardi-Muslim symbiosis.

For Freyre, the cultural efflorescence in Pernambuco during that first century was catalyzed by the melded synergistic energies of the Jews and the Dutch. He cites the example of Jewish influence in literature: "There are those who are of the opinion that Bento Texeira Pinto of Pernambuco, the first poet to sing the beauties of Brazil and the glory of Portugal in the sixteenth century, was himself a Jew. And Jewish literature on the American continent began in Pernambuco with poems written by Aboab de Fonseca in the seventeenth century" (Freyre 1963, 222)—in other words, centuries before another well-known North American Sephardi poet, Emma Lazarus. Freyre also saw as a Sephardi trait the mania for eyeglasses and pince-nez, worn "as an outward mark of learning or of intellectual and scientific achievement" (Freyre 1956, 233).

At the same time, Freyre sees Sephardi/Semitic "blood" as an integral part of the national mix:

> [T]he fact that certain of the best of families [in Minas Gerais] have typically Semitic features would justify the conclusion that there was a strong admixture of Jewish blood in the old diamond region. Historical records bear out the fact that not a few persons, and even whole families, in the captaincy of Minas, especially in Vila Rica, Serro Frio, and Paracatú, were condemned by the Inquisition for persisting in the practice of Judaism. (Freyre 1956, 233)

The Sephardi for Freyre is thus foundational to Brazil's economy, science, and culture, and even to its sanguine hybridity. Ironically, if the *limpieza de sangre* aimed to purify the religious Iberian culture of the traces of the Jew, Freyre symbolically injects some of that very same cleaned up Jewish "blood" into the very veins and arteries of Brazil. Freyre thus deploys the discourse of blood to reclaim a Sephardi genealogy for Brazil. In this sense he subverts not merely the Inquisition's theological purification-of-blood discourse but also the scientific-biological racist discourse which was still strong at the time of his writing, in which religion became racialized and race theologized. In general, Freyre acknowledges that the Brazilian elite sees Indians and blacks, as well as Jews and Moors, as inferior. But in the latter case, the inferiority had to do not simply with racial purity but also with their lack of Catholic affiliation.

> Undoubtedly, there were among the old Christians of the colony, whites or near whites, those who were too set in their habits of masters and Christians to feel at ease rubbing shoulders with the new members of the aristocratic brother-hoods whose hands were still calloused from their base callings, or who were still tainted by the practice of Israelite rites, which were also considered debasing. Hence the existence of brotherhoods which were very strict not only in the matter of candidates' racial purity, but also of their length of tenure as Catholics and gentlemen. (Freyre 1956, 252–253)

Some sixteenth-century "Brotherhoods" established by young unmarried men, such as the Brotherhood of Our Lady of Refuge in Olinda, Freyre points out,

> required that [their] candidates be not only "young and unmarried" but free of all taint of Negro, Jew, or mulatto "for three generations back" . . . In Sousa a Brotherhood of the Blessed Sacrament could not be as exacting with regard to the unimpeachable whiteness of a candidate as in Olinda or Salvador or Recife, where the investigation went back three generations, thus safeguarding the brotherhood from the presence of persons having Negro, mulatto or Jewish blood, an also, in certain cases, Moorish. (Freyre 1956, 252–253)

Here Freyre acknowledges that the discourse about blood, then, could be simultaneously religious, racial, and social.

At times, Freyre absorbs aspects of anti-Semitic discourse. For Freyre, a Jewish-inspired economic upsurge also took place in Portuguese-dominated eighteenth-century Minas Gerais, where "the Jewish infiltration was less apparent and probably more commercial than social or intellectual" (Freyre 1956, 222). The trade in diamonds and precious stones, thought to have been "controlled by Jews," generated special relations between Minas Gerais and northern Europe, leading to greater (non-Iberian) Europeanization of this Portuguese-dominated region (Freyre 1956, 222). Freyre writes somewhat uncritically that Dutch markets helped a Minas principally "under the control of Jewish techniques and finance" (Freyre 1956, 217). Here again he adopts prejudicial language about powerful Jewish secret networks:

> [I]t must also be borne in mind that among those of Hebrew origin, scattered throughout various countries and engaged in all of them in different, but related, forms of trade and moneylending, there existed then—as, up to a point, today—a kind of Freemasonry. A kind of secret society of commercial interest, linked to those of a persecuted religion or race, that functioned with special efficacy in moments of great adversity. (Freyre 1956, 212)

In other words, while Freyre praises the Sephardi contribution to Brazil's modernization—inverting the anti-Semitic views of Jews as exploiters—he also reproduces anti-Semitic tropes of "infiltration" and "control." Freyre relays some of the slurs addressed to Jews as "shrewd dealers" and "Conveyancers" (metaphorically "moneylenders"), a term "which applied in the mining area to this bogeyman, not of children but of grown-ups; this hobgoblin, not of the forest but of the city, for whom the miners developed the same horror as the child for those fearsome figures" (Freyre 1956, 14–15). Freyre's discourse about the Sephardi thus oscillates between a Luso-Brazilian nationalist view of Jews as "us" and a more xenophobic view of Jews as "them," as "outsiders" infiltrating what is "ours."

The Sephardi Jew is thus seen simultaneously as religious outsider and cultural insider. The Sephardi especially becomes more closely allied with the Brazilian nation, however, when viewed in relation to the more visible figure of the European (Ashkenazi) Jew. In this sense, Freyre's discourse about Jews obeys an ethnic split. Freyre contrasts what he sees as "the niggardliness, the avarice, the rapaciousness" of Ashkenazi Jews with the more generous, festive, and cultivated Iberian style of the Sephardis, redolent of the pleasures of "rich clothes of silk and velvet for festive occasions, an abundant table, [a] love of learning,{an] intellectual bent" (Freyre 1956, 221). Moreover, he contrasts the "pure" Hebrew of the Sephardis with the "garbled" version of the Ashkenazis (Freyre 1956, 214–215). One has the impression that for Freyre the Sephardis are "our Jews" and the Ashkenazis "their Jews."

Written during the 1930s, a period of massive Eastern European Jewish immigration to the Americas, including to Brazil, Freyre's early books reflect a discourse toward Ashkenazi Jews tainted by anti-Semitic imagery of a kind that became common in the Vargas era, while the Sephardi becomes "the good Jew" reclaimed for Ibero-American culture. In this kind of ethnic splitting of co-religionists, the Ashkenazis become alien and menacing, while the Sephardis remain an organic, even foundational, part of the Brazilian national family.

Thus Freyre both invokes and criticizes anti-Semitic discourses, depending on which branch of the Jewish family he is treating.[19] Stated differently, Freyre's partial adoption of anti-Semitic discourse is ultimately subordinated to his larger project of highlighting the Sephardic contribution to Brazil's modernization, and even to its very construction as a nation.

In a sense, Freyre celebrates the Sephardiness of Brazil, which crossed the Atlantic not only with the Portuguese (and the Spanish) but also with the Dutch, as integral to the Iberianized culture of Brazil. He returns the Sephardis to a neo-Iberian space, a kind of transatlantic Andalus, this time located/dislocated in the Americas. In Freyre's culturalist discourse, the brief exile in Holland had not eroded the Sephardis' deep allegiance to Iberian culture. Therefore, this apparently exotic colonization by the Sephardis (via the Dutch) in Brazil—people whose Portuguese names persisted, in however mangled a form, even in Amsterdam—was in reality a colonization by people, as it were, of the same cultural family. Freyre's Lusophication of Dutch Brazil via the Portuguese Jews, the very same Jews who escaped from Portugal to Holland, has the Portuguese Jew "return" not to old world Portugal but to its American extension—Brazil.

In sum, the Sephardi, for Freyre, forms a Janus-faced figure, refracted through discourses that oscillate between nostalgic romanticism and enthusiastic modernism, between sensuous Latin/Catholic and hardworking Protestant/Anglo-Saxon, as well as between prejudicial and affectionate images of the religious "other." Although Freyre barely addresses the Inquisition that persisted throughout the Catholic-dominated regions of the Americas, his embrace of the Sephardi can be seen, centuries after their expulsion, as a tacit mea culpa or retrospective "welcome back" of the Sephardis into the Latin fold. And if in some passages Freyre celebrated the racial flexibility of the Latin (as inflected by the Moor/Sephardi) in contrast with the rigid Anglo-Saxon, in other passages he praises the equally flexible Dutch acceptance of the Sephardi, but now in contrast to the Portuguese. The Dutch chapter in Brazil's history is not completely detached from the Iberian past, however. Freyre "Lusophies," as it were, the Dutch presence in Brazil via the Portuguese Jews, refugees of the Inquisition who had escaped to Holland in order to be free to practice Judaism. He gives the Portuguese Jews of Pernambuco a central role as in-between figures who contributed to the modernization of Brazil, but who at the same time maintained the Luso-Latin inheritance. Freyre reclaims Dutch history in Brazil as in some sense also culturally Portuguese thanks to the Sephardis. Within Freyre's ambitious project, the Sephardi figure becomes the agent of the de-peripheralization of northern Brazil vis-à-vis the cultural triangle of Rio–Minas–São Paulo. Freyre recuperates the Sephardi, while the figure of the Sephardi, in return, recuperates Freyre's region within the national mosaic.

## From Moorish Longing to De-Orientalization

The fraught perception of the Sephardi and the Moor already in Iberia in some ways continued in Latin America, although not necessarily with the same emphasis or accent or social valence. Despite their otherness, within the new landscape of the Americas, the "old world" Sephardi and the Moor were nonetheless familiar and linked figures. The Sephardi and the Moor were both subjected to a split discourse, associated simultaneously with order and progress, on the one hand, and with undisciplined backwardness, on the other; with romanticist nostalgia for lost origins and at the same time with a desire for modernity that required the elimination of those very same origins. Moorish longing within this transatlantic Andalus came at the same time under the shadow of the new Brazilian republic's desire for scientific modernity associated with the France of Enlightened republicanism. The peak of Freyre's work comes in the wake of a century of the institutionalization of French models in Brazilian civic life, especially in the capital of Rio de Janeiro. At the same time, his search for Moorish traces can be seen as an indirect lament for a vanished past in the wake of modernization.

Freyre's sensuously amorous description of the persistent traces of Moorish culture points to an often forgotten lineage within cultural debates in Brazil. In the older cities of Brazil, Freyre writes,

> the streets preserved a kind of medieval-guild quality; in some, certain artisans had their place of business, if not exclusively, by preference; in others, dealers in certain articles, such as meat or fish. Or certain races: Jews or gypsies. There was the Street of the Coopers. Blacksmiths Alley. Street of the Fishmongers. Jew Street. Goldsmiths Street. Street of the Gypsies. (Freyre 1956, 37)

Similarly "the Negro and mulatto mechanics and artisans" in places like Olinda "carried on the peninsular tradition of the Moors, or the African of their forefathers" (Freyre 1956, 67). In Recife and in Rio de Janeiro, Moorish influences were visible in gardens dotted with fountains, especially in elegant mansions and small-scale Alhambra-like palaces where the water was "falling all day" and the tiles were "gleaming amidst the plants and fountains" (Freyre 1956, 151). To the Moors, Freyre suggests poetically, can be attributed the love of fountains, so frequent in the gardens and courtyards of the city residences of Recife, of public fountains with their spouts around which the lower middle class of Salvador gathered at night to enjoy the cool, to bathe, and wash their feet. The river bathing even beside the bridges. Especially in Pará, where Kidder, and years later, Warren, saw so many naked people—men and women, old folks and children—delighting in their river bath within sight of the whole city. There are those who attribute this to our Indian heritage; but it is also a Moorish trait. (Freyre 1956, 145–146)

Here Freyre, whose work was concerned with the historical legacy of "the Indian," also links certain cultural practices, at times even the very same practices, to the Moor.

Moorish, African, and Asiatic characteristics could also be discerned in other strata of the social and aesthetic landscapes and geologies:

The house, with the eaves of the red roof in the shape of a pigeon's wing, recalled those of Asia and Asia Minor, with their projecting balconies and the window divided into small lozenges; the means of travel of the wealthy—palanquins and litters—were those of Asia; the fondness for painted tiles on the front of the houses, the dado of the halls; the fountains and the wells—were Moorish. (Freyre 1956, 204)

Freyre's almost Proustian concern with the aesthetic also touches on questions of urban life and bodily cleanliness. In this context, he credits the Moorish and Muslim influence, whether via Portugal or via Afro-Brazil, with a positive impact on health:

We must never forget the influence of the Moors by way of the Portuguese, nor that of the Mohammedans by way of the Negro, on the cleanliness of body and house in the Brazilian cities. It was this that made up to a degree for the lack of public hygiene in cities so filthy that the cleaning of streets, yards, beaches, and roofs was left almost officially to the vultures or the tides. (Freyre 1956, 146)

Freyre's multifaceted and richly textured account even touches on an aesthetic preference for the erotic-exotic body: "The ideal woman, plump and pretty with big breasts and hips, was that of the Moors" (Freyre 1956, 204). Rituals and habits also betray Moorish traces, such as "the feminine habit of sitting cross-legged on mats and carpets, at home and even in church" and the habit of "covering the face, and leaving only the eyes exposed" (Freyre 1956, 204). In the churches, "the ladies clung to the bonnets, capes, shawls, mantillas, covering part of their face. Capes, formerly much used in Portugal and Spain, also survived in Brazil, pointing to the resistance of the Moorish fashion to

European penetration" (Freyre 1956, 224). Brazilian women retained Moorish customs in decorum and modesty, cultural zones which for Freyre became arenas for holding out valiantly against English and French influences (ibid.). Freyre's gendered mapping of sartorial and bodily practices underlines the persistence of Moorish-Iberian culture across the Atlantic, while also revealing its impact even in the most intimate spheres. Moorish women here come to allegorize Brazil's resistance to French and British cultural penetration through Moorish-Iberian authenticity. In his defense of Luso-Brazilian syncretism through a compendium of Moorish traces, Freyre demonstrates a vital investment in a Moorish genealogy for Brazil.

At the same time, Freyre, forgetting the patriarchal tendencies within Brazil's other source cultures, attributes the negatives of Luso-Brazilian patriarchy largely to Moorish Iberia. In the late eighteenth century, Freyre points out, doctors blamed the insalubrity of Rio de Janeiro "to the supposedly Moorish-influenced anti-hygienic life of women, more confined than men to living quarters, to boudoir, to bedroom; more sedentary, without exercise, in houses that were almost Moorish or Oriental; weakened by the daily warm bath, which further enervated these already languid women" (Freyre 1956, 93). Although Freyre associated Moorish heritage with cleanliness, he also describes the control over female bodies as typically Moorish. He therefore suggests that the life of the daughter of the city mansion, for example, was limited to the house "with the aphrodisiac head-rubbing by the slave maid which perhaps made her think of herself as the 'enchanted Mooress,' with some charm hidden in her hair, as in the tales told by the old Negro women" (Freyre 1956, 30). Here Moorishness and blackness are at once exoticized and eroticized, in a way that recalls French Orientalist depictions of Maghrebian *hamam*s and Turkish harems.

If the rejection of "the Moor" in Latin America extends the Iberian "cleansing" project, it also has its tropical specificity given the colonial settlers' inferiority complex vis-à-vis Europe, and especially toward France and Britain and, later, the United States. The persistence of the rejection of this cultural inheritance is reflected in the history of architecture as a metonymy and metaphor for social transformation in Ibero-America. Early city houses, Freyre writes, featured "the barred Moorish type of dwelling [where] the exaggerated desire for privacy of the patriarchal family protected it in Oriental fashion from contacts with the street. But after the arrival of the Prince Regent, the city house underwent a more rapid Europeanization, and not always for the better." Thus a more general Luso-Portuguese-Brazilian identity crisis can be said to be allegorized through the figure of the Moor. The imitation of "the

North," whether in Europe or in the Americas, echoed dominant Iberia's own (self-)rejection of its centuries of Moorish-Sephardi syncretism, overlaid in Ibero-America by the "encounter" with "the Indian," "the black," and other communities. Freyre's romanticization of the Moor must be viewed, then, in relation to the post-independence suppression of this inheritance in the name of westernizing modernity.

If nudity, associated with indigenous Americans, was regarded as shameful, Moorish "overdressing" also had negative connotations; both practices, although apparently opposite, were deemed worthy of eradication. Freyre provides a rich store of examples having to do with these sartorial-cultural battles. Modernizing, as a form of rejecting Moorish residues, was officially enacted within the visible public sphere. A Rio de Janeiro police order, for example, put an end to shutters, which disappeared from mansions' windows in a period of eight days.[20] Westernizing ideologues sought "unshadowing"—the literal removal of shutters—as a way to eliminate the Moorish-Iberian past. But "unshadowing" came to include very diverse practices in different areas of social life: replacing the Orientally covered lattices and curtains with English glass in houses and carriages; designing wider Haussmann-style boulevards instead of the casbah-like winding alleys of Rio de Janeiro, Salvador, Recife, São Paulo, and Olinda; discarding women's capes, mantles, mantillas, or shawls in favor of the transparent French veils (that "did not hide the charms of face and bosom of the young ladies"); and using English scissors and razors to remove the heavy beards variously described as Moorish, "Turkish," or "Nazarene" (Freyre 1956, 278). The "unveiling" of Moorish Brazil thus took varied forms, ranging from sartorial display to architectural design. Within westernizing discourse, the disappearance of Brazil's "Oriental" features in a wide range of areas figured a new *reconquista* in the Americas, a new battle of the Cristianos and the Moros, a decisive victory of the West over the East, in a centuries-long civilizational clash, this time within Brazil (Freyre 1956, 277). Freyre's recovery project seems to reflect a Luso-Brazilian ambivalent relation to the Sephardi and the Moor.

Although Freyre sometimes analyzes the Moorish and the Sephardi presence distinctly and separately, the two groups are more often linked in his prose. Freyre acknowledges that many Brazilians "felt a vague hostility" toward both "Jews" and "Moors," which he attributes to the Portuguese legacy of the Christian struggle against the infidels. The Jew and the Muslim were not merely neighboring, parallel figures within anti-Semitic/anti-infidel discourse, however. In contrast with what they later became, they had long been seen not as antonymic but rather as closely linked in a Judeo-Muslim syncretism. In the context of comparing the situation of Sephardis in the Dutch versus the Portuguese regions of Brazil, Freyre writes:

> Dutch Recife seems to have had a kind of ghetto, with its Street of the Jews, its synagogues, and its illustrious rabbis. Among us, the Jews for the most part concealed their origin, secretly practicing their rites, observing their customs, their dietary laws, and enjoying their gold, silver, and precious stones, thus avoiding the severe penalties of the Inquisition. However, not on this account should the Jew be dismissed as more or less secret agent of Orientalism, stressing only their internationalism. (Freyre 1956, 297)

Here clearly Freyre acknowledges not so much the rejection of "the Jew" per se but rather the rejection of the Sephardi as an agent of "Orientalism," not in the Saidian sense of the word but rather as a symptom and transmitter of the Moorish legacy. The historical alliance and cultural affinities between the Sephardi and the Moor, dating back to the *Convivencia*—the relatively harmonious existence of Muslim, Jew, and Christian in Al-Andalus—meant that the Sephardi presence in Latin America perpetuated the Moorish/Semitic heritage. Within the nineteenth-century Europeanizing project, furthermore, the Sephardi/Moor secret sharer was not merely a religious other to be expelled but also a racial other to be cleansed in the name of progress. Thus even in the absence of actually visible Moors and Sephardis (since many continued to live in secrecy), there was a need for a symbolic expulsion, a kind of a second *limpieza de sangre,* or in this case, a *limpieza de cultura.*

Discourses about the Moor have historically been always already entangled with discourses about the Jew, while the Jew can be said to have always already been a Moor. Against the background of the goal of cleansing Brazilian blood and culture of its Sephardic-Moorish traces, Freyre's work constitutes a revisionist project. Freyre significantly does not reduce that presence to the New Christians or *conversos* who arrived with the *conquistadores;* rather, he also calls attention to the Portuguese Jews who arrived later with the Dutch in northern Brazil. As with his discussion about the Indians and blacks, Freyre's discourse about the Moor-Sephardi is often contradictory, moving between romantic elegies for a disappearing culture to praising the very modernization that "disappeared" the culture being elegized.

By acknowledging the Moorish and Sephardic inheritance of Brazil, Freyre contests centuries of denial rooted in a desire for Europe as Brazil's ego ideal. Yet, his nationalist grid tends to sidestep certain violent aspects within Brazilian history. He writes that there were Jews who in the privacy of their homes scoffed at Our Lord, Negro witch doctors, converted Indians. But neither the Jews or the Negroes really showed hostility toward the Catholic faith; great diplomats of compromise, as is the case with peoples, and the more intelligent women and children, who suffer oppression, for the most part they effected a kind of substitution or transfer, conferring on their saints or rites Catholic names and outward attributes though they remained inwardly different. (Freyre 1956, 5–6)

While acknowledging oppression, then, Freyre also undermines that acknowledgment by citing syncretism as a proof of a lack of hostility on the part of domineering Christianity. Freyre fails to see syncretism as a survival strategy (for Jews and Africans) against anti-Semitic and anti-black violence, and thus ultimately encodes an acceptance of the fait accompli of religious-colonial brutality.

Yet by "unveiling" the role of the Moor and the Sephardi in Brazilian history, Freyre brings to the surface of the discussion a forgotten element in the making of Brazilian identity. He recuperates "the Sephardi/Moor" but in the name of a broader nationalist miscegenation apologia; Sephardi/Moorish traditions become just one more element in the variegated mixing that generates Brazilian identity. In this sense, the rejection by the elite of the Moor/Sephardi is also partially a self-rejection in the context of a conscious de-Orientalizing project, but where the very same group could be recuperated for the sake of another Freyrean-based ideological project, one that assumed miscegenation and syncretism as a source of pride within a kind of national *moreno* exceptionalism.

### Figuring Islam within *Mestiçagem*

Today the metanarrative of racial-cultural harmony through mixing is commonly understood to be central to the conceptualization of the Brazilian nation, indeed even the source of a kind of exceptionalist idea of uniqueness, or mestizo essentialism. But when intellectuals such as Mario de Andrade and Oswaldo de Andrade lauded syncretism, *mestizaçem,* and "anthropophagy" in the 1920s, their theories were mocking colonizing ideologies that mimicked European norms and sought to "correct" a mixing that was already well established, whether through de-Orientalization programs or later through selective immigration policies that encouraged "white" immigration. At the same time, the texts that have been crucial in shaping a nationalist discourse premised on the unifying notion of racial and cultural *mestizaçem* were more comfortable with addressing the traces of a Sephardi-Moorish past than with actually embracing Muslims in Brazil. While Moorish and Sephardic cultures largely "traveled" to Brazil via Portuguese and Dutch colonization, Islam arrived in Brazil through a different route: via enslaved Africans. Freyre does refer to the fact that the slave rebels in the north were "nearly always African-born Negroes—mainly from areas which had come under Mohammedan influence—and not the creoles or Brazilians" (Freyre 1956, 331–332). However, he does not deeply delve into its impact in the shaping of Brazilian syncretism. His account of the de-Orientalization of Brazil focuses on the traces of Moorish civilization, but "disappears," as it were, the actually existing Muslims of nineteenth-century Brazil. In this sense, his nostalgic lamentation about the Moor only accentuates the anxiety about stirring Muslims and Islam into the Brazilian *feijoada*. So in Freyre's work, ironically, the disappearance of Moorish culture in the wake of post-independence modernization, largely ends the story of Muslim Brazil, exactly at the historical moment that Muslims were in the forefront of the rebellions.

If Freyre looked at colonial Brazil from the perspective of the Casa Grande (the Big House), the contemporary historian João José Reis has tried to imagine and incorporate the perspective of Senzala (the slave quarters), and especially that of the enslaved Muslims largely silenced in the writing about Brazil. In *Slave Rebellion in Brazil: The Muslim Uprising of 1835 in Bahia* (1993), Reis meticulously explores the role of Islam in Afro-Brazilian history and specifically in slave rebellions. During the more than two hundred years of the slave trade preceding the nineteenth century, many of the slaves from West Africa were "Mohammedans," or more specifically Malinkes, known in Bahia as *mandingos*. At the turn of the nineteenth century, a large contingent of Muslim Africans arrived from West African areas where Islam had expanded, including in Yoruba kingdoms. Out of the seven thousand enslaved Hausas (which became synonymous with Malês, or Muslims) and Yorubas (Nagôs) shipped annually to Bahia, the majority were Muslim. While some masters were tolerant of their slaves' religion, others prohibited the practice of Islam. The religion became more visible with the growing rebellions, which in their turn provoked as their corollary the repression of Islam as well. Reis's thorough account of rebellions and their repression, we would argue, offers a different context for the project of de-Orientalization/Europeanization, as not merely a new edition of the *reconquista*'s *limpieza de sangre,* but also the expression of a nineteenth-century fear about the spread of Islam, now associated with fierce uprisings of enslaved Africans.

While Reis notes that vigorous proselytizing and conversion to Islam was common in Bahia, especially during the key period of rebellion in the 1830s, he also combats any view of a "jihadist" Islam that would reduce the Bahia rebellions to mere Islamic militancy. Instead, he highlights an Islamic tradition of conversion through revelation that fostered reading from the Quran, while also suggesting that the written word, used by the Hausas/Malês, exerted seductively charismatic power over Africans of oral cultural background. Most of the Hausa/Malê rebels knew how to read and write Arabic; they met to pray and to memorize Quranic verses, as well as to teach and learn Arabic. The elders produced prayer slips, and preached in a language that served both religious and communication purposes, while also expressing a desire for peace and justice, which in that context implied the end of slavery. Writing and reading, then, helped to memorize Quranic texts, but also facilitated Muslim integration of enslaved Africans by initiating the participation in collective prayers (Reis 1993, 97–107). Although Freyre had already noted the superior literacy of the Muslim slaves in *Casa-Grande e Senzala,* it is Reis who explores its role in the agency and subjecthood of Africans in Brazil.

After the defeat of the rebellion, Reis points out, the police collected a vast store of papers inscribed with Arabic, called "the Arabic papers," which generated a profound impression at the time. (For the mostly illiterate whites, it was virtually unimaginable that African slaves possessed such sophisticated means of communication.) These papers, which exhibit accomplished calligraphy and impeccable grammar, testify to the thorough knowledge of Quranic Arabic on the part of the enslaved, supporting the argument that they had been members of the wealthy merchant classes in Africa. Yet the "Arabic papers" were not exclusively the product of educated Malês but also of common people testifying to the "dynamic pace of Muslim conversion and education in Bahia on the eve of the 1835 rebellion" (Reis 1993, 106–107). The Reis narrative undoes a number of prejudices about the Afro-Brazilian diaspora. Inverting the image of uneducated contemporary black Brazilians, Reis depicts their ancestors as what could be called (in our words) an intelligentsia in chains. By demonstrating the popular appeal of Islam, he also subverts the view of an Islam imposed by violence, a view that would excise Islam from the national metanarrative of an all-embracing syncretism.

Although not focusing on contemporary vestiges of Afro-Muslim culture, Reis's narrative can be read as a call for a syncretic reading of these "other" non-Iberian Muslim traces. Muslim culture, he shows, also impacted non-Muslim Afro-Bahians, as Islamic religious artifacts also "travelled" to Brazil with enslaved Africans. Malê charms, reputed to have extraordinary protective powers, were used by Muslims and non-Muslims alike, especially since using them did not necessarily signal a commitment to Islam on the part of the wearer. Even at the end of the nineteenth century, Afro-Bahians regarded Malês as "wizards" familiar with "high magical processes" (Reis 1993, 98–99).[21] In Bahia, literate Malês produced such amulets; their makers, *alufás*, were presumed to possess *baraka* (Arabic for "blessing"), a transcendental power embodied in the *alufá*'s amulet. Whether in Africa or in the Brazilian diaspora, amulets inscribed with Muslim prayers and Quranic passages were deemed to be vital shields against evil spells. Another visible sign of the Islamic presence in the African diaspora community was the wearing of a long white robe called an *abadá* in Bahia, an *aqbada* or *agbada* in Yorubaland. Bahia's *abadá*, according to Reis, was worn only in private in order to thwart the watchful eyes of authorities on the lookout for unusual "subversive" practices. During the 1835 rebellion, the *abadá* made its public debut in the streets of Salvador, in a "spectacle of hundreds of sons of Allah dressed in white," resulting in the authorities calling the *abadás* "war garments" (Reis 1993, 103). In combating the jihadist view of a violent Islam, Reis's text offers the possibility of a different reading of contemporary cultural syncretism of Brazil that would allow for the tracing of cultural practices not merely to a general Afro-diaspora, but specifically to a Muslim Afro-diaspora.

Apart from the disappearing of Muslim genealogies that Brazil inherited from Iberia, Brazil itself generated its own form of "disappearing" Islam, resulting in a kind of amnesia about Bahian, and thus Brazilian, syncretism. The de-Orientalizing modernization carried out by what could be called a neo-*reconquista* in the Americas meant that Jews and Muslims within Catholic spaces continued to be subjected to policing, generating new *conversos* and Moriscos. (Indeed, the historical telenovela *A Muralha* [2000] stages the story of one Sephardic character who escapes the Inquisition to Brazil only to experience a sexualized sadomasochism on the new continent.) Eating practices and food habits were at the core of state and church discipline and punishment—for example, the policing of Jewish households for the colanders that were used to drain blood from the salted meat in respect for the kosher prohibition against cooking and consuming bloody meat. For West African Muslim slaves, meanwhile, the policing was not merely cultural-religious but also racial-economic, threatening the sociopolitical order. For enslaved Muslims the new Brazilian context introduced novel challenges for those who would maintain basic Islamic principles of conduct, especially given culinary taboos and holiday celebrations mandated by the Muslim calendar. To abide by a strict halal diet was challenging since the slaves had little control over their food, even in the relatively flexible environment of urban slavery.

Nonetheless, according to Reis, the Malês' effort to organize communal suppers represented the desire not merely to consume food prepared by Muslim hands and thus avoid non-halal foods, but also to gather for rituals of solidarity, nourishing dreams of independence and rebellion. It was also at table that Malês celebrated their main religious holidays, culinary gatherings that indicated Islam's spread in Bahia. That Islam was visibly on the rise, daring to show its face in public, suggested that slaves and freedmen were enthusiastically joining a religion that represented an alternative to the Catholicism associated with Brazilian slaveholding society. In this sense, Islam was regenerated within a specific Brazilian context where it became appealing not merely because of Quranic notions of equality and sympathy for the discriminated and the persecuted, but also because of the contrast with the oppressive social role of the dominant religion. One could argue that engaging in different rituals than those of Catholicism allowed for agency over the body in a context where the enslaved was merely a vessel to be controlled by the master.

Religious articles, texts, and rituals were vital to the 1835 uprising, which was short-lived yet nonetheless left a deep mark on Brazil. The uprising, in Reis's words,

> was the most effective urban slave rebellion ever to occur on the American continent. Hundreds of Africans took part. Nearly seventy were killed. And more than five hundred, according to a conservative estimate, were sentenced to death, prison, whipping, or deportation. If an uprising of equal proportions were to happen today, in a Salvador with over 1.5 million inhabitants, it would entail the sentencing of over twelve thousand people. (Reis 1993, xiii)

The Malê organizers of the 1835 rebellion were heirs to a rebellious tradition whose valor was manifested already in the well-organized 1807, 1809, and 1814 uprisings. Hausas, both enslaved and freedmen, played a major role in the 1807 uprising that aimed to capture ships in Bahia's harbor for a massive voyage back to Africa. Hausas also performed a key role in the 1809 rebellion, which established a worrying precedent for Bahian slave owners, since Jeje (Aja-Fon) and Nagô (Yoruba) slaves joined the Hausas. Although a growing Islam at times provoked opposition from other Afro-Bahians, the new alliance indicated that ethnic and religious differences no longer constituted an impediment to slave rebellions. Diverse ethnic and religious groups (including Nagôs) joined forces under the command of Muslim Hausas, some reputed to be *malumi,* a Hausa term designating a Muslim preacher, deriving from the Arabic word *mu'allim* or "teacher."

The uprisings were timed to coincide with privileged moments in the Muslim ritual calendar. The 1835 rebellion was planned to begin at the symbolically charged date of the end of the holy month of Ramadan, a moment designed to bring out collective emotions and therefore one that could generate a significant political impact (Reis 1993, 115). The Malês were celebrating the feast at the end of Ramadan, *Lailat al-Qadr* ("Night of Glory" or "Night of Power") that commemorates the Quranic revelation to Mohammed, marking the birth of Islam. On this night, it was believed, humanity's destiny was cast for the coming year. In West Africa, more specifically, it was believed that it was on that night God imprisoned the *jinns* and overcame evil spirits in order to reestablish cosmic order. The Malê rebels believed that the end of Ramadan could be an ideal time to triumph over the forces of evil, in this case the slave owners (Reis 1993, 119). The rebellion indicated that Muslims went beyond purely symbolic subversion rituals to a politically revolutionary act.

Although the rebellions were undeniably violent, including against mulattoes and Brazilian-born blacks allied with established power, Reis disputes the view of the rebellions as either purely ethnic or purely jihadist. While undoubtedly led by Malês, the uprising itself necessitated non-Muslim participation. In other words, Islam may have furnished the discursive glue and organizational infrastructure, but diverse Afro-diasporic groups contributed to the mobilization. The alliance between Malês and non-Malês was also facilitated by common West African historical and cultural roots, which undermine the notion of a "holy war" against all non-Muslims. The rebellion did of course have a religious aspect, and some might have regarded it as a holy war, but it was not, for Reis, a classic "jihad of the sword" (Reis 1993, 126–127). And even if the Malê rebellion were found on some level to be a jihad, historically jihads have also risen out of socioeconomic oppression. Although Islam, like Catholicism, was a transethnic "universal" religion capable of uniting diverse ethnic groups, in the context of a slaveholding society, it nonetheless had a useful political role in opposing the Catholic slave owners who often used an ethnically based divide-and-conquer strategy toward African slaves. Among the many political and cultural alternatives available to Africans at the time, Reis concludes, Islam was attractive among Afro-Bahians not simply because it had promoted social revolution but also because it fostered a revolution in the lives of its followers, endowing them with pride and dignity.

In the wake of the failed rebellion, Islam was subjected to increased repression. The police confiscated dozens of writing slates used by Malês, affecting the ability to practice Islam and making its practitioners vulnerable to further surveillance. As in Iberia, Islam had to be lived in secrecy, but in Latin America it was no longer merely a matter of extending the Inquisition to the Americas. This *limpieza* was not of the Moors of Iberia but of the blacks of West Africa, who in the official view required another cleansing to stabilize a social order premised on both Catholicism and slavery. Reis credits Islam as an ideologically unifying force, while also crediting the West African roots of the Malês as shaping a unique culture of resistance in which Islam flourished. Reis sees Islam as part of a broader syncretic West African culture that was further syncretized in Bahia. The widespread cultural intercourse between Islam and traditional African religions becomes obvious, for example, in the syncretism between tribal spirits (*anjonu*) and Muslim *jinns*. For members of *orixa* terreiros, Allah was allied with the *funfus* divinities, especially Orisalá, known as Oxalá in Bahia. The priests of Ifá, the divining god, identified African Muslims as the sons of Oxalá. It even became common, according to Reis, for *babalaôs* to direct people toward Islam in instances where it was relevant to their divinatory practice, and even to recommend conversion to Islam.

Despite the repression, in other words, Islamic and Yoruba syncretism persisted among enslaved Africans, even while Catholicism reigned as the official religion. The relationship between the various religions is more clouded in the present now that African Islam as a distinct organized religion (at least up to the last two decades' recent immigration) has disappeared in Brazil, even though it has survived in the encoding of diverse rituals in everyday language, in the usage of terms such as *Malê, Allah,* and *alufá* sprinkled throughout the religious chants. Although largely excised from the Bahian collective memory, Malê cultural values have persisted in Bahia's collective unconscious, surviving in the form of ongoing celebrations and the Africanized carnival groups called *blocos-Afros*. The still-thriving ritual washing of the steps for Bonfim Church celebrations, with its white ceremonial dress, for example, might actually be a reminiscence of a Muslim holiday (Reis 1993, 125–126). (Here we are reminded of another festivity, the millions of revelers, all dressed in white attire reminiscent of the *abadás,* in homage to Iemanjá—celebrating New Year on Itapua or Copacabana beaches).

Reis's emphasis on scriptural syncretism challenges the common view that regards the Bahian Muslims as cultural separatists:

> Beside religious communion, there were other forces of social solidarity and integration in Africans' lives: their Africanness, their ethnicity, and their very situation as slaves and freemen who were exploited and discriminated against ... The Malês never posed a threat to that plurality, and there is no proof that a monopoly on religion was their principal objective in 1835; or at any other time. (Reis 1993, 111)

Reis's project reflects an investment in "Brazilianizing" Islam in Bahia through the lens of exceptionalist syncretism. First, the Islam that arrived in Bahia was of the West African variety, less jihadist, in his view, than the North African or Middle Eastern variety. Second, rather than a religion simply transplanting itself in a new site, Islam underwent an indigenization, a kind of metamorphosis in the new situation. The new context necessitated an innovative retooling of Islam for a new situation. And Islam in Brazil, already syncretized in West Africa, was further transformed in the Brazilian diaspora. Thus the boundaries separating West African religions from Islam are not easily demarcated. Reis assumes the nationalist discourse of Brazilian flexibility and adaptability, but in contrast to a discourse that acknowledges Catholic/candomblé syncretism, Reis's project disinters another cultural stratum in the form of the Muslim contribution to the Bahian mix. Reis, in this sense, shares with Freyre an emphasis on Brazilian flexibility, adaptability, and pluralism, but unlike Freyre, he focuses on subaltern syncretism, hybridity from below.

In different ways Freyre's and Reis's distinct texts could be read as suggesting that Brazil's Europeanization project was formulated in counterdistinction to Islam, but while for Freyre it is a question of an Iberian-Moorish Islam, for Reis it is a question of actually existing Muslims practicing Islam in Bahia. At the same time, Reis defends Brazilian Islam by splitting it off from another Islam, implicitly viewed as inflexibly jihadist. In a sense, Reis's effort to recuperate Islam as part of Brazilian history resists a de-Orientalizing, modernizing conception of Brazil as Eurotropic.[22] However, by assuming that Bahian/West African Islam is flexible, Reis's text seems to leave uncontested certain Orientalist axioms concerning another, normative non-Brazilian Islam that is presumably rigid, even if West African Islam and its Bahian diaspora are seen through a revisionist lens.

Despite the neo-*reconquista* and de-Orientalizing modernization project in Brazil, and despite the suppression of an Islam blamed for slave rebellions, Muslim culture never completely disappeared. In his *Black Crescent: The Experience and Legacy of African Muslims in the Americas* (2005), Michael Gomez, while nodding to Reis's work as foundational, focuses on the ways in which Muslims continued to practice their religion even after the suppression of rebellions, often having to go into hiding, not only in Bahia but also in other regions, such as Rio de Janeiro. As occurred with the *conversos* and the Moriscos of Iberia, non-Christian religions came under severe pressure in Brazil. But the association between Islam and slave rebellions made Muslims highly vulnerable to the policing of cultural practices, leading to reducing the numbers of its followers. The cultural impact remained, however, even if in diluted or submerged form. Some church interiors, for example, followed a Morisco pattern, with Moorish arches, including "an Arabic inscription that

reads, 'Behold, This is the Miracle of God and This is the Door of Heaven'"
(Gomez 2005, 127). The art historian Henry Drewal, similarly, speaks of the
Church of Lapina in Salvador, designed in the 1860s by Manoel Friandes, a
Malê architect who combined a "subdued, quiet, Christian exterior" with an
"exuberant Islamic" interior with Moorish arches, decorative tiles, and Arabic
script etched into the walls (1999; 2008). Islam thus persisted within the cultural
syncretism with Christianity and the Afro-Brazilian religions of candomblé,
even when not recognized as such.

These revisionist projects thus must be understood against the backdrop
of the writing out of history of Brazil's Muslims. The chapter of repression,
meanwhile, could be viewed as another de-Orientalization project that took
place in relation to Brazilian Muslims. While the discourses about religious
syncretism in Brazil often highlighted the marriage of convenience between
West African *orixas* and Catholic saints, it is equally important to highlight
Islam as another vital element in this syncretism. While the arrival in Brazil
of Arabs largely from the Ottoman Empire (hence the misnomer *"turcos"*) and
especially from "Greater Syria" at the end of the nineteenth century and early
twentieth century has been acknowledged and even celebrated as part of the
national mix, the West African Muslims have been relegated to the margins
of the national story. In contrast to the Muslim slaves, the *turcos,* who were
for the most part Christian immigrants, did not pose a similar threat to the
religious and racial order. Unlike West African Muslims, they were not viewed
as doubly dangerous. It is perhaps not a coincidence that some novels by the
celebrated Bahian writer Jorge Amado incorporate *turco*/Arab characters as
part of the Brazilian mélange; but whether portraying Christian, or at times
Muslim, Arabs, for example in such novels as *Gabriela, cravo e canela* (1958;
*Gabriela, Clove and Cinnamon*), *Showdown* (1984), and *A Descoberta da
América Pelos Turcos* (1994; *How the Turks Discovered America*), his thoroughly
hybrid Brazil peripheralizes the West African Muslims of his native Bahia.
This forgotten dimension of Brazilian syncretism underlies a specific anxiety
about black Islam, which could simultaneously coexist with a penchant for
Sephardi-Moorish Iberian longing.

## Submerged Genealogies and the Contemporary Rendezvous

Contemporary fascination with "the Orient" in Brazil reveals that despite
popular "intuitions," the performance of public fascination does not always
acknowledge these genealogies. Despite Brazil's Sephardi-Moorish Atlantic
history, its enchantment with "the Orient" tends to be performed in a man-

ner reminiscent of French Orientalist voyeurism. The contemporary Brazilian infatuation with harems, veils, *nargilas, dança do ventre,* and even such music/dance fusion genres as the "belly samba" does not simply date back to the arrival of immigrants from the former Ottoman Empire, but also traces back to the complex relations within the *longue durée* of interconnection between Muslim Moors, Sephardi Jews, and sub-Saharan Muslim Africans that we have examined here. It is against this backdrop that the significance of the presence of the Middle East in contemporary popular culture can be fully appreciated.

The hugely popular telenovela *O Clone* (2001), for example, shuttles back and forth between Fez in Morocco and Rio de Janeiro to tell its tale of the forbidden yet enduring love between a Catholic Brazilian man and a Muslim Moroccan woman.[23] In contrast to the post-9/11 U.S. media, *O Clone* does not offer an Islamophobic representation but rather an Orientalist exoticism rooted, as we have seen, in a tropical imaginary long marked by a fraught fascination with a distant Moorish/Iberian past. While Europe's sense of identity was partially constituted in relation to the anxiety over the power of Islam—French history, for example, is often recounted as going back to the anti-Muslim battle at Poitiers—Brazil's national identity is much more ambivalent about Islam and the Moor. Furthermore, in the wake of the history of official erasure of Moorish/Sephardi culture as well as the suppression of African Malê/Muslim culture, the exoticism of the Middle East in *O Clone* cannot be dismissed as mere "play" with a distant geography; it is the symptom, rather, of a long-standing fascination with a cultural intimate. Indeed, our charting of a Sephardi-Moorish Atlantic is meant to draw such complex affective itineraries, whether acknowledged or not, for contemporary representations.[24]

The foundational idea of "the Orient," in Brazil, is simultaneously desired and rejected, recognized as part of "us" and rejected as an inconvenient reminder of a distant "other." In *O Clone* the Arab/Islamic world is associated with the stereotypical fatalism of *maktub*—literally, that is which is written, or destiny—as opposed to the clone title of the theme song composed by Marcus Viana—while Brazil, through the cloning frame narrative, is associated with science, especially, and with triumphing over an irrational idea of Fate. In the struggle between *maktub,* on the one hand, and scientific innovation, on the other, Brazil has now come to embody modernity's refusal to simply accept that which has been foreordained. The notion of a scripturally predetermined Destiny, within the Orientalist imaginary, operates in tandem with other topoi and tropes, such as "Oriental despotism" and the essentialism of Oriental fatalism, all alongside the formulaic binarism of an active, agential, modern West and a passive, traditional East. Positive portrayals of Arab/Islamic culture, in such instances, simultaneously reproduce a number of paradigmatic Orientalist tropes and binarist oppositions.[25]

In contrast to Freyre's celebration of the Moorish-Sephardi contribution to Brazilian *mestiçagem,* contemporary representations of Islam can be seen both as the end product of a successful de-Orientalization of Brazil and as a re-Orientalization of Brazilian popular culture. And, in contrast to Reis's revisionist foregrounding of the language, discourse, and agency that Islam offered the rebels, and despite the persistence of Islamic traditions, Brazilian popular culture (*O Clone,* for example) tends to depict the encounter between the Brazilian/Catholic and the Arab/Muslim as a first-time historical rendezvous between complete strangers. In *Viver a Vida* (2009), the exotic Arab desert, also the site of a major accident that befalls one of the protagonists, haunts the mixed romance between white and mulatta, while the Arab veins of Latin America remain to be disinterred. *Belíssima* (2005), meanwhile, features tensions between Turkish and Greek characters who discover, in the end, that they are related by blood—a historical rivalry that Brazil's mixing seems capable of resolving. Not only is the ambivalent relation to the Orient on full display in contemporary popular telenovelas, but so is a certain amnesia about Brazil's own Moorish heritage.

Brazil, we have been suggesting, has never ceased being fascinated by the Moor, the Sephardi, the New Christian, the *turco,* the Arab, but this fascination has often been mediated through an Orientalist lens, as though Brazil were mimicking an imperial France looking down superciliously at its non-European "other." Some of the Orientalist imaginary in Latin American popular culture, meanwhile, is mediated less via French representations and more via American Hollywood's spectacular fantasies. Just as the musical numbers in the Mexican film *Aventurera* (1950) reproduced the harem mise-en-scène typical of Hollywood films, so did the Brazilian *chanchadas* such as *Nem Samsao Nem Delila* (1954), *De Pernas pro Ar* (1957), and *Barnabé, Tu és Meu* (1952), but this time in a parodic-satiric vein.[26] Yet Brazilian popular culture, especially Afro-Brazilian Carnival performances, has displayed a good-humored affection for the Orient. A classical 1941 Carnival *marchinha* song, "Allah-la-ô," by Haroldo Lobo and Nassara (of Lebanese origin), mingled Arabic and Muslim references (Allah, Egypt) with Afro-Brazilian references ("ioio," "iaia"") in a parodically Orientalist desert décor (the Sahara):

Allah-la-ô, ô ô ô ô ô ô
Oh what heat, o, o, o, o, o
We crossed the Sahara desert
The sun was hot

And burned our face
Allah-la-ô, ô ô ô ô ô ô
We came from Egypt
And often we had to pray
Allah, Allah, Allah, my good Allah
Send water for ioio
Send water for iaia
Allah, my good Allah[27]

A similar spirit of Carnivalesque hilarity also animated the contemporary performance of "Bin Laden's Harem," which included sambistas rhythmically lifting their burqas to reveal skimpy Brazilian *tangas* underneath.[28]

Narratives of new rendezvous with Arab Islam can also be said to be in themselves a kind of return of the repressed. And even when the encounter is staged as new, it carries also subterranean Moorish memories. We have argued that Brazil and North Africa/the Middle East, within the fluid currents of the Sephardi-Moorish Atlantic, are not strangers but rather secret relatives. Indeed, other popular representations have consciously shaped the image of an intimate stranger incorporated into the Brazilian mélange. We find a Sephardi character in *A Muralha* (2000), a historical telenovela set during the Portuguese expansion in what came to be Brazil, viewed in relation to a history of repression, and thus narrating precisely this ambivalent reencounter within the Sephardi-Moorish Atlantic. Jom Tob Azulay's 1995 film *O Judeu* (*The Jew*) recounts the historical experience of the Marrano dramatist Antonio Jose da Silva, known as "The Jew." The music video *Alma Não Tem Cor* (*The Soul Has No Color,* 1997) by the band Karnak, led by André Abujamra, meanwhile, features a musical mélange of Brazilian regional rhythms mixed with Arabic, Jamaican, and Russian influences, while Chico Buarque de Holanda's CD *As Cidades* (*The Cities,* 1998) celebrates the multiplicity of Brazil, where the cover has morphed versions of himself as variously blond, black, Japanese, *moreno,* and *turco*/Arab in a turban and *abaya*. Such representations echo a three-dimensional world where Christian Arabs and Sephardi Jews ("Arab-Jews") live together in a new diasporic *convivencia* in neighborhoods like Sahara in Rio de Janeiro, or Bom Retiro and Bexiga in São Paulo.

What has hopefully become evident over the course of this chapter is that tropes of mixing—whether religious (syncretism), genetic (miscegenation), botanical (hybridity), culinary (*feijoada*), or linguistic (creolization)—have become over many decades a kind of default national discourse. The most diverse cultural strains are put into the ideological blender called syncretism, proposed as an explanatory principle for the most diverse and contradictory phenomena. In this sense, these discourses of mixture reflect the process by which ethnic groups are constantly remodeled and reframed as they brush up against one another in changing urban contexts. Like Macunaima, Mario de Andrade's chameleonic Paulistano "hero without any character," race and ethnicity and culture exist in constant mutation. The Middle Easterner arrives, as a popular saying has it, first as a *turco,* and then becomes a more respectable *Sirio,* and with greater success, becomes a *Libanese.* Just as many Jewish immigrants changed their names but retained echoes of the original, in Brazil, as Jeff Lesser points out, "Taufik became Teofilo, Fauzi became Fausto, and Mohamed became Manuel" (1999, 52).

Both Freyre and Reis, as we have seen, despite their different perspectives, appeal to the idea of syncretism, whether, as in Freyre's case, to an overarching syncretism formative of the Brazilian nation, or in Reis's case, to a religious-political syncretism between Islam and Afro-diasporic spirit religions. Brazil's contradictions are "resolved," at least provisionally, through the underlying metanarrative of celebrating the *contributions* of the diverse non-European cultures—the Moorish, the Sephardic, the African, the Indian—to the Brazilian nation. The past in present-day culture is acknowledged and recuperated, but the desire for modernizing progress requires a transcendence of that heritage. In many ways, then, Freyre's project becomes one of celebrating the cultural diversity of Brazil, but resignified under the aegis of the modern nation-state.

Thanks to thinkers like Freyre and Reis, despite their differences, the racial hybridity once demonized by many nineteenth-century Brazilian philosophers is now lauded as a source of national pride. Antonio Risério, crucially, distinguishes between Portuguese *miscigenação* as a simple biological mixture and *mestiçagem* as a mix of biology and culture, a discursivization of mixture. In this sense, one might also contrast the "top-down miscegenation" carried out by the *bandeirantes* and *mamelucos* as part of a demographic imperative of territorial domination with the lateral miscegenation between enslaved Africans, Indians, and poor whites, along with a few Muslim and Jewish Arabs, as practiced in Palmares in the seventeenth century and that continues in new forms to the present day. The Brazilian dictatorship, meanwhile, deployed ideologies of harmonious miscegenation in order to promote an organically fascist order and disqualify black demands for political, economic, and cultural rights. The mainstream discourse of Brazilian miscegenation often conflates these very different phenomena.

For our part, we have tried to show that the contemporary Brazilian imaginary of the Orient can be productively viewed against the backdrop of a Moorish-Sephardi unconscious. We have tried to highlight not only the positive transatlantic historical, discursive, and cultural links between "the Orient" and "the Occident," but also the anxieties that such links provoked. This transatlantic Muslim space must be viewed as always already Jewish as well, within shared cultural geographies that are part and parcel of the Americas. The transatlantic Sephardi-Moorish space inaugurated with the two 1492s carried over the ocean hegemonic Iberian discourses about Muslim and Jews. In short, we have highlighted the uneasy tenderness that the Moor and the Sephardi, as Janus-faced figures, have provoked in the Americas, in ways that disturb any facile dichotomy between East and West, and North and South.

**Notes**

We would like to thank the following for an ongoing dialogue about Brazil over the years: Ismail Xavier, Joao Luis Vieira, Luis Antonio Coelho, Carlos Augusto Calil, Esther Hamburger, and Zé Gatti. We would also like to thank Fulbright for the research/lectureship fellowship for Ella Shohat focusing on the cultural intersections between Brazil and the Middle East. We also thank the students at University of São Paulo for their engaged comments on these issues.

1. Jeffrey Lesser and John Tofik Karam are some of the scholars who have closely examined the history and anthropology of Jewish and *turco*/Arab immigration to Brazil. See Lesser 1995 and 1999, Karam 2007, and Khatlab 2002. The journal *Tiraz: Revista de Estudos Arabes das culturas do Oriente Medio,* based at the University of São Paulo, has contributed significantly to the growing research on the Middle Eastern diaspora in Brazil.

2. The notion of Orientalism as constitutive of the Americas was made in previous publications. See Shohat 2009, 2006a, 2000, and 1997a.

3. This argument here about the discursive links between the two 1492s is based on a series of our publications. See Shohat 1992–1993 and 1999. Also reproduced in Shohat 2006b and in chapter 2, "Formations of Colonialist Discourse," of Shohat and Stam 1994.

4. For a historical overview of José Martí's statement and other Latin American references to the Moors, see Aidi 2003 and 2006, and "A Moorish Atlantic," unpublished paper sent by Aidi to Ella Shohat.

5. See Freyre 1956, especially the chapter "The Portuguese Colonizer."

6. See Freyre 1963, chapter 9. For more on the notion of the Moorish-Sephardic Atlantic and the question of Orientalism, see Shohat 2012.

7. For more discussion on these issues, see Stam 1997.

8. There is some debate on the nature of Boas's anti-racism, with some finding a certain paternalism in his work. For a strong defense of Boas, see Lewis 2001.

9. On the double-axes geographical imaginary, see Shohat and Stam 1994.

10. Gilberto Freyre, *Novo Mundo nos Tropicos* (São Paulo: Edusp, 1969), 180. Apart from the problematic idea of praising any form of slavery, it is noteworthy that Freyre

reserves his praise for the slaveholders; he allows for no agency or creative flexibility on the part of the enslaved.

11. See Vianna 2001.

12. This refusal of agency was reflected, moreover, in Freyre's consistent hostility, over many decades, to any form of black militancy, whether found in Brazil or, for that matter, in Angola and Mozambique, all of which he dismissed as dangerous and unnecessary American "imports" alien to the tolerant spirit of Luso-Tropicalism.

13. While Freyre sometimes found New York City hard on his nerves, he also saluted the general dynamism of American culture—"one of the most vibrant in the modern world"—and noted the brilliance of American universities, which for him were "graced with the best social science departments in the world." Freyre also contrasted the relatively democratic and informal atmosphere of American universities with the pomp and circumstance of Brazilian university life in the same period. At the same time, he was critical of American pseudo-patriotic bluster and the militaristic illusion of superiority over other nations.

14. See chapter 9, "Orient and Occident," in Freyre 1963.

15. The reference to the hyphen between "the Arab" and "the Jew" and Judeo-Muslim cultural affiliation is based on Shohat 1997b; 1992; (1989) 2010, especially the chapter on "The Representation of the Sephardim" and the postscript chapter to the 2010 edition; and 1988, especially the section on "The Theft of History."

16. See Veltman 1983. A documentary, *Eretz Amazonia,* by David Salgado, treats the subject of Moroccan Jews in the Amazon. See also Bentes 1987.

17. The Inquisition within the Catholic Americas provides the subject of historically based feature films such as the Mexican *El Santo Oficio* and the Brazilian *O Judeo,* as well as the documentary *The Rock and the Star,* about the migration of Sephardi Jews from Recife to New Amsterdam, where they formed the first synagogue in what was to become New York.

18. See Shohat and Stam 2012.

19. It is worth noting, in this context, that the Portuguese verb "*judiar*" and the noun "*judiação,*" both derived from the word for Jew, evoke an unfair victimization of someone. Even when the reference has nothing to do with Jewishness, it carries the traces of a negative stream of association with an ethno-religious group.

20. An exception was made in the case of shutters of "single-story houses, which do not affect the beauty of the view" (Freyre 1956, 277).

21. Reis writes that Arab merchants "carried about with them scraps or sentences of the *Koran* which they distributed to the natives, who generally fastened them on the end of sticks near their doors as charms against witchcraft" (1993, 98).

22. On the notion of "Eurotropic" in the context of "the protocols of Eurocentrism," see Shohat and Stam 2012.

23. For a closer analysis of the telenovela *O Clone,* see Shohat and Alsultany 2013.

24. On Brazil and Latin America's Moorish longing and Moorish unconscious, see also Shohat 2013. The notion of a multiply raced Atlantic, i.e., "the Rainbow Atlantic" that includes the black, red, white, brown, etc., is developed in Shohat and Stam 2012.

25. The telenovela mixes customs and traditions from diverse regions and communities, subjecting the varied regions of the Middle East and North Africa to what we elsewhere call "topographical reductionism," (*Unthinking Eurocentrism*, 1994) which elides the significant differentiations within Arab Islam's multiple geographies. While the telenovela's theme did feed into a growing Latin American curiosity about Islam, it also provoked discontent about its penchant for a presumably ethnographic representation of polygamy, harems, and veils.

26. For more on parody in the *chanchadas*, see Vieira 1987, as well as Vieira's essay on the *chanchada* in Johnson and Stam 1997.

27. Translation from the Portuguese is by the authors:

Allah-la-ô, ô ô ô ô ô ô
Mas que calor, ô ô ô ô ô ô
Atravessamos o deserto do Saara
O sol estava quente, Queimou a nossa cara
Allah-la-ô, ô ô ô ô ô ô
Mas que calor, ô ô ô ô ô ô . . .
Viemos do Egito
E muitas vezes Nós tivemos que rezar
Allah, Allah, Allah, meu bom Allah
Mande água pra ioiô
Mande água pra iaiá
Allah! meu bom allah

It should also be pointed out that Nassara was of Lebanese origin, just as the band that played in *Barnabé, Tu és meu* was the São Paulo Arab orchestra.

28. Information supplied by the Brazilian film scholar João Luis Vieira in conversation with Ella Shohat, Rio de Janeiro, Spring 2003.

## References

Aidi, Hisham. 2003. "Let Us Be Moors: Islam, Race and "Connected Histories." In *Middle East Report*, no. 229. Marti made the declaration "Seamos Moros" in support of the Berber insurrections against Spanish rule in North Africa.
———. 2006. "The Interference of al-Andalus: Spain, Islam, and the West." In "Edward Said: A Memorial Issue," ed. Patrick Deer, Gyan Prakash, and Ella Shohat. Special issue, *Social Text* 87 (Summer).
Amado, Jorge. (1958) 1987. *Gabriela, cravo e canela* [*Gabriela, Clove and Cinnamon*]. Rio de Janeiro: Editora Record.
———. 1984. *Tocaia grande* [*Showdown*]. Rio de Janeiro: Editora Record.
———. 1994. *A Descoberta da América Pelos Turcos* [*How the Turks Discovered America*]. Rio de Janeiro: Editora Record.
Bentes, Abraham Ramiro. 1987. *Das Ruínas de Jerusalem a Verdejante Amazonia*. Rio de Janeiro: Edicões Bloch.

Benzaquen de Araújo, Ricardo. 2005. *Guerra e Paz: Casa-Grande e Senzala e a obra de Gilberto Freyre nos Anos 30*. São Paulo: Editora 34.

Drewal, Henry John. 1999. "Memory, Agency, and the Arts: The African Diaspora in Brazil." Paper presented at the Global Diasporas Conference, University of Wisconsin, Madison, October 29.

———. 2008. *Mami Wata: Arts for Water Spirits in Africa and Its Diasporas*. Seattle: University of Washington Press.

Faoro, Raimundo. 1958. *Os Donos do Poder: Formação do Patronato Político Brasileiro*. São Paulo: Editora Globo.

Freyre, Gilberto. 1956. *The Masters and the Slaves*. Trans. Samuel Putnam. New York: Alfred A. Knopf. Originally *Casa-Grande e Senzala* (Rio de Janeiro: Maia e Schmidt, 1933).

———. 1959. *New World in the Tropics: The Culture of Modern Brazil*. New York: Alfred A. Knopf.

———. 1963. *The Mansions and the Shanties*. Trans. Harriet de Onís. New York: Alfred A. Knopf. (Portuguese title: *Sobrados e Mucambos*.)

———. 1969. *Novo Mundo nos Tropicos*. São Paulo: Edusp. The English version, *New World in the Tropics*, was published in 1959 by Knopf.

Fuentes, Carlos. 1999. *The Buried Mirror*. New York: First Mariner Books.

Gomez, Michael. 2005. *Black Crescent: The Experience and Legacy of African Muslims in the Americas*. Cambridge: Cambridge University Press.

Holanda, Sérgio Buarque de. 1956. *Raízes do Brasil*. Rio de Janeiro: J. Olympio.

Johnson, Randal, and Robert Stam. 1997. *Brazilian Cinema*. New York: Columbia University Press.

Karam, John Tofik. 2007. *Another Arabesque: Syrian-Lebanese Ethnicity in Neoliberal Brazil*. Philadelphia: Temple University Press.

Khatlab, Roberto. 2002. *Mahjar: Saga Libanesa no Brasil*. Zalka, Lebanon: Mokhtarat.

Lesser, Jeffrey. 1995. *Welcoming the Undesirables: Brazil and the Jewish Question*. Berkeley: University of California Press.

———. 1999. *Negotiating National Identity: Immigrants, Minorities, and the Struggle for Ethnicity in Brazil*. Durham, NC: Duke University Press.

Lewis, Herbert S. 2001. "The Passion of Franz Boas." *American Anthropologist* 103(2) (June).

Marti, José. "España en Melilla." In *Cuba: Letras*, vol. 2. Havana: Edición Tropico.

Merquior, José Guilherme. 1972. *Saudades do Carnaval*. Rio de Janeiro: Forense.

Morse, Richard. 1988. *O Espelho de Próspero*. São Paulo: Companhia das Letras.

al-Mūsili, Elias. 2003. *An Arab's Journey to Colonial Spanish America: The Travels of Elias al-Mūsili in the Seventeenth Century*. Translated from the Arabic and edited by Caesar E. Farah. Syracuse, NY: Syracuse University Press.

Nimer, Miguel. 2005. *Influências Orientais na Língua Portuguesa*. 2nd ed. Edited by Carlos Augusto Calil. São Paulo: Editora de Universidade de São Paulo.

Pallares-Burke, Maria Lúcia Garcia. 2005. *Gilberto Freyre: Um Vitoriano dos Tropicos*. São Paulo: Unesp.

Prado, Paulo. 1928. *Retrato do Brasil.* Rio de Janeiro: F. Briguiet.

Reis, João José. 1993. *Slave Rebellion in Brazil: The Muslim Uprising of 1835 in Bahia.* Baltimore: Johns Hopkins University Press.

Shohat, Ella. 1988. "Sephardim in Israel: Zionism from the Standpoint of Its Jewish Victims." *Social Text* 19/20 (Fall).

———. (1989) 2010. *Israeli Cinema: East/West and the Politics of Representation.* New York: I. B. Tauris.

———. 1992. "Rethinking Jews and Muslims: Quincentennial Reflections." *Middle East Report.* September–October.

———. 1992–1993. "Staging the Quincentenary: The Middle East and the Americas." In "The Wake of Utopia." Special issue, *Third Text* 21 (Winter).

———. 1997a. "American Orientalism." *Suitcase* 2 (1&2).

———. 1997b. "Columbus, Palestine, and Arab Jews: Toward a Relational Approach to Community Identity." In *Cultural Readings of Imperialism: Edward Said and the Gravity of History,* ed. Keith Ansell Pearson, Benita Parry, and Judith Squires. London: Lawrence & Wishart in association with New Formations (Britain).

———. 1999. "Taboo Memories, Diasporic Visions: Columbus, Palestine and Arab-Jews." In *Performing Hybridity,* ed. May Joseph and Jennifer Fink, 131–156. Minneapolis: University of Minnesota Press.

———. 2000. "'Coming to America': Reflections on Hair and Memory Loss." In *Going Global: The Transnational Reception of Third World Women Writers,* ed. Lisa Suhair Majaj and Amal Amireh, 284–300. New York: Garland Publishers.

———. 2006a. "Gendered Cartographies of Knowledge: Area Studies, Ethnic Studies, and Postcolonial Studies." In *Taboo Memories, Diasporic Voices,* 1–16. Durham, N.C.: Duke University Press.

———. 2006b. *Taboo Memories, Diasporic Voices.* Durham, NC: Duke University Press.

———. 2009. "On the Margins of Middle Eastern Studies: Situating Said's *Orientalism.*" In "On *Orientalism* at Thirty." Special section of *Review of Middle Eastern Studies* 43(1) (Summer). Published plenary session lecture, MESA 2008.

———. 2013. "The Sephardi-Moorish Atlantic: Between Orientalism and Occidentalism." In *Between the Middle East and the Americas: The Cultural Politics of Diaspora,* ed. Evelyn Alsultany and Ella Shohat. Ann Arbor: University of Michigan Press.

Shohat, Ella, and Evelyn Alsultany. 2013. " The Cultural Politics of 'the Middle East' in the Americas: An Introduction." In *Between the Middle East and the Americas: The Cultural Politics of Diaspora,* ed. Evelyn Alsultany and Ella Shohat. Ann Arbor: University of Michigan Press.

Shohat, Ella, and Robert Stam. 1994. *Unthinking Eurocentrism.* London: New York: Routledge.

Sommer, Doris. 1991. *Foundational Fictions.* Berkeley: University of California Press.

Stam, Robert. 1997. *Tropical Multiculturalism: Comparative Race in Brazilian Cinema and Culture.* Durham, NC: Duke University Press.

Stam, Robert, and Ella Shohat. 2012. *Race in Translation: Culture Wars in the Postcolonial Atlantic.* New York: New York University Press.

Veltman, Henrique. 1983. *Os Hebraicos da Amazonia.*

Vianna, Hermano. 2001. "A Meta Mitologica da Democracia Racial." In *O Imperador das Ideias: Gilberto Freyre em Questão,* ed. Joaquim Falcão and Rosa Maria Barboza de Araujo. Rio de Janeiro: Topbooks.

Vieira, Joao Luis. 1982. *Hegemony and Resistance: Parody and Carnival in Brazilian Cinema.* PhD diss., Cinema Studies, New York University. Adviser: Robert Stam.

———. 1987. "A Chanchada e o Cinema Carioca." In *Historia do Cinema Brasileiro,* ed. Fernão Ramos. São Paulo: Art Editora.

# 7

# Slave Barracks Aristocrats
## Islam and the Orient in the Work of Gilberto Freyre

*Alexandra Isfahani-Hammond*

Isfahani-Hammond explores how Gilberto Freyre invokes Islam and the Orient—via a certain Africa—to theorize a national history constituted by the Oriental luxury of the plantation economy and a cultural synthesis based on eroticized systems of domination. It argues that Freyre's work represents an intermittent celebration of the power of black writing and of sensualism of Moorish North African Arab-Berber civilization. Though he produces a model of seigniorial subjectivity that speaks for both masters and slaves, the Malê, with his *tiá* and his "blue ink," also speaks within his narrative, disrupting it and acting in opposition to it even as Freyre struggles to seize the power of the rebel Malê and the sensuality of the female Moor and to insert these subjects into a civilizational trajectory that begins in the East, via Africa, and ends in Brazil.

~

In *Orientalism* (1978), Edward Said charts European representations that produce the East not only as the differential marker of Europe but as inherently subject to the West. In Gilberto Freyre's sociology of Brazilian plantation society, *Casa-Grande e Senzala* (The Plantation Manor and the Slave Barracks, 1933),[1] he argues that Brazil has a unique racial democracy based on the "slack balance of antagonisms" between masters and slaves that is the legacy of Moorish domination of the Iberian Peninsula.[2] The resonance of the West's imaginative geography of the Orient and Freyre's imaginative genealogy of Brazilian society is enlightened by juxtaposing two key dimensions of *Casa-Grande e Senzala:* the syncretic, "Afro-European" character of the Portuguese following five hundred years of Moorish rule and the impact of the

East via the Malês, the enslaved and freed African Muslims who organized the most formidable urban slave uprising in the history of the Americas in 1835 in Salvador da Bahia.[3]

Rather than an historical or sociological account of the impact of the Moorish empire or of the *Revolta Malê* (Malê revolt), literary analysis provides a method for fleshing out the symbolic interplay between these terms in Freyre's invention of Brazilian cultural identity. This discursive untangling—an analysis of the internal logic of Freyrean Orientalism vis-à-vis racial democracy—is crucial since his interpretation of plantation relations is the dominant paradigm for Brazilian cultural identity. Sérgio Costa calls racial democracy the "civil religion of Brazil" (2002), while for Carlos Guilherme Mota, *Casa-Grande e Senzala* is the "crystallization of an ideology which, until today, to a greater or lesser extent, continues to inform the notion of *Brazilian Culture*" (1977, 57).

Gilberto Freyre (1900–1987) was a prolific sociologist from the northeastern city of Recife, Pernambuco. The descendant of Pernambuco's plantation aristocracy, he made a career of celebrating the northeastern slavery economy as the seed for a preeminent civilization. His apology for the northeastern *engenho* (plantation) responded to two principal threats: the southeast's steady overshadowing of the northeast as the nation's political and economic center from the mid-nineteenth century onward, and the U.S. hegemony which relegated Brazil to a decidedly inferior status both within the Americas and globally. For Freyre, Brazil's singularity derives from its master/slave synthesis. In *Casa-Grande e Senzala,* he replaces eugenic lamentations about the effects of miscegenation with a redemptive reading of the fusion of European and African cultures during the sixteenth and seventeenth centuries. Freyre identifies the paternalism of the northeastern plantation economy as the origin for a society that is free of the kinds of racial tensions and violence that plague the United States. Premised on Portugal's unique accommodation of non-European difference, *Casa-Grande e Senzala* constitutes what Carlos Guilherme Mota calls a model for African-European contact realized within a patriarchal order, whose epicenter is the *casa-grande* (58). Integral to Freyre's formulation is the idea that Brazilian slavery is distinguished from other slavery economies by the sensuality of master-slave relations and by the fact that Brazilian masters *identify* with slaves (Azevedo 1995, 24).

Freyre's model has mediated systems of domination both within Brazil's borders and without, since it became a key defense for the perpetuation of Portuguese colonial rule in Africa in the 1970s. Produced at a moment when Brazilians were concerned with delineating national character in the aftermath of abolition and independence, racial democracy has consistently been wielded as a panacea against Americanization, most recently by critics of affirmative action, who employ arguments about the sensuality and ambiguity of Brazilian race relations to dismiss the imposition of United States–inspired models for redressing race-based socioeconomic disparities.[4] Because Freyre emphasizes the cultural and atmospheric transmission of identity, his analysis has been widely heralded as initiating a transition from biological to cultural models of national identity. What critics have failed to note is that he employs these non-biological forms of assimilation to produce a symbolically Africanized, genetically white figure as the prototype for "interracial" synthesis. The most important implication of this figure's emblematic status is the exclusion of sociohistorical blacks and *mestiços* (mixed-race people) from the activities of representing and interpreting Brazilian culture. In *White Negritude: Race, Writing and Brazilian Cultural Identity* (2008), I interrogate this displacement through readings of his previously understudied literary criticism, wherein Freyre's treatments of white canonical writers provide critical insight into his eugenically informed paradigm for hybridization.

Thinking about this paradigm in relation to the East, two contradictory impulses emerge. A mythical, feminized Orient connects Brazil, via the Iberian world, to the source of Western civilization. For Freyre, this mythical locale is also the origin for Brazil's unique synthesis of European and African cultures during slavery. The Moor's conquest of Iberia in a mythologized past is remembered in the figure of the "enchanted" female Moor. By contrast, the Malê revolt against slavery in nineteenth-century Brazil represents a form of living, oppositional Islam that upsets his premise of master-slave equilibrium. Freyre negotiates this contradiction by incorporating the Malês as part of a recurrent Oriental substrain that informs Brazilian culture, engaging Malê literacy as a renewal of the erudite Moors' will to power. Given the defiance of U.S. hegemony that informs his analysis of Brazil's colonial and plantation history, and the interface of his invocation of the East with Anglo-Saxon Orientalism, how might we compare Freyre's interpretation of the Malê revolt with Western definitions of Islam as jihad? If the West depicts the East as "mythic origin" by contrast with Africa, a "blank darkness" omitted from the trajectory of civilizational history, how does Freyre's peculiar genealogy stand up to this dialectic?

## The Civilizing Orient

In *Casa-Grande e Senzala*, Freyre maps Brazil as the culmination of a history that, via the Moors, symbolically begins in the East. This gesture is illuminated by Edward Said's reminder that the Orient is "the place of Europe's greatest and richest and oldest colonies, the source of its civilization and languages" (1978, 1). Freyre thus employs a positive form of Orientalism to circumvent eugenic condemnations of the effects of miscegenation, though he paradoxically articulates an alternate racial essentialism wherein the introduction of Arab-Berber and African blood into the Iberian Peninsula "fortifies the stock." Freyre also uses the Moorish domination of Portugal to establish a natural affinity between Africans and Portuguese, claiming that the Moors were driven by empathetic identification with the Portuguese and the wish to "enliven the color" of their pale cousins. As Freyre states:

> As to that which is looked upon as the autochthonous base of a population that is so constantly changing, it is to be found in a persistent mass of dark-brown dolichocephalic individuals whose color Arabian and even Negro Africa have more than once come to enliven with traces of the mulatto and the black as they overflowed large populations of the peninsula—it was as if they felt this people to be intimately their own by remote affinities, merely grown a trifle paler, that is all, and as if they did not wish to see the stock obliterated by superimposed Nordic layers or transmuted by a series of Europeanizing cultures: all that invasion of Celts, Germans, Romans, Normans, the Anglo-Scandinavian, the H. Europaeus L., feudalism, Christianity, Roman law, monogamy—it all suffered a restriction or refraction in a Portugal influenced by Africa, conditioned by the African climate, and undermined by the sensual mysticism of Islam. (Freyre [1933] 1946, 5–6; translation modified)[5]

Characterizing the "overflowing" African occupation of the peninsula as a form of blood transfusion that saves it from the extreme influences of "Nordic obliteration," Freyre counters scientific race theories about the "mongrelizing" effects of the introduction of Africans into Brazil. He also establishes a kinship affiliation between North Africans and the Portuguese that lays the foundation for master-slave equilibrium. In another passage, he refers to the "Moorish or black blood running through a great, light-skinned mulatto population" (5) and insists that this blood transfusion diminished the conflict and coercion of Portuguese colonization and enslavement. At the same time, the Afro-European, Moorish identity of the Brazilian slaveholder establishes slaves' purported identification with the enslavers who were once their subjects and who are themselves, after all, black: "it was as though they felt this people to be intimately their own by remote affinities, merely grown a trifle paler." (6). In an even more dramatic reversal of systems of domination, Freyre argues that "the African influence boiling beneath that of the European" produced a colonial situation in which Africa, rather than Europe, was dominant: "Europe reigned but without governing; it was first Africa that governed" (5).

Laying the groundwork for his narrative of Brazilian plantation culture, Freyre invents a history of oscillating relations of power between the Iberian Peninsula and North Africa, mollified by Oriental sensuality and aggression. The "sensual mysticism of Islam"—the eroticized, mysterious Orient, via the Moors—softens European institutions and produces a model of Luso-Brazilian character whose essence is European and Catholic, but which includes Africa and Islam within it. Freyre stresses that sexual and cultural intercourse between Iberians and North Africans mitigates the tension between oppressor and oppressed: There might be a constant state of warfare (which, incidentally, does not by any means exclude miscegenation or a sexual attraction between the two races, much less an intercourse between the two cultures), but the victor would find relaxation from the intensity of his military exertions by falling back upon the agricultural and industrial labor of war captives, the enslavement or semi-enslavement of the vanquished. These hegemonies and states of servitude were never perpetuated but tended always to alternate, as in the incident of the bells of Santiago de Compostela: the Moors had them borne to the mosque of Córdoba on the backs of Christians, and the latter, centuries later, had them returned to Galicia on the backs of Moors (4–5).

By contrast with the common sense of U.S. national identity, in which plantation slavery is characterized as an historical aberration or, to quote Barnor Hesse, a "disaster" out of synch with the emergence of modern capitalism (Hesse 2002, 157), Freyre's sociology locates master-slave relations as the origin for Brazilian culture's pattern of shifting antagonisms in equilibrium. Like the bells of Santiago de Compostela, first upon Christians' backs, then upon Moors,' the enslaved Africans in Brazil are simply saddled with the burden that was once that of their masters. Africans and Europeans are bound to one another by mutual awareness of their shared history of alternating relations of dominance and subordination.

In addition to mutual recognition, Freyre appeals to a seductive Orient to describe the Portuguese as Afro-Europeans in whom antagonisms waver between fatalism and "bursts of energy," "love of progress" and a "voluptuous indolence that is very Oriental" (8).[6] He insists upon the attraction between non-European women and Portuguese men, employing the "voluptuous indolence" of the Orient to invert colonial systems of domination. Freyre claims that Portuguese men's memory of the *moura encantada* (enchanted Mooress) drove their imperial expeditions in search of brown-skinned women (indigenous and, later, African):[7]

> Long contact with the Saracens had left the Portuguese the idealized figure of the
> "enchanted Moorish woman," a charming type of brown-skinned, black-eyed

woman, enveloped in sexual mysticism, roseate in hue, and always engaged in combing out her hair or bathing in rivers or in the waters of haunted fountains; and the Brazilian colonizers were to encounter practically a counterpart of this type in the naked Indian women with their loose-flowing hair. These latter also had dark tresses and dark eyes and bodies painted red, and, like the Moorish Nereids, were extravagantly fond of a river bath to refresh their ardent nudity, and were fond, too, of combing their hair. What was more, they were fat like the Moorish women. Only, they were a little less coy and for some trinket or other or a bit of broken mirror would give themselves, with legs spread far apart, to the "caraibas," who were so gluttonous for a woman. (12–13)

Freyre repeats a familiar cliché of eroticized colonial contact. He effaces the gendered violence of the conquest by emphasizing indigenous women's eager reception of the Portuguese colonizers. Their "ardent nudity" and "legs spread far apart" recall American discovery myths of submissive indigenous aides to the explorers (from Pocahontas to *La Malinche*) as well as the "foundational" interracial romances (as analyzed by Doris Summer, 1991) that inform Latin America's mestizo national identities, from José de Alencar's *O Guaraní* (1857) and *Iracema* ([1865] 1942) to Gertrúdis Gómez de Avellaneda's *Sab* ([1841] 1993), José Eustácio Rivera's *La Vorágine* (The Vortex, 1924), and Rómulo Gallegos's *Doña Bárbara* (1929). What is distinct about Freyre's national romance is that he situates a mythical Moorish-Oriental past as the antecedent for the symbolic Africanization of the Portuguese that mollifies colonial and slavocratic systems of domination.

## The Malê Revolt

For Freyre, the civilizing legacy of the Moors both ennobles the Portuguese and transforms them into Afro-Europeans uniquely suited to colonizing the tropics. The feminized Orient of the *moura encantada* (reembodied by indigenous and African women) provokes a sensual drive for expansion and enslavement, softening plantation relations and connecting masters and slaves through historical kinship affiliation. In contradistinction to this positive Orient, Freyre posits the living, masculine Islam of the Malê revolt:

[I]n the dark of the slave huts, with teachers and preachers from Africa to give instruction in reading the books of the Koran in the Arabic, and with Mohammedan schools and houses of prayer functioning here . . . slaves who were schooled in the Koran preached the religion of the prophet, setting it over against the religion of Christ that was followed by their white masters, up above in the Big Houses. (315)

Ignited in "Mohammedan schools" and through reading and writing instruction "in the dark of the slave huts," the Malê revolt constitutes Islam not as a floating signifier belonging to a distant time and place but in distinctly oppositional relation to the *casa-grande*. While the Malês challenge Freyre's claims about the harmonious nature of slavery in Brazil, they pose an even deeper threat due to their association with relatively high levels of literacy. Freyre's concern with this phenomenon must be understood in the context of the role of the written word among Bahian slaves in the nineteenth century. In addition to conducting prayer services, the learned, devout *malams* (scholars of Quranic studies) and *alufás* (black Muslims), both freed and enslaved, were educators who provided instruction in reading and writing to slaves and ex-slaves. In *Slave Rebellion in Brazil* (1993), João José Reis explains that though most of the rebels didn't read or write Arabic fluently and the conspiracy was planned and organized by word of mouth, there were highly literate Muslim slaves and ex-slaves among them. Moreover, Muslim and non-Muslim blacks had both taken to wearing *tiá*, amulets containing Quranic verses written on small pieces of paper and worn in leather pouches around their necks for protection (Reis 1993, 99). In a context where most slaveholders were illiterate, the function of written texts in the uprising caused consternation among Bahia's white community. Reis notes that in the inquisition which followed, "The police found many pieces of paper with Arabic writing, and these papers made a deep impression at the time. In a society where even the dominant whites were largely illiterate, it was hard to accept that African slaves possessed such sophisticated means of communication" (Reis 1993, 100). The fact that the Malês were widely admired among enslaved and freed blacks in Bahia caused additional anxiety within the slaveholding community.

Malê literacy bears further weight for Freyre since it undermines a key dimension of his analysis of hybridization. To understand this, we need to look at the relationship between race, slavery, and authorship in Freyre's many prefaces to canonical Brazilian race texts. In these, he produces the *senhor do engenho* (plantation master) as symbolically Africanized through plantation sexual relations and the assimilation of an ambulatory quality he calls "Afro-Brazilian reality." This quality is in nature, in the hot air of the tropics, in Afro-Brazilian food and in the "softened" vocabulary of the enslaved. Detached from sociohistorically Afro-Brazilian identity, it is a floating signifier that is incorporated and interpreted by the plantation master, producing a model of national character that is at once "hybrid" and genetically white, seigniorial and universal.[8]

Freyre's model is frequently decontextualized. Read independently, there are passages in which he appears to be engaged in a critique of fixed identity.

But it is necessary to attend to his adamant insistence that people of African descent cannot properly write.[9] In his preface to Jorge de Lima's "Poemas Negros" (Black Poems, 1947), he attributes Lima's authentic articulation of blacks' "joys, hopes, delights and fears" to his seigniorial upbringing (158). By contrast, Freyre claims that "black blood" prohibits the genuine interpretation of black "reality," given that black authors speak to white audiences and are motivated by the desire to improve their socioeconomic status (Lima 1958, 160; Freyre 1962, 122). Of Joaquim Nabuco's *O Abolicionismo* (Abolitionism, 1883), he states that the white abolitionist was the best spokesman for blacks given his plantation incorporation of blacks' aspirations for freedom and the fact that so many slaves foolishly "desired the continuation of the regime of the whip and of the stake" (Freyre 1962, 18). In "Reinterpretando José de Alencar," Freyre dismisses mixed-race writers, arguing that *mestiço* identity prevents Machado de Assis from interpreting and articulating the dialectic of Brazilian culture; for Freyre, Machado turns his back on the "slave barracks lamentations" (Freyre [1955] 1962, 61) but can never hope to adopt the "gaze of the young white master" (122).

In *Gilberto Freyre: Um Vitoriano dos Trópicos* (Gilberto Freyre: A Victorian in the Tropics, 2005), Maria Lúcia Pallares-Burke unearths Freyre's ambivalent adoption of Franz Boas's culturalism alongside the white supremacy he came to revere as a young man studying at Baylor College, in Waco, Texas, between 1918 and 1921. She discusses his defense of the Ku Klux Klan (Pallares-Burke 2005, 314), his praise for the "Anglo-Saxononic ethnocentric mystique" (273), and his opportunistic alliance with Boas's theories, particularly in relation to the revision of his 1925 master's thesis, in which he weeds out passages that reflect admiration for eugenic theories (268–270). Pallares-Burke calls special attention to how Freyre's ambivalence is played out in the realm of literary criticism when she cites his review of René Maran's *Batouala* (1921) in the *Diário de Pernambuco* (Pernambucan Daily) in 1922. Freyre suggests that the Martinican's talent is a victory over his physiological maladaptation to literacy, characterizing him as a "pure black—a black with a nose so flat that one is shocked to see balanced upon it, as though by miracle, a respectable *pince-nez*" (305). In addition to Maran, in this same article he cites Alexandre Dumas, Machado de Assis, Aleijadinho, and Ruben Dario as examples of "mixed-race" literary genius that debunk racist expectations. This tribute to *mestiço* authorship is undermined by Freyre's condescending description of Maran's "miraculous" use of a pince-nez as well as by his denunciation of black and mulatto writers in the above-cited essays. How can we map the boundary between Freyre's idealization of African-European synthesis and his depictions of African descent as an obstacle to literacy?

Freyre's exclusionary hybridism is further enlightened when he contrasts white-authored black Brazilian text with black U.S. authorship, which he argues is emblematic of segregation:

> Fortunately, there is no "African poetry" in Brazil like that in the United States, of which James Weldon Johnson and other critics have spoken: curt poetry almost always in an attitude of defensiveness or aggression; poetry which is almost always in comic dialect for the ears of whites, no matter how bitter or sad the themes. What there is in Brazil is a region of poetry more colored by the influence of the African, an African already greatly dissolved into a Brazilian. A zone to which are connected, by virtue of their regional upbringing, some of our most rigorously white and aristocratic writers and poets: the Pernambu- cans Joaquim Nabuco and Manuel Bandeira, for example. (*Poemas Negros,* 160)

The distinction Freyre draws between "black literature" produced by blacks in the United States and "black literature" produced by whites in Brazil is informed by his argument about Brazil's uniqueness, constituted above all by cordial, postplantation social relations and the incorporation of elements of African culture by the *senhores do engenho.* Celia Azevedo summarizes Freyre's argument in *Casa-Grande e Senzala:* "In contrast with American so- ciety, where two inimical parts constantly confronted each other—the white and the black, the ex-slaveholder and the ex-slave—Brazil presented two fra- ternal parts whose distinct values and experiences had been long interacting in a mutually enriching process that required no sacrifice of one element to the other" (Azevedo 1995, xii–xiii).

Malê literacy destabilizes Freyre's paradigm of textually inscribed, hybrid- ized seigniorial subjectivity and, thereby, his discourse of master-slave inter- dependence. When he refers to the Malês' *tiá* confiscated after the uprising, he shares the astonishment of the chief of police who, upon investigation of the detainees, discovered "so many manuscripts written by slaves" (Freyre 1984, 299). Freyre further announces his consternation by linking their writing practices to sorcery against whites:

> Manuel Querino also speaks of a "blue ink" imported from Africa of which the Malês made use in connection with their sorceries or charms. With this ink they would make cabalistic signs on a blackboard; and then they would wash the board and give the water to drink to the one whose body they desired to charm; or else they spilled it in the path of the one on whom they wished to work their sorcery. (317)

For Freyre, the Malê's blue ink is the medium not only for conspiring against his master but for practicing witchcraft and casting charms. The ink loses its purpose as a marker of scholarly erudition to become a potion used for "black magic." This cliché of the dreadful African supernatural registers panic about black politicization and the potentially subversive role of black writing at the same time that it provides a solution: by substituting metaphysics for politics, Freyre produces black agency as an irrational force that must be contained. Freyre also intermittently downplays the Malês' subversive potential, disjoining the revolt from substantive strategies for sociopolitical empowerment when he claims that the "masochistic masses" rarely rebel and even then only in "sacrificial, messianic movements" (71), and that "[t]he atmosphere that preceded the movement of '35 in Bahia was one of intense religious ardor among the slaves" (105).

My point is not to diminish—or, much less, to depoliticize—the "magical" dimension of Muslim writing. The problem is that Freyre's treatment of magical black writing and magical black uprising links them to the metaphysical world in contradistinction to the realm of reason and politics. In *Infectious Rhythm: Metaphors of Contagion and the Spread of African Culture* (1998), Barbara Browning connects the emphasis upon black "soul" and spirituality with justifications for coercive policing. Freyre's reference to the Malês' "sacrificial messianism" can be traced vertically and horizontally, from the criminal ethnology of the Bahian medical doctor Raimundo Nina Rodrigues to Fernando Ortiz's theorization of metaphysical, subversive blackness in *Hampa Afrocubana: Los Negros Brujos; Apuntos para un Estudio de Etnologia Criminal* (Afro-Cuban Underworld: The Black Witches; Notes for a Study of Criminal Ethnology, 1906). Alejo Carpentier's magical realist adaptation of the Haitian revolution in *El Reino de Este Mundo* (The Kingdom of This World, 1949) is another potent example of this genre. Widely celebrated for promoting "Afro-Caribbean culture as the true, magical heartland of the Caribbean imagination" (Dash 1998, 88), Carpentier articulates an unwieldy, metaphysical blackness, casting the black rulers of the Haitian state as mimics of their former masters.[10] In *El Reino, vaudun*, communion with flora and fauna and the adoption of animal forms link blacks to the natural world—as animals to be domesticated and consumed—and to the other world, where they exercise their legitimate powers. Likewise, in *¡Ecue Yamba-O!* Carpentier "features *ñáñigo* dances and religious ceremonies as 'therapeutic' alternatives to the culture sugar created during the tumultuous first decades of the twentieth century, when sugar production was so closely tied to U.S. economic, political, and cultural imperialism" (Kutzinski 1993, 141). Haitian dictator François "Papa Doc" Duvalier and Haitian ethnologist Lorimer Denis identified *vaudun* as "the supreme factor for Haitian unity," providing a reminder of the potential conflation of black metaphysics with state violence and criminality, posing a startling point of reference for understanding how and at what point the emphasis on "soul" becomes repressive and exclusionary. In "Race, Nation and the Politics of Servitude in Haitian *Noirisme*" (2005), Valerie Kaussen shows how Duvalier and Denis produce the *noiriste* state as the incarnation of the slave's rebellious energy while at the same time insisting upon the essentially violent nature of the black race and its need for order, hierarchy, and preventive punishment.[11]

There are parallels between Freyre's acclimated—that is, "Africanized"— Euro-Brazilian national prototype and James Clifford's observation of ethnography's self-justifying gesture of salvaging cultural practices threatened by extinction: "Ethnography's disappearing object is, then, in significant degree, a rhetorical construct legitimating a representational practice: 'salvage' ethnography in its widest sense. The other is lost, in disintegrating time and space, but saved in the text" (1986, 112). Whereas Clifford points to how ethnography legitimates itself as the guardian of non-European traditions in decline, the relationship between writing and the vanishing other is inverted in Freyre's oeuvre. That which is "saved in the text" are the cultural and discursive remnants of black identity that are absorbed by the white writer at the same time that sociohistorical blackness is targeted for elimination. This proprietary anthropological usurpation is inextractable from eugenics and police action. Indeed, criminal ethnographer Raimundo Nina Rodrigues (1862–1906) was the first in a genealogy of "specialists" to document Afro-Brazilian cultural influences. Originating with Rodrigues's endeavor to catalogue and regulate the unruly African "element" in his influential studies including *Os Africanos no Brasil* (The Africans in Brazil; written between 1890 and 1905 and published posthumously in 1932) and *O Animismo Fetichista dos Negros Baianos* (The Fetishist Animism of Bahian Blacks, 1896–1897), Afro-Brazilian studies evolved into a "celebratory" enterprise crystallized by Freyre's *Casa-Grande e Senzala*, replacing sociohistorical blackness with a discourse *about* blackness—what Derrida calls "obliterating the proper" ([1974] 1988, 110).

A provocative illustration of this exclusion is encountered in the intersection of two works in the field of Afro-Brazilian studies, Edison Carneiro's *Antologia do Negro Brasileiro* (The Anthology of the Brazilian Black, 1950) and Abdias do Nascimento's *O Negro Revoltado* (The Revolted Black, 1980). The first essay in Carneiro's anthology, Arthur Ramos's "Os Estudos Negros e a Escola de Nina Rodrigues" ("Black Studies and the School of Nina Rodrigues"), observes that Nina Rodrigues's *O Animismo Fetichista dos Negros Baianos* informed, "na sua quase totalidade" (in virtual totality) (20), the study of the Brazilian black. Ramos's and Rodrigues's production of blackness as animistic and fetishistic constitutes it as that which is chaotic and needs to be contained, but also in opposition to the "natural" whitening body that will consume and erase it. In another essay in this volume, "O negro—objeto de ciência" (The Black—Object of Science), Sílvio Romero calls for a study of the Brazilian black that will exceed and exclude European ethnography: "Quando vemos homens, como Bleek, refugiarem-se dezenas e dezenas de anos nos centros de Africa somente para estudar uma língua e colegir uns mitos, nós que temos o material em casa, que temos a Africa nas nossas cozinhas, como a America em nossas selvas e a Europa em nossos salões, nada havemos produzido neste sentido! E uma desgraça" (When we see men, like Bleek, taking refuge for dozens and dozens of years in the centers of Africa only to study a language or collect some myths, we who have the material at home, who have Africa in our kitchens, like America in our jungles and Europe in our salons, have produced nothing in this sense! It's a disgrace) (22). Romero articulates the proprietary stance of Afro-Brazilian studies both in relation to black "material" and European social science. Unlike Europeans, "we" Brazilians have Africa in "our" kitchens. At the same time, writing about that blackness, Brazilian ethnographers confirm their Europeanness—located in "our" salons—as exceeding in their ownership of subaltern raw matter men like Bleek who must travel to Africa to scrutinize black "objects of science." Like Caribbean celebrations of blackness as a tool against Yankee imperialism—Alejo Carpentier's ¡Ecue-Yamba-O! (1933) comes to mind—Romero's defensive aggression toward European ethnography speaks to the critical status of the black object in Brazil's cultural nationalism and poses the intriguing paradox of how, whereas Afro-Brazilian studies and Afro-Cubanism have been duplicitously employed as tools against postcolonial domination, U.S. civil rights have more recently been associated with the conservation and dissemination of U.S. hegemony.

In his exploration of ethnography's impetus of containment in *Hybrid Cultures* (1995), Nestor Garcia Canclini discusses Mexican museums' cataloguing of indigenous culture, a gesture that illuminates Freyre's simultaneous incorporation and erasure of blackness:

> Although they contribute to conceiving a solidary beauty above geographical and cultural differences, [the museums] also engender a uniformity that hides the social contradictions present in the birth of those works. The statues are no longer invoked, and in those museums it is impossible to know how and why they used to be invoked. It seems as if the pots had never been used to cook with, nor the masks for dancing. Everything is there to be looked at. (Canclini 1995, 120)

Like Canclini's indigenous artifacts, Freyre's insistence upon the seigniorial embodiment of blackness—verified by white authors' incorporation of black/

slave "motifs"—requires that "African survivals" be dissociated from the sociohistorical contexts and contradictions in which they originate and, indeed, from the people who produce, mediate, and implement them. In an essay describing his own writing process, "Como e Porque Escrevi Casa-Grande e Senzala" (How and Why I Wrote *Casa-Grande e Senzala*, 1968), Freyre refers to his contact with the black supernatural and to African "survivals"—*xangôs, candomblé*, and *babalorixás*[12]—situating blackness both as remnant and as immaterial and unnatural.[13] In this same essay, the eugenic resonance of Freyre's forays into the "splendid laboratory" of the public plazas and streets of Rio de Janeiro underscores the exclusion of African descent and his own supernatural embodiment of dehistoricized blackness.

But in addition to repressing black dissent as irrational and metaphysical, Freyre's thinking about the Malê revolt is complicated by a contradictory admiration for the insurgents; their literacy resonates with what he has argued is Luso-Brazil's erudite Moorish legacy, a powerful element of his arsenal against U.S. supremacy. This tension comes to the foreground when he refers to the Abbé Étienne's account of the uprising in "Le Secte Mussulman des Malês du Brésil et leur Révolte en 1835." He uses this document to argue with himself: on the one hand, the Malê revolt is a sophisticated feat of political mobilization that registers the resurrection of Moorish civilization, the return of a repressed—and culturally superior—Islam; on the other, it presents a threat to his model of harmonious master-slave interdependence such that it needs to be dismissed as a "messianic, masochistic" impulse fueled by blind religious furor:

> The Abbé Étienne reveals to us some aspects of the Malê uprising in Bahia in 1835 that identify this supposed slave revolt as an outbreak or eruption of a more advanced culture downtrodden by another, less noble one. Let us not romanticize. This was purely a Malê or Mohammedan movement, or a combination of various groups under Mussulman leaders. One thing is certain, it is to be distinguished from slave revolts in colonial times. It deserves a place, indeed, among the libertarian revolutions of a religious, social, or cultural nature. The report of Dr. Francisco Gonçalves Martins, Chief of Police of the province of Bahia, on the occasion of the uprising, lays emphasis on the fact that all the rebels were able to read and write in unknown characters. Characters that "were like the Arabic," adds the learned commentator, who is naturally astounded at so many manuscripts written by slaves. "It is not to be denied that there was a political end in view in connection with these uprisings, for they did not commit robberies nor slay their master secretly." The truth is: in the slave sheds of Bahia in 1835 there were perhaps more persons who knew how to read and write than up above, in the Big Houses. (Freyre 1946, 298–299; translation modified)[14]

Freyre wavers between celebrating the Malê revolt as part of a history of syn-
thesized European and Afro-Oriental cultures and quashing it by portraying
it as an impulsive, apolitical act of religious fervor, between characterizing
the revolt as purely Mohammedan ("Let us not romanticize. . . . [I]t is to be
distinguished from slave revolts in colonial times") and political ("there was a
political end in view in connection with these uprisings"). Freyre identifies the
Malês' "supposed slave revolt" as religious but thereupon declares its political
nature, conceding that it "deserves a place among the libertarian revolutions."
On the one hand, these living, fearsome, Muslim slaves appear to be the negative counterpart to the feminized Orient that is mythical and past. In other
words, if the Moorish imperial legacy is the seed for "Luso-Brazilian civilization," that inheritance seems to consist solely in a mythical recollection.[15]
But Freyre's past and present Islams do not neatly oppose one another, for he
intermittently seizes the Malê revolt as further evidence for his celebratory
history of Luso-Brazilian civilization. The Malês come to signify not only that
Brazilian slaves have not degenerated the national body but also the symbolic
return of the nation's "original," estimable Moors. Upsetting his own model
of universalized, Afro-European seigniorial consciousness, Freyre identifies
the Malê revolt with the drive to correct an historical error, the enslavement
of literate Africans by the semiliterate Portuguese slaveholders. With the "return" of the Malês, the original Arabic literary models are brought back within
the grasp of Brazilian society:

> They came from the kingdoms of Wurno, Sokotô, and Gandô, which possessed
> an advanced form of political organization, a well-defined religious literature
> with native works composed in Arabic characters, and an art that was strong
> and original, superior to the anemic Portuguese imitations of Moorish models.
> (Freyre 1946, 315)

Freyre symbolically situates the insurgents as the descendants of the same
Moors to whom he credits the origin for the slack balance of antagonisms
that made the Portuguese softer, gentler colonizers and slaveholders. Indeed,
Freyre's patriarchism—and with this, his longing for the colonial, slavocratic,
pre-industrial era—informs his interpretation of the Mohammedan Fuláhs
and Haussás who led the slave revolts. He writes that "[s]ome were like slave
barracks aristocrats" (Freyre 1946, 310) and indicts the unnatural subordination
of this "truly Malê elite" (308), whom he also identifies as "the African colonists of our country" (308), to their inferior Catholic masters: "Slaves such as
these could not be expected to conform to the role of mere artistic puppets for
the Portuguese, nor could the holy water of Christian baptism all of a sudden

extinguish the Mohammedan fire that was in them" (315). Whereas at other points Freyre characterizes the Malês as an overwhelming "messianic" force in need of containment, he now exalts the Malês' "Mohammedan fire" as the symbol for an irrepressible will to power that revivifies Brazil and resituates it on the path to civilization.

## The Clash of Civilizations

There is a long history of comparative reflection on race and slavery in Brazil and the United States, but an account of the representation of Islam vis-à-vis the two nations' imperial imaginaries is a topic that remains to be explored.[16] Though the paradoxes of Freyre's script reflect the specific legacy of Portuguese colonialism and the aftermath of southern hemisphere geopolitics, it is none-theless tempting to venture some preliminary reflections on Freyre's discussion of the Moors and of Islam in relation to contemporary Western Orientalism and U.S. empire building. As in Freyre's narrative, in the Anglo-Saxon imaginary, a sensual, feminine, pre-Islamic Orient coexists with a present-day, unthink-ing "axis of evil" that threatens Western civilization. By extension, the U.S. media consistently equate Islam with jihad: from the Iranian hostage crisis to the Gulf War, the World Trade Center attacks, the Palestinian *intifada* and the hunts for Osama bin Laden and Saddam Hussein, Muslim "religious hys-teria" and "blind obedience to authority" are invoked to depoliticize defiance of U.S./Western domination. Analyzing the symbolic significance of Islam in the West, Mahmood Mamdani explicates the manipulations behind this representation: "Modern Western thought, strongly influenced by Crusades-era ideas of 'holy war,' has tended to portray *jihad* as an Islamic war against unbelievers, starting with the conquest of Spain in the eighth century" (2004, 50). Middle East experts like Bernard Lewis efface Islam's parallel clerical and political structures to cast Middle Eastern resistance as irrational and unwieldy. By contrast, Freyre's portrayal of the Malê's "Mohammedan fire" is at times reverential, belying an effort to reconcile the Malê revolt with an oscillating narrative of empire between Portuguese and Africans, Christians and Muslims.

A further distinction between Freyrean and Anglo-Saxon Orientalism is the place of Africa in their respective historiographies. Where Western civili-zational history posits the East as the origin of the West—relegating Africa to a "blank darkness"[17]—Freyre casts a certain "Africa" at the beginning and end of his genealogy of Brazilian society. He uses the Moorish empire to displace the historical darkness of black Africa and to establish that part of the African influence on Brazil ensues from the Muslim, Arab, literate Moors. Invoking

Moorish Africa to transform (genetic) black/blank Africa into the African "soul" of white subjects—vis-à-vis the African cultural incorporation he claims legitimates white authority, producing Portuguese colonizers, then Brazilian slaveholders, as Afro-Europeans—Freyre does not so much overturn scientific racism as constitute a symbolically, nongenetically Africanized seigniorial figure as the embodiment of Brazilian hybridity. In other words, he substitutes a symbolic African legacy for sociohistorical blackness in the evolution of the *mestiço* national subject.

The distinction between mystical, literate Moorish Africa and the real, historical Malês is not reliable. Though Freyre dismisses contemporary black writing, his intermittent celebration of Malê literacy counters not only eugenic lamentations about the African introduction into Brazil but also the West's patronizing evaluation of African "ineptitude" by contrast with the fearsome Islamic Orient. For Europe and the United States, Islam is a source of fear that reenacts a prior anxiety about the Islamic empire: "For Europe, Islam was a lasting trauma," symbolizing "terror, devastation, the demonic, hordes of hated Barbarians" (Said 1978, 59). Freyre, for his part, invokes Islam, and the Orient—via a certain Africa—to theorize a national history constituted by the Oriental luxury of the plantation economy and a cultural synthesis based on eroticized systems of domination. If the Malê revolt epitomizes the fearsome antagonism of the enslaved that compels Freyre's inversion of power relations—his insistence upon the slave who recognizes in his master "remote, slightly paler affinities" and his universalized, Afro-European *senhor*—it also instigates his intermittent celebration of the power of black writing. Though he produces a model of seigniorial subjectivity that speaks for both masters and slaves, the Malê, with his *tiá* and his "blue ink," also speaks within his narrative, disrupting it and acting in opposition to it even as Freyre struggles to seize the Malê's power and to insert him into a civilizational trajectory that begins in the East, via Africa, and ends in Brazil.

**Notes**

1. This is the literal translation of *Casa-Grande e Senzala*, though it was translated into English by Samuel Putnam as *The Masters and the Slaves* in 1946.

2. Though Freyre did not coin the term "racial democracy," it has consistently been associated with his work. See César Braga-Pinto, "The Sugar Daddy: Gilberto Freyre and the White Man's Love for Blacks" (2005) for a discussion of racial democracy's origin in the English translation of Freyre's *Sobrados e Mucambos* (1951).

3. Though this chapter focuses on *Casa-Grande e Senzala*, descriptions of the Moorish rule of Portugal and the influence of Islamic slaves in Brazil are found throughout

Freyre's writing, including *Sobrados e Mucambos* (1951), *Inglêses no Brasil* (1948), and *Como e Porque Sou e Não Sou Sociólogo* (1968).

4. For example, see Hermano Vianna's "Cotas da Discôrdia: O risco da reserva de vagas nas universidades do Brasil" (*Quotas of Discord: The Risk of Reserving Spaces in the Universities of Brazil*, June 27, 2004), wherein he warns that affirmative action would threaten Brazil's syncretism, invoking a Freyrean narrative about the singularity of Brazil's mixed-race sensuality to counter the imposition of U.S. identity politics.

5. I have edited Samuel Putnam's translation of Freyre's "intimamente seus" as "their own" to include the word "intimately" ("intimately their own").

6. In *Casa-Grande e Senzala*, Freyre equates bisexuality with the ethnic indeterminacy of the Iberian Peninsula (1984, 7). For Freyre, bisexuality, like other aspects of the Luso-Brazilian's "slack equilibrium of antagonisms," is the legacy of both Moorish domination and the plantation economy. For a discussion of homosexuality in *Casa-Grande e Senzala*, see Braga-Pinto 2005.

7. See Contreiras 2004 for further discussion of the legend of the "enchanted Mooress." I am grateful to Dr. Isabel Cardigos of the University of the Algarve for calling my attention to this text.

8. For further discussion, see Isfahani-Hammond 2008.

9. For further discussion of Freyre's dismissal of Afro-Brazilian writing in relation to eugenic theories and his exclusionary hybridism, see Isfahani-Hammond 2008.

10. Estranged from their African roots, the quadroon establishment is doubly illegitimate because their power derives from their artificial whiteness. Like Freyre, Carpentier constitutes the sociopolitical aspirations of African descendants—especially *mixed-race* Afrrican descendants—as indicative of false blackness whereas authentic black power is metaphysical and, paradoxically, grounded in nature.

11. The *noiriste* dictatorship casts itself as slave and master in one, the embodiment of both the slave's desire for liberty and revenge and the administrative body of the controlling master (Kaussen 2005). *Noirisme* emerged in response to the U.S. occupation of Haiti between 1898 and 1902, just as for Afro-Cubanists, the mythic black "underworld" was a rebuke against Yankee imperialism, "the antidote to Wall Street"—for Kutzinski, "the only Cuban space seemingly beyond the reach of the U.S." (145)—and Freyre's celebration of Brazilian assimilationism proposes an alternative to North Americanization.

12. Xangô is perhaps the most popular of the Orixás, Afro-Brazilian religious deities. Candomblé is an Afro-Brazilian syncretic religious tradition. *Babalorixás* are spiritual leaders of candomblé.

13. In addition to dissociating African "survivals" from sociohistorical black subjects, the supernatural quality of blackness effaces Freyre's totalizing incorporation. Indeed, his contact with *xangôs, candomblé*, and *babalorixás* suggests that his assimilation of African culture is a spell cast by blacks, like the initiation into candomblé through which the "doors of Afro-Brazilian secrets" open to him ("Como e Porque Escrevi Casa-Grande e Senzala," 1968, 133).

14. I am using my translation of "tanto manuscrito escrito por escravo" (Freyre 1984, 299) as "so many manuscripts written by slaves" rather than Samuel Putnam's "such literary ability on the part of the slave" (Freyre 1946, 299).

15. I am grateful to Paulo Gabriel Hilu da Rocha for suggesting this opposition between "feminized, positive" and "negative, masculine" Orients, and for helping me articulate the unfamiliar, conflicted place of the East in a narrative that celebrates Catholicism as the umbrella for synthesizing differences.

16. As Brazil and the United States were the two largest plantation societies in the Americas, analysis of slavery and race relations in the two polities has an extensive tradition, from the late-nineteenth-century pro-slavery advocacy of Lothrop Stoddard and Madison Grant to the abolitionist manifesto of Joaquim Nabuco, to the twentieth-century cross-dissemination of scientific race theories and the pervasive trend to think of Brazil's positive resolution of racial difference in contrast with the haunting of slavery and perpetuation of legal then de facto segregation in the United States. Although the pervasive analysis from the late nineteenth century onward has been that Brazil had a relatively gentler slavery economy that led to the formation of a racial democracy, unlike the United States' harsh slavery system and rigid racial stratification, recent studies have deconstructed the myth of Brazilian racial democracy and the concomitant myth of the United States' singularly cruel regime. See Hanchard 1994, Isfahani-Hammond 2007, and Telles 2004.

17. Mamdani (2004) points to the "blank darkness" of Western civilizational history—comprising Africa, the pre-Columbian Americas, and the lands of the Pacific, excepting of course Egypt and Ethiopia (28–29)—said to lack history because it had neither great texts nor great monuments: "In other words, the notion of the 'West' went alongside two peripheries: whereas 'the Orient' was visible, Africa and the others were simply blanked out into a historical darkness" (29).

## References

Alencar, José de. (1865) 1942. *Iracema.* Oxford, OH: Miami University Press.

Avellaneda, Gertrúdis Gómez de. (1841) 1993. *Sab.* Lewiston, NY: East Mellen Press.

Azevedo, Celia Maria Marinho de. 1995. *Abolitionism in the United States and Brazil.* New York: Garland Publishing.

Benzaquen de Araújo, Ricardo. 1994. *Guerra e Paz em Casa-Grande e Senzala e a Obra de Gilberto Freyre nos Anos 30.* Rio de Janeiro: Editora Nova Fronteira.

Braga-Pinto, César. 2005. "The Sugar Daddy: Gilberto Freyre and the White Man's Love for Blacks." In *The Masters and the Slaves: Plantation Relations and Mestizaje in American Imaginaries,* ed. Alexandra Isfahani-Hammond. New York: Palgrave Macmillan.

Browning, Barbara. 1998. *Infectious Rhythm: Metaphors of Contagion and the Spread of African Culture.* New York: Routledge.

Canclini, Nestor García. 1995. *Hybrid Cultures: Strategies for Leaving and Entering Modernity.*Minneapolis: University of Minnesota Press.

Carneiro, Edison. 1950. *Antologia do Negro Brasileiro.* Rio de Janeiro: Edições de Ouro.

Carpentier, Alejo. 1994. *El Reino de Este Mundo.* Rio Piedras: Editorial de la Universidad de Puerto Rico. Originally published in 1949.

Clifford, James. 1986. "On Ethnographic Allegory." *Writing Culture: The Poetics and Politics of Ethnography.* Berkeley: University of California Press.

Contreiras, Maria da Rocha. 2004. "As Lendas das Mouras Encantadas." Unpublished
  dissertation, Universidade do Algarve.
Costa, Sérgio. 2002. "A Construção Sociológica da Raça no Brasil." *Estudos Afro-Asiáti-
  cos* 24 (January–April).
Dash, Michael. 1998. *The Other America: Caribbean Literature in a New World Context.*
  Charlottesville: University Press of Virginia.
Derrida, Jacques. (1974) 1998. "The Violence of the Letter." *Of Grammatology.* Baltimore:
  Johns Hopkins University Press.
Freyre, Gilberto. (1933) 1946. *The Masters and the Slaves.* Trans. Samuel Putnam. New
  York: Alfred A. Knopf.
———. 1947."Prefácio." In *Poemas Negros,* by Jorge de Lima. Rio de Janeiro: Lacerda
  Editora.
———. 1948. *Inglêses no Brasil.* Rio de Janeiro: José Olympio.
———. 1951. *Sobrados e Mucambos.* Rio de Janeiro: Livraria José Olympio Editora.
———. (1955) 1962. "Reinterpretando José de Alencar." *Vida, Forma e Cor.* Rio de Janeiro:
  José Olympio.
———. 1968. "Como e porque escrevi Casa-Grande e Senzala." In *Como e Porque Sou e
  Não Sou Sociólogo.* Brasília: Editora Universidade de Brasília.
———. 1968. *Como e Porque Sou e Não Sou Sociólogo.* Brasília: Editora Universidade de
  Brasília.
———. (1933) 1984. *Casa-Grande e Senzala.* Rio de Janeiro: José Olympio.
Haberly, David. 1972. "Abolitionism in Brazil: Anti-Slavery and Anti-Slave." *Luso-
  Brazilian Review* 9(2): 30–45.
Hanchard, Michael. 1994. *Orpheus and Power.* Princeton, NJ: Princeton University Press.
Hesse, Barnor. 2002. "Forgotten like a Bad Dream: Atlantic Slavery and the Ethics
  of Postcolonial Memory." In *Relocating Postcolonialism,* ed. David Theo Goldberg.
  Oxford, UK: Blackwell.
Isfahani-Hammond, Alexandra. 2005. "Writing Brazilian Culture." In *The Masters and
  the Slaves: Plantation Relations and Mestizaje in American Imaginaries,* ed. Alexan-
  dra Isfahani-Hammond. New York: Palgrave Macmillan, 2005.
———. 2008. *White Negritude: Race, Writing and Brazilian Cultural Identity.* New York:
  Palgrave Macmillan.
Kaussen, Valerie. 2005. "Race, Nation and the Symbolics of Servitude in Haitian Noir-
  isme." In *The Masters and the Slaves: Plantation Relations and Mestizaje in American
  Imaginaries* ed. Alexandra Isfahani-Hammond. New York: Palgrave Macmillan.
Kutzinski, Vera M. 1993. *Sugar's Secrets: Race and the Erotics of Cuban Nationalism.*
  Charlottesville: University Press of Virginia.
Lima, Jorge de. 1947. "Poemas Negros." In *Obra Completa.* Rio de Janeiro: José Aguilar.
Mamdani, Mahmood. 2004. *Good Muslim, Bad Muslim.* New York: Random House.
Mota, Carlos Guilherme. 1977. *Ideologia da Cultura Brasileira.* São Paulo: Editora Atica.
Nabuco, Joaquim. 1988. *O Abolicionismo.* Recife: Editora Massangana.
Nascimento, Abdias do. 1968. *O Negro Revoltado.* Rio de Janeiro: Edições GRD.
Ortiz, Fernando. 1998. *Hampa Afrocubana: Los Negros Brujos; Apuntos para un Estudio
  de Etnologia Criminal.* Miami: Ediciones Universal. Originally published in 1906.

Pallares-Burke, Maria Lúcia Garcia. 2005. *Gilberto Freyre: Um Vitoriano dos Trópicos.* São Paulo: UNESP.

Ramos, Arthur. 1950. "Os Estudos Negros e a Escola de Nina Rodrigues." In *Antologia do Negro Brasileiro,* ed. Edison Carneiro. Rio de Janeiro: Edições de Ouro.

Reis, João José. 1993. *Slave Rebellion in Brazil: The Muslim Uprising of 1835 in Bahia.* Baltimore: Johns Hopkins University Press.

Rodrigues, Raimundo Nina. 1935. *O Animismo Fetichista dos Negros Baianos.* Rio de Janeiro: Civilização Brasileira.

———. 1988. *Os Africanos no Brasil.* São Paulo: Nacional.

Romero, Silvio. 1950. "O negro—objeto de ciência." In *Antologia do Negro Brasileiro,* ed. Edison Carneiro. Rio de Janeiro: Edições de Ouro.

Said, Edward. *Orientalism.* 1978. New York: Random House.

Schwarcz, Lilia Moritz. 1993. *O Espetáculo das Raças: Cientistas, Instituições e Questão Racial no Brasil, 1870–1930.* São Paulo: Companhia das Letras.

Sommer, Doris. 1991. *Foundational Fictions.* Berkeley: University of California Press.

Telles, Edward. 2004. *Race in Another America.* Princeton, NJ: Princeton University Press.

# 8

# Islamic Transnationalism and Anti-Slavery Movements
## The Malê Rebellion as Debated by Brazil's Press, 1835–1838

*José T. Cairus*
*Translated by Eduardo Viana da Silva*

The slave rebellion staged by African Muslims in 1835 in Salvador, Bahia, had an enormous impact on Brazilian society. Cairus looks specifically at the coverage of the uprising in the Brazilian press. The national debate that followed the rebellion occurred against a background of internal political turmoil and increasing pressure from the British to end the transatlantic slave trade. The debate reveals the Brazilian elites' concerns about the future of the new nation, which was at the time economically dependent on slave labor. It also unveiled the tragic vicissitudes of the slave trade through the lens of captive Africans' struggle for freedom as well as their connections to Muslim political enlightenment and militancy in West Africa.

∾

## Introduction

In 1835, in the city of Salvador, the capital of the province of Bahia, a few hundred Africans challenged paradigms established by centuries of slavery in Brazil. Their leaders were clerics affiliated with revivalist Islam in West Africa, as confirmed by Salvador's chief of police after the rebellion, who stated, "There are [West African] scholars among them teaching and masterminding the rebellion" ("Relato" 1835). What the police chief was partially acknowledging was the fact that these Muslim leaders of the slave uprising were culturally sophisticated individuals and polyglots who had had experience as adults leading political change and social uprisings on their home continent before being captured and forced into slavery in Brazil. These realities contradicted Brazilian racist images of "beasts of burden" brought to perform hard work in European colonies. Moreover, they further challenged the system by refusing to be assimilated or become "ladino," as Europeanized slaves were called in the jargon of the slave trade (Klein 2010, 13). Assimilation into the master's milieu could sometimes mitigate the severity of the ordeal endured by Africans who were kept at the lowest rank of colonial society. But the Muslims in Bahia rejected what Orlando Patterson calls "slave social death" and enthusiastically preached the Islamic gospel among their brethren (Patterson 1982, passim). In the trial that followed the rebellion, the dialogue between the leader Licutan, also known by his Christian name Pacífico (the peaceful), and the Brazilian judge best illustrates the resilience of Muslim identity. After being ordered by the judge to state his name, Licutan replied: "My name is Bilal." The judge became angry because he thought Licutan was lying. The Muslim leader then defiantly answered, "It is true that my name is Licutan, but I can take whatever name I want" ("Devassa" 1968, 84). In fact, Licutan subtly declared his identity by giving a quintessentially Muslim name in a country where Catholicism was the official religion and Africans were forcibly baptized through the adoption of Christian names.

The historical setting of the slave rebellion was shaped by centuries of slave trade that brought the political and religious movements of the *dar-al Islam* (abode of Islam) to Brazil. The events in Bahia during the first decades of the 1800s thus illustrate like no other the experience of Muslims in the history of slavery in the Americas. But the Muslim experience in Brazil also reveals a paradox created by a system based on violence and exploitation of man by man. If the spiral of violence unleashed by militant Islam contributed to fueling the slave trade either in West Africa or in the Atlantic, the very jihads themselves gave captives a powerful ideology with which to fight slavery in Brazil.

### The Malê Revolt

The beginning of the nineteenth century brought many changes to Brazil, with the nation gaining independence in 1822 and subsequently establishing an imperial monarchy under the rule of the House of Braganza. After the initial period of turmoil that preceded independence, Brazil experienced a decade of relative stability that ended with the abdication of its first emperor in 1831. During this time, however, the demand for African slaves remained constant

(Mishida 2003, 244). The system of slavery established by Portuguese colonizers in the middle of the sixteenth century made Brazil entirely dependent on
slave labor continuously brought over through the transatlantic slave trade.
Salvador, Bahia, had been the capital of Portuguese Brazil from 1549 to 1763
and was the last city to accept Brazil's independence from Portugal after Don
Pedro I declared the founding of the Brazilian empire in Rio de Janeiro in 1822.

Change and instability were not much different in other parts of the Atlantic
world. In Spanish America, colonies struggled for independence as Europe
suffered the effects of the Napoleonic Wars (1803–1815). In the region known
as Central Sudan, which corresponds to Nigeria today, society was also rapidly
changing due the collapse of local political systems under attack of a militant
Islam.[1] The intense warfare that ravaged Central Sudan in the first decades of the
1800s produced a large number of prisoners of war, many of them Muslims,
who were enslaved, sent to the coast, and traded to Brazil. So African captives
arrived in Brazil already politicized. The province of Bahia, in northeast Brazil, received the bulk of enslaved Muslims due to its trade network with slave
entrepôts along the coast of the Bight of Benin (Lovejoy 1994, 2). In Salvador,
the capital of Bahia, as well as in the province's hinterland, these Muslims became protagonists in several revolts during the first four decades of the 1800s.

The last and largest rebellion occurred in 1835. It began with a group of Africans who were sharing a meal in the basement of a house in downtown Salvador
on the evening of January 24. They were having the *iftar*, which is the evening
meal that breaks the daily fast during the month of Ramadan. For that group
of Africans, the date on the Islamic calendar was Ramadan 24, 1250 AH. That
evening, they were also making preparations to celebrate the Lailat al-Qadr
(Night of Power). According to Islamic tradition, this is one of the last ten
odd nights in the month of Ramadan. It marks the beginning of the Quranic
revelation, and Muslims spend it in meditation and prayer. The Gregorian
calendar only mattered for those African Muslims because January 25 was the
Catholic holy day of Nossa Senhora da Guia (Our Lady of Guidance), which
fell on a Sunday in 1835. They plotted an insurrection for the next morning,
when they expected to catch white Catholics off guard as they were celebrating their holy day.

Employing dates from different calendars symbolized the imposed coexistence of two worlds that were in opposition because of slavery, two worlds that
were about to collide. The plot was given away and a police patrol raided a house
where plotters were based, interrupting the celebration of Lailat al-Qadr. As
the fight ensued, the Muslims gathered at the house were forced to initiate the
rebellion before the planned time. They attacked government buildings and

facilities housing the provincial security forces. Out of the few hundred Africans that fought in the streets of Salvador, around seventy were killed. The rebels were finally defeated after a prolonged battle that lasted until dawn; however, through their actions, they paralyzed and spread panic in the second-largest city of the Brazilian empire. For this, they were sentenced to incarceration, whipping, deportation, and death. This group of Africans, formed by slaves and freed slaves, became known in Bahia by the ethnonym "Malê." During the 1830s in Bahia, this denomination was used to identify Muslims who were brought to the Bight of Benin in general and Yoruba Muslims in particular. "Malê" was also a diasporic version of the original "Imale," which became synonym for "Muslim" in Yorubaland and other parts of West Africa (Law 1993, 68, 85, 86).

## The Brazilian Press at the Time of the Malê Revolt

In order to analyze the impact of the "Malê revolt" on the Brazilian press during the period 1835–1838, I conducted research on Rare Collections Section of newspapers held at Biblioteca Nacional do Rio Janeiro (Rio de Janeiro National Library). I selected articles dealing with topics related to slavery and the slave trade at the time of the Muslim rebellion in Salvador. The newspapers are from different parts of Brazil, including Rio de Janeiro and the capitals of other provinces, as well as towns in the countryside. Newspapers were the most effective mode of communication at the time, and perhaps it is this that explains the high number that were in circulation at the time of the Muslim uprising. Furthermore, newspapers enjoyed a great degree of freedom after the right to free press was granted in 1821, prior to Brazil's independence. Rio de Janeiro alone had 2,000 newspapers in circulation between 1808 and 1896. The province of Bahia had around 700 between 1811 and 1899 (Galvao 1974, 15). Although many of these newspapers were short-lived, Brazil's press in the nineteenth century was nonetheless impressive.

The press constituted a public space for socialization and conflict. It represented the views of a variety of political groups with different ideologies, and its content ranged from anonymous letters to personal accusations. The line between public and private debate often became muddled. It was not so much a question of censorship as one of a sheer lack of democratic debate due to the despotism of the political system. The main newspapers of that time were all familiar with the rhetoric used, whether they were of academic, religious, or no affiliation. There was not a well-informed public opinion that could influence debates. Instead, there were personal duels among newspaper writers (Carvalho 1998, 12). Newspapers in the nineteenth century were accessible to only a small literate elite. The press promoted liberal ideas and a new political vocabulary. But the news reached other segments of society through conversations, discussions, and rumors that would take over the cities (Basile 2000, 206).

Newspapers became a battlefield for different ideologies, shaped by specific groups' interests (Basile 2000, 206). The political atmosphere of the time was particularly charged. Brazil was being temporarily governed by the regency that followed the abdication of Pedro I in 1831. In the absence of a strong executive as personified by the emperor, political and regional rivalries grew strong, provoking a long period of anarchy throughout the nation. To make matters worse, Brazil was economically dependent on the British, who increasingly pressed the Brazilian government to outlaw the slave trade. During this period, political views and ideologies became more radical. Political parties used a variety of media outlets to promote their ideologies, including the press.

The fear of "Africanization" of the Brazilian population worried the elites who were not benefiting directly from the slave trade. In 1823, the leading Brazilian politician José Bonifácio, who was instrumental in the process of independence, claimed:

> It is more than time to end the barbaric and butcher-like traffic of slaves. It is also time to gradually erase the last vestiges of slavery among us in order to have a homogeneous nation in a few generations. Without this, we will never be entirely free, respectable, and happy. It is necessary to put a stop to this physical and civil heterogeneity; we have to wisely combine discordant and contrary elements. By "amalgamating" so many different metals, we aim to have a "whole" homogeneous and compact product, something that does not crumble when it is touched by a minor political upheaval. (Silva 2000, 24–25)

The "Patriarch of Independence" was hoping to make the Brazilian population more homogeneous by ending the slave trade. His analogy between racial and social inequalities of the population and chemical processes refers to his mineralogy studies in France and Germany. Given his long experience living in Europe, José Bonifácio understood progress as occurring only within a uniform civil society. According to him, "not only is the slave inferior to his slave master, but blacks are also inferior to whites" (Silva 2000, 24–25).

## The Revolt's Aftermath in the Brazilian Press

*1835*

The February 10, 1835, edition of the Rio de Janeiro newspaper *Jornal do Commercio* included the report of Salvador's police chief, Francisco Gonçalves

Martins, describing the slave rebellion that took place on the night of January 24 ("Relato" 1835, front page). The report was originally addressed to the president of the province, Francisco de Souza Martins, and the article may have been originally published in *Diário da Bahia* only six days after the event. In any case, the document became important because it was the first official report made by an authority who had directly participated in the event. It was published in other northeastern newspapers, including Pernambuco's *Quotidiana Fidedigna* on February 11, 1835, and Maranhão's *Echo do Norte* on March 6, 1835. It is important to note that news from the rebellion had a greater impact on Rio de Janeiro and on the northeastern provinces of Brazil than in the southeast, including São Paulo. Rio and the northeast had a high concentration of enslaved Africans, which may explain why they took such interest in the events in Bahia.

Gonçalves Martins's report became the foundation for future interpretations of the Muslim uprising in 1835. His report made it possible to glean details of what happened in Salvador on the night of January 24. The document offers some important clues: the fanatical determination of outnumbered and outgunned rebels fighting against government troops, the existence of a sophisticated plan, the Hausa-Yoruba alliance, the ostensive presence of Islam, and the rebels' hostility toward other Africans. The report also described how the slave trade had a direct effect on the ethnic makeup of the city of Salvador and its hinterlands. In the following excerpt, the police chief highlights the ethnic alliance, Muslim literacy, and the demographic shift that made the Yorubas the majority among the slave population in Bahia: "They are able to read and write in an unknown alphabet that resembles Arabic, used by the *Ussás*, who have now combined with the *Nagôs*. The former nation was the one that in another time came to this province and was later replaced by the *Nagôs*" ("Relato" 1835). Hausa Muslims disembarked in great numbers before the 1820s as a direct result of jihads in Central Sudan, and they had a prominent role in leading slave rebellions at the time. The Yorubas, who in Brazil were known as "*Nagôs*," replaced the Hausas not only in numbers but as leaders and rank-and-file rebels in the slave uprisings after the 1820s (Law 1997). This change in ethnic makeup reflected the expansion of warfare in the Yorubaland. Such state of permanent conflict produced a large number of captive Yorubas (mostly non-Muslims) who were sent to Bahia through the transatlantic connection, linking the Bight of Benin to Salvador (Reis and Mamigonian 2004, 80). Yet the "Yorubarization" of Bahia's slave population did not change the prevalent pattern of rebellion that was previously established by Hausa Muslims. Instead, during the early decades of the 1800s, in Salvador and its environs, more than in any other region in the Americas, the presence of militant Islam became a synonym for relentless resistance to slavery.

The report goes on to emphasize the strong role of religion in the rebellion. According to the chief of police, "Many books have been found, some of which are religious in nature, incorporating verses, especially from the Quran. It is clear that that religion has a played a role in the uprising" ("Relato" 1835). Many rebels knew Arabic, and others attended Quranic schools organized by clerics (Rodrigues 1935, 53). In the 1820s, scores of young Yorubas converted to Islam in Bahia due to the active proselytism of Muslim clerics. This phenomenon, however, could be seen as part of a broader process of Islamization among Yorubas that was occurring simultaneously on both sides of the Atlantic (Rodrigues 1935, 79).

The report reveals other issues as well, for instance, that the British merchants who lived in Salvador may have supported the African Muslim rebellion: "It was also noticed that a large number of rebels were slaves of Englishmen, and they were better armed. This is probably due to the fact that less precaution is taken among these foreigners, who are accustomed to living among freemen" ("Relato" 1835). Such suspicions were based on two premises. One was the great degree of involvement in the rebellion of Yoruba Muslims belonging to the British merchants. The other premise was rooted in conspiracy theories of the time, which accused the British of encouraging slave rebellions in order to weaken Brazilian resistance to ending the slave trade. In any case, the Yorubas held by the British were devout Muslims. They observed Islamic holy days by attending religious ceremonies in a small mosque that was built in the backyard of the house of one of the British masters and displayed an intolerant attitude toward non-Muslim Africans. Such outward demonstrations of faith, considering their lack of rights within a slave society, made them victims of persecution by local authorities (Cairus 2002, 191–192). Brazil's Constitution of 1824 established Catholicism as the official religion of the empire. Other Christian denominations followed by free persons had the status of cults and their rituals were performed in secrecy. Non-Christian religions were explicitly banned, which made any public display of faith performed by Muslim slaves a crime.[2] Yet no concrete evidence was found of a possible collaboration between British merchants and Muslims in the uprising. But the rise of quotidian tensions between African Muslims and local authorities certainly contributed to the rebellion's outbreak.

On the same day that the aforementioned article was published in *Jornal do Commercio*, the Rio de Janeiro newspaper *Pão D'Assucar* reported a letter from a witness of the rebellion (*Pão D'Assucar* 1835). The anonymous letter revealed important details of the rebellion on the night of January 24, 1835. The secrecy surrounding the event is once again highlighted:

> Rebels would set fire to the lower part of the city. Once people started gathering there, as usually happens, the massacre would then take place on the defenseless and unprepared crowd. To assure the success of this mission, they kept the plan a secret. Only on the night of the uprising would all black non-members of their group become aware of their plan (*Pão D'Assucar* 1835).

The idea of Africans plotting against the slave system was always a major concern. It is possible that the secrecy surrounded the rebels' plans, their audacity in plotting against their masters, and even their ability to mobilize non-Muslims at the last minute accentuated the desire to punish them in order to set an example for the majority of non-Muslim Africans in Bahia.

The author of the anonymous letter went on describing the clothing and weapons used by the rebels: "They arrived with shaved heads and wearing similar clothing. Some had papers that I suppose were speeches or amulets. They carried swords and wore silver rings around their left thumbs" (*Pão D'Assucar* 1835). The Yoruba historian Samuel Johnson described the silver ring called *kende* as a symbol of distinction wore by jihadist warriors in their conquest of northern Yorubaland. This symbol consisted of two big rings, one for the thumb and another for the middle or the ring finger of the left hand. Members of this brotherhood greeted each other by touching their rings and saying *"O re kende si mi okan na ni wa"* (He greeted me as a *kende*, together we are one) (Johnson 1937, 194).

The anonymous observer also noted the shaved heads of the Africans. This was possibly part of a warfare tradition brought from Central Sudan jihads, where professional warriors (*jarumai*) had long hair and Muslim leaders shaved their heads (Last 1988, 184). Finally, the observer mentioned amulets used by the rebels, which seem to appear in all reports of the rebellion. The use of talismans or *gris-gris* by Muslims was a common practice in several parts of the Islamic world (Diouf 2004, 81). In Central Sudan, identical amulets were used by jihadists. Clerics involved in the war effort crafted amulets known as *ondè yfunpá*, among other war amulets (Danmole 1992, 52). These talismans had inscriptions reproducing Quranic verses and esoteric formulas written in Arabic as well as in *Ajami* (local languages written in Arabic); the use of amulets by the faithful in both Central Sudan and Bahia aimed to boost their power.

Lastly, the symbolism described by the anonymous author as well as the distinct forms of organization that I found throughout the trial records produced after the rebellion may indicate the existence of Sufi guilds, a type of organization similar to those found in the Islamic world. Expressions such as "partners," "non-partners," and descriptions of rituals of initiation not found in orthodox Islam suggest the existence of Sufi brotherhoods, among many other Islamic traditions brought over by the Muslims and recreated in Bahia (Dobronravin 2004, 15).

The newspaper *Astro de Minas* published an article on March 14, 1835, titled "Reflections on the insurrection of black Africans that broke out on the night of January 24, 1835" ("Reflexões sobre a sublevação dos negros Africanos, que rompeo na noute de 24 para 25 do corrente [1835]"). This newspaper was published in the town of São João Del-Rey, in the heart of the mining country of the southeastern province of Minas Gerais, which was heavily populated by Africans (Bergad 2006, 105–107). The article establishes a causal relationship between the transatlantic slave trade and the rebellion in Salvador. The author regrets the arrival of thousands of "barbaric" Africans every year and criticizes Brazilians who have a hostile attitude toward Europeans. According to him, Brazil should have followed the example of the United States in encouraging European immigration. He believes that blacks would feel intimidated if the majority of the Brazilian population were white. The article praises the law ending the slave trade approved on November 7, 1831, and criticizes authorities as well as the population for complying with the ongoing illegal slave trade. In the author's view, every African who landed in Brazil was a potential enemy in future rebellions. The newspaper suggests that the Brazilian government should make efforts to create a colony for freed slaves in Africa. The article warns that Brazilians are "calmly sleeping on top of a volcano that could erupt at any time."

Slaves living in urban spaces were also the subject of concern. Slaves enjoyed more autonomy in urban areas, which made it difficult for masters to control them. In 1835, the minister of justice, Euzébio de Queiroz, wrote a letter ("Reflexões" 1835) to the chief of police in Rio de Janeiro expressing his concern and asking for "tight control in order to prevent slaves from participating in conspiracies aiming at freedom that could jeopardize social peace, as in the case of Bahia" (Chalhoub 1990, 188).

The slave population of Bahia increased significantly in the first third of the nineteenth century. The city of Salvador received around seven thousand Africans per year, according to a conservative assessment (Reis 1993, 6). Slaves made up 40 percent of the city's population and Africans alone made up 60 percent of the slave force (Schwartz 2006, 249). In many cities in Brazil, the distinction between slaves and freed men was not always clear. Thus, whites tended to live in a permanent state of fear of blacks, which explains why control and repression were major concerns in the "Reflexões" letter. Euzébio de Queiroz acknowledges that "Africans were humans, thus, they had aspirations for freedom and control." He went on to observe that "our blacks are not stupid" and concluded with a warning about the danger of blacks being controlled by someone "possessing more intelligence than a barbarian," which sounds like a clear reference to the African Muslims in Bahia ("Reflexões" 1835).

On March 21, 1835, the newspaper *Jornal do Commercio* published a message from the Provincial Assembly of Rio de Janeiro: "The slave rebellion threatens not only Bahia, but also other provinces and therefore we cannot ignore it" ("Mensagem" 1835). The central government felt threatened by the slave uprising in Bahia. The danger was not only in the "beautiful portion of the empire," as Bahia was known, but also in other provinces, including Rio de Janeiro. This concern with the imperial capital was justified on the grounds of Rio's relatively close commercial and political connections to Bahia and by both cities' having vast African enslaved populations.

The members of parliament chose freed Africans as "scapegoats." The Provincial Assembly's message also raised concerns regarding the dangers represented by the propagation of "Haitian doctrines" among slaves in Brazil. The slave insurrection in Haiti (1791–1804) haunted slave owners throughout the Americas during the nineteenth century. As the only successful slave rebellion leading to state takeover and independence from colonial masters in the history of slavery in the Americas, the example set by Haitian rebels were often cited by Brazilian authorities. The Muslim uprising unleashed widespread panic that generated fear of combined revolts that would bring together slaves in Bahia and Rio de Janeiro (Brazil 1909, 70–91). The province of Rio de Janeiro sent police forces to Bahia and set up a blockade to prevent Africans sold by northeastern provinces from entering Rio de Janeiro without official authorization. Any African caught trying to break the blockade would be arrested and deported to other provinces. The slave trade became an issue of national security, demanding from the authorities "justice and energy" (*Jornal do Commercio* 1935).

The newspaper *Recopilador Mineiro,* from the province of Minas Gerais, published an article from the Bahian newspaper *Astro da Bahia* on April 24, 1835 ("Decreto" 1835). Like other journalists at the time, the author uses the press and the impact of the Malê revolt to criticize slavery and to promote his ideas. Slave traders were called "horrific enemies of our society" and African slaves are compared to "bloodthirsty beasts." The author based his analysis of slavery on European and American intellectuals affiliated with the Enlightenment such as Charles Dunoyer and Thomas Jefferson. At the end of the article, the author concludes that "slavery corrupts and depraves Brazilian society."

The *Recopilador Mineiro* on May 2, 1835, also reported that local businesses in Salvador were paralyzed and the population was in a constant state of alert ("Post Scriptum" 1835). The news was obtained through a letter written by a merchant in Salvador and sent to the newspaper by the captain of the British brig *Trafalgar*. In the column "Bahia 29 de Março," from the same newspaper, it was announced that Bahia had suspended civil rights for thirty days. The decision was taken by the president of the province and aimed to give local authorities power to arrest suspicious individuals and search homes without a warrant. This decision caused great surprise and made the population uneasy. Furthermore, the dramatic tone accused the rebels of plotting to overthrow the monarchy. The article ends with a pessimistic remark: "Given the circumstances, we do not know how this situation will turn out."

The July 25, 1835, edition of *O Echo do Norte,* from the province of Maranhão, published nine laws, two of which related to the uprising in Bahia ("Bahia" 1835). The first law suspended civil rights. The second authorized the provincial government to deport freed African rebels and foreigners suspected of supporting uprisings. Yet in the same edition, the newspaper announced the execution of five Africans found guilty for participating in the Malê revolt. They were sentenced on May 14, 1835, and they did not appeal. The five rebels were initially condemned to execution by hanging, but the justice was unable to find executioners to carry out the task. The authorities tried without success to recruit executioners in prisons. In the end, the sentence was carried out by a military firing squad. The rebels' solidarity and perhaps their power of intimidation forced authorities to give the Muslims a soldier's death rather than hanging them like ordinary criminals.[3]

The journalist warned the readers about the possibility of riots after the sentences were carried out. This represented the final act of the Muslim uprising, but the African Muslim ringleaders were still at large and remained untouched by authorities (Cairus 2002, 54). The rebels' execution in Salvador did not eliminate the collective fear. The Rio de Janeiro newspaper *O Fluminense* reported a slave rebellion planned for October 3 in Salvador. But the plot was discovered, preventing the Yoruba from staging another revolt. Whether these rumors were real or only the product of collective paranoia, Africans in general emerged as a serious threat to society and fear spread throughout Brazil. In the province of Pará, in the Brazilian Amazon, the commander of the naval forces declared "Africans declared war on whites" ("Coluna Bahia" 1835). The article also criticized local judges and police for the supposedly high degree of freedom enjoyed by Africans in the city of Salvador. The author accuses the authorities of being too confident in slaves' submission to their masters and warned of the risks of such misplaced confidence.

It is true that local authorities in Rio de Janeiro kept the slave population under tighter control (Chalhoub 1990, 66). But it would be misguided to believe that authorities in Salvador did not have an accurate perception of the situation as the article suggests. A few years earlier, in 1830, a slave revolt had taken place in Salvador and the local authorities had been able to contain the rebellion. After all, slave uprisings in Bahia dated back to the colonial period. Furthermore, Rio de Janeiro and Salvador shared very similar demographic patterns with regards to the high number of Africans brought by the slave trade. But in contrast to Salvador, the absence of slave rebellions in Rio was remarkable. The phenomenon of slave rebelliousness, therefore, cannot be explained solely by the high percentage of Africans living in the cities. Rather, the reasons behind the state of persistent rebelliousness in Salvador lay in the background of the Africans sent to Bahia.

*1836–1837*

The August 5, 1836, edition of the Rio de Janeiro newspaper *O Atlante* published an article that was part of a campaign against the slave trade and in favor of deporting Africans back to Africa ("Africanos" 1936). The story used terms like "barbarian slaves" and "semi-barbarian freed slaves," which correspond to the traditional categorization of slaves as *ladinos* and *boçais*. For the author, the process of "civilizing" Africans would only be complete with the full assimilation of Western values imposed by the masters. But the great commotion felt by Brazilians perhaps could be understood in light of the fact that African Muslims challenged some of the basic principles of Western slavery. The British anthropologist Jack Goody has argued that African Muslims in Brazil belonging to a culture of written tradition based on Islamic values had what he calls "technologies of the intellect." He claims that Islam provided rebels with an intellectual apparatus of resistance, as demonstrated by the weight and scope of religion in the Muslim uprising. Jack Goody concludes by comparing the role of Islam in Brazil to that of the Enlightenment for French revolutionaries in 1789 (Goody 2000, 197).

The newspaper described negotiations between Brazil, Great Britain, and the United States regarding the deportation of Africans to Sierra Leone and Liberia. This would mitigate the potential for rebellion and would give Brazil the opportunity to receive immigration of "worthwhile" people. The British offered the island of Trinidad in the Caribbean as a place to host the deported Africans, and the United States offered Liberia through the Philanthropic Society. The newspaper, however, argued that none of these alternatives were convenient for Brazil. In any case, more than one hundred freed Africans accused of being involved in the Malê revolt were deported to Lagos and Dahomey in West Africa. A Brazilian ship left the Africans in the Upper Guinea at their request, where they were received by a *sovah* (prince of the land). A community was rapidly built by the returnees thanks to the presence of carpenters and other skilled workers among the deported Africans. Given the success of this deportation, other Africans in Brazil returned to their continent on their own, resulting in the issuing of more than four hundred passports. The article referred to approximately three trips by ship to the same area in the coast of Africa "where Africans lived peacefully, safe and free." The author suggested the creation of Brazilian colonies in Africa as a strategy to get a rid of undesirable Africans and to use them to promote "our businesses and our new industry" in the region. In fact, the Brazilian government planned on establishing a colony for freed slaves in Angola ("Africanos" 1836). A Brazilian consul was sent to Luanda in 1834, but he was prevented from landing by Portuguese authorities, and plans to establish a colony in Angola were put to an end (Verger 1987, 361–362).

On July 8, 1837, the Rio de Janeiro newspaper *Seminário de Cincinato* published the first article of a series which compared African slavery and European immigration as solutions for solving Brazil's labor shortage. The title is suggestive: "Does slavery benefit Brazil or is it dangerous for the country? Is European colonization harmful or helpful for Brazil? "("A escravatura convém ao Brasil ou é-lhe perigosa" 1837). The author expressed his concern about the tension inherent to the master-slave relationship: "Could a slave befriend his master? How could a slave love the one that dominates him? He certainly has a terrible hatred against his master. . . . The examples are here to attest to what we have said. How many times have we seen slave masters being assassinated by their slaves?" ("A escravatura convém ao Brasil ou é-lhe perigosa" 1837).

## Conclusion

On August 7, 1838, the Bahian newspaper *Correio Mercantil* reported an attempt to steal arms from Jiquitaia Fortress, which was disclosed by a slave living nearby ("Uzeiros e vizeiros no offício da malêzada" 1838). Six Africans were arrested in the fortress and in a boat anchored in waters close to the fortress. Two of the prisoners belonged to a local slave owner called Falcão and had supposedly taken part in the Malê revolt in 1835 along with other slaves of the same master. They were accused of planning another violent rebellion. The article criticized the negligence of local authorities for leaving a fortress abandoned with a cache of weapons.

This event happened in 1838, just three years after the Malê revolt. This time, however, Salvador was rocked by another revolt known as Sabinada (1837–1838). Radical liberals, militia, and army officers raised arms against the imperial government. The rebellion was widely covered in local newspapers and was a great concern for local authorities. The article relates the Muslim uprising of 1835 to the Jiquitaia Fortress burglary. Two Africans were identified by authorities by their Christian names: Thomé and Sebastião. Both were arrested after the uprising of 1835, but had escaped punishment. The newspaper urged authorities to take action since the memory of what happened in 1835 was still alive.

The impact of the Muslim uprising promoted an intense debate about slavery and the transatlantic slave trade. This discussion was highly controversial. The slave trade was considered vital to the maintenance of slavery as a result of high mortality rates and due to the difficulties of slaves reproducing naturally under dreadful life conditions. On the other hand, the arrival of more Africans represented the risk of future rebellions, and in post-independence Brazil, elites worried about the future of a modern nation heavily populated by blacks. Yet after the initial wave of indignation generated by the events in Salvador, the illegal slave trade continued, even under tremendous British pressure, bringing over a half million Africans to Brazil between 1835 and 1850 (Bethell 2009, 395). Furthermore, the high labor demand fueled by sugar and coffee plantations combined with the political stability achieved by the crowning of Emperor Pedro II in 1842 provided the raison d'être to justify the illegal trade until its de facto termination in 1850. And slavery as a whole (not just the importation of new slaves) was not abolished in Brazil until 1888.

African Muslims were stigmatized and became the target of the authorities after 1835. They were regarded as dangerous and prone to rebellion, and therefore as a threat to the system. In addition, in the following decades, Brazil's economic activity became heavily concentrated in the southern provinces. Consequently, an intense internal trade linking the northeastern provinces to Rio de Janeiro brought African Muslims from Bahia to this region. Such a dangerous development of the internal slave trade did not pass undetected by Rio de Janeiro authorities. They devised an operation aimed at identifying Muslims arriving in Rio de Janeiro to prevent any attempt to reproduce in the nation's capital the events that had occurred in Bahia (Soares 2001, 358–359). Muslim communities reportedly survived in Rio de Janeiro, Bahia, and a few other places

in northeasten Brazil after the termination of the slave trade in 1850. But their
numbers decreased rapidly without the slave trade and through their gradual
assimilation into the Afro-Brazilian population, as well as through religious
syncretism (Silva 2001, 83–90). As the numbers of African Muslims in Brazil
decreased in the late nineteenth century, Islam was renewed in the nation by
the arrival of Levantine Arabs leaving behind a crumbling Ottoman Empire
in the early twéntieth century.

## Notes

1. The jihad of the reformer Fulani Uthman dan Fodio began in 1804 and was followed by a number of conflicts, such as the Muslim uprising of 1817 in Ilorin, the Owu
War in the 1820s, the Nupe wars in 1825–1826, and the Muslim revolt in Borgu in 1835.
2. The Constitution of 1824 declared Catholicism Brazil's official religion in Article 5.
*Constituição Política do Império do Brazil* (March 25, 1824).
3. João Reis decreased to four the number of rebels executed by firing squad (1993, 17).

## References

"Africanos." 1836. *O Atlante.* August 5.
"Bahia." 1835. *O Echo do Norte.* July 25.
Basile, Marcelo Otávio. 2000. "O Império Brasileiro: Panorama Político." In *História
Geral do Brasil,* ed. Maria Yedda Linhares. Rio de Janeiro: Campus.
Bergad, Laird W. 2006. *Slavery and the Demographic and Economic History of Minas
Gerais, Brazil, 1720–1888.* New York: Cambridge University Press.
Bethell, Leslie. 2009. *The Abolition of the Brazilian Slave Trade: Britain, Brazil and the
Slave Trade Question.* Cambridge: Cambridge University Press.
Brazil, Etienne Ignace. 1909. "Os Malês." *Revista do Instituto Geografico e Historico
Brasileiro* 72.
Cairus, Jose. 2002. *Jihad, Cativeiro e Redenção: Escravidão, resistência e irmandade,
Sudão Central e Bahia (1835).* Master's thesis, History, Universidade Federal do Rio de
Janeiro.
Carvalho, José Murilo de. 1998. *Pontos e bordados: Escritos de história e política.* Belo
Horizonte: Editora UFMG.
Chalhoub, Sidney. 1990. *Visões da liberdade: Uma historia das ultimas decadas da es-
cravidão na corte.* São Paulo: Companhia das Letras.
"Coluna Bahia." 1835. *O Fluminense.* November 3.
Danmole, H. O. 1992. "Crises, Warfare, and Diplomacy in the Nineteenth-Century
Ilorin." In *Warfare and Diplomacy in Precolonial Nigeria,* ed. Toyin Falola. Madison:
African Studies Program, University of Wisconsin.
"Decreto." 1835. *Recopilador Mineiro.* April 29.
"Devassa do Levante de Escravos Ocorrido em Salvador em 1835." 1968. Arquivo Público
do Estado da Bahia.

Diouf, Sylviane. 2004. "African Muslims in Bondage: Realities, Memories and Legacies." In *Monuments of the Black Atlantic: Slavery and Memory,* ed. Joanne M. Braxton and Maria Diedrich. Münster: LIT Verlag.

Dobronravin, Nikolay. 2004. "Escritos Multilingues em Caracteres Arabes: Novas Fontes de Trinidad e Brasil No Seculo XIX." *Afro-Ásia* 31.

"A escravatura convém ao Brasil ou é-lhe perigosa." 1837. *Seminário de Cincinato.* July 8.

Galvao, Walnice Nogueira. 1974. *No calor da hora: A Guerra de Canudos nos jornais.* São Paulo: Atica.

Goody, Jack. 2000. *Power of Written Tradition.* Washington, D.C: Smithsonian Institution.

Johnson, Samuel. 1937. *The History of the Yorubas: From the Earliest Times to the Beginning of the British Protectorate.* Lagos: C.M.S. Bookshop.

Klein, Herbert S. 2010. *The Atlantic Slave Trade.* Cambridge: Cambridge University Press.

Last, Murray. 1988. "Charisma and Medicine in Northern Nigeria." In *Charisma and Brotherhood in African Islam,* ed. D. B. Cruise O'Brien and C. Coulon. Oxford, UK: Clarendon Press.

Law, Robin. 1993. *Contemporary Source Material for the History of the Old Oyo Empire, 1627–1824.* Ibadan: Institute of African Studies, University of Ibadan.

———. 1997. "Ethnicity and the Slave Trade: 'Lucumi' and 'Nago' as Ethnonyms in West Africa." *History in Africa* 24.

Lovejoy, Paul E. 1994. "Background to Rebellion: The Origins of the Muslim Slaves in Bahia." *Slavery and Abolition* 15(2).

"Mensagem Que A Assembleia Provincial Do Rio De Janeiro Por Intermedio Do Presidente Da Provincia Dirigio Ao Governo Central." 1835. *Jornal do Commercio.* March 21.

Mishida, Mieko. 2003. *Slavery and Identity: Ethnicity, Gender, and Race in Salvador, Brazil, 1808–1888.* Bloomington: Indiana University Press.

*Pão D'Assucar.* 1835. February 10.

Patterson, Orlando. 1982. *Slavery and Social Death: A Comparative Study.* Cambridge, MA: Harvard University Press.

"Post Scriptum." 1835. *Recopilador Mineiro.* May 2.

"Reflexões sobre a sublevação dos negros Africanos, que rompeo na noute de 24 para 25 do corrente." 1835. *Astro de Minas.* March 14.

Reis, J. J. 1993. *Slave Rebellion in Brazil: The Muslim Uprising of 1835 in Bahia.* Baltimore: Johns Hopkins University Press.

Reis, J. J., and Beatriz G. Mamigonian. 2004. "Nagô and Mina: The Yoruba Diaspora in Brazil." In *The Yoruba Diaspora in the Atlantic World,* ed. Toyin Falola and Matt D. Childs. Bloomington: Indiana University Press.

"Relato do chefe de policia Francisco Gonçalves Martins." 1835. *Jornal do Commercio.* February 10.

Rodrigues, Raimundo Nina. 1935. *Africanos no Brasil.* Rio de Janeiro: Companhia Editora Nacional.

Schwartz, Stuart B. 2006. "Cantos and Quilombos: A Hausa Rebellion in Bahia, 1814." In *Slaves, Subjects, and Subversives: Blacks in Colonial Latin America,* ed. Jane Landers and Barry Robinson. Albuquerque: University of New Mexico Press.

Silva, Alberto Costa. 2001. "Buying and Selling Korans in Nineteenth-Century Rio de
Janeiro." *Slavery & Abolition* 22(1).

Silva, José Bonifácio de Andrada e. 2000. *Projetos para o Brasil.* São Paulo: Companhia
das Letras.

Soares, Carlos Eugênio Líbano. 2001. *A capoeira escrava e outras tradições rebeldes no
Rio de Janeiro, 1808–1850.* Campinas: Editora da UNICAMP.

"Uzeiros e vizeiros no offício da malêzada." 1838. *Correio Mercantil.* August 7.

Verger, Pierre. 1987. *Fluxo e refluxo do tráfico de escravos entre o Golfo do Benin e a Bahia
de Todos os Santos, dos séculos XVII a XIX.* 2nd ed. São Paulo: Editora Corrupio.

# 9

# A Transnational Intellectual Sphere
## Brazil and Its Middle Eastern Populations

*María del Mar Logroño Narbona*

María del Mar Logroño Narbona explores the transnational cultural and political sphere of the first generation of Middle Eastern migrants in Brazil in the 1910s and 1920s. In particular, she looks at how the Arabic press in Brazil during these decades, and more broadly in the *mahjar* (the term used to designate collectively the geographical locations of Arab migration), created a truly transnational sphere as it facilitated communication flows between distant segments of populations with shared political goals. She concludes that this generation of Middle Eastern migrants lived through a moment in history of political transition when political mobilization was not confined to a geographical location. As first-generation migrants they dreamt of transforming their homelands into the spaces they imagined would welcome them back after their "sojourn."

∾

### Transnationalism as a Condition of the Past

In the historic neighborhood of Botafogo, in Rio de Janeiro, stands the house of Rui Barbosa, a well-known lawyer, politician, and public intellectual of early-twentieth-century Brazil. Today his residence has become the seat of the Rui Barbosa Foundation, a public research center and library specializing in Brazilian literature that houses an important library and archival collection donated by Brazilian personalities, featuring Barbosa's personal library and an archive of documents he wrote. Barbosa was an avid collector of books during his lifetime; his personal library amounted to around thirty-seven thousand volumes, with particular interest on publications from around the world about jurisprudence.[1] Barbosa's literature collection included titles that connected the cultural universe of turn-of-the-century Brazilian elites to that of European elites, including a passion for Orientalist writings such as an 1888 edition of Gustav Flaubert's *Salammbo* and a green leather-bound copy of FitzGerald's *Rubáiyát of Omar Khayyam*. Among the more unusual holdings, Barbosa's library included a 1609 edition of the book by Dominican missionary João dos Santos, *Ethiopia Oriental e varia historia de cousas, notaveis do Oriente* (Oriental Ethiopia and Other Notable Things of the Orient).

While Rui Barbosa acquired many of the books in his collection, his shelves also contained books given to him during his lifetime as a public servant for the Ministry of Finance and the Ministry of Foreign Affairs. One such present was an Arabic translation of a *History of Brazil* done by Jurj Atlas, a Syrian writer who had migrated to São Paulo in the early years of the twentieth century. Jurj Atlas dedicated his book to Barbosa on April 4, 1919, months before Barbosa was offered the chance to represent Brazil at the League of Nations, an appointment he never accepted due to political disagreements with the Brazilian government.[2] In this context, Atlas's present to Barbosa was not disingenuous. As the following pages explain, Middle Eastern migrant intellectuals in Brazil were part of a dynamic transnational community ready to mobilize political support wherever it was needed at a time when French and British colonial aspirations in the Middle East were reaching their apex.

In contrast to views by sociologists and anthropologists, migration historians have argued that transnationalism is not a phenomenon of the present time (Harzig and Hoerder 2009, 83). Historian Nancy Foner has noted how "transnationalism has been with us for a long time, and a comparison with the past allows us to learn just what is new about the patterns and processes involved in transnational ties today" (ibid.). Although technology has made exchanges faster and more intense, scholars need further dialogue on how these new technologies affect the lives of migrants today in contrast with experiences from the past.[3]

Population movements from the Middle East into the Americas have been a reality since the last decades of the nineteenth century. This migration was due to a combination of economic, religious, social, and political factors that took migrants to Egypt, Europe, West Africa, and the Americas.[4] After the United States, Argentina and Brazil were the second and third most frequent destinations for Syrian and Lebanese emigrants, an order that reversed itself after the end of the Second World War, when Brazil became the most important destination.[5] In terms of their social background, these migrants have been described as mostly male and Christian, and as belonging to the poorest classes from the

Ottoman territories of Greater Syria and Mount Lebanon.[6] However, it is worth remembering that women, non-Christian populations, and a myriad of liberal professionals (doctors and lawyers), intellectuals, and merchants also moved to the Americas in an effort to improve their economic and social conditions.[7]

Following a general trend in migration studies that dates back to the 1920s, research about Middle Eastern migrant communities in Brazil has focused on "the ways in which migrants adapted themselves to their place of immigration rather than upon how they continued to look back to their place of origin."[8] In particular, scholars have looked into questions of group formation and assimilation into Brazilian society. In their findings they have described a progressive process of social stratification within Middle Eastern migrant communities defined by the economic success of some of these migrants that resulted in a highly stratified community, at the top of which stood a set of rich immigrant families whose wealth mostly derived from their commercial and entrepreneurial activities in Brazil. Closely related to wealthy merchants or high bourgeoisie were the intellectuals who, by virtue of their outstanding educational background, enjoyed important social prestige within the community but had a much lower economic status. Finally, at the bottom of this hierarchy were the majority of migrants, many of whom arrived as poor guest workers and in most cases found their first jobs at the businesses of their wealthier compatriots.[9]

In spite of the economic success of some of these migrants, most of them faced racial and ethnic biases within their host communities that made their process of assimilation difficult. As Jeffrey Lesser and Ignacio Klich have explained, "*turcos,*" as these migrants were popularly known in Brazil and other Latin American countries, was "an imposed rather than self-constructed label" created "in the minds of Latin America's elites" (1996). *Turco* did not denote any particular national identity but a mix of *exoticized* perceptions, or as Klich and Lesser noted, a purposely mistaken label that came to signify "a multiplicity of various even conflicting regional, national and/or ethnoreligious backgrounds" (1996). Arab immigrants in Brazil, like their Jewish counterparts, found themselves to be subject of a particular situation: they "fell outside of the desirable category and thus posed a particular challenge because, while not banned from entering most Latin American countries until the late 1920s, they were also never expected to migrate" (Lesser and Klich 1996, 6). Arabs, in the minds of Brazilian elites, were not white enough to improve the "racial stock" of their host countries.[10]

While scholars of Middle Eastern migration to Brazil were delineating the contours of the history of group formation and assimilation of these communities, in the early 1990s a "transnational turn" took place among scholars of migration that has since produced important results in the field of migration history.[11] In these new narratives, historians have begun to explore the transnational condition of migrants, understood as the "continuities in migrants' experiences," with a particular emphasis on "the simultaneous living of aspects of different cultures," and its consequences in the formation of multifaceted cultural and social identities.[12]

In this vein, the pages that follow explore one important aspect of the transnational condition of Middle Eastern migrants in Brazil in the early twentieth century by looking at the existence of what could be defined as a "transnational public sphere." Composed of intellectuals whose lives were embedded in multilocality and readers who were aware of their "diasporic consciousness," the Arab "ethnic press" in Brazil provided a privileged site that enhanced multiple geographical connections between Arab migrant communities and the world around them.

## "Unbounding" the Arab "Ethnic Press" in Brazil

Among scholars interested in "unbounding" the nation-state,[13] the Internet has become the preferred medium that defines transnationalism. Castells has convincingly argued the Internet's importance in transforming aspects of social life, and it is unquestionable "that advances in transportation and electronic technologies, and especially the Internet, have resulted in a transformation, a compression if not collapse, of time and distance, as well as altered conceptions of hierarchy, territory, sovereignty, and the state."[14] In contrast to the transnational nature of the Internet, the "ethnic press" has traditionally been considered a one-way link between the migrant communities and their homes (Rhodes 2010, 39). For instance, in a study about the Irish in Ireland and America, social historian G. W. Potter argued how the information published in this press shed light on "what was important to the immigrants, how to interpret current events in the home and new countries, and how they defined their role in their new countries of settlement," among other things (Potter 1960, cited in Rhodes 2010, 42). Written in the 1960s and 1970s, most of these works were driven by questions of assimilation of migrants into their host communities and did not look into concepts that today concern scholars of transnationalism and the transnational condition of migrants such as "simultaneity" of experiences or "awareness of multilocality." Yet, that same "old ethnic press" still stands as the medium that enhanced the transnational condition of these migrants.

In his *Ma'asat al-Harf al-'Arabi fi al-Mahajir al-Amrikiyya*, the Arabic writer Ilyas Qunsul states that the largest number of Arabic periodicals before the Second World War were published in the United States, Argentina, and Brazil (Qunsul 1980, 28). The *Ma'asat*, Written during the 1970s, at a point when Arab migration flows had slowed down significantly, and when assimilated populations in the Americas were often no longer able to express themselves in Arabic, Qunsul's words were a nostalgic cry to vindicate the splendid period of Arabic writings in the Americas.[15] Beyond nostalgia, his words convey a glimpse into the active editorial life of these communities in Brazil, where it has been documented that 140 Arabic newspapers and magazines were published during the period preceding World War II with approximately three hundred persons working as journalists.[16] In just the two decades from 1910 to 1930, there were more than thirty-five publications.[17]

Beyond its sheer numbers, the Arabic press in Brazil was defined by its transnational condition: it was produced by intellectuals whose personal trajectories were inextricably linked to multiple geographies, and it served communities with political, economic, social, and cultural links to the Middle East, Europe, and the Americas at large. The result was more than the added value of a long list of publications and editors in Brazil. As the content of these publications highlight, it was a written expression of the existence of a culturally, politically, and socially interconnected world of Middle Eastern citizens to their homelands and their surrounding world.

## *The Arabic Press in Brazil as a Site of Transnational Political Mobilization*

The Arabic press of the early twentieth century in South America, and in the particular context of Brazil, was the most important medium that helped organized migrant communities socially and politically. At a time of heightened political tensions when parties and factions needed popular support, the press fulfilled the necessary function of informing communities, enabling coordination, and sometimes even encouraging the participation of political actors across borders.

In the years prior to the First World War, at a time of growing regional nationalist tensions among the Ottoman provinces of Greater Syria and Mount Lebanon, the Arabic press in Brazil was a venue for expressing, disseminating, and advancing the ideas of decentralization, regional nationalism, and Ottomanism among Middle Eastern migrants.[18] The case of the Lebanese Renaissance (*Al-Nahda al-Lubnaniya*) is particularly interesting as it shows the interconnectedness of prewar migrant communities in Brazil. The Society of the Lebanese Revival, an organization founded in 1908 in Jounieh, demanded the independence of Lebanon under Ottoman suzerainty. The society's goals were supported not only in Mount Lebanon but also among Ottoman migrants around the world. In Cairo, Daud Barakat, the editor of *Al-Ahram*, established a local branch of the society under the name of the Lebanese Union (*Ittihad Lubnan*), and in 1909 the society elected Iskander Ammoun, a lawyer from Deir al-Qamar with experience in the Egyptian judiciary, as its president. Ammoun's brother, Daoud Ammoun, presented the society's list of demands to the French government in Paris in 1912, and helped found a third sister society, the Lebanese Society of Paris (Tauber 1993, 72–88). The world connections of the Ammoun brothers did not stop in Paris, but moved on to São Paulo, where their brother Khalil Ammoun lived. Beginning in 1896 and until his return to Cairo at the request of his brother Iskander, Khalil did editorial work for *Al Brazil*, a weekly publication in São Paulo (Duoun 1945, 235). Although it has been impossible to locate the issues of *Al Brazil* edited by Khalil Ammoun, the January 1916 issue shows as its chief editor Ilyas Massarra, who, before working for *Al Brazil*, had collaborated on *Abu al Hawl* (The Sphinx), a publication that stood behind the idea of the creation of a greater Lebanon under the auspices of France.[19] *Abu al-Hawl* was one of the newspapers that we know printed the program of the fourth sister association of Ittihad Lubnan, the Centro Rinascenza Libano created in São Paulo in 1912 by As'ad Bishara.[20] Even more interesting to our story of transnational flows in prewar Brazil is the fact that two years after its founding, *Al Manar*, the Egyptian publication of Rashid Ridda, reprinted from *Abu al-Hawl* the program of the Centro Rinascenza Libano within a series of articles questioning the "Ottoman nationality."[21]

During the years of the First World War the press became an even more important venue of political mobilization that was used not only by migrants, but also by Ottoman authorities and European colonial powers alike. An important instance that highlights the transnational world of these migrants in Brazil was an episode that involved recruiting Middle Eastern troops from among their diaspora for what was known as the Légion d'Orient. As I have explained elsewhere,[22] in the final stages of the First World War, the French government developed a sustained interest in the Syrian and Lebanese emigrant communities for several reasons, including the Sykes-Picot Agreement, concluded on May 16, 1916, which, far from reconciling the competing French and British colonial ambitions in the Middle East, actually exposed how deep the inter-allied divisions were, mostly due to Britain's military preeminence in the Middle East in contrast with the numerical and structural weaknesses of French military presence in the region.[23] Taking this strategic inferiority into account, alongside the potential that Syrian and Lebanese communities abroad offered as some sort of counterweight, the French wartime coalition government moved to formalize its relationship with those émigré committees in Paris sympathetic to French claims on the Levant. This initiative crystallized in the creation of the Comité Central Syrien in May 1917.[24]

The creation of the Comité Central Syrien was a new departure in French efforts to manipulate Syrian and Lebanese elite opinion overseas. Among the tasks assigned to the new committee's members, two of the most significant were, first, to coordinate the claims for self-determination made by those Syrians abroad who were amenable to French political protection and, second, to organize the recruitment of a military section, the Légion d'Orient, composed of loyal émigrés willing to fight alongside French forces in defeating the Ottoman Turks (Tauber 1994, 171–180). The Légion d'Orient, formally created by ministerial edict on November 15, 1916, was to consist of "Arab, Syrian, or Armenian volunteers" recruited mostly in the Americas and Europe. It would be a volunteer force that would serve under the orders of a French commander and would be paid for by the French government. Those coming forward for enlistment were first expected to formalize their recruitment in France, after which they would later be sent either to Cyprus or to Port Said in Egypt, where they were to receive their military apparel (Tauber 1994, 171–180). In order to fulfill its new mandate, the Comité Central Syrien picked a team led in part by Jamil Mardam Bey to travel to Brazil and Argentina. The delegation aimed to unite those sympathetic to France by canvassing for volunteers to the Légion d'Orient and putting in place local branches of the Comité Central Syrien. The delegates' arrival was widely publicized in emigrant community newspapers, thereby advancing its propaganda and organizational goals, but it was also highly criticized among those who opposed French control over Syria and Lebanon, particularly among the Arabic press in Brazil where much of the discussion took place.[25] Although the Légion d'Orient never became a military force of sufficient size to compete with the British military power already entrenched in the Middle East, it recruited thirty-seven combatants from Brazil.[26] Most important, the episode highlights yet again the transnational condition of these migrants beyond communication flows, as well as the role of the press in forming public opinion.

As the ebb and flow of Syrian and Lebanese migration between South America and the Middle East continued in the context of postwar French mandates in Syria and Lebanon, the Arabic press continued to shape a vibrant and very politicized transnational public sphere. On the one hand, the Arabic press produced in the Middle East continued to be read by migrants either through subscriptions or through texts that were reproduced in locally edited Arab

publications. For instance, *Al-Afkar,* one of the most important newspapers
in São Paulo, edited by Sa'id Abu Jamra, regularly included articles from the
Egyptian publication *Al Muqattam* or invited collaboration by journalists and
intellectuals in the Middle East. On the other hand, the Arabic press produced
in the Americas was not subject to the same censorship mechanisms imposed
in the context of colonial Syria and Lebanon, so it offered a venue to develop
political dissent against the new colonial order that eventually found its way
back to the Middle East.

Aware of the relevant role of the Arabic press as a medium that influenced
transnational public opinion, French colonial authorities spared no effort to
control and monitor closely the Arabic press around the world. The French
mandate authorities in Syria and Lebanon passed numerous regulatory laws
to extend control over the content and distribution of newspapers and journals among its colonial subjects not only within the mandate territories but
also overseas. In exercising full control over France's Levantine colonies, the
French authorities imposed an active policy of censorship in terms of both
content and distribution of what was considered politically dangerous. The
office of General Security (Sûreté Générale) reported periodically to Paris on
the state of the press within Syria and Lebanon. Acknowledging the dynamic
communication flows between migrant populations and their homelands and
the role of the press in shaping public perceptions of French colonial rule over
its Levantine provinces, but unable to impose any censorship, the French consul in São Paulo, Gucciardi, was asked as early as 1921 by the French Ministry
of Foreign Affairs (Quai d'Orsay) to report on the different political trends
expressed in the Arabic press in Brazil. Aware of the anxiety of the French
colonial authorities, the French consul proceeded to map the publications
according to their pro- or anti-French stances, after which he concluded that
"there were no more than 7,000 issues of these publications circulating in
Brazil the most widely read being *Al-Brazil, Fatat Lubnan, O Livre Pensador/
Al-Qalam Al-Hadid, Abu Al-Hawl/O Sphynge"* and *Amerika.* All except the
last were considered to be pro-French.[27] Gucciardi's dimissive words regarding the total number of issues being published as well as his positive spin on
the pro-French role of the Arabic press in the conclusion to his report were
simply not accurate. Those "no more than 7,000" was certainly meaningless
considering the reading practices at the time, as it chose not to take into account the potential community of readers that perused each of those individual
newspapers as it circulated. More important, however, was the fact that his
report chose to diminish the value of well-established anti-French publications
like *Al-Afkar,* published by Sa'id Abu Jamra; *Al-Jarida,* published by Khalil

Saadeh; and *Al-Ittihad Al-'Arabi,* published by Jurj Atlas. These also had a broad audience among migrant populations in Brazil.

When it became impossible for French authorities to control content, either by censorship or by subsidizing pro-French publications,[28] the common practice followed by mandate authorities was simply to ban the distribution of certain publications. Although the French mandate in Syria and Lebanon had very strict customs regulations that forbade the entry of publications, violations of custom laws happened frequently enough that the authorities were forced to produce lists of newspapers that needed to be banned from entering mandate territory. In the seven-page *arrête* published on May 1, 1933, at least seven publications from Brazil were banned, an act that highlighted the fluid communication with seemingly distant geographical locations,[29] as well as the strength and pervasive role that the French authorities believed that the press could have in their colonial territories.[30]

## From *"Intelectuais da colônia"* to "Builders of Transnational Communities"

Writers, editors, and journalists made the existence of this transnational public sphere possible with their work and writings. The approach to the study of these intellectuals in Brazil has been twofold: on the one hand, critics of Arabic literature have considered them second-class when their work is compared with that of their fellow writers in North America in advancing Arabic literature.[31] On the other hand, Brazilian sociologists have defined them as *intelectuais da colônia* (intellectuals of the community), as they relied on the wealthy members of the migrant Syrian and Lebanese communities to develop their intellectual activity (Truzzi 1997, 106) The patron-client relationship that indeed defined the work of these *intelectuais da colônia* resembles Gramsci's description of "urban intellectuals," or those who worked to legitimize the wealthiest sectors of society (Gramsci 1999, 3–23)

Although these class-based characterizations are justifiable, they wrongly confine these intellectuals to their local immigrant geographies in Brazil, thus missing an important aspect of their works and lives: their cosmopolitan trajectories. Many of these intellectuals were seasoned writers and journalists with academic backgrounds going back to their lives in Lebanon and, in some cases, complemented by studies in either Europe, the United States, or Brazil. Through their personal trajectories, these individuals accumulated a transnational social and cultural capital that was inevitably reflected in their work in Brazil.

One fine example was Saʻid Abu Jamra, the editor of *Al-Afkar*. Born in al-Kfeir, Hasbaya, on April 21, 1871, in 1884 he moved to Beirut, and in 1892 he graduated with a bachelor's degree in arts and sciences from what was then the Syrian Protestant College (SPC) in Beirut.[32] Abu Jamra taught at a secondary school in Beirut for three years, while he collaborated in the editing of newspapers such as *Lisan al-Hal* and *Lubnan*. He then decided to continue his education and pursued a degree in medicine, first at SPC in 1896, and then at St. Louis University in the United States, from which he graduated in 1899. Upon his graduation Abu Jamra left for Brazil, following in the steps of family members who had previously emigrated there. Once in Brazil, he settled in São Paulo and started publishing *Al-Afkar* in 1903, a work that he combined with the publication of several medical works in Cairo. The editorial work of Abu Jamra on *Al-Afkar*, although despised by the French for its anti-mandate attitudes, was well regarded within the community, which probably helped made *Al-Afkar* one of the longest-lasting Arabic publications in Brazil.[33] It also seems that his editorial life led him to contribute "at least one article on anarchism to *al-Hilal*" before the First World War, completing the common circles of collaboration among intellectuals at that time (Khuri-Makdisi 2011, 52)

In addition to his editorial work, medical practice, which the French characterized as a *dangereux morticole* (dangerous quackery), Abu Jamra acted as the vice president of the American University in Beirut (AUB) alumni association in São Paulo, which he helped to found in 1923. The president of the association was Naami Jafet, one of the wealthiest, if not the wealthiest, Lebanese industrialist in São Paulo (Duoun 1945, 189) Not much is known about his personal life other than the fact that he was married and had four sons and one daughter. He died in 1955 (Saideh [1957] 1999, 453)

Abu Jamra's cosmopolitan profile was not unique, but rather was similar to that of the many intellectuals who made up the Arabic public transnational sphere in Brazil. Tawfiq Fadl Allah Duoun is another good example of the cosmopolitan trajectories of these intellectuals. Born to Syrian parents on October 21, 1883, in the Lebanese city of Zahle in the Bekaa Valley, his mother was Greek-Syrian, since his maternal grandfather was originally from Cyprus but got married in Damascus (Duoun n.d., 23). His father was the "efendi" of the village, a civil servant who was versed in accounting and law had some musical inclinations as well, as he recited poetry and played the oud. Until he was twelve, Duoun was always a good student: he entered the local school at the age of four; got his first school degree at five; at ten he was the substitute for the local teacher, and he entered the Syrian Protestant College (SPC) in the fall of 1895 with a scholarship that covered half of his tuition, since the missionaries already knew his excellent academic record (Duoun n.d., 29–33).

Despite his inclination for studying and his love for the city of Beirut, he did not adapt well to the new environment, and failed most of the subjects, as he himself explained. His father then decided he would be educated in Zahle until he was ready for Beirut. So it wasn't until 1901 that he registered once more at the SPC in order to get a degree that would enable him to pursue his plans of working for the British administration in Egypt and Sudan (Duoun 1944, 65). Duoun first arrived in Egypt on his way to Sudan, and while in Egypt he had several menial jobs until he became a teacher at a school for both poor and rich Jewish children (Duoun 1944, 84–85).

In 1904 he finally left Cairo for Khartoum, where he lived until 1914. There he worked for the Sudanese government, and then he migrated to São Paulo.

In Brazil he first worked in trading businesses, which he combined with his editorial collaborations.[34] However, as he himself wrote, Duoun arrived at the time of the economic crisis produced by the war, which made trading a difficult and unprofitable business. Because of the lack of employment in this sector, he resorted to teaching and eventually collaborated simultaneously with various newspapers of opposing ideological trends, such as *Fatat Lubnan* and *Amerika* (Saideh [1957] 1999, 431–432). After a couple of years Duoun and Ilyas Farhat worked together as journalists in *Al-Miqra'a/A Chibata* and *Al-Jarida,* both of which had anti-French leanings ('Awdat and Shukr 1991, 63). After an unsuccessful editorial stint at *Al-Jarida,* he then started and edited *Al-Watan al-Hurr* in 1920, which was the mouthpiece of As'ad Bishara's nationalist party. But the new editorial adventure did not last long, and so from 1923 until 1928 he published *Al-Dalil,* a monthly periodical that focused on the economic life of Syrians and Lebanese in Brazil ('Awdat and Shukr 1991, 106). In 1930 he moved to Chile for two years. Upon his return to Brazil in 1932 he participated in the foundation of *Al-'Usba al-Andalusiyya,* which was both a journal and a literary circle, and continued with his literary activity until his return to Lebanon in the mid-1950s. He died in 1966. He was married and was the father of two daughters ('Awdat and Shukr 1991, 63).

Both Abu Jamra and Tawfiq Duoun were members of the AUB alumni association, and so were other writers and journalists such as Tawfiq Qurban, or Sami Raci (editor of *Al-Jalia*), all of whom shared similar cosmopolitan trajectories. As AUB alumni, they gathered periodically for conferences and dinners that served as a catalyst for exchanges with Brazilian and Arab intellectuals, some of whom were invited from distant locations, as was the case of AUB alumni and, later on, the Princeton University professor Philip Hitti.[35]

**Coda: The Transnational Public Sphere in History**

In her critique of the profuse way in which scholars have used the term "transnational public spheres," Nancy Fraser has emphasized how "the concept of the
public sphere was developed not simply to understand communication flows
but to contribute a normative political theory of democracy." Fraser argues that
"a public sphere is conceived as a space for the communicative generation of
public opinion and . . . as a vehicle for marshaling public opinion as a political
force" (Fraser 2007). As this chapter has addressed, the Arabic press produced
in Brazil during the 1910s and 1920s, and more broadly in the *mahjar* (the term
used to designate collectively the geographical locations of Arab migration),
created a truly transnational sphere as it facilitated communication flows
between distant segments of populations with shared political goals. More
important, this was a transnational public sphere for, in Fraser's words, "marshaling public opinion as a political force." Examples like the summoning of
forces for the Légion d'Orient, or the instrumental approach used by French
colonial authorities in regards to the content and distribution of Arabic publications within their colonial territories and among the migrant communities,
helps the historian advance the idea that transnationalism is not only a process
of the present but one firmly rooted in the past. These populations, after all,
lived through a moment in history of political transition, when territorial sovereignty in the Middle East was a bleak concept, to say the least, and political
mobilization was not confined to a geographical location, but rather found a
better medium in the reality of a highly dispersed population, most of whom,
being first-generation migrants, dreamt of transforming their homelands into
the spaces they imagined would welcome them after their sojourn.

Last but not least, the writers, journalists, politicians, and more generally the
elites who helped create this transnational public sphere also deserve attention.
Most narratives of Middle Eastern migrant communities in Brazil have provided a narrow understanding of the social background of these populations.
In some cases, scholars have taken at face value the information contained in
some of the narratives produced by members of the communities in the 1940s
and 1950s, without questioning these works. These works provided a typical
narrative of success, presenting the individuals of these migrant communities
as "self-made men in a land of opportunity."[36] In these works, written with
the intention of elevating the role of these communities in the eyes of general
Brazilian audiences, there is no emphasis on the complex personal trajectories
of these individuals, or on the role that the Middle East played in shaping the
lives of these individuals. However, it is important to remember that for many

of these intellectuals and merchants, migration was not merely a stepping-stone out of poverty, no matter what these narratives may present, but a way to improve their opportunities to develop their own professional careers. It is only by looking at the rich and complex trajectories of these individuals, however, that we can understand how an Arabic translation of a general history of Brazil could find its way as a gift into one of the most important personal libraries in Rio de Janeiro.

**Notes**

1. http://www.casaruibarbosa.gov.br/interna.php?ID_S=108.

2. For a detailed biography of Rui Barbosa, see, among others, *Rui Barbosa: Cronologia da vida e da obra* (Rio de Janeiro: Edicoes Casa de Rui Barbosa, 1999).

3. Steven Vertovec acknowledges that new technology has intensified transnationalism but not caused it. And yet, it is that intensity that seems to define "transnationalism" in his view. For further analysis, see Vertovec 2009, 3–15.

4. Among the works that diminish the role of religion to explain this migration and emphasize a multiplicity of factors are Charles Issawi, "The Historical Background of Lebanese Emigration," *The Middle East Economy: Decline and Recovery* (Princeton, NJ: Marcus Wiener Publishers, 1995) and "Lebanese Migration in the Context of World Population Movements," in *The Lebanese in the World: A Century of Emigration* (London: Centre for Lebanese Studies in Association with I. B. Tauris & Co., 1992), ed. Albert Hourani and Nadim Shehadi; Akram Fouad Khater, *Inventing Home: Emigration, Gender and the Middle Class in Lebanon, 1870–1920* (Berkeley: University of California Press, 2001); and John Tofik Karam, *Another Arabesque: Syrian-Lebanese Ethnicity in Neoliberal Brazil* (Philadelphia: Temple University Press, 2007).

5. Claud Fahd Hajjar (1985) estimated that there were 300,000 *turcos* in Brazil in 1920, but more reliable studies taken at the local level provided by the French consular authorities established an approximate figure of 140,000 Syrian and Lebanese in Brazil around 1921.

6. For further information on the social makeup of the migration see Khater 2001 and Truzzi 2006.

7. This socio-occupational division of the highest ranks of emigrants parallels the findings of Thomas Philipp for the Syrian emigrant community in Egypt. See Philipp 1985, 96.

8. In reference to the trend in migration studies that started since the 1920s see Vertovec 2009, 13.

9. This is the work of peddlers described in Truzzi 1991 and Klich 1992, 243–284.

10. See Lesser 1995 for further explanations of the racial paradox that these Levantine migrants faced.

11. See the introduction to Vertovec 2009.

12. This last part is one of the definitions used that I embrace in this article. See Harzig and Hoerder 2009, 83–84.

13. In reference to Glick-Schiller, Basch, and Blanc 1994, entitled *Nations Unbound*.

14. Vertovec 2009, 22, citing Resnau 2003.

15. For a detailed description of Qunsul's work see Civantos 2006.

16. The estimate comes from Raddawi 1989, 106.

17. This is a personal estimate based on my research of primary sources, contrasted with a chronological breakdown of the most relevant secondary sources: 'Awdat and Shukr 1991 and Raddawi 1989.

18. The literature on Arab nationalism and the different regional nationalisms is extensive. See for instance Kais Firro, *Inventing Lebanon: Nationalism and the State under the Mandate* (London: I. B. Tauris, 2003), or Tauber 1993.

19. Hardan 1989, 62. Hardan describes *Abu al-Hawl*'s relationship with the French as one in which "it published anything that the French wanted."

20. This mention of As'ad Bishara can be found in Tauber 1993, 88, but contradicts other Arabic sources that do not consider Bishara to have been politically active until 1920, when he founded the *Hizb al-Watani al-Suri*. See, for Duoun 1945, 388.

21. In particular see the article *"Al-Jinsiyyat fi al-mamlaka al-'Uthmaniya"* in *Al-Manar,* June 23, 1914.

22. I have developed this argument in full in Logroño Narbona 2011, 144–167.

23. For detailed background on British military supremacy see Hughes 1999.

24. It was an offshoot of the Comité de l'Orient, which had previously enjoyed the backing of the French colonial party.

25. *Al-Maqr'a,* May 1917, 5–6.

26. *Al-Zahrawi,* June 4, 1917, 2. It provides the names of fourteen individuals who went from the province of São Paulo.

27. Ministère des Affaires Étrangères (MAE)/Paris/ Série E-Levant, Carton132, fols. 26a and 26b. Following original French transliteration.

28. The pro-French leanings of *Abu al-Hawl* (*The Sphynx*) were so strong that the journal was described by a contemporary observer as one that "published anything that the French wanted." See Hardan 1989, 62.

29. MAE/Nantes/Syrie-Liban, Carton 907.

30. See for instance *arrête* no. 147, article 19 (1925) on the right to ban the circulation of publications produced abroad in MAE/Nantes/Syrie-Liban/1er Versement/ Carton 907. The practice of banning publications is recorded in Thomas 2005. For the case of Tunisia see 268 and for Algeria 298–301.

31. This is a common approach by scholars when addressing *mahjar* writers. See for instance Paul Starkey, *Modern Arabic Literature* (Washington, DC: Georgetown University Press, 2006), and Saideh (1957) 1999.

32. For a history of the American University of Beirut see Betty Anderson, *The American University of Beirut: Arab Nationalism and Liberal Education* (Austin: University of Texas Press, 2011), 48–50, for the meaning and chronology of changing the name from SPC to AUB in 1920.

33. MAE/Nantes/ Syrie-Liban/ 1er Versement, Carton 419, Report "Syrians in São Paulo," 1928; see also Duoun 1945, 297.

34. This is mentioned in several sources, see for instance Saideh, *Adab wa Adabuna fi al-Mahjar,* 431–432; see also Tawfiq Fadl Allah Duoun, *Sirat hayati kitab yatadamman ahamm ma jara li min al-hawadith fi Suriya wa-Misr wa-al-Sudan,* (São Paulo), 65–66.

35. *Al-Jalia,* edited by Sami Raci, and *Al-Afkar,* edited by Sa'ad Abu Jamra, included references to these meetings whenever they occurred.

36. This has been the case, for example, of the work of Tawfiq Duoun, whose *A Emigração Sirio-Libanense à Terras de Promisao* has been extensively used by scholars of Arab migration to Brazil.

## References

'Awdat, Husayn, and Yasin Shukr. 1991. *Al-Mawsu'ah al-Suhufiyah al-'Arabiyah.* 3 vols. Tunis: Jami'at al-Duwal al-'Arabiyah, al-Munazzamah al-'Arabiyah lil-Tarbiyah wa-al-Thaqafah wa-al-'Ulum, Idarat al-Thaqafah.

Civantos, Cristina. 2006. *Between Argentines and Arabs: Argentine Orientalism, Arab Immigrants, and the Writing of Identity.* Albany: State University of New York Press.

Duoun, Tawfiq. 1944. *A Emigração Sirio-Libanense à Terras de Promisão.* São Paulo: Confissões.

Duoun, Tawfiq Fadl Allah. N.d. *Sirat hayati kitab yatadamman ahamm ma jara li min al-hawadith fi Suriya wa-Misr wa-al-Sudan.* São Paulo.

———. 1945. *Dhikra al-hijrah: risalat al-muhajirin al-Suriyin wa-al-Lubnaniyin ila ikhwanihim al-mutakhallifin.* São Paulo.

Fraser, Nancy. 2007. "Transnationalizing the Public Sphere: On the Legitimacy and Efficacy of Public Opinion in a Post-Westphalian World." Online at http://eipcp.net/transversal/0605/fraser/en.

Glick-Schiller, Nina, Linda Basch, and Cristina Szanton Blanc. 1994. *Nations Unbound: Transnational Projects, Postcolonial Predicaments, and Deterritorialized Nation-States.* Newark, NJ: Gordon and Breach.

Gramsci, Antonio. 1999. *The Prison Notebooks: Selections from the Prison Books.* Edited by Quintin Hoare and Geoffrey Nowell Smith. New York: International Publishers.

Hajjar, Claude Fahd. 1985. *Imigração Árabe: Cem Anos de Reflexao.* São Paulo: Icone, 1985.

Hardan, Nawwaf. 1989. *Sa'adah fi al-Mahjar.* Beirut: Dar Fikr lil-Abhath wa-al-Nashr.

Harzig, Christiane, and Dirk Hoerder. 2009. *What Is Migration History?* Cambridge, UK: Polity Press.

Hughes, Matthew. 1999. *Allenby and British Strategy in the Middle East, 1917–19.* London: Routledge.

Karam, John Tofik, 2012. "Diasporic Histories of Area Studies: Philip Hitti, Brazil, and the Reimagining of the Arab World." Unpublished manuscript.

Khater, Akram. 2001. *Inventing Home: Emigration, Gender, and the Middle Class in Lebanon, 1870–1920.* Berkeley: University of California Press.

Khuri-Makdisi, Ilham. 2011. *The Eastern Mediterranean and the Making of Global Radicalism.* Berkeley: University of California Press.

Klich, Ignacio. 1992. "Criollos and Arabic Speakers: An Uneasy Pas de Deux, 1888–1914." In *The Lebanese in the World: A Century of Emigration,* ed. Albert Hourani and Nadim Shehadi. London: Centre for Lebanese Studies in association with I. B. Tauris.

Lesser, Jeffrey. 1995. *Welcoming the Undesirables: Brazil and the Jewish Question.* Berkeley: University of California Press.

Lesser, Jeffrey, and Ignacio Klich. 1996. "Introduction." In "'Turco' Immigrants in Latin America," *The Americas* 53(1): 1–14.

Logroño Narbona, María del Mar. 2011. "Information and Intelligence Collection among Imperial Subjects Abroad: The Case of Syrians and Lebanese in Latin America, 1915–1930." In *The French Colonial Mind*, vol. 1, ed. Martin Thomas, 144–167. Lincoln: University of Nebraska Press.

Potter, G. W. 1960. *To the Golden Door: The Story of the Irish in Ireland and America.* Boston: Little Brown.

Qunsul, Ilyas. 1980. *Ma'asat al-Harf al-'Arab fi Al Mahajir al-Amrikiyya.* Damascus: Manshurat Ittihad al-Kuttab al-'Arab.

Raddawi, Majid. 1989. *Al Hijra Al 'Arabiya ila al Brazil, 1870–1976.* Damascus: Dar Tlas.

Resnau, James. 2003 *Distant Proximities: Dynamics beyond Globalization.* Princeton, NJ: Princeton University Press.

Rhodes, Leara D. 2010. *The Ethnic Press: Shaping the American Dream.* New York: Peter Lang Publishers.

Saideh, George. (1957) 1999. *Adab wa Adabuna fi al-Mahjar al-Amerikiya.* 4th ed. Lebanon.

Starkey, Paul. 2006. *Modern Arabic Literature.* Washington, DC: Georgetown University Press.

Tauber, Elizer. 1993. *The Emergence of the Arab Movements.* London: Frank Cass.

———. 1994. "La Légion d'Orient et la Légion Arabe." *Revue française d'histoire d'outre-mer* 81(303): 171–180.

Thomas, Martin. 2005. *The French Empire between the Wars: Imperialism, Politics and Society.* Manchester: Manchester University Press.

Thomas, Philipp. 1985. *The Syrians in Egypt, 1725–1975.* Berliner Islamstudien, Band III. Stuttgart: Steiner-Verlag.

Truzzi, Oswaldo. 1991. *De mascates a doutores: Sírios e libaneses em São Paulo.* São Paulo: Editora Sumaré.

———. 1997. *Patrícios: Sírios e libaneses em São Paulo.* São Paulo: Editora Hucitec.

———. 2006. "Libanais et Syriens au Brésil." *Revue européenne des migrations internationales* 18(1). http://remi.revues.org/document1694.html.

Vertovec, Steven. 2009, *Transnationalism.* New York: Routledge.

## Newspaper Sources

*Abu al-Hawl*
*Al-Jalia*
*Al-Manar*
*Al-Maqr'a,*
*Al-Zahrawi*

## Archival Sources

Ministère des Affaires Étrangères (MAE)/Paris/ Série E-Levant
Ministère des Affaires Étrangères (MAE)/Nantes/ Syrie-Liban

# 10

# The Politics of Anti-Zionism and Racial Democracy in Homeland Tourism

*John Tofik Karam*

Karam explores the phenomenon of "homeland tourism" among Brazilians of Syrian and Lebanese descent. He explores ways in which trips to the homeland are often used as opportunities to promote anti-Zionism. While some heritage tourists reproduce this discourse, others are critical of it. Using Brazilian nationalist precepts that are typically exclusionary, many tourists undermine the ideology often presented to them on these trips.

~

Since the late nineteenth century, Brazilians of Syrian and Lebanese descent have visited their homelands. Yet, during the late twentieth and early twenty-first centuries, the marketing strategies of airline enterprises and state powers both reproduced and transformed their practice of traveling to the eastern Mediterranean. In addition to becoming a "target market" (*público alvo*) for European-based transnational airlines, Syrian-Lebanese descendants in Brazil attracted Syrian and Lebanese state powers that imagined diaspora as a resource to strengthen domestic travel industries. During their tour of the homeland, though, descendants encountered memorialized sites of past Israeli attacks in Syria and Lebanon. In 2001, as part of an eighteen-month-long project among Syrian-Lebanese in São Paulo, I participated in one of these tours to Lebanon. I found that while some heritage seekers reproduced anti-Zionism, others criticized it as encouraging "prejudice" among Arabs who relate well with Jews in a purported "racially tolerant" Brazil.[1] Using the exclusionary language of Brazilian nationalism, they undermined anti-Zionist ideology in homeland tourism. Their reactions reveal that nationalist precepts can counter the very logics of exclusion that derive from them.

Such a journey requires us to take a different approach to the idea of racial democracy, a bastion of Brazilian nationalism. First published in 1933, Gilberto Freyre's *Casa-Grande e Senzala* argued that miscegenation among Indians, Africans, and Portuguese created a society that "balanced racial antagonisms" (1977, 126). Freyre's oeuvre gave rise to the idea of Brazil as a *democracia racial,* a "racial democracy" with supposedly little or no racial tension. Since the mid-twentieth century, this myth has been questioned by scholars and activists alike (Andrews 1991; Cardoso and Ianni 1960; Hasenbalg 1979; Nascimento 1977; Wagley 1952). Today many everyday citizens still claim that racial discrimination is tenuous in Brazil or related to socioeconomic inequality. I argue that this still-dominant nationalist myth of racial democracy continues to mask enduring racism in Brazil but that it is also used to disrupt absolutism elsewhere, namely in the Middle East. In Arab state-sponsored tourism, heritage seekers used the language of racial democracy to counter anti-Zionism, expressing "an unnamed cosmopolitanism in the space of a very specific institutional site" (Schein 1998, 190). Such nationalist mythology must not be romanticized but rather contextualized as a salient lens through which diasporic subjects experience the homeland.

Circular routes of travel from Brazil to the Arab world have a much longer, if particular, history. Like their counterparts throughout the world, migrants from the eastern Mediterranean as well as their descendants in Brazil have periodically visited or returned to their lands of origin since the late nineteenth century. Contemporaneous foreign observers as well as present-day interlocutors took note of the red-tiled roofs of houses built by return or circular migrants as well as the single women betrothed to male migrants from Brazil (Gulick 1955, 62; Khater 2001, 2; Safady 1972; Salibi 1976, 116; Williams 1968, 98, 105). Indeed, this history of persons circulating between homeland and diaspora is central to understanding the making of twentieth-century Lebanon and Syria (Gualtieri 2009; Khater 2005).

Since its very start, this movement of persons between Brazil and the eastern Mediterranean was enabled by transportation lines as well as travel agents. But by the mid-twentieth century, an increasingly greater share of passenger traffic took not ships but rather airplanes. In 1951, for instance, Air France took out a large advertisement in the popular Arab-Brazilian newspaper *A Pátria,* characterizing itself as "the oldest air transport company between Brazil and the Orient" for both "trips and remittances to Lebanon and Syria."[2] In the same newspaper, a travel agency announced "wonderful trips to the Middle East" for an upwardly mobile middle-class readership interested in "Oriental marvels."[3] By post–World War II times, Brazilians of Syrian-Lebanese origin purchased tickets to travel to Middle Eastern homelands not only to fulfill financial or marital strategies but also as an option for leisure and tourism.

Newly independent Arab states reached out to "their emigrants" as well. In 1960, Lebanon hosted the First World Congress of Lebanese Emigrants. Five years later, the Syrian state likewise convened the First Congress of Syrian Emigrants. Dr. Riad Cury, a Brazilian of Syrian-Lebanese background who participated in the 1965 congress, related that the Brazilian delegation was brought to "museums, mosques and churches, famous ruins, such as Saidenaia, Palmira, and Bona" [sic] as well as the villages of "Homs, Hama, and Aleppo," where many of the delegates traced their origins to.[4] As Syrian and Lebanese states tapped into their diasporas in the 1960s, willing participants from Brazil started to consume the homeland as "heritage," or in Dr. Cury's words, they embarked on a "discovery of the new in the old world."[5]

In the late twentieth and early twenty-first centuries, second-, third-, and fourth-generation Syrian-Lebanese narrated similar desires and motivations in what I would call homeland tourism. Most spoke of wanting to both "know [one's] origin" as well as to "know a different place." Middle-aged Sr. Abidão explained that "I wanted to know the land of my parents, my grandparents." He stressed that his mother "transmitted" to him and his siblings a connection with Lebanon, "a love for Lebanon," and especially "a love" for their small village in South Lebanon, called Mimes. In a shaky voice, he recounted that

> Mimes peopled our infancy . . . because she [Abidão's mother] would speak about Mimes, Mimes, and we would stay imagining what would Mimes be like, right? She would speak about how it was located on the top of a mountain, really beautiful . . . and she didn't get it wrong. The first time that I went there, I saw Mimes on top of the mountain, those clear houses surrounded by olive groves. I mean, beyond beauty, it was really moving (*muito emocionante*).

In a parallel fashion, twenty-something Ahmed noted that "we travel first to better know our relatives . . . and to know various cities, historical and new." He highlighted sites like Baalbeek, Beitedine, and others that "have much history." Dr. Said, a medical doctor in his thirties, explained that "first, I liked seeing the relatives again . . . and also coming to know Lebanon. I visited more places . . . I liked Baalbeek, I liked Jouneih and I liked South Lebanon." Another thirty-year-old, Beto, noted that during a trip to Lebanon in 1999, he visited paternal relatives, as well as ruins in Baalbeek and the Jeita Grotta. Like the Brazilian heritage consumers of Syrian-Lebanese origins in the 1960s, contemporary

Arab-Brazilian experiences of familial villages and state-regulated sites over-
lapped in homeland tourism.

Anti-Zionism, not surprisingly, was originally absent in such travel plans.
Arabs in Brazil never specified a desire to visit the sites of past Israeli attacks.
Generally, conflicts in the Middle East were contrasted with the so-called "coexistence" between Arabs and Jews in Brazil. Following a similar professional
trajectory, Arab descendants recounted that many of their associates were
Jews. "Who is living there [in the Middle East]," explained Rafael, "doesn't
believe in what is happening here. But this doesn't mean that the Jew who goes
to the store of the Arab will invite the Arab to his home . . . It depends." Yet,
this ambivalence was often overlooked. As Sr. Mário idealized, "Arabs and
Jews integrated themselves a lot here . . . Brazil can break the structures of all
sectarianisms . . . Brazilians, and Brazil, are able to transform all rancor." This
celebration of Arab-Jewish relations in Brazil reflects the ideology of racial
democracy, a national mythology which simultaneously works against Afro-
Brazilians and anti-racism in Brazil.

Nationalist politics aside, flows of people from Brazil to the Middle East continue to draw the attention of European-based transnational airline companies
today. In my visits to the São Paulo branches of Alitalia and KLM (before its
merger with Air France in 2004), managers seemed more than familiar with
the quantified databases of Brazil–Middle East flight patterns. They easily
accessed numerical representations of such routes, stored in the mainframe
computers of the airlines' European headquarters. In 2000, a KLM manager
related, almost 25,000 passengers flew between the two regions, for a profit of
$31 million. This, however, was only 2 percent of all the airline tickets sold in
the world. Viewing such a paltry number, I asked why enterprises would be
interested in a market segment so evidently small. "We're interested because
it's sales," responded the manager from Alitalia.

Air France is interested too, but in ways that differ from their mid-twentieth-
century advertising campaign. In 2000, Parisian headquarters informed the
branch office in Brazil that part of its budget should be allocated to *publici-
dade étnica* (ethnic advertising). Brazilian executives subsequently "elected"
three *colônias* (communities) as target groups: Arabs, Germans, and Jews. Air
France's transnational advertising agency, Carrillo Pastore Euro RSCG, ran the
campaign for each community. An archetypal advertisement was designed to
fit into each ethnic press, notwithstanding different destinations. The full-page
ad featured a green highway sign with white trim and lettering. Its background
was a blue sky and white fluffy clouds. The sign had two arrows, but instead of

denoting either eastern or western directions, each respectively pointed downwards to "Brazil" and upwards toward the sky. The downward arrow pointed to "São Paulo" and "Rio de Janeiro." The skyward arrow indicated the cities abroad to which the given readership would be destined. In Arab community magazines,[6] the ten cities in white script included Beirut, Amman, Cairo, and Damascus. In German magazines, three of the twelve cities were Berlin, Frankfurt, and Hamburg. Only Tel Aviv and Paris were listed in Jewish magazines.[7] Flying high above the highway sign in the blue sky was an Air France plane with the message "Air France: never have the continents been so close."

Marketing, however, is not only the domain of airlines. Not unlike its earlier initiatives, the Syrian state has co-sponsored seven excursions since the early 1990s, generally called the *Encontro com as Raízes,* "Roots Encounter." Respectively bringing together three dozen youth and/or adults of Middle Eastern descent, the tourist program became a familiar, if intermittent, leisure opportunity for Brazilians during winter vacation months. In an akin albeit more systematic fashion, the Lebanese state has sponsored annual excursions for second and third generations, the so-called "emigrant youth camp." Since 1996, it has brought together "Lebanese" youth from Africa, Asia, and the Americas, including Brazilians (the largest delegation in 2001). For three weeks every July, the Lebanese Ministry of Foreign Affairs and Emigrants escorts teenagers and twenty-somethings to tourist "marvels." In doing so, it hopes to persuade youth to recurrently vacation there. Soon after the 2001 camp came to an end, for instance, one official reflected that "we want them to come back to Lebanon," qualifying that participants will feel compelled to return not to live, but to visit. The state also recruited youth to publicize, if only by word of mouth, the "good side" of Lebanon. In the camp's opening ceremony in 2001, an official beckoned to participants: "We are faithful to you and we count on you to be an ambassador of Lebanon in your host country." Another director later added that "the Lebanese government wants you to *divulgar* (publicize) Lebanese culture and tourism . . . in your countries of emigration." Publicity is useful to airline companies and states alike.

This advertising approach to diaspora was made clear in the perspective of the publicity director in the Lebanese Ministry of Tourism, Mme Boushra. In her words, there is a necessity "to realize a campaign for Lebanese descendents in Brazil." She explained that

> Brazil is home to the first largest Lebanese community . . . I'm sure that they'd be happy to come to Lebanon . . . because they've heard about the homeland from their parents and grandparents who keep beautiful images of Lebanon,

who always speak about their villages and homeland. And so their children and grandchildren have these beautiful images, this myth of Lebanon in their heads. And when they come here, they will see the Lebanon that they have always heard about.

Descendants' aforementioned desire to visit the village of their emigrant parents or grandparents forms part of the market strategy of the Lebanese state itself.

With this in mind, the Lebanon-based executive, Mr. Amir, planned an advertising campaign in Brazil promoting Lebanon's tourism. One of his projects included an excursion for youth of Lebanese descent. With the support and stamp of the Lebanese Ministry of Tourism, he created a pamphlet in Portuguese. He then distributed it to Lebanese-Brazilian clubs, negotiated with major tourism operators in Brazil, and asked two journalists to write op-ed pieces about the excursion. Asked "Why Brazil?," Mr. Amir's reply was direct: it "has the biggest reserve of Lebanese descendants . . . There is no other country in the world that has so many . . . [and] it's a virgin market." As the campaign got under way in early 1999, though, Israeli planes bombed Lebanon. The negative publicity generated by the attacks, concluded Mr. Amir, "made everything difficult" and the project was indefinitely shelved.

But the very sites of past Israeli attacks were transformed into memorial shrines. One site in this tourism of turbulence is the southern Lebanese village of Qana. As Israel launched a sixteen-day artillery attack on South Lebanon in 1996, Qana found itself caught in the crossfire. Called "Operation Grapes of Wrath," Israeli military forces allegedly aimed to stomp out Hezballah bases, but "mistakenly" dropped bombs on a United Nations shelter in the village of Qana, killing more than one hundred innocent civilians and UN peacekeepers. In order to "remember" the brutal attack, the Lebanese government made the bombed-out UN compound into a memorial shrine. Today, Lebanese tourist agencies and even the *Lonely Planet* guide instruct heritage seekers to visit the Qana Memorial in the newly liberated South. It was also one of the sites visited by the emigrant youth camp, in which I also participated, in July 2001.

Our tour buses ground to a halt beside an almost completely destroyed building. On its unsteady tower was written "UN." Two intimidating tanks were parked nearby. As sixty members of the Brazilian delegation made their way off the buses, several boys climbed on the tanks and asked friends to take pictures. The festive entourage continued into the memorial, despite signs that read "The New Holocaust: 18 April 1996 United Nations Hospital." No one took note of the six or seven eight-meter-long marble tombs in which rested the remains of the 106 people killed. One tour guide lost patience and screamed for everyone to show respect in such a solemn site. "This is the place of the holocaust of the twentieth century," he bellowed. "This is where the Israelis massacred 106 Lebanese . . . the number one criminal for the Lebanese is the Israelis who killed 106 unarmed civilians here in 1996."

Silenced, the youth walked among the memorial's tombs and spaces. Inside an adjacent room, there were two walls full of photographs taken in the aftermath of the bombing raid. Images of strewn body parts and women grasping the spilled entrails of children shocked everyone. One Brazilian friend pointed to a picture where a baby's head was blown off. The group then shuffled toward another area where the remains of a church lay behind glass windows. As we gazed inside, an official professed, "This is our resistance." The memorial—its white tombs, bloody photographs, and broken cement remains—brought youth face-to-face with a war that they neither did nor could experience firsthand. Like other tourists, however, we were soon escorted back onto buses and brought to the next site: nearby Christian rock carvings that may suggest that present-day Qana is biblical Cana. In this fragmented sense, the destroyed UN compound was just one of many tourist sites visited that day in South Lebanon.

In the next week, the emigrant youth camp visited the most grisly site in this tourism of turbulence, the al-Khiam prison near the Israeli border. Historically, it was here that Israel and its proxy army, the South Lebanese Army (SLA), tortured Lebanese resistance fighters. After Israel withdrew from South Lebanon in April 2000, the prison was turned into an "impromptu museum and memorial for its victims" (Jousiffe 2001, 240). Entering the camp, we were soon enveloped by signs in English and Arabic which indicated the bathrooms to be used by tourists and where prisoners were once tortured: on the right was the "Men's Bathroom"; on the left, the "Room for Investigation and Torture by Electricity." Passing by detainee cells, some emigrant youth in their teens and twenties knelt down into the caged cubicles. Camera flashes lit the dark festive air. Everyone "played prisoner" for the day. The tourist glee, however, again turned into silence as bearded men, former prisoners, spoke of their experience in the camp. In an open courtyard within the camp, Brazilians struggled to listen while tour guides tried to translate the ex-prisoners' stories from Arabic to Portuguese. "They [Israelis] passed electrical shocks on our face, on our body," began one man. "We suffered a lot. They would beat us until we couldn't walk. They'd throw water on us and then whip us." Another ex-prisoner reassured his listeners: "This prison is known in the entire world and now you will know it." If emigrant youth traveled to Lebanon "to know their origins," they would surely leave also knowing the misdeeds of Zionism as well.[8]

A few weeks after the youth camp ended, I met with the officials who over-saw the program in the Lebanese Ministry of Foreign Affairs and Emigrants. Very conscientious of these intense experiences in homeland tourism, one director explained:

> Our objective is not only a tourist one. It is to introduce the youth to their nation, and so the camp has a national dimension. Lebanon has suffered a lot with Israel. It has been attacked. Its citizens have been killed. Since Lebanon has suffered a lot from Israel, we of course would include these national symbols. There is a lot to be learned visiting Khiam and Qana, national symbols . . . In doing the camp, we wanted to let third and fourth generations know the way Lebanon has suffered, the way it bleeds . . . and . . . to know the deeds of Israel in Lebanon.

In strengthening the identification of Arab-Brazilians with the national home-land, however, Lebanese authorities sought to inculcate in them an absolute rejection of Israel.

Similar dynamics characterized the half dozen or so tourist excursions to Syria. Participants spoke of being brought to Quneitra, a village that was completely destroyed with the Israeli pullout after the 1973 war and has since been "preserved" as a material testament to Zionist aggression. With official guides and permits, excursion members were escorted around the "ghost-town." Exhibited were the remains of bombed houses whose rooftops still lay on the ground, a hospital that was "like a skeleton" after being used for bomb drills by the Israeli army, and other razed structures. As part of the tour, visi-tors were also brought into a small house wherein stood a small replica of the hundreds of houses and streets of the town before Israel leveled them.[9] At-tentive to the ideological agenda of the tour, one elderly participant, Dr. João, sardonically noted that "they [the Syrian authorities] wanted to show us what the Jews (*judeus*) did."

Back in São Paulo, most spoke at length about the horrors of the destruc-tion exacted by the Israelis. At a dinner organized for the "Roots Encounter" participants to Syria, a speaker paused to denounce such a "violent act of hate." Those sitting at my table nodded their heads in agreement. Even a middle-aged businessman commented that he "didn't see anything standing" in the once well-populated village. He added, "It's as if one day to the next, all the build-ings on Avenida Paulista [a main artery in São Paulo] would be destroyed." Another middle-aged participant, Sr. Ismail, later noted, "We went there . . . to this place, out of this world (*fora de série*). It shows how the war was, that war that they had [pause]. I even have a book [about it] that I brought from there. I have the book from there." In this tourism of turbulence, diasporic visitors could consume history books and other mementos memorializing Israeli aggression.

Lebanese-Brazilians also spoke of such experiences after their return to Brazil. Sandro, a second-generation high school student, noted that the tours around Qana and al-Khiam were his favorite part of the trip. In his own words, "I was happy to know that the mouse wasn't afraid of the cat, because . . . the people would say, 'I am Lebanese. I am not afraid of countries that judge [themselves] to be superior to us.'" These sites, he continued, were part of the government's desire "to show Arab descendants that they were sort of blind-folded (*meio-tapados*), which were the majority [of them], and that they weren't really inside of the situation to understand what was going on." Sandro concluded that "for sure now I know who I am. I am Lebanese and Lebanese do not bow to anyone. I am not inferior to anyone . . . I am Lebanese." Although recognizing that the tours were "kind of staged" (*meio-orchestrados*), this youth did not simply reproduce the government line, but also captured the ways that Israeli violence continues to mark Lebanese self-understandings much further afield than the homeland itself.

Others took issue with the tours in Qana and al-Khiam. The point of contention concerned both the motives of Lebanese state officials and the "one sided" view of Arab-Israeli relations. After being shown the photographs of decapitated women and children in the memorial shrine in Qana, for instance, one Arab-Brazilian youth commented to me in a very low voice, "This is brainwashing." Several cohorts made the same statement during the trip and afterwards in Brazil. In a similar vein, a high school student commented: "They [Lebanese state officials] want us to be angry at Israel." A university student, Melissa, added, "But there's no use. There isn't this prejudice in Brazil." Likewise, Isabella, a high school student, opined:

> I found the political tours sort of revolting (*meio-revoltante*) because, in my opinion, they intended to create in us hate toward the Israelis. But, in Brazil, our culture does not permit this kind of racism due to our miscegenation. They [Lebanese state officials] can show us the effects of war, but not motivate us to hate a country or a culture.

Questioning the motives of state officials and anti-Zionist tourism, Isabella and others articulated critiques in the Brazilian nationalist language of racial democracy and mixture. Rather than dwell on the consequences that such claims carry for Afro-Brazilians and the anti-racist struggle in Brazil, homeland tourists surmised that Arab and Jewish relations in an alleged racially tolerant country were not fraught with the "prejudice" and "racism" that severed them in the Middle East. Nationalist precepts thus potentially countered the logics of exclusion that derive from them.

Equally important, Isabella launched into another self-reflective commentary about the camp and how it related to her own lifestyle in Brazil. She explained:

> On the trip, I came to know the city of my great-grandfather . . . It was a little sad because this city was . . . destroyed by the war. But it's interesting to know that I am not simply Brazilian. I have another past in another country. . . . My future project will be to . . . put together a genealogical tree.

Both overtly political and profoundly personal, this intensified identification with the homeland was not limited to introspection, but was put into practice within the diaspora as well. Upon his return to São Paulo, a third-generation Lebanese-Brazilian boy, Carlos, took it upon himself to give a public presentation about his travel experience. The idea for the event came from Lebanese state officials who stressed the importance of "publicizing" the "good side" of the country. In the *oficina cultural* of a middle-class neighborhood center in São Paulo, Carlos's family organized a table lined with pamphlets of Lebanese tourism, bills and coins of the national currency, and foods. Maps were taped on the walls. A large Lebanese flag hung from a post. For around twenty people, Carlos spoke for more than two hours about Lebanon as a "crossroads" of civilization, as the land of the mythic Phoenicians, as a country beholding natural and cultural marvels. He assumed the responsibility imparted to him by the Lebanese state: becoming an "ambassador" and "spokesperson" for Lebanon in São Paulo.

In the middle of the presentation, however, Carlos grew nervous. He had touched on the "political aspect" of the country's history. Toward the end of the youth camp, he explained, tourists were brought to the "Liberated South" in Lebanon. It was there, Carlos pointed out, that everyone visited the village of Qana, where a UN compound had been bombed in 1996, and the al-Khiam prison used by "Israelis" until their withdrawal in 2000. Recounting some of the ex-prisoners' stories, Carlos stated that the latter "saw less than ten minutes of sun each day. They were whipped with the insides of tires." Though the details varied, the overall sentiment was conveyed: the Lebanese suffered at the hands of the Israelis in South Lebanon. Carlos thus fulfilled his role as ambassador of Lebanon in Brazil—or did he?

What caught my attention during this part of Carlos's talk was exactly that which was not stated. Long before the public presentation, he confided to me (and his family and friends) that, though absolutely adoring the emigrant youth camp and Lebanon, he felt troubled by the politicized tours in Qana and al-Khiam prison. Recalling his own sentiment immediately after visiting the sites, Carlos ironically pointed out that he himself, "who couldn't kill even a fly," came to feel resentment toward Israel. He concluded that these tourist sites were "pure politics to have us be angry at Israel." Notwithstanding this muffled criticism of the clear intentions of Lebanese state officials, however, Carlos's presentation tacitly reproduced their anti-Zionist representations, even though he himself expressed ambivalence about them.

At 9:00 PM, the presentation came to an end. The flag was brought down. The map folded. The kafiya worn by Carlos's younger brother was removed, rolled up, and placed back in a bag. As the young tourist, his family, and I made our way into the cool night's breeze, his mother volunteered, "Son, I am very proud of you." Questions about whether Carlos collaborated with the Lebanese state's anti-Zionism, or whether he should have clarified his personal ambivalence about it, were not matters of great concern to Carlos or his family. As a fifteen-year-old boy who spoke eloquently about the country whence stemmed his paternal grandfather, his family was proud of him. Indeed, this was an exercise of the intensified identity which Carlos was still getting used to: being Lebanese in Brazil.

Travel flows between Brazil and the Middle East are hardly a novel phenomenon, but the techniques and targeted advertising employed by states and corporations are as unprecedented as they are unpredictable in terms of their outcomes. While they may increase Brazil–Middle East ticket sales as well as enrich the domestic tourist industries in Syria and Lebanon, Arab-Brazilians put to use such travel practices in their own particular ways. Amidst the increasing acceptance of the false binary between "Arab" and "Jew," their voices resound that there are indeed culturally creative, and particular, ways to disrupt absolutist impositions. Such disruptions, however, are hardly liberating in and of themselves, but are rather part of an edifice of inequality within Brazil itself.

Arab-Brazilian self-understandings lend some empirical grist to a "cosmopo- litical" agenda (Cheah and Robbins 1998, 9). Although still largely unacknowl- edged and ambivalent, Arab-Brazilians used nationalist precepts to counter the exclusionary logics that stem from them. In rejecting anti-Zionist ideology through Brazilian racial ideology, they help us to see that "the journey that might take us beyond the nation must first pass through" it (Chatterjee 2010, 165).

## Notes

This essay is based on research funded by a Fulbright-Hays Doctoral Dissertation Award in 2000–2001. I am greatly indebted to and wish to thank both Paul Amar and Paulo

Gabriel Hilu da Rocha Pinto for their critical suggestions for this essay and for all their work articulating, organizing, and legitimizing scholarship on the Middle East in Brazil. The essay was prepared for their seminar "O Oriente Médio no Brasil, o Brasil no Oriente Médio: Perspectivas Transnacionais e Comparativas," at the Universidade Federal Fluminense (UFF), Niterói, RJ, Brazil, in October 2003. A later version of this essay was presented at the 102nd Annual Meeting of the American Anthropological Association (AAA) in Chicago, in November 2004. I wish to thank my panel's organizer, O. Hugo Benavides, for his words of encouragement. Finally, I want to thank Bela Feldman Bianco for inviting me to present this work for the Departamento de Antropologia and the Centro de Estudos de Migrações Internacionais (CEMI) at the Universidade Estadual de Campinas (UNICAMP) in 2006. Portions of this chapter were published in an earlier version in John Tofik Karam, *Another Arabesque* (Philadelphia: Temple University Press, 2007).

1. I do not mean to confuse the Zionist state of Israel and Jewishness. However, Arab-Brazilians themselves used "Israel" and "Jews" as synonyms. This conflation of Zionism and Judaism is not dealt with here.

2. "Air France: A Pioneira do Atlantico Sul," advertisement in *A Pátria* on October 13, 1951, 2.

3. "Viagem maravilhosa ao Oriente Médio e à Europa," advertisement in *A Pátria* on October 13, 1951, 4.

4. Riad G. Cury, "Brevíssims impressões sôbre uma viagem ou a descoberta do novo num velho mundo," *Homs,* November/December 1965. This entire issue of the Club Homs magazine is dedicated to the Brazilian delegation that participated in the 1965 congress in Syria.

5. Ibid.

6. In the Arab-Brazilian community, the three magazines chosen were *Al-Urubat, Chams,* and *Orient Express.*

7. Meeting with the president of Amet, who is the editor in chief of a popular Jewish community magazine, I raised the possibility that many Jewish Brazilians were from Arab cities and nations (and, implicitly, Arab as well as Jewish). But the magazine editor replied that Jewish Brazilians were Jewish, not Arab, *ponto final* ("end of story").

8. As emigrant youth were escorted back toward the buses, many of us passed by a "souvenir" stand. A large yellow and green sign read "Site where donations for the Islamic Resistance are Accepted." The souvenirs sold included Hezballah flags in three sizes, Hezballah baseball caps, postcards of Hezballah's leader, Nasrallah, VHS tapes of bombing raids and the homecoming of displaced families after liberation, key chains with Hezballah insignia, and coloring books that recounted Hezballah and Lebanon's struggle, as well as dozens of other items. Like sight-seeing in any other tourist site, this "tour" had its own unique mementos.

9. It was also said that tourists were shown the water-rich territory just south of Quneitra that was occupied by Israel in 1973. Seeing the rich pastures, one participant reflected that Israel would never return the land because of its fertility.

## References

Andrews, George Reid. 1991. *Blacks and Whites in São Paulo, 1888 – 1988.* Madison: University of Wisconsin Press.

Appadurai, Arjun. 1996. *Modernity at Large: Cultural Dimensions of Globalization.* Minneapolis: University of Minnesota Press.

Cardoso, Fernando Henrique, and Octávio Ianni. 1960. *Côr e mobilidade social em Florianopolis.* São Paulo: Companhia Editora Nacional.

Chatterjee, Partha 2010. *Empire and Nation: Selected Essays.* New York: Columbia University Press.

Cheah, Pheng, and Bruce Robbins. eds. 1998. *Cosmopolitics: Thinking and Feeling beyond the Nation.* Minneapolis: University of Minnesota Press.

Freyre, Gilberto. (1933) 1977. *Casa-Grande e Senzala.* Rio de Janeiro: José Olympio Editora.

Gualtieri, Sarah M. A. 2009. *Between Arab and White: Race and Ethnicity in the Early Syrian American Diaspora.* Berkeley: University of California Press.

Gulick, John. 1955. *Social Structure and Culture Change in a Lebanese Village.* New York: Wenner Gren.

Hasenbalg, Carlos. 1979. *Discriminação e Desigualdades Racias no Brasil.* Rio de Janeiro: Graal.

Jousiffe, Ann. 2001. *Lonely Planet: Lebanon.* Singapore: SNP printing.

Khater, Akram. 2001. *Inventing Home: Emigration, Gender, and the Middle Class in Lebanon, 1870–1920.* Berkeley: University of California Press.

———. 2005. "Becoming 'Syrian' in America: A Global Geography of Ethnicity and Nation." *Diaspora: A Journal of Transnational Studies* 14(2) (2005): 299–331.

Lesser, Jeffrey. 1996. "(Re)Creating Ethnicity: Middle Eastern Immigration to Brazil." *The Americas* 53(1): 45–65.

———. 1999. *Negotiating National Identity: Immigrants, Minorities, and the Struggle for Ethnicity in Brazil.* Durham, NC: Duke University Press.

Nascimento, Abdias do. 1977. "Democracia racial: Mito ou realidade." *Versus* 16 (November).

Safady, Jamil. 1972. *Panorama da Imigração Árabe.* São Paulo: Editora Comercial Safady.

Salibi, Kamal Suleiman. 1976. *The Modern History of Lebanon.* London: Greenwood Press.

Schein, Louisa. 1998. "Importing Miao Brethren to Hmong America: A Not-So-Stateless Transnationalism." In *Cosmopolitics: Thinking and Feeling Beyond the Nation,* ed. Pheng Cheah and Bruce Robbins, 163–191. Minneapolis: University of Minnesota Press.

Skidmore, Thomas. 1974. *Black into White: Race and Nationality in Brazilian Thought.* New York: Oxford University Press.

Wagley, Charles, ed. 1952. *Race and Class in Rural Brazil.* New York: Unesco.

Williams, Judith. 1968. *The Youth of Haouch El Harimi, A Lebanese Village.* Cambridge, MA: Harvard University Press.

# 11

# Rio de Janeiro's Global Bazaar
## Syrian, Lebanese, and Chinese Merchants in the Saara

*Neiva Vieira da Cunha and Pedro Paulo Thiago de Mello*
*Translated by Silvia C. Ferreira*

The Saara, a popular commercial region in Rio de Janeiro, has been largely defined by the presence of the many immigrants who have made it a thriving commercial hub and a center for multi-ethnic residence. While the region was historically a Syrian and Lebanese enclave, the arrival of a new wave of Asian immigration in the 1990s generated important changes and ethnically marked tensions. A social-historical and anthropological analysis of conflict and resolution in the Saara sheds light on different notions of identity and commerce in Rio de Janeiro's bazaar district, often referred to as a "mini United Nations."

～

## Introduction

The Saara is at once Rio de Janeiro's most enduring and most vibrant popular commercial area. It comprises eleven city blocks and 1,250 stores (Ribeiro 2000; Worcman 2000), and is frequented daily by many people from all over the city. According to the president of its principal organization, about 150,000 people a week come to the area. Located in the center of the city, near primary administrative and business centers, and not far from the major seaport, the Saara's customers are attracted by both the wide variety and the low prices of its products. First established by immigrants at the turn of the twentieth century, the area quickly became a stronghold for migrants who have imbued it with several layers of distinct character. Besides Portuguese and Spanish immigrants, there has also been a marked presence of Syrians, Lebanese, and Armenians, as well as Jews of various origins. More recently, the area has become home to Chinese and Korean immigrants as well. All of these groups tended to make their livelihood through commerce.

The Saara derives its name from the organization that represents the local merchants—the "Association of Friends of Alfândega Street and Adjacent Areas." The term "Saara" refers to both the commercial area and the association. In order to differentiate between the two, we will use "Saara" to refer to the place and "SAARA" in all capital letters to refer to the merchants' organization. The fact that "Saara" is pronounced the same way in Portuguese as "Sahara" has stimulated over the years an endless flood of "Arabian Nights" and "Oriental Bazaar" jokes and caricatures. This zone is characterized by buildings that are designed to combine home and workplace. Businesses consist mainly of vending stalls and retail stores, as well as some small tailor shops and bakeries. Its proximity to the Atlantic port in Guanabara Bay also contributes to the area's unique configuration. In the nineteenth century, Rua da Alfândega was the main route around which the city developed and home to one of its principal crossroads. At that time, the area was inhabited mostly by Portuguese merchants. The region as a whole was characterized by the presence of large wholesale companies, as well as warehouses for the storage of goods—primarily drinks, foodstuffs, textiles, and odds and ends. The goods were distributed by merchants or peddlers, who supplied the capitals as well as the smaller cities in the interior of the province (Blyth 1991; Elhajji 2008). With the advent of industrialization in Brazil, during the first decades of the twentieth century, business on Rua da Alfândega began to change. Industries began to distribute their goods directly to storeowners, allowing for retail commerce to develop (Ribeiro 2000; Worcman 2000).

Saara's evolving cultural identity has reflected the shifting diversity of the ethnic groups that make it up. The immigrants that would definitively influence the area began arriving as early as the end of the nineteenth century, and continued to arrive in large numbers until the 1920s. According to the Instituto Brasileiro de Geografia e Estatística (IBGE)'s Demographic Census of 1920, there were 50,246 Syrian-Lebanese immigrants in Brazil at that time. Among the many motivations for this migration were the economic crisis suffered by the silk industry in Lebanon, World War I, and the French and English imperial presence in the Middle East (Pinto 2010). In the case of the Syrians and Lebanese, many migrated because they were expelled from their homelands by Ottoman imperial expansion. Sephardic Jews also began leaving the Middle East for Brazil during this time, as did Ashkenazi Jews from Eastern

Europe. Both groups sought to escape persecution and ethnic discrimination in the hopes of building better lives in the Americas. The presence of different ethnic groups—especially Sephardic Jews, Syrian and Lebanese Maronites, Christian Orthodox, and Catholic Armenians—each of which specialized in different commercial activities gave the Saara the semblance of an oriental market like a *suq* or bazaar. All of these groups coexisted with other ethnic groups as well, such as the Portuguese, Greek, and Spanish. This diversity led the merchants themselves to refer to the marketplace as "Rio de Janeiro's mini-UN" (Bittencourt 2004). In the 1940s, efforts by the city to clear out and modernize huge swaths of the downtown's built environment led to the birth of collective action among threatened merchants in the area. The construction of Avenida Presidente Vargas, which was part of the plan to remodel Rio de Janeiro designed by the French urban architect Alfredo Agache, would have countless consequences for the city. It particularly affected the continuity of the urban landscape that characterized the Saara area. Intrusive interventions in urban renewal did not stop with the construction of Avenida Presidente Vargas. The construction of the Avenida Diagonal, which was also part of the original Agache Plan, began to be discussed by the end of the 1950s (Blyth 1991; Elhajji 2008). These violent changes to Rio de Janeiro's urban space threatened to destroy the Saara's thriving market.

In this context, the merchants decided to create an organization that would officially represent their collective interests, as well as ensure their continued presence in the region. The Association of Friends of Alfândega Street and Adjacent Areas was created in 1962, at which time its first governing board was formed and the current borders of the commercial area were delineated (Blyth 1991; Worcman 2000). Still in existence today, this organization is a nonprofit with the objective of administering local affairs, such as street cleaning, garbage collection, transportation of goods, advertising, parking, and local security. The organization of these services demonstrated the merchants' powerful ability to mobilize both politically and socially, and reaffirmed their common interests.

## History of Arab and Chinese Communities

Syrian and Lebanese immigrants first arrived at the port Cais Pharoux, situated in the current-day square Praça Quinze in the last two decades of the nineteenth century and the first decades of the twentieth (Elhajji 2008; Pinto 2010). The majority of them were Orthodox Christian or Maronite, with a minority of Muslims. As they arrived with Ottoman passports in hand, they were mislabeled *turcos* (Turks). The large-scale migration to Brazil that occurred in the 1920s comprised mostly Syrian and Lebanese immigrants, who initially established themselves on Rua da Alfândega and in the area around the square Praça da República. Jews of diverse origins were the next to arrive, with Sephardic Jews arriving from the Middle East and Ashkenazi Jews from Central and Eastern Europe. The Ashkenazi Jews, who generally came from Poland, Russia, and Romania, also arrived mainly in the 1920s. They first established themselves in Praça Onze, and only later in the area around Rua Senhor dos Passos.

When the immigrants first arrived, networks of family relations played a fundamental role for them. Immigrants tended to already have a few relatives established in the area who could serve as mediators for them. These relatives would house the newcomers and facilitate their assimilation into their new life. They would help them find work, sometimes by establishing them in their own trades as tailors, shoemakers, or cobblers, as was common among Jewish immigrants (Elhajji 2008; Pinto 2010). Or they would establish the newcomers as peddlers, providing them with a variety of goods—buttons, ribbons, ties, perfumes, textiles, yarn, needles—which were to be transported in suitcases or trunks and sold door-to-door. It was through these familial networks that newcomers were able to secure goods on credit, paying for them only after they had sold them.

Despite the predominantly economic motivations of this migration, the first generations of these immigrants claimed that they intended to return to their homelands as soon as political circumstances allowed it. Meanwhile, as time went by, they grew accustomed to their new home. As they married and started families in Brazil, returning to the homeland became nothing more than a lost dream (Grün 1992; Truzzi 1992). Immigrants of Arab origin had often been farmers in their homelands. But they did not turn to farming in Brazil, as the nation's large-scale agricultural system was completely unlike the small-scale subsistence farming that they knew. The plantation-style farming that was the norm in Brazil meant access to the land was no simple matter. Instead, as they toured the countryside with their suitcases and trunks full of wares, these immigrants established themselves as peddlers. They would bring products from the city to the countryside and vice versa, often fulfilling specific requests for products.

Even though Portuguese and Italian merchants had previously filled the role of peddler in Brazil, immigrants of Arab origin introduced new business models to the commercial activity, including higher-quality goods, high product turnover, sales and clearances, and sales made on credit (Ribeiro 2000; Worcman 2000). As their profits increased, peddlers were able to open stores in bigger cities, and different ethnicities began to specialize in the sales of different goods. As business prospered, the immigrants were able to help bring over relatives from the homeland and to help them the way they had been helped. They would help newcomers acquire goods that they could then hawk. Many of these new immigrants established themselves in the vicinity of Rua da Alfândega, often living in the apartments above their stores.

As their businesses prospered and new generations of their families were born in Brazil, the immigrants' intention of returning to the homeland effectively disappeared. This happened as their children and grandchildren embraced a Brazilian identity while still maintaining familiarity with their ethnic origins. The biggest difference and source of conflict between the generations can be found in the process of choosing a successor for the family business. Generally, children were prepared to participate in the family business by older generations, who would socialize them in the various inner workings of the business from an early age. They would normally begin by assisting in general services, then move on to first the gift-wrapping station, then the cash register, then accounting, until they were finally deemed ready to run the store. From the point of view of the older generations, it was necessary for their children to experience these various intermediary stages before gaining full control of the store. However, many of the younger children did not wish to become merchants and instead aspired to professions that would provide them with more social capital.

## The Chinese and the Koreans

The 1960s saw the arrival of new groups of immigrants who would change the urban landscape as well as local business. It was during this period that the first Chinese immigrants arrived, followed by the first Korean immigrants, although it is difficult to give precise numbers.

In the mid-1990s, large numbers of Asian immigrants began arriving in the Saara. They were all subsumed under the general category of "Asian." The majority were Chinese immigrants from Taiwan and the south of mainland China, speaking mostly Mandarin and Cantonese. South Koreans and Japanese immigrants also came to the Saara, although in much lower numbers. In 2012, the Chinese consulate in Rio estimated that the Chinese population in Brazil numbered around 150,000 (Shu 2012). Asian immigration happened so rapidly that at the time it was deemed by other local merchants to be an invasion of sorts. Asian immigrants tended to come from São Paulo, where the business sectors in which they specialized—the selling of gifts, stationery, and sweets—

were already too crowded. The majority of them did not speak Portuguese. They had generally entered Brazil through the city of Foz do Iguaçu, having journeyed first from Asia to Ciudad del Este in Paraguay.

The phenomenon of Asian immigration constitutes a diaspora. In the case of the Chinese, they generally left Taiwan and mainland China for a journey that would ultimately bring them to North America or Europe. But there were a number of unique characteristics that distinguished this diaspora from that of the Syrians and the Lebanese. It was marked, for example, by a high degree of mobility. This means that the Chinese tended to immigrate to places temporarily, rather than putting down permanent roots. Their migration was also marked by a constant, strong relationship with their hometowns in China, maintained through a complex system of solidarity between familial and clan networks. Chinese immigration was not entirely composed of cheap labor, either. It also included many entrepreneurs, who arrived with sufficient finances and resources to set up shop in their new nations. This was made possible by their aforementioned familial and clan networks (Liu 2000; Ma and Cartier 2003; Zhang 2001). More than 90 percent of Brazil's Chinese and Korean population had originally established itself in São Paulo, in the area surrounding the commercial street Rua 25 de Maio and in the Liberdade and Bom de Retiro neighborhoods. The rest were scattered throughout Brazil, predominantly in Rio de Janeiro, Paraná, and in areas with international ports.

The Asian presence in the Saara in Rio meant more competition for local merchants. But aside from new commercial practices, the Chinese also brought with them distinct methods of financing and their own culture. They were often perceived by local merchants as closed and as unable to master the Portuguese language. But these immigrants continued to arrive in large numbers, and eventually Asians became the third-largest ethnic group in the Saara—outnumbered only by the Syrio-Lebanese and the Jewish community, according to SAARA's data.

For the Chinese, this quick ascension was made possible by the availability of resources, which allowed them to buy and rent stores, including some of the more historical storefronts. This availability was sustained by a credit system that was based on cooperatives. This system influenced the Chinese and Asian economy in the twentieth century and is considered one of Asia's most successful economic models, even in Japan. The model is based on the formation of networks structured by familial and clan connections, leading to the creation of financial institutions that are similar to banks (Chung 2000). These networks then form relationships with one another, thus multiplying their financial capacity and their labor pool.

In other words, the merchants of Chinese origin were not tied to the conventional financial and credit models of Western capitalism. The Chinese system functions under certain rules of conduct, under which cooperation through familial or clan networks reduces competition. It does not eliminate competition altogether, but favors collaboration over the individual development of a group or business. This leads networks to leverage their available resources in order to finance commercial ventures. According to some studies, these networks are behind China's current private businesses and are one of the mainstays of that nation's high productivity rate (Chung 2000).

**Conflict and Dispute**

The arrival of Asian immigrants in the Saara set off a series of conflicts and disputes between them and other ethnic groups. Local business was affected by the chronological distance between the different groups of immigrants, perceived cultural differences in commercial practices and in more general behaviors, and perceived differences in adaptability and degrees of assimilation, as well as by a general stereotype that Asian immigrants were part of the "Chinese mafia," a representation that was very common in the local press as well as among Saara's merchants, especially after a series of stories about Chinese merchants in São Paulo accused them of selling illegal products (see, for instance, *Isto É Brasil* 2001). For the traditional merchants who had been established in the area since the beginning of the twentieth century, the arrival of the Asian immigrants in the 1990s and 2000s constituted a social drama. It was a particularly difficult time, as local commerce was already feeling the effect of Brazil's economic crisis in the 1990s, high interest rates for financing, and one of the highest tax rates in the world. Although the family ties among the traditional merchants in the Saara meant high employee productivity rates, this proved insufficient to save their businesses from the supposed "invasion" of Asian immigrants. (In 1996, *Jornal do Brasil* published an extensive report about the "sudden" arrival of Chinese and other Asian immigrants at the Saara marketplace, "A invasão chinesa do Saara" [The Chinese Invasion of Saara's Marketplace]. See also Ribeiro 2000.) The new immigrants sold new goods at prices with which others could not compete. This meant that many Arab and Jewish merchants were forced to sell their businesses to Asians, who were almost always willing to pay cash up-front, according to Enio Bittencourt, the SAARA's president, and other merchants (Bittencourt 2004).

One of the business strategies employed by the Asian merchants was the opening of the dollar store. The local merchants from other ethnic groups reacted strongly to this practice, as they viewed it as a disloyal form of competition. Since they considered the Asian merchants to be a closed group that was unable to master the Portuguese language, they did not form bonds with them. In fact, Asian merchants tended to not establish relations beyond the strictly commercial vendor-client one, thus failing to conform to local social norms that treated the market as a public arena for the performance and definition of identities. The Asian business model, which is also based on family-run businesses, makes use of more extended networks of solidarity and financial support. It was this economic model that permitted the Chinese to arrive in the Saara with financial resources, labor, and a high-productivity business model. Their relationships with suppliers, for example, were also mediated through such networks, and thus allowed them to acquire merchandise at very low costs (Chung 2000). As a result, Asians were able to sell products extremely cheaply and in many cases to even practice dumping (liquidation of products at prices below their value, normally done to kill competition).

Another important factor in the success of Chinese entrepreneurs in the diaspora can be found in the work contracts of their employees. While merchants of Syrian or Lebanese origins tended to have familial or personal relations with their employees, relationships between Asian merchants and their employees were often based on debts, financial or otherwise. This meant that the merchants could expect dedication from their employees (Chung 2000). Many go so far as to consider the relationship one of servitude. The result is that the productivity of an Asian employee tended to be higher than that of one who was protected by Brazilian labor laws. Furthermore, the environment in these workplaces was much stricter, and many employees complained about not being allowed to have conversations during work hours and being expected to be constantly in motion.

The issue of gender also seems to have influenced the productivity of Asian employees, particularly the productive role played by businesswomen and female shopworkers. This visibility of women in Chinese businesses distinguished them from other ethnic groups that were already established in the Saara. We noticed that the role of women in stores run by Arabs was mostly reserved for behind-the-scenes work, with some exceptions, as our ethnographic research showed. In general, the store hierarchy can be said to begin with those responsible for general maintenance and cleaning, followed by the "scouts," vendors, clerks, and cashiers, up to the managers and owners (with this last group responsible for opening and closing the store). In stores run by Arabs, women generally only occupied the top of this pyramid in the absence of available men. But in the case of the Chinese, it has been observed that women participate actively in the administration of the store. They can be seen at cash registers and helping customers. Meanwhile, men tend to do the heavier work, such as security and the monitoring of the products.

There is yet another characteristic that distinguishes the Asian merchants from those of other ethnicities: they are always in transit (Ma and Cartier 2003). In other words, they are enmeshed in a system of mobility and circulation. This does not mean that some of them did not establish themselves in the Saara on a more permanent basis. However, the fact is that the supposed Chinese "invasion" has all but disappeared today. The Asian presence in the Saara dissipated almost as rapidly as it emerged. As was discussed earlier, the ultimate objective of this migratory flux was often to gain access to markets in developed nations in North America and Europe. Moreover, the choice of Brazil seems to have been related to the facilities offered them by the local authorities, which allowed them access to the most prestigious ports. As restrictions on immigration and on both licit and illicit business have tightened since 2000, these groups changed routes in favor of less restrictive nations (Ma and Cartier 2003).

Previous waves of immigrants had arrived in the Saara with the idea of eventually returning to their homeland, but had ended up establishing themselves in Brazil and assimilating themselves into its culture instead. Asian immigrants, on the other hand, were constantly in motion. They were distinguished by their mobility and constant circulation, which enormously affected their perspective on assimilation to the local culture. Immigrants of Syrian and Lebanese origin sought to establish themselves in local commerce, and maintain the family business by preparing their children to succeed them and maintaining the expectation that they would continue the family legacy. But Chinese immigrants did not seek to establish themselves in local business, and instead pushed their children to seek positions in multinational businesses run by Asians but not in Japanese or Chinese enterprises run by more assimilated Asians who had migrated to Brazil in earlier waves a century before. Such enormous differences in perspective no doubt played a role in the animosity that other groups harbored toward the Asian immigrants. Even today, when there is no longer such a marked presence of Asians in the Saara, local merchants continue to refer to the Chinese as "them." The president of the SAARA association sums up local perceptions of the Chinese best when he says: "They are extremely closed. They came and opened their stores here but without trusting anybody" (Bittencourt 2004).

In some ways, the later arrival of Chinese immigrants in the Saara brought the issue of integration to the forefront. Already in their second and third generation, immigrants from other ethnic groups were mostly assimilated into the local culture and had firmly established themselves in the prevailing social order. But the presence of the Asians inaugurated a new succession process that seems to repeat the cycle of ethnic relations suggested by Ezra Park (Park [1916] 1967). Furthermore, the Chinese did not share the local memories of assimilation and mobilization. For example, they did not share the memory of mobilizing against the construction of Avenida Diagonal in the 1960s. These shared collective memories are an important component of the identities of the local merchants. The arrival of the Chinese and the Koreans led to changes in the social fabric as well as the cultural forms of the Saara. New forms of relations and social interactions were subsequently introduced in the region.

## The SAARA

While the Saara has neither gained the cultural relevance of a Middle Eastern bazaar nor become the city's Chinatown, it has important ramifications for Rio de Janeiro. It is simultaneously an economic enclave and an arena of dispute and definition of identities. The Saara can be said to be the site of the construction of shared values that result in a prevalent sense of belonging. This sense of belonging gains in significance when considered alongside the diversity of diasporas that have brought merchants to the area. It is thus possible to consider it a type of *moral region* (Park [1916] 1967), one that is built upon a work ethic and that is distinguished by the different processes of succession adopted by distinct ethnic groups.

In this context, it is easy to see why the SAARA (the merchant association) was attributed such importance. The organization was directly linked to the possibility of permanence and continuity of the economic activities that the immigrants had developed in that marketplace. However, the significance of the Saara seems to transcend economics. The Saara has necessitated the development of particular social relations, as evidenced by the solidarity and mutual assistance between merchants of diverse origins that have come to characterize the network of local relations. The interactions between different ethnic groups that share the space thus became a fundamental element in the construction and reconstruction of the Saara's identity.

However, the above-cited statement made by the president of the SAARA about the supposedly closed nature of the Chinese also demonstrates that the discourse of unity and consensus in Rio de Janeiro's so-called mini-UN is not without its conflicts and daily disputes. The organization prides itself on an efficient security system with about forty agents that can be found sprinkled throughout the consumer public. These private security guards are police officers who work the Saara during their days off, but remain directly linked to the local station. This security structure has contributed to the Saara's low level of violence. The most common crimes are pickpocketing and shoplifting, according to Bittencourt (2004), citing SAARA's data. The security structure has also prevented the accumulation of street vendors, beggars, and street children in the area. The SAARA is also active in regulating the conduct of the merchants, and this has no doubt minimized the impact of cultural differences between the Asian and the Syrian and Lebanese immigrants. If a merchant breaks one of the organization's rules, he risks having a security guard physically prevent him from working. It is rare but not unheard-of for the private guards to block the entrance of a store so that customers cannot enter in retaliation for the breaking of such a rule. This means that, to a certain extent, all ethnic groups have had to conform to local rules and business models.

However, this does not prevent the SAARA from turning a blind eye to certain behaviors that contradict the local laws, such as displaying merchandise outside of the stores and even selling pirated goods. (However, according to Bittencourt [2004], the responsibility to follow such laws falls on the owners, and the SAARA does not get involved in cases where the police seizes goods or punishes merchants.) The SAARA thus plays a fundamental role in the area, as on the one hand it imposes certain rules upon the merchants, and on the other hand it defends the interests of those same merchants against external actors such as tax collectors, police officers, competing street vendors, and mafia groups. The organization also acts as mediator of internal conflicts that result from cultural differences. It even mediates external conflicts at times, as in the episode in which its security guards were involved in the arrest of two members of the tongs[1] who had come to the Saara to extort Chinese merchants (Bittencourt 2004). Nevertheless, there are also other groups to which the merchants belong that will defend their interests, such as the networks so common to the Asian merchants. These organizations can be based on ethnicity, religion, affinity, or familial bonds.

All of this points to the complexity of the structure and social organization of business in the Saara, which is governed by webs of affiliation and belonging that crisscross and often overlap. The Saara's merchants thus have various organs at their disposal when it comes to negotiating their interests and settling their disputes. In such cases, the SAARA plays a fundamental but not exclusive role. It cannot stop new alliances from being made or broken as a result of conflicts. Networks of alliances formed in this way may establish their own parameters or morals that may or may not coincide with the Saara's norms.

The Muslim *hisba,* which establishes moral norms that regulate the markets of the Middle East, and the Chinese *guanxi,* which maintains relations based on trust, are examples of the distinct values that govern these groups' business practices and are part of the Saara's daily reality.

## Notes

An earlier version of this chapter was published in Portuguese as *"Libaneses & chineses: sucessão, conflito e disputa numa rua de comércio no Rio de Janeiro,"* in *Anuário Antropológico/2005* (Rio de Janeiro: Tempo Brasileiro, 2006), 155–169.

1. Tongs are Chinese gangs that have an armed branch that resembles a mafia group. According to the local police, all five Taiwanese mafia families—14k, Sun Yee On, Bamboo Union, Fuchien, and Flying Dragon—have a strong presence in Brazil.

## References

Bittencourt, Enio. 2004. Extensive fieldwork interview with the president of SAARA (Association of Friends of Alfândega Street and Adjacent Areas). 20–21 April 2004.

Blyth, Annabella. 1991. "Cristalização espacial e identidade cultural: Uma abordagem da herança urbana (O Saara, na área central da cidade do Rio de Janeiro)." Master's thesis, Geography Institute. Universidade Federal do Rio de Janeiro (UFRJ).

Chung, Wai-keung. 2000. "Institutional Transformation and the Creation of Chinese Entrepreneurial Networks." Paper presented at Corfu pre-conference session X: Diaspora entrepreneurial networks, 1000–2000, at 13th International Economic History Congress, Buenos Aires, July 22–26.

Crespo, Paloma Gómez. 1993. *Comprar y vender.* Madrid: Eudema.

Duneier, Mitchell. 2001. *Sidewalk.* New York: Farrar, Straus and Giroux.

Elhajji, M. 2008. Organização Espacial e Resistência Cultural: Saara, um acampamento étnico no coração do Rio de Janeiro. In *Comunidade e Contra-Hegemonia: Rotas de Comunicação Alternativa,* ed. Raquel Paiva and Cristiano Ribeiro dos Santos. Rio de Janeiro: Mauad.

Fausto, Boris. 2000. *Negócios e ócios: Histórias da imigração.* São Paulo: Companhia das Letras.

Geertz, Clifford. 1979. "Suq: The Bazaar Economy in Sefrou." In *Meaning and Order in Moroccan Society: Three Essays in Cultural Analysis,* ed. Clifford Geertz et al. Cambridge: Cambridge University Press.

Gerson, Brasil. 2000. *História das ruas do Rio.* Rio de Janeiro: Lacerda Ed.

Gomes, Laura Graziela. 2002. "'Comércio étnico' em Belleville: Memória, hospitalidade e conveniência." *Revista Estudos Históricos* 29. FGV.

Grün, Roberto. 1992. *Negócios & famílias: Armênios em São Paulo.* São Paulo: Editora Sumaré.

*Isto É Brasil.* 2001. "A Máfia Pirata." Edition 1671. October 10.

Jacobs, Jane. 2001. *Morte e vida de grandes cidades.* São Paulo: Martins Fontes.

*Jornal do Brasil.* 1996. "A invasão chinesa na Saara: Aos poucos os comerciantes orientais vão ocupando as lojas do centro comercial carioca, tradicional reduto de árabes e judeus." September 1, 1996, cover and p. 30. Rio de Janeiro.

Joseph, Isaac, and Yves Grafmeyer. 1984. *L'École de Chicago.* Paris: Aubier.

Liu, Xin. 2000. *In One's Own Shadow: An Ethnographic Account of the Condition of Post-Reform Rural China.* Berkeley: University of California Press.

Ma, Lawrence J. C., and Carolyn Cartier. 2003. *The Chinese Diaspora: Space, Place, Mobility, and Identity.* New York: Rowman & Littlefield.

Mello, Marco Antonio da Silva, et al. 1993. *A galinha d'Angola: Iniciação e identidade na cultura afro-brasileira.* Rio de Janeiro: Eduff/Editora Pallas.

Misse, Michel. 1997. "As ligações perigosas: Mercado informal ilegal, narcotráfico e violência no Rio." *Contemporaneidade e educação* 1(2): 93–116.

Park, Robert Ezra. (1916) 1967. "A cidade: Sugestões para investigação do comportamento humano no meio urbano." In *O fenômeno urbano,* ed. Gilberto Velho. Rio de Janeiro: Zahar Editores.

Peraldi, Michel. 2001. *Cabas et conteiners: Activités marchandes informelles et reseaux migrants transfronteliers.* Paris: Maisonneuve et Larose.

Pinto, Paulo Gabriel Hilu da Rocha. 2004. "Negociando o público: Retórica, trocas e identidades religiosas no suq al-Medina de Alepo, na Síria." Paper presented at XXIV Reunião Brasileira de Antropologia. Recife.

———. 2010. *Árabes no Rio de Janeiro—uma identidade plural.* Rio de Janeiro: Editora Cidade Viva.

Ribeiro, Paula. 2000. *Saara: Uma paisagem singular na cidade do Rio de Janeiro (1960–1990).* Master's thesis, History. Pontifícia Universidade Católica/PUC-SP. São Paulo.

Shu, Chang-Sheng. 2012. *Imigração Chinesa: Chineses no Rio de Janeiro.* In *Revista Leituras da História: Portal Ciência & Vida.* Vol. 55. São Paulo: Editora Escala.

Truzzi, Oswaldo. 1992. *De mascates a doutores: Sírios e libaneses em São Paulo.* São Paulo: Editora Sumaré.

Turner, Victor. 1957. *Schism and Continuity in African Society.* Manchester, UK: Manchester University Press.

Valentin, Andreas. 2010. *SAARA.* Rio de Janeiro: Francisco Alves.

Worcman, Susane. 1996. *Relátório Projeto Memória do Saara.* Rio de Janeiro: Programa Avançado de Cultura Contemporânea (PACC) / UFRJ, 1993–1996.

———. 2000. *Saara.* Rio de Janeiro: Relume Dumará (Coleção Cantos do Rio).

Zhang, Li. 2001. *Strangers in the City: Reconfigurations of Space, Power, and Social Networks within China's Floating Population.* Stanford, CA: Stanford University Press.

# 12

# Muslim Identities in Brazil
## Engaging Local and Transnational Spheres

*Paulo Gabriel Hilu da Rocha Pinto*

Pinto presents case studies of Muslim communities in Rio de Janeiro and the Tri-Border Region in order to explore how the process of identity formation in these communities intersects with local as well as transnational imaginaries of Arabness and Muslimness. He demonstrates that despite their homogeneous representation in the media, Muslims in Brazil are a decidedly heterogeneous group whose identities play out differently in the many cultural arenas in which they participate.

∾

Brazil has one of the largest Muslim communities of the Americas,[1] which has been formed by diverse waves of migration from the Middle East (Syria, Lebanon, Palestine) since the nineteenth century and by the conversion of non-Arab Brazilians. The Muslim community is mostly urban, with large concentrations in Rio de Janeiro, São Paulo, Curitiba, and Foz do Iguaçu. The majority of Muslims in Brazil are Middle Eastern Arabic-speaking immigrants and their descendants. Nevertheless, there is a growing number of non-Arab Brazilians who convert to Islam.

The first Islamic institutions in Brazil started to appear in the 1920s, but they only gained strength in relation to "Syrian-Lebanese" or Palestinian ethnic and/ or national associations in the 1980s.[2] As most Muslim immigrants to Brazil came from the Arab Middle East—mainly Lebanon, Syria, and Palestine—they were identified with the large Arab community that exists in Brazil (Karam 2007, 10–13). The Arabic-speaking immigrants who came to Brazil in the first half of the twentieth century were mostly Christians, and they managed to overcome or minimize the effects of the widespread racism and discrimination directed at them in the 1930s and 1940s, such as their stigmatization as backwards, fanatical, and greedy "orientals," who were referred to as "*turcos*" (Turks) by a large part of the Brazilian intellectual elite (Lesser 2000, 87–135). This was done through economic success and a strong investment in cultural capital, such as higher education for their sons and daughters, which created an impressive upward social mobility (Truzzi 1997).

Throughout the 1950s and 1960s, economic success and an intense investment in acquiring social distinction allowed the descendants of the Arabic-speaking immigrants from the Middle East to be gradually incorporated as "whites" in the scheme of racial classification of Brazilian society. However, the process of "whitening" the Arabs always remained incomplete, as they continued to be marked as a culturally different and somewhat "foreign" group in Brazilian society. This was exemplified by the constant mobilization of the stigmatizing stereotypes associated with the term "*turco,*" which was often mobilized to denounce or vilify politicians of Arab descent after the end of the military dictatorship and the beginning of the process of democratization in 1985. Arab immigrants and their descendants in Brazil therefore reached the final decades of the twentieth century having achieved successful social integration, which allowed them to be present in all spheres of social life but was accompanied by the persistence of a mild version of the processes of cultural exclusion by some sectors of Brazilian society.

The media discourse on terrorism after September 11 made more present some of the tensions underlying the ambiguous insertion of Arabs in Brazilian society as whites who are, nonetheless, "marked" by cultural differences. This became more acute in the case of Muslims, who became targets of transnational political discourses that tried to link them with international conflicts and define them as a security threat (in particular the Muslim community in Foz do Iguaçu). These discourses had clearly negative effects on the situation of Muslims in Brazil. Many informants told me that they were harassed on the streets, and were the target of verbal abuses such as "terrorist" or, in the case of women, "Bin Laden's wife." There were also a few cases of physical aggression in Rio and São Paulo.

However, the stigmatization of Arabs and Muslims as "terrorists" was challenged by other discourses that define the Brazilian nation in opposition to what is perceived as the imperialistic policies of the United States and its allies.[3] This tense relation with the USA in the Brazilian nationalist discourse made a large portion of the Brazilian public opinion view the 9/11 terrorist attacks as "retaliation" provoked by the very imperialist policies that are fostered by Americans in the Middle East.

In this sense, Muslim identities in Brazil inherited the ambiguous position of Arab/Syrian-Lebanese ethnic identity, to which more dramatic symbolic and political meanings were added. With this broader context in mind, I will analyze the construction of Muslim identities and codifications of the Islamic tradition in Rio de Janeiro and Foz do Iguaçu as a way of understanding how different articulations between Arab ethnicity and Muslim identities emerges as the result of processes that construct and objectify the Islamic tradition.

## Between Textual Universalism and Ethnic Distinction: The Muslim Community of Rio de Janeiro

Rio de Janeiro is Brazil's second-largest city, with about nine million inhabitants in its metropolitan area. The Muslim community in Rio has its religious center in the Muslim Charity Association of Rio de Janeiro (Sociedade Beneficente Muçulmana do Rio de Janeiro [SBMRJ]). Until 2007, the SBMRJ had a prayer hall (*musala*) in a commercial building in downtown Rio. It has since moved to a new mosque, the Mesquita da Luz (Mosque of the Light), which the religious authorities of the community also refer to by its Arabic name, Masjid al-Nur. The Mesquita da Luz was built in the Tijuca neighborhood in the northern part of the city. While its prayer hall (*musala*) was already finished in 2007, other parts of the building, which include classrooms and a conference hall, have been gradually built since then. This is the only mosque currently operating in Rio de Janeiro, as an older one which was built in the neighborhood of Jacarepaguá in 1983 was abandoned due to its location in a place too distant from the residences and workplaces of most members of the Muslim community, and is now slowly turning to ruins. There is also one *musala* downtown and another in Copacabana.

The SBMRJ estimates a total of five thousand Muslims in the entire state of Rio de Janeiro, with its members constituting only a fraction of this number. The community organized around the religious activities of the SBMRJ is a multicultural and multiethnic group that brings together Arabs and their descendants, Africans (many of whom are in Brazil for studies, in addition to the economic immigrants from that continent), and non-Arab Brazilians who have converted to Islam from other religious traditions.

The non-Arab Brazilians are, in fact, the majority in the community, while Arabs and their descendants make up only 10 percent of the membership. The number of non-Arab Brazilian converts has increased dramatically since 2000, when they constituted about half of the members of the community (Montenegro 2000), reaching 85 percent of the total membership in 2007. In socioeconomic terms, most of the members belong to the middle or lower middle class, with merchants, public servants, employees in commerce, and a number of university students and professionals (lawyers, veterinarians, and so on) constituting the majority of the community.

The multiethnic character of the Rio community created a complex process of construction of Muslim identities in interaction both with Arabic linguistic and cultural traditions and with Brazilian social and cultural reality. The Arabic language is valued as a key element of the religious universe of Islam, but not as one that determines Muslim identity. There is an emphasis on teaching the language to members of the community who are not of Arab origin (and even to those who are but have not mastered the classical Arabic of religious texts), in order to give them direct access to the sacred text of the Quran.

Nonetheless, the lingua franca for religious activities, such as sermons or courses, is Portuguese, with the exception of ritual formulas and quotations from the Qur'an that are always pronounced in Arabic. This shows the SBMRJ's leadership efforts to construct a religious and linguistic milieu that is, to some extent, integrated into the local cultural context. Even the verses of the Quran that are quoted in Arabic during the Friday sermon are immediately followed by a Portuguese translation.

Nevertheless, the symbolic value of the Arabic language and Arab identity makes them markers of religious distinction within the community. During the informal gatherings that follow the religious rituals, it is common to see Arabic speakers use that language in their interactions, marking an ethnic boundary that separates them from the rest of the community. Those who have Arab origins but do not speak the language are constantly the target of subtle teasing and jokes that reinforce the value of Arabic as a cultural diacritic constitutive of the ethnic boundary between the Arab community and other groups in the larger Brazilian society.[4] In fact, the vast majority of the descendants of Arab immigrants do not speak Arabic, although in the last decade there has been a renewed interest among Brazilians of Arab descent, both Muslims and non-Muslims, in learning the language.

Beyond that, it is also significant that most of the positions of power and status within the community are occupied by Arabic speakers, clearly setting up an ethnic hierarchy. Abdu, a Sudanese man who was president and imam (prayer leader) of the SBMRJ until 2007, also defined himself as Arab, notwithstanding the emphasis that he placed on his African origin after 2006 in order create a greater connection with the African immigrants and black Brazilian converts that make up a significant part of the community at the SBMRJ. Since 2007, the presidency of the SBMRJ has been in the hands of an Egyptian, Muhammad. The role of imam has also been performed by a Brazilian of Syrian descent who speaks Arabic and has pursued religious studies in Saudi Arabia.

Despite the relation between hierarchy and Arab ethnicity in the division of religious labor within the SBMRJ, the leadership's public discourse promotes the dissemination of Islam and the incorporation of the converts into the community, a fact that is demonstrated by the centrality of educational activities, such as courses about Islam or "Muslim culture." Courses tend to focus on the challenges that Brazilian society and culture pose for Muslims, particularly for the converts or for recent immigrants. These courses touch upon subjects such as the use of the veil, the prohibition against drinking alcohol or eating pork, and interaction with non-Muslim friends and family members. These themes are mixed with other ones of global and transnational scope, such as the image of Islam and Muslims in the media, which is generally considered as holding hostile and misinformed views on these topics (Montenegro 2002a), the conflicts in the Middle East, and the terrorist attacks of September 11.

The SBMRJ also offers spaces and forms of sociability as alternatives to Brazilian cultural traditions that are seen as "un-Islamic," such as Carnival, which is particularly present in the everyday life of Muslims in Rio. During Carnival there are activities of "Islamic camping" or "spiritual retreat" that are usually held in farms or hotels in the countryside. On these occasions, those who want to can retreat to an "Islamic" environment where leisure activities, such as sports or hiking, are mixed with praying and the study of Islam.[5] Other traditions linked to urban middle-class culture, such as Mother's Day or Children's Day, sometimes also receive an "Islamic" version in the SBMRJ or become the object of commentaries in the sermon about how a Muslim should behave during their celebration.

On the other hand, the missionary character of the community makes it very conscious of its position in Rio's religious field, in which the Muslim community tries to inscribe itself as part of the local "religious diversity" with a discourse of tolerance and coexistence. Since 2008, a delegation of the Muslim community participates in the annual "March against Religious Intolerance," where it shares a space of identification with religious traditions such as the African-Brazilian religions (*candomblé, umbanda*) which, from the point of view of the leadership of the SBMRJ, would be considered condemnable polytheist practices. Muslim identities in the SBMRJ are not only constituted in contrast to the beliefs and practices of non-Muslims but also produced by the contrast among the different Islamic traditions that are represented by members of the community according to their diverse origins. The number of converts increased steadily, gaining momentum after 2001 when the greater visibility that Islam gained in the cultural imaginary of Brazilian society enhanced the dynamics of conversion.[6]

In the period between 2000 and 2012, converts became the larger group in the community, changing its cultural and religious character. The process of conversion to Islam in the Muslim community in Rio is centered on the acquisition of a Muslim identity through an individual commitment to a set of Islamic beliefs, practices, rules, and norms. Therefore, the increase in the number of converts led to an individualization of Muslim religiosity in Rio de Janeiro.

Indeed, the individual is the target of the official religious discourses that circulate in the community. The sermons emphasize individual responsibility, rational choice, and conscious intention as the bases of faith. All collective rituals—such as saying daily prayers, fasting during Ramadan, or making the pilgrimage to Mecca (the hajj)—are the object, at the appropriate period of the religious calendar, of sermons that emphasize that their religious merit is only valid if they are performed with the full rational and emotional engagement of the individual. It is a recurrent theme in the discourse of the leadership of the community that Muslim identity is not inherited, but rather something that is achieved through the acquisition of religious knowledge and the conscious shaping of one's behavior according to the moral rules of Islam.

This kind of religiosity that connects religious knowledge is based on the codification of Islam that is fostered by the leadership of the SBMRJ. The leaders of the Muslim community in Rio define their understanding and practice of Islam as deriving from the Salafiyya.[7] According to them, Islam is a definite and bound set of beliefs, rules, and moral norms that are inscribed in the Quran and the Hadith. Sami, brother of the imam and teacher of the "Islam" courses of the SBMRJ, summarized this position during one course that he taught in 2008, by saying that

> all Islam is what is stated in the Qur'an and in the traditions of the Prophet, peace be upon him. That is the Islam of the revelation. After that because of historical reasons and influence of culture and other religions, people started to interpret and add things, creating variation and deviation from the original message. Here in the SBMRJ we think that these other practices and beliefs might seem correct to those who follow them, but we don't accept them for us.

Other religious traditions of Islam, such as Shi'ism and Sufism, are often criticized and pointed to as examples of "deviations" from the Prophet's message. Also, Sunni religious traditions that do not have explicit references in the sacred texts—such as the celebration of the Mulid al-Nabawi (the Birth of the

Prophet)—are also rejected as innovations that moved the Muslim community away from its mythical unity.

In that sense, one can say that the multiethnic character of the Sunni community in Rio de Janeiro has generated an awareness of doctrinal and ritual differences among various Islamic traditions, because there was the need to codify Islam as an abstract religious system that could be taught to the new converts and should be mastered by all Muslims. This led to a search for the "true" Islam within the framework of a Salafi interpretation of Islam centered on the transmission of doctrines through preaching and the study of the textual tradition.

Nevertheless, the religious authorities of the Sunni community in Rio de Janeiro have a very particular interpretation of the Salafiyya, which for them is mainly the idea that all aspects of Muslim religiosity should be grounded in the Quran and the Hadith. They do not follow the literalist or the political trends of the Salafiyya (Rougier 2008, 15–19), framing their interpretation of Islamic doctrines as a moral discourse centered on the individual who aims to insert him- or herself into the larger society as a pious Muslim. This orientation toward creating a Muslim religious life in a non-Muslim society leads the leaders of the community to adopt positions that could be better classified as "modernist" rather than "Salafi," usually drawing inspiration from European or North American Muslim sources.

One example of that is the official position of the SBMRJ on women converts who were already married to non-Muslim husbands before their conversion. According to Munzer, who does the Friday sermon (*khutba*), as there is no consensus among Islamic scholars on the issue of whether the marriage would still be valid or not, it is up to each individual female convert to decide if she will remain married to her non-Muslim husband or not. This opinion is inspired by a similar decision by the European Council of Fatwas. Similar issues of whether it is licit or not to work in a bar, to celebrate one's birthday, or to eat in non-Muslim houses where pork is served with other food are also left up to the conscience of each member of the community. This "Salafi minimalism" is possible because the community has traditionally refused to receive *shaykh*s appointed by other religious institutions, in particular those from Saudi Arabia.[8]

The importance of the efforts to create a religious codification of Islam and a mechanism for its transmission (sermons and texts in Portuguese, courses) that were adapted to the local social and cultural conditions of the community must not prevent us from seeing that they are associated with other mechanisms that point to transnational religious horizons. This is particularly true with the converts, whose socialization in the doctrines, practices, and values of Islam goes together with the construction of a transnational religious imagination centered on the Middle East and its holy sites. Several Friday sermons talk about the past and present religious and political situations of the Middle Eastern societies. Examples from Muslims living in Europe, China, or the USA are also used frequently as moralizing stories in the sermons.

Many converts take courses in the Arabic language, aiming to read the Quranic text in its original version, but also to acquire enough linguistic competence to be able to interact with Middle Eastern cultural and religious realities. Others go spend some time living in Syria, Egypt, or Saudi Arabia in order to study Arabic and "learn how life is in a Muslim society," as summarized by one convert who had lived in Syria. The hajj is another occasion for the converts to add an experiential dimension to the transnational religious imagination that connects them to the sacred sites in the Middle East. All these experiences provide the converts with the cultural capital of direct knowledge of the Arab Muslim societies of the Middle East, which allows them to affirm their Muslim identity and their belonging to the 'umma on equal terms with those born Muslim.

Therefore, the disciplinary practices developed by the SBMRJ's religious authorities (sermons, courses, normative texts, and the like) have produced a process of "objectification" of Islamic tradition, generating a "purified" religious system of cultural and social practices that serves as a conscious normative point of reference in the life of the faithful. This "objectified" Islam presented as a local form of the Salafiyya facilitates the integration of the converts into the community, downplaying the cultural differences between individuals and allowing the construction of an inclusive Muslim identity that connects the local realities of the Muslims of Rio de Janeiro with the transnational horizons of their religious imagination.

## Both Local and Transnational: The Muslim Community in Foz do Iguaçu

The Muslim community in Foz do Iguaçu, in the state of Paraná, is almost totally constituted by Lebanese and Palestinian immigrants and their descendants. The Lebanese constitute a large majority within the community. While there are no reliable statistics on the number of Muslims in Foz do Iguaçu, the religious leaders of the community advance numbers that range from 18,000 to 22,000 Muslims in the Tri-Border Region (*Tríplice Fronteira* in Portuguese, *Triple Frontera* in Spanish). This area comprises the confluence of the national borders of Brazil, Argentina, and Paraguay and has three cities, one in each country, that have different levels of integration with one another. The economy of this region is oriented toward transborder commerce and tourism, for it harbors the Iguazu Falls on the border between Brazil and Argentina, which is a major tourist attraction of both countries.

While Paraguay has no major tourist attraction in this area, its city, Ciudad del Este, with about 170,000 inhabitants, developed as a major commercial hub that feeds the Brazilian market with imported electronics and luxury goods from Asia, Europe, and the USA. Commerce in Ciudad del Este is mainly controlled by Arab and Chinese immigrants and their descendants. Many Brazilians also work in Ciudad del Este. Foz do Iguaçu on the Brazilian side is the largest city of the region, with about 300,000 inhabitants. The economy of Foz do Iguaçu is fully integrated with that of Ciudad del Este, with people and goods constantly flowing between both cities. The Arab Muslim community is spread between both cities, with those who are better off economically tending to live in Brazil and those who recently arrived living in Paraguay. Puerto Iguazú on the Argentinean side, with 32,000 inhabitants, is the smallest of the three cities and the least integrated in the transborder economy; it has no Arab/Muslim community.

There are Islamic institutions in both Foz do Iguaçu and Ciudad del Este. In Foz do Iguaçu there is the Mesquita Omar ibn al-Khattab, which belongs to the Sunni community, and a Husayniyya in the Sociedade Islamica de Foz do Iguaçu, which belongs to the Shi'a community. In Ciudad del Este, the Shi'a community has the Mesquita del Profeta Mohammed, and the Sunni community has a prayer hall (*musala*) in a commercial building. While there is a great circulation of people between the institutions belonging to the same sectarian group, with the mosque and prayer hall in Paraguay functioning more during working hours and the mosque and the Husayniyya functioning for celebrations and collective prayers at night or during the weekends, there is almost no circulation of Sunnis to Shi'a religious institutions and vice versa.

The existence of separate institutions reveals the importance of the sectarian boundaries for the Muslims in Foz do Iguaçu. While both communities present a discourse of Islamic universalism, stressing the unity of Islam and the irrelevance of sectarian divisions, there is a great awareness of the existence of two Muslim communities with discrete understandings and practices of the religion. Despite their differences and rivalries, the Sunni and the Shi'a communities agree in their identification of Muslim and Arab identity. The leaders of both communities see their role as the maintenance of the Arab Muslim identity of their community and its transmission to the new generations.

This was summarized by *shaykh* Ahmad of the Sunni mosque of Foz do Iguaçu when I asked him if his community had any plan to spread Islam in Brazilian society. He responded:

> No, we have no plans for *dawa* [preaching and spreading Islam] among the non-Muslims. Actually our main concern is to create conditions for the Muslims to remain Muslims, and for the new generations to not go away from Islam. If we manage to do that, we can say that we were very successful.

Indeed, neither the Sunni nor the Shi'a community has any plan for attracting new converts to Islam, which shows a complete identification between Islam and Arab ethnicity in their definition of Muslim identity. The transnational connections with the Middle East are very active, with an intense circulation of people, goods, and ideas from Brazil to Lebanon and back. Many marriages occur with grooms and brides from Lebanon, where some of the wealthier families send their sons and daughters in order for them to learn Arabic and the cultural traditions of their region of origin. These transnational ties are important symbolically and economically, as many families have property and business both in Lebanon and in Brazil. While there are some cases of marriage with non-Muslim Brazilian and Paraguayan women, I did not came across any mixed Sunni-Shi'a couples, which shows again the strength of the sectarian divide.

However, the very construction of Islam as a cultural heritage that, in principle, is shared by all Middle Eastern immigrants and should be transmitted to their descendants enhances the awareness of the sectarian differences between Sunni and Shi'a Muslims. In order to be able to transmit a general "Muslim identity" that is defined as specific cultural content, the community had to reach a consensus about the doctrinal and ritual elements that constitute it. Therefore, the various doctrinal and ritual references that mark the boundaries between Sunni and Shi'a constructions of the Islamic tradition were seen as deviations from the cultural consensus that should prevail in the community and, in the end, led to its division along sectarian lines.

*Shaykh* Muhammad Khalil, who became the leader of the Shi'a community in Foz do Iguaçu in 2005 after leading the mosque in Curitiba, sees in the division the effect of the introduction of Wahhabi-influenced understandings of Islam into the Sunni community, which forced the Shi'a to create their own religious institutions. According to him, the religious consensus that existed in the community due to the fact that they all shared cultural understandings of Islam as it was practiced in the Middle East was broken by the introduction of what he saw as an intolerant religious ideology by non-Lebanese *shaykh*s.

On the other hand, *shaykh* Ahmad, who was born in Brazil and did his religious studies in Saudi Arabia, blamed the Shi'is for the division of the Muslim community, saying:

> We were all together in this mosque until the Shi'is built their Husayniyya. Then it was impossible to keep the community together, because they would perform rituals [of the 'Ashura][9] there that are not acceptable to us. They preferred to maintain these rituals than to continue with us. It is better this way, they have their religion and we have ours.

There were nonreligious institutions, such as the Clube da Unidade Árabe (*Nadi al-Itihad al-Arabi* or Arab Unity Club), which managed to gather the Sunnis and Shi'is on an ethnic basis as Arabs. However, the club was closed a few years ago due to financial problems. The end of the club also provoked mutual accusations from the Sunni and the Shi'a communities, with the Sunnis saying that the Shi'is were responsible for the club's bankruptcy and the Shi'is accusing the Sunnis of closing the only institution where members from both communities could interact as Arabs.

The Sunni community has the Escola Árabe Brasileira (Arab-Brazilian School), which functions in a building near the mosque, and the Shi'a community has the Escola Libanesa Brasileira (Lebanese-Brazilian School). There is also a Shi'i Lebanese school in Paraguay. The main purpose of these private schools is to teach Arabic to the descendants of the Muslim immigrants in order to allow them to keep their linguistic and cultural ties with the Middle East.

However, despite the obvious purpose of maintaining the transnational character of the Muslim community, the schools also serve as an instrument of cultural localization in Brazilian (and Paraguayan) society. Both schools teach the regular national curriculum common to all Brazilian schools, public or private, together with a large number of hours for Arabic (and English) as a foreign language. Therefore, while the Arab school enables the new generations of Muslims to maintain transnational cultural connections, it also clearly sets them into the Brazilian educational and economic context.

This complex interaction between transnational and local elements in the constitution of Arab Muslim identities is even more clear in the Lebanese-Brazilian Scout Group (Grupo de Escoteiros Líbano-Brasileiro), which was created in 2005 by the Shi'a community and functions in a building next door to the Husayniyya. The president of the group, a member of the Shi'a community, stressed that the Lebanese-Brazilian Scout Group was very much part of the scene of youth associations in Foz do Iguaçu, having intense relations with the other two scout groups in the city and participating in the activities of the União dos Escoteiros do Brasil (Brazilian Union of Scouts). In this sense, the scout group is an instrument of insertion of the Muslim community into the local social context and even into the Brazilian nation-state.

However, this affirmation of belonging to the local society is articulated with the affirmation of cultural diacritics that delimit the boundaries of the Arab Muslim community as a particular group within the Brazilian nation-state. The president of the Lebanese-Brazilian Scout Group expressed this double process when he explained the purposes that informed the creation of the group. He said:

> The idea to create the scout group was to provide our youth with a space for healthy entertainment, where they could meet and get to know one another, as well as other kids who are not from the community. It is very important to teach them [the young ones] social responsibility and respect for nature and the environment. In this sense the scout group can be seen as part of the education of our sons and daughters as Muslims and as citizens. Of course, the idea to create a group for the Lebanese and the rest of the Arab community comes from the need to allow the young generations to live a normal life while teaching them to respect the customs that define us as Muslims and Arabs. We have boys and girls in all the activities, but we make sure that everything goes within the boundaries of Islamic morality, particularly while camping. But, of course it just reinforces a healthy and respectful atmosphere that is the essence of scouting.

In this statement we can see that Arab and Muslim identities are treated as having equivalent or, at least, overlapping cultural meanings, as both are referred to a set of "customs" and moral values related to the Middle East societies. The activities of the group use both Portuguese and Arabic as their linguistic contexts. This identification between ethnic and religious identities was stressed by the president of the group, who pointed out that while most members are Shi'is, the group also gathers Sunni, Druze, and Christian descendants of Arab immigrants, who see in it a space where Arab identities can be reinforced among the new generations born in Brazil. Therefore, we can say that the scout group fosters identities and creates cultural competences that allow its members to negotiate their insertion into the local society, into the Brazilian nation-state as well as into the transnational social networks and symbolic systems that connect them to Middle Eastern societies.

These multiple layers of local, national, and transnational social imaginaries that are fostered by the Lebanese-Brazilian Scout Group are condensed and expressed in their honorary patron, Akil Merhei. Merhei was the president of the Lebanese-Brazilian Scout Group until he was killed together with his wife and two children in the indiscriminate bombing of South Lebanon by the Israeli army in the 2006 war. The figure of Akil Merhei condenses several layers of meaning in the symbolic rendering of his life and death.

Of interest to this analysis, he simultaneously represents a local public figure, known and loved by many, who fostered the insertion of the Arab Muslim community into the society of Foz do Iguaçu; a transnational Arab-Brazilian who lived and worked in Brazil as well as maintained his cultural and personal ties with Lebanon, where he took his family for vacations and to visit relatives; and a "martyr" (*shahid*) who became a victim of the regional and global conflicts that involve the Middle East. In this sense, the figure of Akil Merhei works as a nodal symbol[10] in the context of the Lebanese-Brazilian Scout Group, allowing the condensation and articulation of a gamut of identities (Brazilian, Lebanese, Arab, Muslim, etc.), which organize the various spheres of belonging through which the members of the group circulate.

Similarly, while the religious imagination of the Muslim community is oriented toward the Middle East, there is a sharp consciousness of its belonging to the local religious field, which means the possibility of exposure of its members to the religious proselytism and transit of identities that characterizes a dominant model of religiosity in Brazil. Thus, the creation in Foz do Iguaçu of the Brazilian Christian Church for the Arabs (Igreja Cristã Brasileira para os Árabes) and of the Arab Evangelical Church (Igreja Evangélica Árabe or *Kinissa Injiliyya Braziliyya*), both of which aim at converting Muslims to evangelical Christianity, is perceived as a threat to the community by some Muslims, while it is accepted as part of the local reality by others.[11] The *shaykh*s of both the Sunni and the Shi'i communities said that the evangelicals were free to preach to Muslims, but they dismissed the idea that this could be a threat to their communities. "A true Muslim would not renounce his faith," said *shaykh* Ahmad of the Sunni mosque.

*Shaykh* Muhammad, the leader of the Shi'i community, elaborated more on this point, saying:

> Well, we cannot do anything about that. Here is not Lebanon, where missionary work is forbidden. Here it is part of our reality. I saw the banners in Arabic [that the members of the Arab Evangelical Church carry on the streets of Foz do Iguaçu] saying "Smile, Jesus loves you" (*Ibitsam Yasu' yuhibbak*). Well, all I can say is that when I see the banner I smile and agree that the sentence is true, Jesus loves us as Muslims because we accept him as a prophet. The evangelicals managed to put a teacher of sports in the [Sunni] Arab school and people in

the [Sunni] mosque were very upset and ended up firing him. I would let him stay, because I believe that the teachings of Islam are stronger than their [the evangelical Christians'] arguments and I bet that after some time he [the teacher] would become a Muslim.

From this statement we can say that the Arab Muslims in Foz do Iguaçu have a sharp consciousness of belonging to the local religious field and of having to play by its rules, while their religious identity contextualizes them within the transnational religious and ethnic identities articulated by the Arab Muslim communities in the Tri-Border Region. The religious identities that are constructed and mobilized in these communities articulate local, national, and transnational spheres of belonging. Islam is objectified by the members of both the Sunni and the Shi'a communities as the religious context of a cultural heritage that connects them to the Middle East as well as gives them a framework for belonging and positioning themselves in Brazilian society.

**Conclusion**

The analysis of these two Muslim communities shows how Islam in Brazil is marked by a plurality of identities, practices, and forms of organization. The connection between Muslim identity and Arab ethnicity is very strong in most Muslim communities in Brazil, with the clear exception of the one in Rio de Janeiro. While the growing number of non-Arab Brazilian converts push for less ethnic and more universalistic interpretations and practices of Islam, the Arabic language and some Arab cultural diacritics remain as signs of religious distinction even among the converts. The appropriation, interpretation, and practice of discrete Islamic traditions in the Muslim communities in Brazil are informed by the local social and cultural context of each one of them, as well as by the multiple connections that they establish with globalized and transnational Islamic discourses and practices.

The ethnographic comparison between these two Muslim communities in Brazil allows us to understand how various constructions of Arab ethnicity and Muslim identities coexist, articulate, and compete in discrete social and cultural contexts. The comparative approach highlights the similarities and differences between these communities, as well as revealing their internal divisions and diversity (Arabs and non-Arabs, Muslims by birth and converts, immigrants and Brazilian-born Muslims of Arab descent, Sunnis and Shi'is, and so on). Therefore, instead of treating "Muslim identity" as a category covering a homogeneous cultural space, we can approach it as spheres of meaning and practice where local, national, and transnational cultural elements and processes are mobilized and engaged by agents who constitute their identities and trajectories in the various social arenas in which they participate in their everyday lives.

**Notes**

1. The census of 2010 estimates that there are 35,167 Muslims in Brazil, while Muslim religious authorities speak of one to two million Muslims. Raymond Delval had estimated that there are 200,000 Muslims in Brazil after surveying various regions of Brazil in 1983 (1992, 201). I have been doing ethnographic research in the Muslim communities of Rio de Janeiro, São Paulo, Curitiba, and Foz do Iguaçu since 2003, and based on my ethnographic experience in these communities, which are the largest ones in Brazil, these numbers do not seem accurate. The mosques and Islamic institutions in which I have done research gather around 70,000 members. Therefore, an estimate ranging between 100,000 (if only the practicing Muslims are counted) and 400,000 Muslims (if all people who consider themselves Muslim are counted) in Brazil seems plausible.

2. The first Muslim association in Brazil was the Muslim Mutual-Aid Association (Sociedade Beneficente Muçulmana) of São Paulo, which was created in 1929. This association also built the first mosque in the country, the Mesquita Brasil (Brazil Mosque), between 1946 and 1960. It was only in the 1970s that other mosques started to be built in Brazil.

3. Perhaps the most famous and more visible nationalist group was MV-Brasil (Movement for the Valorization of the Language, Resources, and Culture of Brazil), which was very active in its campaign "in defense of the Brazilian culture" between 2002 and 2009. This group gathered sympathizers and members from both right and left on the Brazilian political spectrum. The organization's official website was http://mv-brasil.org.br/index2.htm (accessed 15 October 2009; this site was deactivated on 11 April 2012).

4. For the role of cultural diacritics in the definition of ethnic boundaries, see Fredrik Barth, "Introduction," in *Ethnic Groups and Boundaries: The Social Organization of Culture Difference,* ed. Fredrik Barth (1969; Prospect Heights, IL: Waveland Press, 1998).

5. The creation of alternative spaces of religious sociability is not exclusive to Muslims, as devout Catholics and evangelical Christians also have "spiritual retreats" in order to avoid the festivities of Carnival.

6. Two events contributed to the change in the perception of Islam in Brazilian society from something exotic and distant to a phenomenon that everyone can relate to or must preoccupy themselves with: the soap opera *O Clone* (The Clone), which portrayed Muslim characters in a positive way, and September 11. On the ambiguous position that September 11 has in Brazilian cultural discourse, see Paulo Pinto, "Arab Ethnicity and Diasporic Islam: A Comparative Approach to Processes of Identity Formation and Religious Codification in the Muslim Communities in Brazil," *Comparative Studies of South Asia, Africa and the Middle East (CSSAAME)* 31(2) (2011): 312–330.

7. The Salafiyya is a Sunni reformist movement that emerged in the nineteenth century and proposes a return to the "original of Islam," which is understood as a set of rules, rituals, and beliefs codified in the Quran and the Hadith.

8. See Montenegro 2002b.

9. The Day of Ashura is the day of mourning for the martyrdom of Husayn ibn Ali, the grandson of the Prophet Mohammad. Husayn, whom Shi'a identify as the legitimate successor to Mohammad and as their spiritual guide, was martyred in the battle of Karbala in AD 690 (year 61 in the Hijra or Islamic calendar). Ashura is one of the most important days in the Shi'a calendar, and is a major national holiday in countries with Shi'a populations.

10. Victor Turner defined the properties of the dominant symbols as condensation, unification of disparate meanings in a single symbolic formation, and polarization of meaning. See his book *The Forest of Symbols* (Ithaca, NY: Cornell University Press, 1967), 30.

11. The Brazilian Christian Church for the Arabs is a branch of the Assemblies of God and was present in Foz do Iguaçu from 2001 to 2006. The church closed that year after failing to convert any Muslim Arabs. The Arab Evangelical Church, which is a branch of the Baptist church, continues its missionary work today and has succeeded in converting a few Shi'is and Druze to evangelical Christianity. See Silvia Montenegro, "Proyectos Misionales y Representaciones sobre La Diversidad Cultural: El Evangelio Transcultural para Árabes em la 'Triple Frontera,'" in Verónica Béliveau and Silvia Montenegro, *La Triple Frontera: Dinámicas Culturales y Procesos Transnacionales* (Buenos Aires: Espacio Editorial, 2010).

## References

Delval, Raymond. *Les Musulmans en Amérique Latine et aux Caraibes*. Paris: L'Harmattan, 1992.

Karam, John Tofik. 2007. *Another Arabesque: Syrian-Lebanese Ethnicity in Neoliberal Brazil*. Philadelphia: Temple University Press.

Lesser, Jeffrey. 2000. *A Negociação da Identidade Nacional: Imigrantes, Minorias e a Luta Pela Etnicidade no Brasil*. São Paulo: UNESP.

Montenegro, Silvia. 2000. *Dilemas Identitários do Islã no Brasil*. PhD diss., Universidade Federal do Rio de Janeiro.

———. 2002a. "Discursos e Contradiscursos: o Olhar da Mídia sobre o Islã no Brasil," *Mana* 8(1). (http://www.scielo.br/scielo.php?pid=S010493132002000100003&script=sci_arttext).

———. 2002b. "Identidades Muçulmanas no Brasil: Entre o Arabismo e a Islamização," *Lusotopie* 2: 59–79.

Rougier, Bernard. 2008. "Introduction" In *Qu'est-ce que le Salafisme?*, ed. Bernard Rougier. Paris: Presses Universitaires de France.

Truzzi, Oswaldo. 1997. *Patrícios: Sírios e Libaneses em São Paulo*. São Paulo: Hucitec.

# Part Three.  Literature and Transregional Media Cultures

# 13

# Telenovelas and Muslim Identities in Brazil

*Silvia M. Montenegro*
*Translated by Anneliese Pollock*

This chapter discusses the treatment of Islam in the Brazilian TV series *O Clone*. It examines how the series positioned its main character, Jade, to provoke national dialogues around the meanings of Muslim religiosity, Arab ethnicity, and associated gender, social, and political issues in the Brazilian public sphere. While the idea for the series was conceived before the attack on the World Trade Center, the controversy that emerged around the show's treatment of the Muslim religion speaks to the heightened public interest in these questions after September 11, 2001. The chapter addresses the public's reaction to the series, as well as the reactions of members of the various Muslim communities in Rio de Janeiro. It also addresses stereotypes presented by the series, and the reactions of both Arab and non-Arab Muslim communities to these stereotypes. A key issue that emerged was the distinction between "religion" and "culture" and between Arab-Brazilians as an assimilated "race" and Muslim Brazilians, particularly recent converts who reject the sensuality identified with assimilated Arab-Brazilians. This chapter ultimately suggests that the telenovela series created a universe where different elements were mixed together that were faithful neither to the "reality" of the Muslim religion nor to the customs of the Arab country that they supposedly presented.

∽

Telenovelas (evening soap operas or serial melodramas) represent the most popular genre of contemporary narrative media in Brazil. They attract more viewers, by far, each night than films, situation comedies, television news broadcasts, and musical programs. Social controversies, political events, and cultural shifts are commented on and implemented through the lens of fictional telenovelas. And specific social campaigns are largely carried out through these shows, such as for vaccinations, AIDS prevention, and birth control, and against drug addiction, by embedding these issues into telenovela plotlines. Notably, the discourses that allude to the elements that supposedly make up "Brazilian identity" are reevaluated, principally through certain shows on the Globo network, or Rede Globo, Brazil's most powerful, profitable, and most viewed television network. In this context, the modern *novela* has emerged as a new genre, mixing fictional characters with current news, sometimes trying to effect changes in models of behavior. In summary, the genre that started in the 1960s by doing cheap Portuguese-language copies of imported Latin American shows became, especially with the efforts of the Globo network, a powerful, high-quality domestic industry, exporting profitable media products to a number of countries well beyond the Lusophone world. Today, the Brazilian telenovela industry represents an important profit source for distributors, and numerous products are derived from them, such as books and soundtracks.

The history of telenovelas in Brazil reflects a gradual process of the nationalization of televised fiction. The first daily soap opera in Brazil was presented in 1963 by the TV network Excelsior. During the early years, the genre was clearly an imported product: local distributors dubbed or adapted series by Cuban, Argentinean, or Mexican television writers. The television production industry had far fewer resources at its disposal than it does today.[1] At the end of the 1960s, the telenovela industry became a realm of competition between rival networks which all began to include *novelas* in their programming. Rede Globo did not yet have the near monopoly on audience that it enjoys today, though its leadership had helped culturally nationalize the genre by the end of the 1960s. With the "Brazilianization" of televised fiction, scripts, topics, and writers were more frequently Brazilian; and by the 1970s the practice of adapting shows from other Latin American countries had come to an end.

Scholars have analyzed these changes in media forms and narratives in relation to the interaction between society and the state beginning in the 1970s (Fadul 1999; Ortiz Ramos and Borelli 1989). The factors that contributed to the transformation and nationalization of soap operas are varied. On the one hand, the fact that consumer society and political life was becoming more complex and contentious affected television, which, as a growing market, placed increasing importance on the themes of daily life and on topical issues of public interest. Also, during this period, Brazilian television consolidated itself as an industry, as the number of TV sets in Brazilian households grew.

As TV shows increasingly seemed to approximate real life, their success in the public eye increased too. The topics included "Brazilian problems" such as racial prejudices, the *jogo do bicho*,[2] corruption, soccer, *coronelismo* or *caciquismo*,[3] and so on. In the 1970s, telenovelas came to receive the highest audience ratings after news programs; and in the 1980s, they surpassed news shows to become the core viewing experience of Brazilian television and the most important profit source in the industry. It was at this time that Rede Globo became the network with the most watchers, and it remains so today without challenge.

In the context of the telenovela's influential status in Brazil, it is possible to state that the fictional treatment of Islam in the fantastically popular Globo telenovela *O Clone* (originally aired from October 1, 2001, to June 15, 2002, with 221 episodes) engaged in a "reciprocal" dialogue between sociocultural reality and media representation, influencing the construction and growth of discussions of identity in Muslim communities, while making it possible to look at the different orientations of Islam in Brazil, as witnessed in the diversity of positions taken by the communities in their reception of the program.[4] The reasons behind these divergent opinions reflect the complexity and fragmentation of the local Muslim communities' identities.

It is important to discuss the plot of the show in order to understand the conflict that caused such diverse reactions among Brazilian Muslims. The main characters were Jade; her uncle Ali; the twins Diogo and Lucas (and later Lucas's clone, Leandro); and Yvete, Lucas's stepmother. Jade is the daughter of two Muslims, but she was born and educated in Brazil. When her mother, Sálua, dies, she is obligated to move to Morocco to live with her uncle Ali, thus causing her to experience conflicts from cultural adaptation. Her uncle requires two things: that Jade cover her head and that she reconcile with Muslim tradition. In the exotic setting of Morocco, she meets Lucas, a Brazilian who is traveling with his twin brother, Diogo, and with their godfather Albieri, a geneticist. Jade and Lucas confront varied obstacles in pursuit of a relationship with one another. Because of conflicts with his father, Diogo returns to Brazil, but he dies in a helicopter accident in Rio de Janeiro. Albieri decides to clone his surviving nephew, taking Lucas's cells to create Leandro. From here, a series of subplots develop that show the problems among the different characters, but what became of most interest to the public was not the romantic plotlines but rather the portrait of "Muslim-ness" as it intersected with gender, religiosity, and national reputation.

From the beginning, the public knew that Jade experienced difficulty passing between two worlds and two cultures, unable to feel either Muslim or Brazilian, and that on multiple occasions she was oppressed by religious customs that she found unjust. Uncle Ali, the patriarch of her Muslim family, studied at Oxford University, where he was a classmate of Albieri. Ali and Albieri remained friends, but did not agree on the subject of cloning. For Ali, genetic knowledge is linked to the "materialism of the Occident" and indicates betrayal of faith and abandonment of God.

Ali clearly embodied "Muslim values," as he took it upon himself to point out what was correct or wrong, and guided the conduct of others. Ali recited Quranic suras and professed Mohammed's teachings. Jade tried to escape and find Lucas, but her uncle had already arranged her marriage to a Muslim man. Sometimes the women in Jade's family allied themselves with her. Sometimes Ali slapped her and threatened her with religious curses.

Although the original script had imagined an Egyptian setting, when the Egyptian government turned down Globo's request for a permit to shoot there, the characters' stories were reset in villages around Morocco, such as in the ruins of the Kasbah Aït Benh Hadou in Ouarzazate. There were episodes that showed caravans of camels and nomads from Erfoud in the Sahara; and scenes in that emphasized the exoticism of the camel market in Marrakesh, as well as the Portuguese-colonized sixteenth-century city of El Jadida. Many scenes were filmed in the medina of Fez, which served as an inspiration for the city reconstituted on the soundstage by Rede Globo.

It should be noted that although the show was set both in Brazil and North Africa, the telenovela's dramatization of conflict around Islamic customs set all these questions not in Brazil itself but in Morocco, which was presented as an exotic universe. The two "cultural milieus" of the program, Rio de Janeiro and Morocco, created a contrast, and each one constantly "othered" or defined itself in contradistinction to the other location. Morocco looked like the universe of rigid customs, completely "culturized," while as a counterpoint Rio de Janeiro appeared as a liberal and mixed universe. But Rio was also the homeland of the darkest aspects of liberal modernity, where secondary characters did drugs, going to look for them in the *bocas de fumo* of the *favelas*.[5]

Even when Jade and the other Muslim characters occasionally appeared in Brazil, the show never referred to existing Muslim-identified locales or peoples of Muslim faith in Brazil itself. This leads to diverse questions that are helpful in following the reactions of some Muslims living in Brazilian communities: Did any views expressed by the series provoke a problem? If everything was set in Morocco, why did some people see the series as an attack on Muslims in Brazil? Why did people come to focus critical attention on the Muslim advisory committee that had been constituted to assist the show's producers and to mediate with the public?

## Themes of *O Clone*

In my previous publications on the relationship between stigmatizing stereo-types in the Brazilian press and on the elaboration of positive identity attri-butes of Muslims (Montenegro 2002a), I underlined that it is possible to isolate recurring themes, that is, limited motifs that repeat themselves and form the focal point of journalistic discourse on Islam in Brazil. These themes, which do not stray far from other Western mainstream journalistic viewpoints on Islam, emphasize the situation of women, the spread of Islamic conversions, the "threat" posed by militant Islamism in Brazil, and assertions that polygamy is a widespread phenomenon among Muslims. All aspects of this phobic "main-stream" repertoire were clearly reproduced in the series with the important exception, in the immediate wake of the World Trade Center attacks, of the link between terrorism and Islam. This repertoire of representations of Islam therefore emphasized the permeability of the borders between television and printed media sources. *O Clone* put forward a specific interpretation of what it means to practice Islam. These representations had significant repercus-sions among Muslims in Brazil. In order to analyze these responses, one must address the specificities of the telenovela genre in Brazil, and recognize its importance in popular culture. At the Globo network, an "expert" advisory committee was convened to analyze the content, plot, character development, and location. This committee worked for six months during *O Clone's* devel-opment and preproduction in order to discuss the portrayal of Muslim roles, institutions, and cultures. In addition to this committee's official pronounce-ments, many Muslim leaders and Arab community spokespeople in Brazil expressed ambivalence. Then, when confronted by pressure from believers, they began rendering much stronger public critiques of images of Islam in Brazil's media and public culture in general, rather than confine themselves to those presented in the series.

## The Rede Globo Network and the Production of "Brazilian Identity"

One of the principal tasks of the telenovelas on Rede Globo was to highlight political themes connected to Brazilian identity. It is important to note that, during the 1970s, the network was closely shaped by direct actions of the state. According to Ortiz Ramos and Borelli (1989), during the presidency of the military dictator Humberto de Alencar Castelo Branco (1964–1967), Brazil's authoritarian state was preoccupied with "subjects of culture," that is, creating directives that favored the development of a "Brazilian culture" or a "national identity" compatible with the administration's coercive vision. These directives combined censorship with economic incentives, creating a political-cultural atmosphere that transformed fictionalized television shows:

> Since the start, Jarbas Passarinho [who served as minister of labor and social providence then as minister of education in the 1960s] underlined that it would be ideal that there exist among us a culture that founds itself on "the belief in nationality" and not an imported culture, or a "form of cultural colonialism." At the same time, the chief of federal censorship reflected on that which should or not be shown on television. In 1975, the document of national and cultural politics shows the preoccupation with creating the "Brazilian man." (Ortiz Ramos and Borelli 1989, 84–85)

During this authoritarian period, television series were one of the principal vehicles used to transmit these ideas about a transformed Brazilian identity, and the distributor responded to the state's demands, taking charge of the production of the genre.

Since the beginning of the 1970s, television production has been dominated by the Rede Globo network, a quasi-monopoly resulting from a combination of President Castelo Branco's governmental protection and his support for business development and national production (Faria and Potter 2002, 23). In this era, Globo began the tradition of broadcasting TV shows based on literary adaptations that illustrate different moments in Brazilian history, as well as shows that treat contemporary topics. More recently, *O Clone* was one of many shows that took up the polemics then present in public opinion and in the media; it made use of these topics in order to interpret "Brazilian identity" in relation to and opposition to the "Islamic world." At the same time, it profited from the Brazilian soap opera genre of "it's you who decide": on the basis of public opinion polls, the show reconfigured itself little by little, never separating itself from the public's expectations of the plot. According to the Rede Globo website:

> Just as much as having a daily and captive public, the telling fact is that the TV show is an open work and under permanent construction, that is to say that the authors write it at the same time as it is diffused. As the plot unfolds, Rede Globo tries to know more intimately the profile of its spectators, know their expectations in order to motivate them. The public's taste is so much taken into account that, in some manner, the television viewers are the co-authors of the series. In summary, the public that shapes the series is responsible as much as the authors, actors, directors, and technicians.[6]

Television programs that air at 8:00 PM, given the potential for large audiences, attract the most successful and famous writers. This is then the most valuable hour for Brazilian television. A television program has twenty episodes taped by the time it is broadcast, plus another twenty are already drafted in loose form. This means that when a show is first aired, it is not yet completely scripted but exists only in the form of general guidelines established in the author's synopsis. This open nature, of which the viewers are well aware, permits a certain level of public interaction (Fadul 1999, 14). This is why, in the case of *O Clone*, Muslims who participated on the advisory committee originally thought that they could demand corrections if they found errors in the interpretation of Islam in subsequent episodes.

## The Plot: Between Morocco and Rio de Janeiro

The show's principal writer, Glória Pérez, produced a successful show by engaging controversial topics. Her stories brought together public themes, stirring national-level debate, and re-created them in televised fiction. In other shows, such as *Barriga de aluguel (Womb for Rent), De corpo e alma (Body and Soul),* and *Explode coração (Explode, Heart),* topics such as organ donors, children with cancer, and missing children were included in the plots. In *O Clone,* Pérez admits to having selected Islam as her topic because public interest in it was growing:

> I like polemical themes, capable of causing debates, of making people reflect on current questions. People have a lot of curiosity about Muslim culture and, in general, this curiosity shows itself only through a prism full of prejudices. In the program, we don't discuss either religion or politics and even less so do we talk about the different interpretations of the Quran. What interests us is to show customs, through the daily life of a family.[7]

*The Image of the Muslim Woman*

When *O Clone* began to air, Rio-based Muslims on the advisory committee withdrew their participation. The first few episodes proved to them that this would not be good for the image of Islam that they were hoping to transmit: Jade danced sensually in her bedroom with her cousins, escaped to the village's ruins to kiss Lucas, and even had sexual relations with him, filmed by another man. In different episodes, topics included the "proof of virginity" exam portrayed as traditionally required in the Islamic faith. In one episode, Jade was shocked when she learned that she had to undergo a virginity exam, and worried when she learned that in the Muslim religion, "one can go so far as to kill the engaged woman" if she is no longer a virgin. Because of this, she cried when the doctor gave her his attestation. Other female characters in the show suffered from the constraints of these tests when, the day after a wedding, the family demanded to see the sheets that proved the loss of virginity on the wedding night. Meanwhile, Uncle Ali threatened transgressors with the punishment of "80 lashes with the whip."

The program also popularized belly dancing. In multiple scenes, Jade and other women danced in an "Arab" style. On other occasions, Lucas's female friends gave him a performance of the same kind. In reality, the popularity of belly dancing had been established during the preceding years with the adoption of "Arabized" rhythms and dances. In Brazil, its roots can be traced in part to the success of the Algerian singer Khaled, rediscovered by deejays in Bahia during the summer of 1999, and at the same time, Brazilian musical groups with large audiences, like *É o Tchan*, put together choreography based on Arab dances to the hugely popular Afro-Brazilian rhythm of *axé bahia*. Also in 1999, in a game/variety show on the TV network Bandeirantes, a "genie" became very popular. She was a blonde model dressed in "Thousand and One Nights" garb, complete with veil and harem pants, who danced for young people and participated in the show's games. The show's success inspired an increase in the number of belly dancers featured on programs on rival networks.

In *O Clone*, Muslim women belly-danced 182 times during the first 132 episodes. This prompted many gymnastics and dance schools to start offering belly-dancing classes (Pereira 2002, 2). Over the life of the program, the image of the Islamic woman became a point of conflict that many Muslims brought up. This was similar to conflicts that arose between cultural customs, specific to Morocco or Middle Eastern countries, and customs from the Muslim religion.

At the same time, in newspapers and magazines Arab and Muslim customs were collapsed into each other. The newspaper *Isto é* wrote:

> The success of *O Clone* is at its apogee. Last week, for every 100 TV sets that were turned on, 74 showed Jade and Léo's kiss. With the popularity of the series, Arab culture is currently surging in the streets and Brazilian houses. To know more about the customs of Morocco, there are websites put up by the Islamic community of Foz do Iguaçu. The page talks about the religion and contains the entire text of the Quran. (*Isto é gente* 2002, 146)

Thus, newspapers presented articles on Moroccan culture, offering as complementary sources the websites of the Muslim communities in Brazil.

The press fueled the increasing popularity of the program, promoting various activities that showed this surge of Arab culture in the Brazilian streets. For example, *Tribuna da Imprensa* announced a program of cultural activities at the University of Vega de Almeida (UVA), including exhibitions, forums, and conferences on Arab culture. The curious part is that these activities were announced as complementary to what the public learned via the program:

> If the program *O Clone,* on the global stage, is not sufficient to understand this group of people, the exposition is, no doubt, a good way to clarify Arab customs and, principally, their cultural manifestations on Brazilian soil. The objects in the exposition are divided into tapestries, tiles, dishes and other curiosities. Beyond the exposition, UVA is today preparing for the "first interdisciplinary cultural forum" on the theme of the Arab community in Brazil. (*Tribuna da imprensa* 2002, 13)

The UVA forum addressed questions such as the entrepreneurial success of the Arab shopkeepers' street in Rio, the Arab presence in Brazilian culture, and women's rights in Islam. Then, tributes to the actors of the show were announced. A belly-dancing group closed the event. According to *Tribuna da imprensa,* the organizer of the event, along with the university co-coordinator of a course on social communication, "chose this theme because she observed the curiosity of people who wanted to know more about relations between Arabs and Brazilians." It is clear from the written press that it was the public who showed enthusiasm for "Arab culture" (*Tribuna da imprensa* 2002, 14).

## Repercussions and Advisory Committees

As *O Clone* scored extremely well in the TV ratings, repercussions from the Muslim community became more explicit. And the press noted the critiques that were being expressed online and in some Muslim community newspapers.[8] Mainstream national newspapers printed testimonials from Muslims who expressed their opinions on the program, saying that *O Clone* reflected, with only a few minor inaccuracies, the reality of the Islamic community. Newspapers like *Isto é gente* published interviews with Brazilian Muslims nearly weekly that showed the supposed enthusiasm of the local communities for the new program. For example, questioned on how Islam should be treated on the show, a Brazilian Muslim woman and member of the Center for the Study and Dissemination of Islam said, "We have a very big advantage: the fact that our religion, which has always been so little or badly understood, enters into all Brazilian houses [via *O Clone*]. But the disadvantage is that, like all TV programs, it is fantasy-like—there are things that don't correspond to reality" (*Isto é gente* 2001, 134).

The article also inquired about errors that might have been made, and the woman responded: "For example, when the uncle slaps the girl in the face. I think that a religious person would never have had an attitude like that. When they speak of the woman, they ask if she is engaged. It's not like this that marriages take place" (2001, 135). It is true that some Islamic communities' newspapers responded to the series with positive reviews, referring to its success in other countries. The newspaper *Jornal Voz Arabe,* a publication of the Muslim community of Londrina, presented an article on the success of *O Clone,* telling readers that the New York–based *Wall Street Journal* had dedicated a long article to the Brazilian TV program:

> *Will Islam separate Jade from Lucas?* It is with this question that the *Wall Street Journal,* one of the most reputable American newspapers in the world, initiated a long article in a supplement of its Market Place section on the series *O Clone* by Glória Perez. With its photos, the text brought to the forefront the fascination that the romance between the two protagonists of different religious faiths is in the process of creating for television viewers. According to the director of the international sales division of Globo TV, Carlos Alberto Simonetti, the distributor decided to look forward to broadcasting the series internationally thanks to the good results it is getting in the United States, where it has been broadcast on the Telemundo network since January 14. "We were contacted with offers from distributors from Eastern Europe, Russia, and South American countries. People's curiosity about Muslim culture has greatly increased since the attacks [of September 11, 2001], and the series that addresses a little its traditions and its people arrived at the opportune moment," Simonetti says. (*Jornal Voz Árabe* 2002, 1)

*Jornal Voz Árabe* did not criticize the program. On the contrary, it seemed to praise this "upsurge of Arab culture" (*Jornal Voz Árabe* 2002, 1). An analysis of the content of this newspaper shows that it also advertised belly-dancing classes, conferences on Islam, tourism to the Middle East, and so on.

The diversity of opinions by Muslim communities in Brazil can be partially explained by the existing social cleavages in the country. Communities that mostly comprised long-assimilated immigrants and their descendants (such as in São Paulo) tended to demonstrate a greater tolerance when faced with the mix of Islamic and Arab customs that the program presented. However, communities that had a high rate of converted Brazilians, such as in Rio de Janeiro, often engaged in a process of "de-ethnification" of their identity discourse. They adhere to a type of "correct" Islam that attempts to dissociate religious identity from Arab ethnicity or from the national origin of its members. In these communities, criticism of the telenovela was much stronger.

In other scholarly research on Brazilian Muslims,[9] it is hypothesized that a principal difference among Brazilian communities stems from the dilemma of defining themselves as either just Muslims or just Arabs, despite the fact that the majority of both groups owed their institutional beginnings to the initiatives of groups that self-identified as Arab Muslims. It has also been shown that, in the discourses on what it means to be Muslim in Brazil, the Arab-centric emphasis conflicted with the emphasis on having an Islamic commonality. Certain communities, such as those in Rio de Janeiro, coordinated with certain international movements that proposed to "de-Arabize" Islam. In this context, "de-ethnification" meant placing religious identity above any emphasis of origin. And, evidently, these communities started to understand that in *O Clone,* Moroccan and Arab customs were mixed with Islam, at the same time as public opinion started to associate belly dancing—considered taboo among the most purist of Muslims—with Islam as a religion rather than with specific Arab cultural practices. As a reaction, these groups wrote articles in newspapers alerting their believers to a new "stereotype" and "stigma" of Muslim customs, Internet forums filled with Muslims criticizing the series, and the Muslim participants in Rio de Janeiro quit the advisory committee.

However, Shaykh Jihad H. from São Paulo continued to work as an adviser because, for him, despite the conflicts, the show represented an opportunity to make the teachings of the Muslim religion known to the Brazilian public. I interviewed Shaykh Jihad H. at the Muslim Center of São Bernardo do Campo, in the ABC. The ABC is a massive industrial urban zone in southern Greater São Paulo.[10] When I asked him why certain Muslims refused to continue on the advisory committee, he stated that he respected the opinion of those shaykhs; however, he thought that as a leader of Islam—because he "did not only represent a local community but Islam at the national level"—it was his duty to participate on the advisory committee and to watch over the images of Islam presented in the series. The shaykh confirmed that, during the six months (so far at that point) that he had participated on the show's advisory committee, the telenovela's principal writer, Pérez, had come to the Muslim center multiple times and that, using these opportunities, he had pointed out errors and the necessity of why they must be corrected in upcoming episodes. The directors of the World Assembly of Muslim Youth (WAMY) confirmed that they had given Pérez the opportunity to meet some Muslim families in the local community and to observe their way of life. The actors had also "done some observation" at the Muslim center. According to the shaykh, the report was positive because the interest in Islam had increased with the series. However, he had to admit that many Muslims felt insulted by the images of Islam presented in the series: "When each episode finished, my telephone didn't stop ringing," he said. To explain the diverse reactions to the series, the spokesperson of the WAMY distinguished two types of Muslims. On one side were those he called "non-practicing Muslims," the descendants of Arab families, who represented the segment who seemed to appreciate the series, not paying attention to the mistakes, and who were enthusiastic about the diffusion of Arab culture. On the other side were "practicing Muslims," who Shaykh Jihad H. admitted were revolted by *O Clone*. Evidently, the shaykh did not hesitate to include the first group of "non-practicing" viewers in what he regarded as the Brazilian Islamic community, which explains why, in his evaluation, the results of *O Clone* were positive.

However, during the series, the pressure of "practicing Muslims" began to grow and more critical advisers of *O Clone* wrote a document to the writer of the series that was published on the homepage of the WAMY.[11] In this document, the advisers attempted to clarify certain controversial points linked to the religious questions presented in *O Clone*. Their largest criticism was on the representation of the role of women in Islam: "In Brazil, seven converts out of ten are women. If Muslim laws were repressive, why would these women convert? It seems to us that certain themes brought up in the series showed either a complete lack of knowledge of the religion (which is unjustifiable, as we, Shaykh Ali and Shaykh Jihad, are always ready to clarify these doubts), or bad faith." [12]

The highlighted controversial points referred to the show's presentation of certain Muslim customs: the use of the hijab (the headscarf worn by women), the Islamic attitude toward the Occidental world, Muslim marriage customs, the question of divorce, the question of whipping as punishment in Muslim law, and the position of women. The document denounced the errors in the treatment of each of these points, including, for example, everything that concerned the use of the Quran. The representatives of WAMY thus stated:

> We have noticed that the Quran is always presented as a joke. A non-Muslim cannot have access to it in Arabic (which is the original), because it is constituted in the words of God and it is not a motif for jokes. To mention it, at any moment, in any situation, is to banalize it, to lack respect for it. We do not allow it. In addition, verses are mentioned and interpreted in an erroneous manner, which leads the public to confusion about the religion and its precepts.

As for the other topics—the concern for affirming virginity, the marriage scenes, the showing of women as "promised," and so on that appeared in the series—they were considered mistakenly attributed to Muslim theology rather than cultural practice. At the end of the document, the shaykhs of São Paulo described the mental state of the Islamic community concerning the reception of the series:

> When they broadcast the last episodes, showing Muslim women as objects, thousands of spectators— converts as well as those of Muslim origin—reacted to the scenes presented and sent us e-mails or called us on our personal lines, in the middle of the night, to protest. They brought up the lack of respect that the series showed, even offering to contact the author of the series so that Glória could see, with her own eyes, how Muslim women live and the respect with which they are treated—respect that they only found in Islam.

During my interview, the adviser admitted to having produced this document on the WAMY homepage, but also declared that, thanks to the Muslim advisory committee, a multitude of mistakes had been avoided. Recalling the beginning of the negotiations, when the show was trying to film "Arab scenes" in Egypt, the adviser referred to the less-than-happy declarations of one of the actresses who in an interview spoke of the oppression of women in this country, insinuating that it was for that reason that Morocco was finally selected.

Samir el-Hayk, a translator of the Quran that is distributed in some Brazilian communities, also indicated in an interview that the advisers had blocked serious errors in the series:

> Globo always exploited feminine nudity and exaggerated polemical themes. But there are multiple themes whose treatment we prevented. Feminine excision is an example. They wanted to cite it in the series as if it were a Muslim religious practice. But it is not. It was practiced by Muslims, Christians, and the faithful of any religion in Africa because women lived nude. The clitoris was cut so that the vagina would be better closed and so that dirt would not enter. This process is, even today, practiced in certain countries. But it is a cultural trait, this has nothing to do with religion. Glória Pérez [the author of O Clone] wanted to present it as a Muslim practice. We formed a team to counsel production and I suggested that she find in the Quran a reference to this theme. She read it and found nothing. She was not convinced and she went to live with a family in Egypt. She did the same thing in Morocco, two countries where excision is practiced. There, she heard a mother say to her daughter that to go through excision was ridiculous, that it was not necessary. But, for the girl, keeping the clitoris was constraining, once all her friends had cut it. (*Revista de Estudos da religião* 2002, 3–35)

Muslims' reactions to Rede Globo's televised fiction were varied. The most critical reaction came from non-Arab-centric religious communities, which ended all collaboration at the beginning of the series and left their advisory roles. For these groups, the series literally disfigured Islam, transmitting a distorted image of its religious practices. Among Brazilian Muslim Shiʿites,[13] comments on the series were particularly negative; they claimed that the image of Islam that appeared was "demonizing." Those Muslims who continued to participate on the program's advisory committee after the first wave of resignations considered themselves to be moderates, but they had to respond to pressure from the faithful with elaborate critical documents. Their strategy gambled that they could utilize the series as a messenger to spread Islam to the interior of Brazil. They remained on the advisory committee in the hopes that they could make sure erroneous versions of Muslim customs did not appear in the telenovela. It should be noted that "non-practicing Muslims" who made the distinction between an identity based on origin (Arab) and on religion—and also those who practiced the religion as linked to Arab origins—were enthusiastic about the series, because it spread knowledge of Arab customs, dances, and food.

It is important to underline that critical discourses referred to the confusion between "religion" and "culture" as a cause of the distorted image of Islam presented in the show. In truth, this is one of the recurring themes in the study of reactions of Muslims to media discourses. From the point of view of Muslims in Brazil, it was always considered that different media outlets attributed certain cultural practices of people—in this case, the people of Morocco—to the Muslim religion. In general, in certain arguments on authenticity, people expect Islam to appear in a sort of cultural void, or at least to exclude any practice that cannot be placed in the religious universe.

However, it should not be forgotten that the series also received criticism from non-Muslims linked to Moroccan culture. These critiques came from the viewpoint opposite to that mentioned above. From this perspective, the problem was that this cocktail of many countries' religious practices created a false and fantastical representation of Morocco. Zélia Adghirni, a journalist and a researcher at the University of Brasília, explains that Glória Pérez's series did not clarify Islamic practices but rather muddled them. Adghirni, who lived in Morocco from 1983 to 1990, and who taught at a school of journalism there, affirms that the women in urban zones that she met possessed the liberty to choose their husbands, as well as to study and have professional careers. She also highlights that to marry a foreigner (as is the case of Jade in the series) was difficult, but not impossible. It sufficed that the husband convert to Islam, which numerous foreigners did. But what seemed the most shocking to her in the series was the "distorted vision" of the feminine universe, the supposed virginity exams and the obsession with belly dancing and with images of dancers wearing fantasy versions of Egyptian clothes. According to her, Morocco was in economic crisis and it had hoped to promote the country through Globo's TV shows and to profit from them:

> What Morocco didn't expect was to see itself presented through the prism of simple exoticism. Women surrounded by walls, obelisks, polygamy, camels, and Tuaregs, these are only a few ingredients that confirmed the stereotypes constructed by misinformation. It may be for this reason that Egypt, which, according to the guide, was supposed to be the original place where part of the series was to take place, refused Globo upon seeing some of some of the series' scenarios. (*Correio Brasiliense* 2001, 32)

The statements above synthesize the general critique of the series: it painted a universe where different elements mixed together, but it was not faithful to the "reality" of the Muslim religion or to the country's customs that it supposedly presented.

## Analyzing Novela Identities

As Esther Hamburger underlines (2000), the tropes, publics, and structures of Brazilian telenovelas have served as the primary concern for scholars of media in that country. Scholars have debated the paradox of a media phenomenon capable of mobilizing national audiences; composed of diverse demographical segments, including social classes, generations, genders, and geographical regions; around a program that mixes melodrama, TV news, entertainment, and newspapers. Thus, a number of academic works have been dedicated to debating the ideological content of such programs in the context of the television industry, and the role of television in the reproduction of dominant ideologies. More recent works have researched the influence of television programs on direct political behaviors such as voting (Hamburguer 2000, 26). Also, innumerable research projects have studied the social impact of television on changes in certain models of behavior (Faria and Potter 2002).

There is clearly a lack of research on the dialogue between the fictional worlds created by the telenovelas and the social worlds of identity groupings and minorities who react to seeing themselves interpreted in a certain manner. Hamburguer's work on "politics and TV series" is an example of the rare analyses that consider the hazy frontiers between TV series and other television genres like the news, documentaries, and reality shows. Hamburguer assumes that the political and social impact of a series is a paradox that highlights the polysemy of the text and the difficulty in finding the meaning in a specific program with supposed ideological content (Hamburguer 2000, 27). In analyzing Globo's 1996 series *O rei do Gado (The King of the Cattle)*, whose content included the question of agricultural reform in Brazil, the show's writer tried to explain how the series crossed into the arena of Brazilian politics, earning front-page treatment in newspapers and provoking legislators to take varying positions.

Many works still insist on the supposed overall effect created by television on political or cultural life. When, as in the case of *O Clone*, it is a question of the construction of a representation of a religious way of life, an analysis centered on the friction between the images created by the series and those that the groups and minorities would like to transmit of themselves, we observe that the repercussions of the image transmitted by television are not monolithic, because the identity discourses inside Islam are equally fragmented, and feed on multiple sources, demonstrating the internal differences between local communities. It is perhaps because of this that it is not possible to detect a collective strategy in confronting the media.

In fact, in the relationship between minorities and the media, certain reactions to images are conveyed. It thus becomes fundamental to clarify the specificities of the modes in which this relationship is established and to demonstrate that negotiations and strategies are produced to bring these communities into contact with the media (Jankowski 1994). Only in the 2000s did a growing body of anthropological work incorporate analyses of different media genres—in their role in transmitting specific "imaginary elements" in the cultural representation of groups or segments of society—and the study of processes engendered by interactions of social groups through the media (Dickey 1997, 9). Works such as those of Lila Abu-Lughod (2005) and Faye Ginsburg, Lila Abu-Lughod, and Brian Larkin (2002) discuss how anthropology approaches the relationship between the media and community identities. They highlight the importance of ethnographic work when analyzing the production and reception of meanings and their influence on the representations and practices of certain groups. What is called "active negotiation," that is, a type of routine practice of creation and refutation of representations of self and others, appears in the "dialogue" provoked by the series *O Clone* between the exotic images on the television and the counterdiscourses of the Muslims.

At the end of the 1970s, Edward Said (1997) in *Covering Islam* analyzed the way in which media and journalistic experts determined how people see the Muslim world. Said's analysis throroughly examines the theme of the media coverage of Muslims. In his view, Islam—as painted by the press, television, and experts—is seen through the prism of a "neo-orientalism" that renders it monolithic. In the view of this study, it is difficult to consider the micropolitical interpretations of Islam without reflecting on the wider representations generated by international geopolitical conflicts.[14] But is this the case of *O Clone*?

With fictional television programs, it is normal to find their center of fantasy and liberty vis-à-vis "historical reality." However, the main fictional character is frequently a point of controversy. For some Muslims, *O Clone* did not reflect the "reality of Islam," the "real way of life of Muslims," or how one really lives in Morocco. In these arguments, the series distorted, "lied," because it was not faithful to reality. More elaborate discourses suspected an intentional ideology: the series was a new perspective on the image of Muslims in Brazil, even it was set in Morocco.[15] For other Muslims, the problems were linked to concerns about what Brazil might think of the Islamic religion and its customs, and that it confused practices like belly dancing with essential forms of Muslim religiosity.

The identity discourses of Muslim communities in Brazil should be understood in the diverse contexts in which they each articulate the relationship between immigrants of Arab origins and their descendants with Brazilians who more recently embraced Islam through conversion.[16] The demographic makeup of these groups, with respect to the number of "Arabs" and "converts" among them, as well as to the juxtaposition or disjunction between Arab and Islamic identities, is also an important factor that informs the identity construction of Muslims. The tension alone between those that strive for identification based on Arab-centrism and those that strive for identification based on religion renders more complex the construction of a homogeneous identity discourse, as much on the level of institutions as on that of the individuals who participate in certain religious associations.

The amalgamation of the sense of being Muslim and the sense of being Arab, subsumed by the notion of the existence of an "Arab-Islamic" cultural origin, provoked dissension among Muslim groups who rejected an axiomatic identity,[17] where the two descriptions appear as two faces of the same coin. The identity discourse that developed among groups in Rio de Janeiro emphasized a universal Islam that was "de-ethnicized" and that could be understood through the heterogeneity of its community members. In this context, the show's mixing of "Arab customs" with Islamic principles was interpreted as a misrepresentation of the "Islamic culture" that these institutions sought to convey. Nevertheless, for other Muslims and their institutions, the juxtaposition of Arab cultural identifies with Islamic identities was the defining feature of their community. In this case, despite the program's mistakes, *O Clone* was seen as an opportunity to spread understanding, not just of Islam but of Arab culture as well.

Beginning in the turning-point year of 2001, Islam and Muslims gained greater visibility in Brazil. But it was not the events of September 11 that brought about this change; it was *O Clone* that introduced positive images of Muslims into Brazilian society (Pinto 2010, 209). It remains to be seen whether this hypothesis will be confirmed, and to what degree the tremendous popularity and visibility of *O Clone* during the time of its broadcast represents a turning point in the diffusion of positive images of Muslims in Brazil and in other Latin American countries where the telenovela aired.

**Notes**

An earlier version of this chapter was published in French as *"Telenovela* et identités musulmanes au Brésil" in *Lusotopie* (2004), pp. 243–260. It was originally translated from Portuguese to French by Victor Pereira of IEP, in Paris. The revision and adaptation were originally done by Michel Cahen of CNRS, in Bordeaux.

1. During this period and up until the 1970s, soap and toothpaste companies, among them Gessy-Lever, Colgate-Palmolive, and Kolynos–Van Ess, sponsored the shows.

2. Translator's note: A popular lottery, most often clandestine.

3. Translator's note: *Caciquisme* is a system of domination of rural populations by an elite political party headed by charismatic strong-men. This is similar to the notion of *coronelismo,* in which a particularly strong leader generates a highly personalized rule, fragmenting political parties around him, and extending networks of clientelism and dependency.

4. The statistics on the presence of Islam in Brazil are still being researched. Local Muslim institutions advance numbers of around 1.5 million believers. A variety of censuses put Islam in the "other" category, a practice that makes it difficult to quantify the community. For an evaluation of the theme, see Waniez and Brustlein 2001. As for institutions, according to our own research, Brazil has fifty-eight Muslim organizations (mosques, charitable organizations, and Islamic centers). The most important institutions, such as the Center for the Dissemination of Islam for Latin America, are located in São Paulo (see Montenegro 2002b).

5. Translator's note: *Bocas de fumo,* literally "mouths of smoke," refers to places where drugs are sold. *Favelas* are shantytowns.

6. Rede Globo, http://redeglobo.globo.com/.

7. Rede Globo, "O Clone," http://redeglobo3.globo.com. Accessed March 4, 2002.

8. One of these websites was *A voz dos muçulmanos na Internet* (The Voice of Muslims on the Internet), which hosts an Islamic chat forum. See http://www.islamismo.org/ghoraba.html.

9. For a specific discussion of the Arabization and Islamization dilemma in the Muslim communities of Rio de Janeiro, see Montenegro 2002b.

10. Interview conducted on December 2, 2002.

11. World Assembly of Muslim Youth in Brazil, http//www.wamy.org.br.

12. The official advisers were Shaykh Jihad H. and Shaykh Ali Abdouni, president of the Latin American desk of the World Assembly of Muslim Youth (WAMY), located in the interior of São Paulo's ABC region.

13. The community is united around the mosque Brás, in São Paulo.

14. See Suleiman 2002 for an analysis inspired by the work of Edward Said that discusses "unconscious" stereotypes directed at Arabs and Muslims in American culture.

15. A recurring question on the modus vivendi of the relationship between the media and Muslims appears to be the location of allusions to global Islam. Thus, in "demonizing" Muslims in faraway places, those in nearby communities are demonized as well.

16. For an analysis of Muslim communities in Brazil, see Pinto 2005. For a study on conversion to Islam in São Paulo specifically, see Ramos 2003. For an analysis of the tensions between those born into Islam and those who convert, see Campos Barbosa Ferreira 2009.

17. For a discussion of the concept of "axiomatic identity," see Obeyesekere 1995.

### References

Abu-Lughod, Lila. 2005. *Dramas of Nationhood. The Politics of Television in Egypt*. Chicago: University of Chicago Press.

Campos Barbosa Ferreira, Francirosy. 2009. "Redes islâmicas em São Paulo: Nascidos e muçulmanos revertidos." *Revista Litteris* 3: 2–27

*Correio Brasiliense*. 2001. "O falso clone de Marrocos." November 12, 32. Brasília.

Dickey, Sara. 1997. "La Antropología y sus Contribuciones al Estudio de los Medios de Comunicación."*Revista internacional de ciencias sociales Unesco* 153: 10–33.

Fadul, Ana Maria. 1999. "Telenovela e família no Brasil." Paper presented at the XXII Congresso brasileiro de ciências da comunicação, Rio de Janeiro. September.

Faria, Vilmar, and Joseph Potter. 2002. "Televisão, telenovelas e queda da fecundidade no nordeste." *Novos Estudos* 62: 21–39.

Fernandes, Ismael. 1987. *Memória da telenovela brasileira*. São Paulo: Brasiliense.

Ginsburg, Faye, Lila Abu-Lughod, and Brian Larkin, eds. 2002. *Media Worlds: Anthropology on New Terrain*. Berkeley: University of California Press.

Hamburger, Esther. 2000. "Política e novela." In *A TV aos 50, criticando a televisão brasileira no seu cinquentenario*, ed. Esther Hamburguer and Eugênio Bucci. São Paulo: Editora Fundação Perseu Abramo.

*Isto é gente*. 2001. "O véu dignifica a mulher." October 5.

———. 2002. "Sob o véu da web." May 20, 146.

Jankowski, Martin S. 1994. "Le Gangs et la Presse." *Actes de la recherche en sciences sociales* 102: 101–117.

*Jornal Voz Árabe*. 2002. "O Clone." March 1, 56.

Montenegro, Silvia. 2002a. "Discursos e contradiscursos: O olhar da mídia sobre o Islã no Brasil." *Mana* 8(1): 63–91.

———. 2002b. "Identidades muçulmanas no Brasil: Entre o arabismo e a islamização." *Lusotopie:* 59–80.

Obeyesekere, Gananath.1995. "Buddhism, Nationhood, and Cultural Identity." In *Fundamentalism Comprehended,* ed. Martin E. Marty and R. Scott Appleby, 231–225. Chicago: University of Chicago Press.

Ortiz Ramos, José Mario, and Silvia Borelli. 1989. "A telenovela diária." In *Telenovela, história e produção,* ed. Renato Ortiz. São Paulo: Brasiliense.

Pereira, Lenora. 2002. "Dança do ventre, o tabu islâmico que encanta em *O clone.*" Paper presented at the XXIII Reunião brasileira de antropologia, Rio Grande do Sul. June. Pinto, Paulo. 2005. "Ritual, etnicidade e identidade religiosa nas comunidades muçulmanas no Brasil." *Revista USP* 67: 228–250.

———. 2010. "Novos espaços do Islã comunidades muçulmanas na Europa e no Brasil." *Islã religião e civilização.* São Paulo: Editora Santuário.

Ramos, Vlademir. 2003. *Conversão ao Islã uma análise sociológica da assimilação do ethos religioso na sociedade muçulmana sunita em São Bernardo do Campo* [Conversion to Islam: A sociological analysis of religious identities in the Sunni Muslim society of São Bernardo do Campo, Brazil]. Master's thesis, Religious Sciences, Universidade Metodista de São Paulo.

*Revista de Estudos da religião.* 2002. "A lei é rígida." Interview with Samir El-Hayek, 33–35. São Paulo.

Said, Edward. 1997. *Covering Islam.* New York: Vintage Books.

Suleiman, Michael W. 2002. "Paradojas en las actitudes occidentales frente al islam y los musulmanes." In *Antropología y antropólogos en Marruecos,* ed. A. Ramirez and López Garcia. Barcelona: Bellaterra.

*Tribuna da imprensa.* 2002. "Uma viagem às Arabias." March 21. Culture Section, 12–14.

Waniez, Philippe, and Violet Brustlein, 2001. "Os muçulmanos no Brasil: Elementos para uma geografia social." *Alceu* 1(2): 155–180.

# 14

# *Turco* Peddlers, Brazilian Plantationists, and Transnational Arabs
## The Genre Triangle of Levantine-Brazilian Literature

*Silvia C. Ferreira*

Ferreira explores twentieth-century Levantine-Brazilian literature by proposing three important genre-shaping literary strategies through which Levantine migrants in Brazil reinvented their embodiment through fiction. From the figure of the peddler, to the plantationist, to the transnational Arab, Levantine migrants' self-representation in the Portuguese language demonstrates diverse engagements with nationalist ideals, often in attempts at discursive distinction or assimilation. In this model, the novel *A Fogueira* serves as a turning point in representing the Levantine migrant as quintessentially Brazilian through an agricultural inheritance.

∾

Since their initial arrival in Brazil at the end of the nineteenth century, Levantine migrants and their descendants have written prolifically in the Portuguese language. While historians have read some of their works as part of the historical archive, little attention has been paid to their production of uniquely evocative literary genres, subgenres, and figurational strategies. An analysis of these dimensions in migrants' cultural production reveals distinct genre-shaping strategies through which migrants reinvented their embodiment through fiction as they sought modes of distinction and assimilation into nationalist ideals throughout the twentieth century. A first strategy prevalent in migrants' earliest works, such as those produced by Tanus Jorge Bastani and Taufik Kurban during the first half of the twentieth century, seek to present the pioneering "turco" peddler migrating to Brazil from the Arabic-speaking

Syrio-Lebanese regions of the declining Ottoman Empire as a "civilizing" element in Brazilian society. While such representations aim to engage nationalist ideals, they are ultimately limited by mainstream exoticization of the itinerant and urban peddler figure and its perceived economic proclivities. A second strategy that emerges in the middle of the twentieth century finds quintessential expression in the often-overlooked novel *A Fogueira*, which reterritorializes the migrant not at the place of origin in the Middle East, nor in the urban commercial milieu, but on the site of the Brazilian plantation. Through the idea of a Moorish agricultural inheritance, this novel engages national ideals that imagine Brazil as the meeting place of (North) African and European races and ultimately represents the Levantine migrant as quintessentially Brazilian. In a third figurational strategy emerging in the late twentieth and early twenty-first century, the literature produced by Levantine-Brazilians like Salim Miguel and Alberto Mussa has rethought the significance of the national categories engaged by earlier works, and focused instead on new connections and circulations. Nevertheless, the importance of these two previous attempts at discursive assimilation remains, and the three strategies intersect. To a certain extent, all of these strategies still exist and are appropriated in different ways in contemporary fiction. They should thus be understood not as categories fixed in time and space, but as a productive set of figurational strategies and genres through which it is possible to interpret the dynamic relationship between the historical facts of Levantine migration and its various literary imaginings in the Portuguese language.

## *Turco* Peddlers

The figure of the pioneering peddler has been an enduring symbol of Levantine migration to the Americas. The peddler is present in migrants' earliest literature in Brazil, and continues to find renewed cultural expression among their descendants today. An analysis of early literary depictions of the figure, such as those of Tanus Jorge Bastani, demonstrates that it is through the representation of the pioneering peddler that Levantine migrants create a dialogue with dominant narratives of Brazilian nationhood, emphasizing the figure's economic success as well as its key role in spreading civilization to remote corners of the nation.

> Were it possible for man's logic to be more loyal and human today, he would build an illuminating monument to those who once were, as many continue to be, the soldiers at the vanguard of civilization and progress: the peddlers! (Bastani 1949, 17)[1]

Levantine migrants' reappropriation of the traditionally marginalized peddler thus imagines peddlers as "soldiers at the vanguard" of the project of Brazilian nation building. But like the *turco* label with which it is associated, the peddler remains a largely peripheral figure whose economic proclivities exclude it from popular imaginings of Brazil's future, imaginings that commonly emphasized agriculture over commerce.

The prevalence of the peddler in imaginings of Levantine migration owes much to the popular historical narrative of new arrivals and their economic activities, which saw a large number of migrants initially take up peddling in their points of arrival in the Americas. While many migrants had been small-scale subsistence farmers in the Levant, when they first began to arrive en masse they were unfamiliar with the type of large-scale agriculture that was common on Brazil's plantations (Truzzi 1997). Most chose to abandon farming for peddling, and the profession is commonly credited with facilitating migrants' rapid upward social mobility in Brazil. The popular historical narrative suggests that through peddling, Levantine migrants achieved levels of economic success that enabled them to become store owners and to continue to climb up the economic ladder (Knowlton 1992).

But Bastani's lament over the peddler's lack of recognition bespeaks the figure's marginal or stigmatized status at different points in Brazilian history. During the first decades of the twentieth century, the nomadic and/or urban profession of selling was often interpreted by Brazil's elites as an affront to what John Tofik Karam describes as the more grounded, sedentary "agriculturally imagined Brazilian nation" (2007, 26). At a time when Brazil sought immigrants to labor on its plantations, most Levantine migrants were moving to cities and engaging in economic activities such as peddling instead. (Lesser 1996; Karam 2007). In his widely read anthropological work *Rondonia*, Edgar Roquette-Pinto compares Brazil's undesirable immigrants to gold miners, as they "arrive hurriedly and toil diligently in order to leave the place as soon as possible" (1950, 66). His comparison illustrates the growing perception among Brazilian elites that many migrants intended to exploit the nation's resources and quickly return to their homelands. The economic integration espoused by the peddler-to-proprietor narrative was thus not accompanied by easy social assimilation, and even proved to be an impediment to that assimilation.

The idea that the Levantine peddler was outside of nationalist ideals is embodied by the othering inherent in the label *turco*. Since the first migrants to arrive in Brazil from the Levant carried Ottoman passports, they were registered by local authorities under terms as varied as *turcos, turco-árabes, turco-asiáticos, sírios,* or *libaneses,* all of which commonly became subsumed under the more general label *turco* (Truzzi 1997, 39). The term was often used pejoratively to identify all "exotic" Easterners (Lesser 1996). Its general ambiguity and failure to reflect identities actually claimed by migrants served to deterritorialize them by robbing them of their cultural specificities. This ambiguity was also reflected in an uncertainty about the *turco*'s race that was cause for anxiety at a time when Brazil's immigration policies actively sought to "whiten" the nation's population (Lesser 1996). The vague misnomer came to be explicitly linked to the commercial activities negatively associated with the Levantine community, as evidenced by a satirical statement made by Brazilian poet Guilherme de Almeida in 1929: "What's the recipe for a Turk? Take the 25 de Março Street cocktail shaker and put in a Syrian, an Arab, an Armenian, a Persian, an Egyptian, a Kurd. Shake it up really well and—boom—out comes a Turk" (qtd in Lesser 1996, 58). The figure of the *turco* was thus specifically linked to migrants' commercial hub in São Paulo—25 de Março Street. This idea was strengthened by the popular claim that the *turco* in general, and the Levantine migrant more specifically, had a hereditary penchant for commerce at a time when the activity was not always valued (Lesser 1992). The discourse surrounding the label *turco* therefore served to to exoticize, deterritorialize, and other the Levantine peddler.

But Levantine migrants have reappropriated the figure of the *turco* peddler in a number of different ways.[2] One way that they have sought to elevate the peddler's peripheral status is through discursive strategies like those in Bastani's book *Memórias de um mascate* (Memories of a peddler). In many ways, his book encapsulates the prevailing discourse surrounding the peddler in Levantine migrants' early literature. Published in 1949, it draws heavily from the earliest decades of migrants' prose writing, a phenomenon that will be discussed in more detail below. Throughout the work, Bastani emphasizes the peddlers' roles as agents of civilization in Brazil's imagined future, a role that is reinforced in the book's very subtitle: *O Soldado Errante da Civilização* (The wandering soldier of civilization). The image of the Levantine peddler fighting valiantly for the nation's progress is maintained throughout the stories in the book, in which peddlers brave the unknown to hawk goods in the remotest corners of the nation. If understood in the context of the aforementioned nationalist discourses, the exaltation of the maligned peddler's contributions to the Brazilian nation can be understood as an attempt at discursive assimilation.

The representation of the peddler's role in "civilizing" Brazil has colonial implications as well. This link is suggested at a moment in the book when the narrator emphasizes the intermingled blood of the Iberian conqueror. He explains, "We are a people formed by races that are diverse but patriotic, most of which spilled their blood on battlegrounds in order to elevate national dignity. Brazilians do not carry in their veins indigenous and African blood only, but also Iberian, Oriental, Jewish, Indo-European, and others, in a wild mix of courage and affection" (Bastani 1949, 57). The idea that Brazilian national identity comprises multiple influences refers to Gilberto Freyre's seminal work *Casa-Grande e Senzala* ([1933] 1963). In Freyre's popular imagining, national identity is defined by the miscegenation of indigenous, African, and Portuguese elements that occurred on the Brazilian plantation. Here, the narrator points to the less frequently cited part of Freyre's argument, that the Portuguese conqueror was already the result of the miscegenation that occurred on the Iberian Peninsula. Freyre argues that Portugal's unique location and history have long led its people to be in contact with diverse influences. The influence that he most focuses on is the Moorish one. He contends, "For if Arabs—Moors, as a young master in the law preoccupied with terminology would more accurately say—did not mix with Lusitanian populations, we are ignoring the very meaning of the word 'miscegenation'" (Freyre [1933] 1963, 264). The miscegenation that Freyre thus posits as the crux of Brazilian identity is modeled on the miscegenation that occurred on the Iberian Peninsula centuries ago. While Levantine migrants find themselves excluded from the miscegenation that comprises Freyre's Brazil, Bastani's work seems to be suggesting an entry point through the Moorish roots of the Iberian colonizer. Bastani posits the migrant's superiority over the indigenous population in particular when he comments, "It was not the indigenous hand that cultivated the land" (Bastani 1945, 11). But according to the historical narrative, it was not the hand of the Levantine migrant that cultivated the land either. This conflicted moment raises a problem with attempts to present the economic figure of the peddler as a type of colonizer of Brazil, a problem for which, the next section will argue, *A Fogueira* attempts to find a resolution.

Bastani's attempt to insert the peddler into narratives of national progress is typical of Levantine migrants' earliest Portuguese-language literature in Brazil. The first prose written by this group belongs to a hybrid genre that appears to be chiefly historical.[3] In pointing to a similar phenomenon in Arab-Argentine literature, Christina Civantos describes the genre as a "mélange of history, legend, anecdote, fictional narrative, philosophical essay and/or philological treatise" (2006, 20). This hybrid genre is perfectly exemplified in Brazil by the community's earliest Portuguese-language works, such as Taufik Kurban's *Os Sirios e Libaneses no Brasil* (The Syrians and Lebanese in Brazil). Published in 1933, the book is a veritable hybrid of all of the elements Civantos identifies. Kurban moves with facility between historical discussions of migration to

Brazil, ancient legends of Phoenician grandeur, and his own nostalgic philosophical musings. Kurban's book even includes an anecdote in which Theodore
Roosevelt finds an Arabic newspaper in the Brazilian backlands; the author is
quick to suggest that this must mean a Levantine peddler had already passed
through the supposedly uncharted territory (Kurban 1933, 111). Like Bastani,
Kurban imagines ways to insert the peddler into Brazilian narratives of nationhood and progress.

While some historians have read Kurban's book and others like it as archival
sources, the unique genre of the works has never been fully explored. Sometimes referred to as autobiographies or "life histories," they are much more
complex than this label suggests. While *A Fogueira* represents a break with
this genre, it in no way signals an end to it, as works like it were still produced
for decades after its publication. T. Duoun's *A Emigração Sirio-Libanesa às
Terras de Promissão* (Syro-Lebanese emigration to the Promised Land) and
Bastani's *O Líbano e os Libaneses no Brasil* (Lebanon and the Lebanese in
Brazil) and *Memórias de um mascate* (Memories of a peddler), among others, continue to borrow heavily from this tradition. Common throughout
most of the works in this genre are an emphatic glorification of Brazil, which
relates to the discursive strategies of assimilation present in Bastani's work,
and nostalgia for the homeland. The fastidious detail with which many of the
works describe Levantine customs and traditions seems to suggest that these
works were meant for a wider Brazilian audience as well. This idea is reinforced by the fact that they are written in Portuguese rather than Arabic.[4] The
works can thus be understood as attempts to restore cultural specificity to the
deterritorialized *turco*. For as Bastani's preface to *O Líbano e os Libaneses no
Brasil* explains, "When the Lebanese emigrated from their country, they were
considered and always known as *turcos* by the people of other nations. Why?
Because geography, history, literature and the didactic books that were used in
schools were lacking" (1945, 11). Bastani thus presents his work as a corrective
to the ambiguous misnomer *turco*.

Yet it is unclear whether works like Bastani's actually succeeded in reaching
a wider Brazilian audience. More attention to the politics of circulation of these
works is needed to definitively assess their trajectories. Preliminary observations
suggest that there is a disconnect between Levantine migrants' prose writing
and that of their Brazilian contemporaries. Many of the works were published
internally by presses that belonged to wealthier Levantine migrants.[5] The works
are also notably absent from prominent discussions of Brazilian literature at
the time. Their genre also serves to set them apart from mainstream Brazilian literature. This suggests that while these works were employing rhetorical

strategies that aimed at assimilation, they were not necessarily able to establish a wider dialogue with Brazilian literature. But there is a fictional imagining that has already provided the link between the migrants' earliest literature and the Brazilian canon. In fact, it is such a convincing Brazilian novel that it has never been discussed on a continuum with the migrant community's earliest work. If *A Fogueira* is read in this context, then it is possible to see a unique imagining of the Levantine migrant in Brazil, one that reterritorializes the deterritorialized *turco* on the site of the Brazilian plantation to imagine an assimilation that the peddler figure alone could not achieve.

## On the Brazilian Plantation

An alternative imagining of the Levantine migrant's place in the Brazilian nation can be found in a novel that has all but escaped critical attention in discussions of this migration. In *A Fogueira*, the deterritorialized *turco* is reterritorialized not at the place of origin in the Middle East, but on the site of the Brazilian plantation. At a time when nationalist discourses were presenting the *turco* peddler as a figure bent on exploiting the nation rather than contributing to its future through agriculture, *A Fogueira* imagines the Levantine migrant as contributing prodigiously to the Brazilian plantation economy.

> [Elias] became jubilant when he saw the magnitude of the lands that were appearing before him. Recovering from his apathy, he gave himself over to his grandiose fantasies once more. How happy he became when he thought that huge chunks of that virgin American land, with its forests, valleys, hills, and rivers, would be his. (Carneiro 1942, 160)

Unlike in the migrants' earlier works, there is no nostalgic longing for the homeland in this novel. Instead, in a return to the site from which Freyre's thesis originally emerges, the Levantine migrant is imagined as a new colonizer on the Brazilian plantation. But at the same time that it imagines this new role for the Levantine migrant, the novel also mimics many of the stigmatizing racial discourses of the time. The tensions between these seemingly contradictory discursive moves drive the plot forward yet are never fully resolved, resulting in a conflicted quality that in many ways refers back to the tensions in Freyre's own work.

*A Fogueira* was written by the Brazilian-born son of Syrian migrants, Cecílio Carneiro (Putnam 1943, 325). He was a prolific and respected writer in the 1940s and '50s. The Instituto de Estudos Brasileiros holds his correspondence with a prominent contemporary, Mario de Andrade.[6] Carneiro also won honorable mention for *A Fogueira* in a pan-American contest meant to promote Latin American literature (Carneiro 1942, 2). In 1944, his novel was translated into English by Dudley Poore as *The Bonfire*. While previous works written by the Levantine community about the experience of migration did not always reach a wider Brazilian audience, *A Fogueira* is the first truly fictional imagining of this experience to take the form of a Brazilian novel and to reach a wider Brazilian and even international audience. For the first time, the topic of Levantine migration is brought center stage in a novel that is in direct dialogue with Brazilian literature through its genre as well as through its engagement with the literary movement of *naturalismo,* which favored socially defined types and scientific determinism. While there may (or may not) be some autobiographical point of departure to it,[7] Carneiro's novel is more significant for the ways in which it deviates from the dominant narratives of migration to imagine a new place for the Levantine migrant on the Brazilian plantation. It is, according to my findings, the first novel to imagine this alternate possibility.

The novel tells the story of Elias Alexandre Arbe, the son of peasant farmers from the Lebanese village of Terbul (near Tripoli). It follows the linear progression suggested by its five parts: "Orient," "America," "The Struggle against the River," "The Daughters," and "The Inheritance." The narration begins by describing the protagonist in his native village. Its characterization of Elias and other characters is typical of *naturalismo* in that it casts them into types that inevitably determine their trajectories. Elias, for example, is defined by his unfaltering honesty and courageousness, as well as by a restlessness that translates into remarkable ambition. The protagonist yearns for more than what he perceives to be the monotony of his small Levantine village. After years of unsuccessfully trying to achieve greatness at home, Elias decides to move with his wife to the Americas. His desire to move is driven by more than social and economic reasons. Elias sees himself as a visionary for the new nation, an image that is made explicit when the narration refers to him as a "new Columbus" (78).[8] He convinces a group of his wary compatriots to join them in the arduous journey to the promised land.

It is in the section "America," when Elias and his group first arrive in "that famous city of foreigners," São Paulo, Brazil, that their trajectories most closely follow the historical narrative of immigration (95). Many of them cluster together with other newcomers in the immigrant neighborhood of Braz, and Elias immediately takes up work as a peddler. The description of his life as a peddler is wholly typical of the historical narrative of Arab migration. From the reference to the 25 de Março Street, to the description of the goods that Elias hawks, right down to the *sonora matraca* or noisemaker that he uses to get his customers' attention, the narrator's description conforms to those found in the migrants' earliest works.

The story of Elias's subsequent ascent from peddler to successful store owner also borrows heavily from this narrative. The narration goes on to explain how Elias uses the same skills he used when selling surplus crops in Terbul to adeptly meet the demands of his customers in Brazil. As in Terbul, he distinguishes himself with his unfaltering honesty and ambition. He is able to quickly transform his small store into a twelve-door emporium. The migrants among whom he lives and works, who "were also making America," recognize him as leader of the community (98). This narrative closely follows the typical peddler-to-proprietor historical one, which saw Levantine migrants rise quickly from peddling, to retail, to wholesale, and often even on to manufacturing.

But not even Elias's remarkable economic and social ascent is enough to satisfy his restlessness; after all, he didn't come to Brazil for either economic or social success. Elias came as a visionary, a "new Columbus," and is thus eager to conquer new challenges (78). He finds that opportunity when he meets José Manso, a self-proclaimed "eighth-generation Brazilian" whose ardor reminds Elias of his own ambition (107). Elias is impressed by Manso's recounting of the vast plantations he owns in the interior. Elias eagerly tells him, "I love Brazil much more than my life and those of my loved ones!" (107). Moved by the migrant's display of enthusiasm, Manso gives Elias the following advice:

> Never forget what I'm about to tell you. You should know that this country of ours is an amazing place for those who know how things work. You can't make a fortune in the public sector, obviously. Commerce and industry also can't fill everyone's pockets, as is clear . . . But the land . . . the land is what gives us everything, understand? Agriculture and livestock, remember that, sir. (108)

Elias takes his Brazilian friend's advice to invest in the land itself very seriously. But it is not the promised fortune he is after, as he is already rich at this point; it is the power and the stature of his very Brazilian idol that Elias desires. Manso gives him one more piece of advice before they part: why not translate his surname into Portuguese? Unable to pronounce the guttural sound in "Arbe," Manso suggests, "There are many Brazilians with the surname 'Guerra'" (109). Equipped with a new Brazilian name that means "war," Elias Guerra sets out on a wild journey to battle São Paulo's harsh uncharted territories. It is precisely at this moment that his story begins to diverge from the conventions of the historical narrative of Levantine migration to Brazil.

In "The Struggle against the River," Elias leads his family on an arduous trek to the new land he has purchased in the *sertão* or hinterlands. The fact that Elias buys this land from a Portuguese man is significant. The narrative describes the Portuguese man as lazy, and as ultimately unable to tame the harsh land he eagerly passes off to Elias. While the Portuguese man is described as sluggishly dozing on and off on the train ride that constitutes the first leg of their trip, Elias stays up planning how he will tame the rough landscape (155–156). Over the next few years, Elias realizes his grandiose dream of conquering and populating uncharted Brazilian territory by effectively transforming inhospitable land that is constantly threatened by flooding from an untamable river into a massive coffee plantation with an innovative irrigation system. Elias's role in the interior of São Paulo represents a radical break with the historical narrative of Levantine migration. If some Levantine migrants did become large coffee plantation owners, they are largely omitted from the historical record. But unlike the historical narrative and early imaginings of the peddler, Elias is imagined as contributing significantly to the nation's agricultural future as a new type of colonizer.

The protagonist's role as a new colonizer of Brazil is reinforced by the description of his plantation. Elias brings migrants from all over to work on his plantation, turning it into a microcosm for the Brazilian nation itself. The narrative reads:

> During those two months, that international crowd worked continuously on the harvest. Those millions of creatures were white, black, Jewish, European, Oriental . . . As they worked, they could be heard singing anthems of the most distant and exotic of nations. And under that intense sun, the strangest and most unexpected unions were born. In the shade of secret corners, humans of the most opposite races and enemy nations would get together. (254–255)

Like Brazil itself, Elias's plantation has become home to a diverse group of migrants eager to contribute to its progress. The image of his plantation as a microcosm for the Brazilian nation is made even clearer by the reference to miscegenation. Here, the narrator returns to the very site of Freyre's imagining of national identity in order to imagine the Levantine migrant at the helm of the nation in formation.

Elias's role in the construction of the Brazilian nation takes on a performative aspect in one particular episode. On the occasion of Rui Barbosa's death, the narrative reveals Elias's passionate admiration for the Brazilian statesman. For Elias, Rui Barbosa is a symbol of intelligence and hard work. His death so moves him that, for the first and only time, he orders work stopped on the plantation so that all can attend the memorial ceremony he holds. Elias pays homage to Rui Barbosa by wrapping his portrait in the Brazilian flag, thus recognizing his fundamental role in the nation's construction. The description of the memorial ceremony is almost comical—all of Elias's migrant workers, knowing only that the portrait symbolizes greatness, venerate the unfamiliar image religiously. Once again, this international group is performing the Brazilian nation under Elias's direction.

In his teary-eyed eulogy, Elias says of Rui Barbosa, "A man that taught English to the English themselves! That, one day, made the entire world remember his nation and race. How great it is to be Brazilian, to be born in the same land as him!" (290). Here, Elias admires his idol's ability to "teach English to the English." When considered in conjunction with his subsequent claim to Brazilianness, this statement can be understood as true for Elias as well. Like Rui Barbosa with the English, Elias has proven himself to be more Brazilian than many Brazilians, bravely bringing civilization to the nation's most remote corners. In fact, the quintessentially Brazilian José Manso later tells him, "This country of ours is very large and full of virgin territory. That's why we need men as stubborn as you" (203). Elias is thus posited as making an impressive contribution to the construction of his adopted nation.

In the final days of his life, as both his plantation and his lucidity begin to fail, Elias dreams of bringing over even more of his compatriots. He muses, "Poor things. They don't have a country to love. They belong to France after having belonged to Turkey . . . Always slaves! Who knows if maybe I could emancipate them from the yoke of other nations? To proclaim the independence of a nation . . . even this might be possible for a man with an iron will" (377). Elias's last musings on greatness display his desire to contribute to the project of nation building both in Brazil *and* in his homeland. This is a desire that is faithful to the historical narrative of Levantine migration.[9] It also speaks to the importance of national identification at this particular moment, one that Elias feels he lacks and must construct for himself on the Brazilian plantation.

Elias's decision to abandon his comfortable, lucrative job as a merchant in order to work the land represents a subversion of the historical narrative of Levantine migration to Brazil. It emerges from the restless ambition that defines his type, as well as his desire to emulate his Brazilian idol, José Manso. But the narration also suggests that agriculture is capable of maintaining Elias's ties to the homeland as well. It reads: "'I was born for agriculture and through it I shall achieve great things,' he thought, vividly remembering how all of his ancestors had worked the land" (111). In this way, Elias imbues agriculture with an ancestral significance. Elias's ancestral connection to the working of the land allows him to envision a new place for the Levantine migrant in Brazil's imagined agricultural future.

Elias works the land with the same unflinching honesty with which he ran his store. He has no knowledge of the financial aspects involved in running a large plantation. This is ultimately his downfall, as he is unable to comprehend the market forces that finally devalue the coffee plants he worked so hard to nurture. It also allows him to be easily swindled by his cousin Saladino, who sells him falsified shares and eventually manages to swindle Elias out of his hard-earned fortune. But, because he has invested in the land itself, Elias is not left empty-handed. As he lies dying, he tells his inconsolable daughters, who now regret their past displays of greed, "Listen! If I die, I won't leave you any money! But I'll leave you a ruined plantation so that you can build it up again, understand? . . . I give you as my inheritance not my money but my labor! You will inherit my labor! Do as I did, sweat as I sweat, tire as I tired . . . and you shall earn your fortune" (413). Despite his financial ruin, Elias is still able to leave an inheritance for the next generation. His decision to return to his agricultural roots ensured that regardless of outside forces, he would always have the land itself, in all of its creative potential.

By imagining a Levantine migrant contributing prodigiously to Brazil's future through a specifically agricultural inheritance, the narrative engages Freyre's formulation of national identity in ways that imaginings of the peddler could not. For Freyre claims that the Iberian conqueror's Moorish roots are what specifically enabled him to undertake the agrarian and slaveholding colonization of Brazil. According to him, it was both invading and captured Moors who introduced the technical expertise and provided the labor necessary for the development of large-scale agriculture on the Iberian Peninsula, a system that would later be transposed onto Brazil ([1933] 1963). As he explains, "The physical conditions in the part of America that fell to the Portuguese required an agrarian and slave-holding colonization. Without the Moorish experience, the colonizer would have probably failed at that formidable task. He would have failed, unable to respond to conditions so outside of his specifically European experience" (Freyre [1933] 1963, 262). Without an agrarian, slaveholding inheritance from the Moors, the Portuguese would not have been able to conquer Brazil. Freyre's problematic claim becomes a portal for the Levantine migrant to enter a configuration of national identity from which he was originally excluded.

While it is tempting to speak only of the celebratory implications of a minority's assimilatory moves, it is important to not shy away from moments of tension within these narratives too. For while *A Fogueira* finds a place for the Levantine migrant in Freyre's imagining of miscegenation, its depiction of race simultaneously expresses ambivalence about that miscegenation. The novel is fraught with racist undertones that mirror many of the stigmatizing racial theories of the time. This becomes apparent in the description of Elias and his brothers with which the novel begins: "[Elias] had delicate features and very light skin and he was ambitious, unlike his brothers, who were cowardly and rough and were dark" (9). The narration immediately links Elias's fair skin to his ambition and his brothers' dark skin to their cowardliness. This depiction of race owes much to the scientific determinism that is often characteristic of *naturalismo*. But in mimicking stigmatizing racial theories of the time, the narrative also points to a more painful and conflicted side of assimilation. The same can be said of the novel's Orientalist undertones. The depiction of the inferiority and passivity of many of the Levantine migrants is reinforced by the fact that both Elias and the narrator exclusively associate civilization and progress with the Americas, and passivity and idleness with the Levant, undeniably valuing the former over the latter. But while the novel's racist and Orientalist undertones seem to go against its attempt at a discursive assimilation through Freyre, this ambivalence can be found in Freyre's work itself.[10] Alexandra Isfahani-Hammond, for example, contends that by even as Freyre links a past biological assimilation (with the Moors) with more recent cultural assimilation (with Africans and indigenous people), he expresses an anxiety with non-white races that is continuous with his earlier racist writings (2008). In this way, it is possible to posit that Carneiro inherits from Freyre not just a celebratory imagining of miscegenation as the core of national identity, but also a simultaneous trepidation in regards to that assimilation.

While the novel can be limited by its deterministic or conflicted qualities, even these achieve something no previous work did by establishing a dialogue with *naturalismo* and the Brazilian canon. By imagining the Levantine migrant contributing to Brazil's agricultural future through an inheritance from the homeland—the working of the land—*A Fogueira* finds a way for the migrant to be more Brazilian than the Brazilians themselves *through* the inheritance of his Levantine roots. While the novel has been either ignored or absorbed by the Brazilian canon, its interpretation alongside other literature produced by Levantine migrants offers a unique perspective to the understanding of rhetorical strategies of assimilation.

## Toward a Reimagining of National Belonging

Levantine migrants and their descendants continue to negotiate a place for themselves in contemporary Brazil through the act of representation. More recent imaginings of Levantine migration have articulated notions of belonging in distinct ways. The theme of later generations' struggle to negotiate their own relationship to their adopted nations, for example, finds masterful expression in Raduan Nassar's *Lavoura arcaica* (1975). Like Carneiro, the author imagines a migrant family that continues to live off the land in Brazil, as it had done in the Levant. Nassar represents this theme in its full complexity, without moralizing or ascribing normative values to any of its aspects. The result is a poignant portrait of loss that questions the viability and seamlessness of an assimilation based on the revival of ancient agricultural talents that is present in Carneiro's novel. Despite the problematization of this assimilation, Nassar's characters never stop searching for fresh ways to articulate belonging in their new homes.

In many ways, Nassar's problematization of this assimilation has set the stage for contemporary reimaginings of belonging. Categories that were fundamental to earlier imaginings are being rethought in a changing global context. The result is that contemporary literary production by Levantine migrants and their descendants has moved away from notions of national belonging to embrace more fluid circulations and connections. An example of this can be found in the articulation of a transnational Arab identity, as exemplified in novels like Salim Miguel's *Nur na Escuridão* (Light in the darkness) (2000) and Alberto Mussa's *O Enigma de Qaf* (The enigma of qaf) (2004). Both novels revolve around characters that mine their pasts not for specifically Levantine roots, but for more transnational Arab ones. In Miguel's novel, for example, the father chooses not to return to Lebanon after migrating to Brazil. Knowing that the specific piece of land he has left behind no longer exists as he remembers it, he imagines himself heir to a transnational Arab heritage instead.[11]

> It is not just the ancient [poets] that he remembers, although he prefers them. There are those from yesterday but also those from today—a Gibran Khalil Gibran and his *The Prophet,* for example. Father pauses again and falls silent, tired, or thinks of something else and says: and the anonymous fables, so rich, of such immense wisdom, the result of a fertile imagination, which return to me intact the pride of being Arab, no matter what kind—from any time, part, sect, or religion. (Miguel 2000, 164)

Authors like Salim Miguel, Alberto Mussa, and Milton Hatoum have done away with essential categories like "Orient" and "America" in order to renegotiate new notions of belonging.[12] Waïl Hassan's reading of Mussa,[13] for example, points to its potential for offering South-South paradigms that can provide new perspectives on transnational literatures. What is clear is that authors with multiple allegiances, like Levantine ones in Brazil, are neither returning nostalgically to the old nor abandoning it for the new. Instead, they are carving unique spaces for themselves in which they can renegotiate both.

Levantine migrants' cultural production in the Portuguese language offers a productive lens through which it is possible to understand different discursive moves that aimed at assimilation or distinction. Representations of the pioneering peddler first sought to create a place for the Levantine migrant in Brazil's nationalist ideals, but the figure's perceived economic proclivities precluded it from imaginings of Brazil's future. If *A Fogueira* is understood on a continuum with these earlier discursive strategies, its mooring of the Brazilian plantation is a turning point within the literary strategies and histories of representation that make up the "Genre Triangle" of Levantine-Brazilian literature, and can be understood as a powerful imagining of how Levantine migrants could be more Brazilian than the Brazilians themselves.

**Notes**

Portions of this paper were presented at the North Carolina State University Khayrallah Program for Lebanese-American Studies conference "The Mashriq and the Mahjar."

1. All translations in this chapter are my own.

2. For example, Karam (2007) analyzes strategies through which Levantine migrants have made their perceived business acumen relevant throughout different stages of the Brazilian economy's development.

3. The earliest Levantine migrants were also prolific journalists. For more on both Arabic and Portuguese newspapers published in Brazil, see Vargas 2006 and Narbona 2007.

4. Maria del Mar Logroño Narbona contends that the content and tone of T. Duoun's Arabic writings differ from those of his Portuguese writings, and that in the latter he omits many of the hardships and struggles he elsewhere claims to have experienced in Brazil. This raises the important question of audience and highlights how many of the Portuguese narratives are constructed as attempts at discursive assimilation (personal conversation, April 20, 2012).

5. For more on the relationships between intellectuals and the business class among Levantine migrants in Brazil, see Narbona 2007.

6. This information can be found in the institute's digital archives (www.ieb.usp.br). The reference numbers of the letters in question are MA-C-CAR185, MA-C-CAR187, and MA-C-CPL-1660.

7. In a footnote to his article, Samuel Putnam describes *A Fogueira* as "an autobiographical novel by a second generation Syrian in Brazil, dealing with the life of his people" (1943, 325). It is unclear where Putnam gets the idea that the novel is autobiographical, other than the fact of Carneiro's Levantine roots. The author himself does not make this link explicit.

8. All unattributed citations from this section are from Carneiro 1942.

9. For more on the contributions that Levantine migrants in the Americas made to the construction of the modern nation-states of Lebanon and Syria, see Khater 2001 and Narbona 2007.

10. For a full theorizing of the eugenic undertones behind Freyre's substitution of a biological assimilation with a cultural one, see Isfahani-Hammond 2008. For the Orientalist implications of his thesis, see chapter 7 in this volume.

11. For a discussion of the social and economic ramifications of Levantine descendants' claims to transnational Arab identities in neoliberal Brazil, see Karam 2007.

12. For more on Milton Hatoum, see chapter 16 in this volume.

13. See chapter 17 in this volume.

**References**

Bastani, Tanus Jorge. 1945. *O Líbano e os Libaneses no Brasil.* Rio de Janiero: C. Mendes.
———. 1949. *Memórias de um Mascate.* Rio de Janeiro: F. Briguiet & Co.
Carneiro, Cecílio. 1942. *A Fogueira.* Rio de Janeiro: Livraria José Olympio Editora.
———. 1944. *The Bonfire.* Trans. Dudley Poore. New York: Farrar & Rinehart.
Civantos, Christina. 2006. *Between Argentines and Arabs.* Albany: State University of New York Press.
Duoun, T. 1944. *A emigração sirio-libanesa às terras de promissão.* São Paulo: Editora Brazil.
Freyre, Gilberto. (1933) 1963. *Casa-Grande e Senzala.* 12th ed. Brasília: Editora Universidade de Brasília.
Ghanem, Sadalla. 1936. *Impressões de Viagem: Líbano-Brasil.* Nictheroy: Graphica Brasil.
Hourani, Albert, and Nadim Shehadi. 1992. *The Lebanese in the World: A Century of Emigration.* London: Centre for Lebanese Studies / I. B. Tauris.
Isfahani-Hammond, Alexandra. 2008. *White Negritude: Race, Writing, and Brazilian Cultural Identity.* New York: Palgrave Macmillan.
Karam, John Tofik. 2007. *Another Arabesque: Syrian-Lebanese Ethnicity in Neoliberal Brazil.* Philadelphia: Temple University Press.
Khater, Akram. 2001. *Inventing Home: Emigration, Gender, and the Middle Class in Lebanon, 1870–1920.* Berkeley: University of California Press.
Knowlton, Clark S. 1992. "The Social and Spatial Mobility of the Syrian and Lebanese Community in São Paulo, Brazil." In *The Lebanese in the World: A Century of Emigration,* ed. Albert Hourani and Nadim Shehadi, 285–312. London: Centre for Lebanese Studies / I. B. Tauris.
Kurban, Taufik. 1933. *Os sirios e libaneses no Brasil.* São Paulo: Sociedade Impressora Paulista.
Lesser, Jeff. 1992. "From Pedlars to Proprietors: Lebanese, Syrian and Jewish Immigrants in Brazil." In *The Lebanese in the World: A Century of Emigration,* ed. Albert Hourani and Nadim Shehadi, 393–410. London: Centre for Lebanese Studies / I. B. Tauris.
———. 1996. "(Re) Creating Ethnicity: Middle Eastern Immigration to Brazil." *The Americas* 53(1) (July): 45–65.
Miguel, Salim. 2000. *Nur na Escuridão.* Rio de Janeiro: Topbooks Editora.

Mussa, Alberto. 2004. *O Enigma de Qaf.* Rio de Janeiro: Editora Record.

Narbona, Maria del Mar Logroño. 2007. *The Development of Nationalist Identities in French Syria and Lebanon: A Transnational Dialogue with Arab Immigrants to Argentina and Brazil, 1915–1929.* PhD diss., History, University of California, Santa Barbara.

Nassar, Raduan. 1975. *Lavoura arcaica.* São Paulo: Companhia das Letras.

Pinto, Paulo Gabriel Hilu. 2010. *Árabes no Rio de Janeiro.* Rio de Janeiro: Cidade Viva.

Putnam, Samuel. 1943. "Race and Nation in Brazil." *Science & Society* 7(4) (Fall): 321–337.

Roquette-Pinto, Edgar. (1917) 1950. *Rondonia.* 5th ed. São Paulo: Companhia Editora Nacional.

Safady, Wadih. 1966. *Cenas e Cenários dos Caminhos de Minha Vida.* Belo Horizonte: Santa Maria.

Said, Edward. 1978. *Orientalism.* New York: Pantheon.

Truzzi, Oswaldo.1997. *Patrícios: Sírios e libaneses em São Paulo.* São Paulo: Editora Hucitec.

Vargas, Armando. 2006. *Migration, Literature and the Nation:* Mahjar *Literature in Brazil.* PhD diss., Comparative Literature. University of California, Berkeley.

# 15

## Multiple Homelands
Heritage and Migrancy in Brazilian *Mahjari* Literature

*Armando Vargas*

This chapter discusses the rhetorical strategies through which *mahjari* literature sought to inscribe the Arab immigrant onto the Brazilian nation. It explores how this literature responds to Brazilian nationalist discourses by reinterpreting the very language and images often meant to exclude them.

~

John Tofik Karam demonstrates in *Another Arabesque* how an Arab identity has been recently embraced as a component of Brazilian culture and society in reaction to increased globalization (Karam 2007). In this chapter, I explore the roots of a multicultural Brazil with a recognized Arab component that lie in an earlier stage of globalization—the era of mass international migration of the late nineteenth and early twentieth centuries. Beginning with the first arrivals, Arab immigrants to Brazil usually aimed to preserve their home identity without seeming disloyal or disrespectful to their Brazilian hosts. However, this liminal identity was unsatisfactory for Brazilian nation build-ers, who criticized this posture as too ambiguous. Despite an initial negative reaction to their presence, early Arab immigrants refused to completely forsake their original culture and language, arguing that their interstitial stance did not represent a threat to the Brazilian nation but was actually complementary with nationalistic ideals of racial democracy.

Arab immigrants in Brazil found in the texts of prominent nationalist au-thors a variety of ideas to support their embrace of a dual identity. Arabs argued that multiple identities were logical in Brazil, because Brazilian writers had acknowledged since early in the nineteenth century that Brazil was a country of diverse peoples.[1] Furthermore, Brazilians could not deny the preponderance of the Portuguese influence on their culture. This was key for the Arab community because Portugal provided a direct link with al-Andalus and the Arab presence in the Iberian Peninsula of the Middle Ages. This historical tie would prove to be the foundation of an entire process of reconfiguration of the nation that would portray the Arab community as quintessential Brazilian. Arabs in Brazil were able to argue for the logic of a double consciousness, both Arab and Brazilian, because the legitimacy of history supported these claims of affinity. Unlike other groups migrating to Brazil, Arabs could claim a common historical and cultural heritage with their hosts. This gave them credibility when claiming their Arabness by helping them assert that Arabness was not foreign to Brazil.

The Arab community in Brazil had various tools at its disposal that allowed for its integration into the nation. These tools helped Arabs rework Brazilian nationalism in their favor. Also, Arabs claimed to have enough commonalities with Brazilians to make a case for the preponderance of similarities over differences between the two groups. Arabs inserted themselves onto the metanarrative of Brazilian identity and history by tracing their presence in Brazil back to a purported Phoenician presence in the Americas, claiming ties to the Africans that were originally shipped to Brazil as slaves, telling tales of Arabs living in the middle of the jungle with native peoples, asserting the presence of Arab sailors alongside the Portuguese discoverers of Brazil, and establishing ties between Arabs and the celebrated frontiersmen (*os bandeirantes*) who went into the jungles in search of adventure and conquest (Khatlab 1999, 32–42). *Mahjar* writers in Brazil also highlight a common Andalusian familial and cultural descent between Arabs and Iberians (Zeghidour 1982, 74). Furthermore, the traveling Arab peddler or salesman (*o mascate*) became an important part of the Brazilian landscape and an important trope of Brazilian literature and national consciousness (Khatlab 1999, 39). Arab immigrants have asserted numerous other historical and cultural ties between themselves and Brazilians. Some are more mythological than factual, but they have all served the purpose of easing the transition of mostly Christian immigrants from Lebanon and Syria to the largest nation in South America. Other supposed ties range from highlighting the accompaniment of Vasco da Gama by Arab navigators, to accounts that the land where the Brazilian imperial house was erected was donated by a Lebanese businessman, Antun Elias Lubus, to Dom João VI upon his arrival in 1808 (Khatlab 1999, 32–33). There are also accounts of Lebanese immigrants living alongside both Father Cícero Romão Batista and another eminent historical figure, Virgulino Ferreira (known as *o Lampião*), in the arid *sertão* of northeast Brazil (Khatlab 1999, 39). Furthermore, studies exist of the links and similarities between the southern Brazilian cowboys (*os gaúchos*) and Bedouin Arabs.[2]

Using multiple aspects of Brazilian culture and history, a concerted effort was made to forge ties between the Arab immigrant community and their hosts. These ties included those between Arabs and important national folk and elite figures, between Arabs and the Portuguese royal and exploratory traditions, and, finally, between Arabs and all geographic regions of the vast country.[3] It was up to the immigrants, and especially the artists and writers among them, to make use of Brazilian nationalist practices to create a narrative that included Arabs. This immigrant narrative, in turn, was integrated into the larger idea of the Brazilian nation to produce what Homi Bhabha would later describe as a basis for nation building, reproducing "the idea of the nation as a continuous narrative of national progress, the narcissism of self-generation, the primeval present of the *Volk*" (Bhabha 1990, 1).

Identity for Arabs in Brazil has always been flexible. Arabs there have had what the scholar of American multiculturalism Mary Waters has termed "ethnic options." They have always claimed full Brazilianness as defined by the elite of European descent, but they have also been able to claim to be ethnic—and therefore different. Mary Waters would describe Arabs in Brazil as "people for whom ethnicity is an option, rather than an ascribed characteristic" (Waters 1990, 7). This type of ethnicity, Waters claims, "is not something that influences their lives unless they *want* it to. In the world of work and school and neighborhood, individuals do not have to admit to being ethnic unless they choose to. Ethnicity has become a subjective identity, invoked at will by the individual" (12). In the context of Arab immigrant communities and despite the potential for upsetting the assimilationist goals of nativist Brazilian nationalists, this type of chosen ethnicity invites the question: Why would Arabs choose to assert their ethnicity in late-nineteenth- and twentieth-century Brazil?

In the Brazilian context, Arab commitment to preserving their original cultural ties is multifaceted. One important reason for this commitment is that they could rely on their Arab identity to prove their historical fraternity with Iberians and, by extension, Brazilians. In this way, they proved their primal role in the nation. Another reason is that the Ottoman provinces from which these immigrants were departing had undergone an Arab renaissance—a renewed celebration and exploration of Arab roots and their rich linguistic and literary tradition.[4] Arab immigrants did not want to abandon an emergent self-confidence that had been so difficult to achieve after centuries of what Arab nationalists perceived as cultural stagnation under the Ottomans. Finally,

Arabs could not divorce themselves from sociopolitical developments in their home countries. Arab nationalism, for example, was deemed a necessary tool against the Ottoman Empire that ruled them for centuries. When large numbers of Arabs first migrated to Brazil, their home communities were still under foreign control. Many writers saw their relative freedom in the Americas as an opportunity to help their countrymen achieve independence. All prominent Arab poets in Brazil were dedicated pan-Arabists who used their craft to inspire both pride and rebellion. After the Ottoman Empire crumbled, Arab nationalism would again be invoked in the struggle against even more powerful European imperialists. For reasons both internal and external to Brazil, Arabs felt a strong desire to maintain and nourish their Arab identity. This was often done at the literary level—especially in poetry. This exploration and definition of identity through literature was also common among Brazilian nationalists of a European background.

In the nineteenth century and beyond, the examination of not only identity but also nationalism and modernity in Brazil was conducted at the textual level. These texts, as Brazilianists like Robert Stam point out, are replete with notions of multiculturalism. The present analysis seeks to recognize and interpret the multiculturalism of these texts. Stam emphasizes that "although issues of race and ethnicity are culturally omnipresent in Brazil, they are often textually submerged. It is therefore important to pay attention to the racial undertones and overtones 'haunting' all texts. The challenge is to render visible, or at least audible, the repressed multiculturalism even of dominant texts" (Stam 1997, 19). These dominant texts are especially relevant for the study of Arabs in Brazil because, as the renowned Brazilian literary critic Antônio Cândido has observed, Brazilian writers have always considered it part of their purpose to address the problem of national identity.[5] Current debates concerning national identity point to the lasting nature of this unresolved issue. Clearly the notion of the nation emanating from the nineteenth century was unsatisfactory for many groups within Brazil. For this reason, the problem of identity is currently still addressed through acts of rereading and reinterpretation. I argue here that these processes began much earlier than the more vigorous movement of the late twentieth and early twenty-first centuries to destabilize the traditional framework of the Brazilian nation as developed by cultural and political elites.

The original Arab immigrants reached Brazil at a time when the Brazilian nation was still in the early stages of its modern conceptualization. In his study of the creation of nation-states in Latin America, James Dunkerley emphasizes that even at the start of the twenty-first century, "all nation-states are still 'in-formation'" (Dunkerley 2002). Presently in Brazilian studies, once dominant ideas of the nation are being destabilized by more nuanced, multilayered identities, such as those that Arabs tried to fashion. As Fernando Arenas has remarked, grand narratives of national identity are being supplanted by an

> upsurge of a multiplicity of smaller narratives of nationhood across various discursive fields, social arenas, and media in contemporary Brazil. Thus, we observe a shift from macrological approaches that have privileged constructs such as "racial democracy," social typologies such as the "cordial man," or geopolitical binaries such as the "national" and "foreign" to micrological perspectives—in some cases, ones developing outside of the intellectual field—that account for a fragmented nation where there are multiple and competing versions of nationhood, democracy, and modernization. (Arenas 2003, 22)

Arab immigrants in Brazil were involved in the way of thinking about the nation described by Arenas long before its theoretical prominence emerged in the late twentieth century. Arabs were able to use the rhetoric of Brazilian nation building, centered on the tripartite definition of the nation as Indigenous, European, and African, to include themselves in the national narrative. At the heart of this project were purported historical ties to each of Brazil's three main racial groups. Arabs in Brazil engaged in a process that Judith Butler variously describes as resignification, recontextualization, and the reversal of meaning.[6] It is a process that takes dominant linguistic tropes and changes their meaning to redress the grievances of those who have been marginalized or maligned by dominant discourses.

Whereas nationalist narratives tend to be homogenizing and restrictive, Arabs in Brazil creatively used the prevalent narrative of Brazilian nationalism to devise an alternative interpretation of the nation. This novel approach made of Brazil a nation much more diverse than many had imagined—one where Arabs could claim their rightful place in society. Through their literary efforts, Arabs in Brazil were able to challenge a restrictive notion of identity while attempting to expand the definition of the nation so that it could be more inclusive. Initially, the Arab challenge to the dominant paradigm of the Brazilian nation knew varying degrees of success—largely because Brazilian nationalism was robust and patently racist at times. For example, Arabs themselves were often the targets of attacks by well-organized nationalistic politicians who decried a "Turkish" Eastern presence in their country. Despite these obstacles, the Arab community eventually thrived by reimagining the nation, inscribing themselves in it and rewriting "foundational fictions" (to use the famous phrase of the Latin Americanist Doris Sommer).[7] The engagement with Brazilian nationalism that Arab writers in Brazil displayed demonstrates their role as complex translators, not only of languages, but also of identities and culture. Arabs were able to interpret and translate themselves into the Brazilian nation by reworking the canonical texts and ideas of Brazilian nationalism as fashioned by the political and intellectual elite in Brazil. Arabs, for example, accepted and used the idea that Brazil was multicultural, except that their notion of multiculturalism was much more expansive than most Brazilian nationalists usually allowed.

Azade Seyhan has discussed the cultural production of immigrant communities as a negotiation of loyalties to nation, language, and ethnicity. She notes that "writing between borders and languages, many writers plot complex strategies of translating" (Seyhan 2001, 8). Through this process of translation, Arabs have been able to take master narratives of nationalism that apparently excluded them and interpret them in such a way that recognizes their presence in the Brazilian nation, its history and culture. They did this without forgetting or neglecting their original Arab identity. This is why they decided to publish in Arabic and constantly refer to their countries of origin in their writing. This was a strategy based on nurturing loyalties to more than one place.

The process of translation undertaken by Arab immigrants to Brazil challenged traditional notions of nationalism and citizenship. This was innovative and daring because the ideas about the nation-state emerging from the nineteenth century did not have room for shared loyalties. Ultranationalists did not tolerate anything that might rival loyalty to the nation. Eventually, extreme forms of these sentiments would evolve into extremist political movements in multiple regions during the twentieth century—including Brazil. Marilena Chaui has noted that any perceived disloyalty to the Brazilian nation negates the image of the "good society," which is "indivisible, pacific and ordered"—an image that nationalists have worked hard to forge. Since any conflict or contradiction (including those related to identity) is synonymous with "danger, crisis and disorder," those outside of the limiting and traditional rubric of the nation receive "a unique response, military and political repression for popular groups and condescending disdain for opponents in general" (Chaui 2000, 92).

Despite the potential for tension and conflict faced by those challenging restrictive notions of the Brazilian nation, Arab intellectuals were motivated by a strong sense of Arab identity, which they did not see as conflicting with Brazilian society. They believed it was possible to share loyalties without compromising the integrity of the nation. They could not and would not disavow their Arab background. For example, they dedicated praise poems to the Arab world just as easily as they did to Brazil. This stance on identity has been asserted more and more among immigrant communities, especially at the end of the twentieth century and the beginning of the twenty-first. These communities are an example of what Salman Rushdie calls "conscious émigrés." He observes that these migrants are "not willing to be excluded from any part of [their] heritage." Furthermore, he exclaims that it is the right of all post-diaspora communities to draw on their roots for art (Rushdie 1991, 15). The Arabs in Brazil thus became what Mike Featherstone has termed "transnational intellectuals." He notes that transnational intellectuals "keep in touch via global cultural flows and . . . are not only at home in other cultures, but seek out and adopt a reflexive, metacultural or aesthetic stance to divergent cultural experiences" (Featherstone 1990, 9).

Arab intellectuals in Brazil provided a cultural consciousness that preceded late-twentieth-century efforts, there and elsewhere, by cultural, linguistic, and sexual minorities to assert alternative identities after difficult struggles against conservatism and intolerant nationalism. It has taken great efforts by those in fields such as cultural and ethnic studies, postcolonial studies, and feminist studies to be able to assert alternative conceptualizations of the self and the nation. To do it in Brazil at the beginning of the twentieth century, previous to that century's civil rights movements, required original thinking such as that described by Seyhan. She contends that "the migrant, exile or voyager not only crosses the threshold into another history and geography but also steps into the role of an itinerant cultural visionary" (Seyhan 2001, 14). Arabs in Brazil were such vanguard thinkers. They provide a valuable example of early challenges to dominant discourses of nationhood as new directions of scholarship are currently emerging in the production of knowledge, such as in the fields of literary and cultural studies.

In the case of the Arab immigrant community in Brazil, a strong sense of group consciousness, migration, and cultural revival combined to produce literary works demonstrating a nuanced, complex sense of self while writers maintained and nurtured their heritage. In naming their literary group and journal *Al-'Usba al-Andalusiyya* (the Andalusian League) and in their literary output, Arabic-language poets in Brazil reflected these dynamics of identity during the latter part of the nineteenth century and the first half of the twentieth. One such poet was Tawfiq Berber, who was born in Lebanon in 1921 and migrated to Brazil in 1938.

Berber expresses in his poetry the possibility of the individual having more than one *waṭan* (homeland, nation) and belonging to both an original homeland and to another place. Berber proudly expresses his strong ties to the Arab world and to Brazil in a poem titled *"naḥnu wa al-brāzīl"* (Us and Brazil):

Brazil the magnificent embraced our dreams,
and they flourished in the most generous of embraces.
Praise be to Him who makes marvels,
having made this country the most marvelous of places.
Have you read about Eden? For this is its sister,
but without a serpent or a Satan.
It joined copious luxury
with the freedom of birds on branches.
Its embraces are a refuge for the stranger [*al-gharīb*] and its breast
a spring of ever-flowing love.
Caress the loving mother—a stranger
who treated you with the greatest loyalty;
A second homeland [*waṭanun thānin* ] for us; and there is no first
in love for one persistently in love, nor second.[8]

Although written by an Arab immigrant, this poem includes much of the imagery and themes of the vast corpus of Brazilian nationalist writings. The fact that this poem is written in Arabic excludes it from mainstream Brazilian literature, but many of the sentiments expressed in it echo classic nationalist texts written by native Brazilians of European descent. They are reminiscent of the poetry of Olavo Bilac, for example. The personification of Brazil in this poem makes the nation deserving of ultimate respect. Brazil is seen as a utopian ideal equated with the eminent status in society afforded the mother in both Arab and Latin American culture. The motherly embrace of Brazil, with its magnanimity, warmth, and protection, takes the individual into a state of loving communion. Its breast nurtures the spirit. The land touches the soul while nature is equated with liberty. The liberty expressed here is both ethereal and political. This idea of political liberty was of great consequence for immigrant Arabs, because the Arab countries had long-standing grievances against foreign control—first against the Ottomans, then against the Europeans.

There are other significant sociopolitical references in Berber's poem. The idea of Brazil accommodating and hosting the foreigner is important in a nation characterized by immigration. Of course, the light in which immigration is cast here is very positive, but this was not always the stance taken by Brazilian intellectuals or politicians toward recent arrivals. This poem adds to the debate about the role of immigrants in Brazil. It passionately argues for their incorporation and acceptance into the embrace of the nation. Berber's poem is descriptive, but it also means to serve as an example of the social ideal. In constructing this social ideal, the Arab poet is promulgating the basic social tenet of hospitality found in his home culture. This is doubly effective because hospitality is also a social ideal of Brazilian society. In this confluence of cultural characteristics, the immigrant reminds the host nation of its own ideals while helping to keep alive his original identity. This convergence of societal norms would help the integration of Arab immigrants in the nation. Through the ideal of hospitality, a welcoming approach to *al-gharīb* (the stranger, foreigner, immigrant) is espoused. This is of great importance, because as many theoreticians of nationalism have argued, it is the stranger, in his or her multiple guises, that poses the greatest threat to the nation-state. This poem addresses nationalistic anxieties as it calls for solidarity between Brazil and its recent immigrants.

Portraying Brazil as the embracing mother, the welcoming paradise and the passionate caretaker deserving of the highest praise and gratitude, is typical of much of the poetry written by Arabs in Brazil. The images of refuge, nature, and moisture, along with the affirmation of life in this poem, are not unlike the text of the Quran itself, which, in the words of Roger Allen, "shows an obvious concern with the rigors of daily life in the way it depicts Paradise as a well-watered garden" (Allen 2000, 8). Perhaps it is its association with Paradise that allows an easier acceptance of a second homeland, because the second homeland is not an equivalent rival to the original homeland, but rather an otherworldly entity above and beyond the terrestrial. The majority of Arab writers in Brazil, and in the rest of Latin America, were committed Arab nationalists; but by casting the countries to which they migrated as beyond the realm of the worldly, the revolutionary idea of fidelity to a second homeland could be espoused. This was novel because it came at a time when the idea of the nation-state, along with its driving force of nationalism, was being strengthened in places like Brazil. However, as an alternative to limited notions of the nation, Arab immigrants posited that although there can only be one birthplace, there can also be more than one homeland—with the inherent multiple loyalties that this idea implies. This comfort in sharing loyalties is one of the major intellectual contributions of these writers. This was done before the advent, toward the end of the twentieth century, of intellectual currents that celebrate a multifaceted, fractured identity (such as postcolonial theory and poststructuralism). These ways of thinking that question dominant tropes have served as a challenge to the types of restrictive nationalism that occasioned such developments as the rise of fascist movements within Brazil, but more prominently in Europe, during the first half of the twentieth century. In traditional conceptualizations of the nation, there is no room for shared loyalties or multiple homelands. The manifestation of these sentiments at the juncture of the nineteenth and twentieth centuries highlights the problematic nature of binary logic and essentialist thinking in the analysis of identity and cross-cultural contact.

Remarkably, the imagery and symbols used to praise the new homeland in Arabic are strikingly similar to the musings in Portuguese of Brazilian nationalists forging a new nation. A similarity of spirit is found in these writings. The renowned Brazilian nationalist Olavo Bilac wrote:

> Love with faith and pride the land in which you were born!
> Oh child! You will never see a country like this one!
> See what sky, what sea, what jungle!
> Nature here is perpetually in celebration;
> It is a mother's breast overflowing in caresses. . . .
> Imitate the grandeur of the land in which you were born![9]

As in Berber's poem, the Brazilian nation is personified by the loving, caressing mother overflowing with care for her children. Her body is a plentiful, nourishing land that is a provider on a large scale. Brazil here is again seen as exceptional, singular in its abundance and unique in its grandeur. The nation is divine and deserving of total loyalty. This text is typical of nationalistic musings—meant to arouse patriotic passions and demanding that its subjects rise to the lofty level of their homeland. The imperative mood marks the immediacy and relevance of the need to support the nationalist cause. In these and other respects Berber and Bilac are of similar spirit. However, upon closer scrutiny, these two poems diverge in one important way. Bilac places enormous emphasis on the place of birth, on an originary relationship between the land and the true Brazilian. This is something that would exclude Berber and the other millions of immigrants to Brazil.

It is worth noting that both Bilac and Berber were writing at a time when immigration was changing the sociopolitical landscape of Brazil. But Berber responds forcefully to the nativism of Bilac. While agreeing with Bilac in many respects, Berber argues that Brazil is so magnanimous, so unique, that its motherly embrace has the enormous capacity to take in even those not born on its soil. Brazil can take other nations' citizens and protect them and nourish them while under its care. Brazil is so loving and grand that it can receive immigrants without concern for their birthplace. This presents a direct challenge to Bilac. Berber takes the image of the mother overflowing with love to assert that there can be no limit to this love.

Berber asserts that love, especially such a special love as Brazil offers, cannot be qualified to include only the native-born. It is difficult to argue against this if there is agreement about the strength of love of the mother. Berber's poem is indicative of the response of Arab immigrants to Brazilian nationalist rhetoric. Arabs do not dismiss these ideas outright, but rather engage them by reinterpreting the language and images often meant to exclude them. At a time when immigration matters divide many nations in the Americas, Europe, and elsewhere, the successful project of Arabs inscribing themselves onto the Brazilian nation is a valuable example of productive coexistence and cultural confluence in the face of periodic adversity.

## Notes

1. Ironically, a non-Brazilian was the first to advocate this concept. As Burns stresses, "it was a foreigner, Karl Friedrich Philipp von Martius, who discovered an important key to the interpretation and understanding of Brazil. The German scientist had spent the years 1817–20 traveling through the country to gather botanical specimens. Two decades later, when the [Brazilian Geographical and Historical Institute] sponsored a contest to solicit answers to the question of how the history of Brazil might best be written, Martius submitted a penetrating essay that displayed a remarkably clear vision of the uniqueness of Brazil. He saw the amalgamation of the three races [African, European, Native American], and their contributions to a single civilization, as the salient Brazilian theme" (Burns 1968, 41–42).

2. Manoelito de Ornellas argues for the cultural cross-pollination between Bedouin Arabs and Brazilian cattle ranchers in his *Gaúchos e beduínos* (1976).

3. Arabs in Brazil managed to incorporate much of the definition of Brazilian nationalism in their narratives. Marilena Chaui notes that nationalists in Brazil defined nationalism as the "spirit of the people," encompassed in the language, in popular and folk traditions, and in race, which, she notes, was a "central concept of the social sciences of the nineteenth century" (Chaui 2000, 18). Language barriers would keep early immigrants from addressing their hosts in a common language, but this would quickly change. Eventually the Lebanese community would produce notable Portuguese-language writers and grammarians. Arabs were adamant about learning Portuguese, and they were inspired by such things as the influence of Arabic on Portuguese (al-Naʿuri 1976, 12).

4. For a discussion of the Arab cultural revival of the nineteenth century (*al-Nahḍa*), see Roger Allen, *An Introduction to Arabic Literature* (Cambridge: Cambridge University Press, 2000), 45.

5. Antonio Cândido explores this issue in depth in his *Formação da literatura brasileira: Momentos decisivos* (São Paulo: Martins, 1959).

6. See Judith Butler, *Excitable Speech: The Politics of the Performative* (New York: Routledge, 1997).

7. See Sommer's *Foundational Fictions: The National Romances of Latin America* (Berkeley: University of California Press, 1991).

8. Quoted in Ahmed Matlub, *Suwwar ʿArabiyya min al-Mahjar al-Janubi*, 12–13. This and all unattributed translations are mine.

9. Quoted in Chaui 2000, 5.

# References

Allen, Roger M. A. 2000. *An Introduction to Arabic Literature*. Cambridge: Cambridge University Press.

Arenas, Fernando. 2003. *Utopias of Otherness: Nationhood and Subjectivity in Portugal and Brazil*. Minneapolis: University of Minnesota Press.

Bhabha, Homi K. 1990. "Introduction: Narrating the Nation." In *Nation and Narration*, ed. Homi K. Bhabha. London: Routledge.

Burns, E. Bradford. 1968. *Nationalism in Brazil*. New York: Frederick A. Praeger.

Chaui, Marilena. 2000. *Brasil: Mito fundador e sociedade autoritária*. São Paulo: Editora Fundação Perseu Abramo.

Dunkerley, James. 2002. Preface to *Studies in the Formation of the Nation-State in Latin America*, ed. James Dunkerley. London: Institute of Latin American Studies.

Featherstone, Mike. 1990. "Global Culture: An Introduction." In *Global Culture: Nationalism, Globalization and Modernity*, ed. Mike Featherstone. London: Sage.

Karam, John Tofik. 2007. *Another Arabesque: Syrian-Lebanese Ethnicity in Neoliberal Brazil*. Philadelphia: Temple University Press.

Khatlab. Roberto. 1999. *Brasil-Líbano: Amizade que desafia a distância*. Bauru: Editora da Universidade do Sagrado Coração.

Matlub, Ahmad. 1986. *Suwwar 'Arabiyya min al-Mahjar al-Janubi*. Amman: Dar al-Fikr.

Na'uri, 'Isa al-. 1976. *Mahjariyyat*. Tunis: al-Dar al-'Arabiyya li-l-Kitab.

Ornellas, Manoelito de. 1976. *Gaúchos e beduínos: A origem étnica e a formação social do Rio Grande do Sul*. 3rd ed. Rio de Janeiro: Livraria Jose Olympio Editora.

Rushdie, Salman. 1991. *Imaginary Homelands: Essays and Criticism, 1981–1991*. London: Granta Books.

Seyhan, Azade. 2001. *Writing Outside the Nation*. Princeton, NJ: Princeton University Press.

Stam, Robert. 1997. *Tropical Multiculturalism: A Comparative History of Race in Brazilian Cinema and Culture*. Durham, NC: Duke University Press.

Waters, Mary C. 1990. *Ethnic Options: Choosing Identities in America*. Berkeley: University of California Press.

Zeghidour, Slimane. 1982. *A poesia árabe moderna e o Brasil*. Trans. Daniel Aarão Reis Filho. São Paulo: Editora Brasiliense.

# 16

# Orientalism in Milton Hatoum's Fiction

*Daniela Birman*
*Translated by Silvia C. Ferreira*

Birman explores Milton Hatoum's appropriations of the concept of Orientalism in the novels *Relato de um certo oriente* (1989) and *Dois Irmãos* (2000). She develops the hypothesis that, as a native of the Amazonian city of Manaus, Hatoum critically explores the distinction between East and West by playfully exposing its limits rather than essentializing it in an Orientalist fashion. Hatoum thus demonstrates that, far from being natural, the differences between East and West are continually transformed by encounters and close contact with the other. Birman also suggests that the author himself assumes a unique border position—both within and outside of the East, the West, and the Amazon—that is similar to the one occupied by Edward Said. She concludes by discussing Hatoum's role in the diffusion of Said's work in Brazil, as well as the importance of so-called Orientalist texts in the author's academic background.

∾

## A "Certain Orient"

Milton Hatoum's debut novel, *Relato de um certo oriente (Tale of a Certain Orient)* abounds with references to popular imaginings of the Middle East. The novel describes typical Middle Eastern delicacies, customary prayers in the direction of Mecca, learning the Arabic language, and stories from *1001 Nights*. These references are intertwined with the descriptions and narrations of the people, customs, and fauna of the Amazon. Despite their differences, the cultures present in *Tale of a Certain Orient* are both susceptible to being read as or transformed into exotic objects—as either Amazonian or Oriental.

Yet the writer generally refrains from exploring the concept of the exotic. The exotic is understood here as a barrier to the encounter with or recognition of the other. If the concept relies on defining the other, it can be said to crystallize difference and thus make it insurmountable. By emphasizing difference, the concept of the exotic prioritizes its irreducibility over its potential for facilitating recognition of the other. However, Hatoum does not emphasize the exotic gaze that freezes and isolates images of the Amazonian, of the Oriental, or of the indigenous groups of the region. Instead, he seeks to explore themes such as fluxes *between* territories and cultures, and to create characters on whom different customs have left their mark.

The title of the novel already indicates that the reader is not dealing with a narration of *the* Orient, but of *a certain* Orient. This choice seems natural, as the plot unfolds mostly in Manaus and not in the Middle East. The author could have, however, opted to affirm the existence of a pure piece of the Middle East in Brazil. Instead, he chose to imbue the region of which he writes with a unique character that is informed by the miscegenation and hybridization of two cultures, Amazonian and Oriental—that is, for those readers who are able to discern that the novel narrates the story of a Lebanese family in Brazil. The "certain Orient" recreated by Hatoum does not have a natural, essential identity. Instead, it is a construction that can be understood as fictitious or not, depending on whether the reader opts for a realist reading of the novel. The northern Brazilian region of which Hatoum writes does not constitute a world closed into itself. Besides immigrants and Amazonians, it is populated by a number of other people from different countries and ethnic backgrounds, all of whom influence and allow themselves to be influenced by one another.

In addition to the title, the reader encounters numerous other examples that the world constructed by the author is in fact a unique place that cannot be reduced to stereotypes of the Amazon or Orient. The border that divides this specific place from neighboring ones can be said to be the product of a constellation of desires and events, a constellation that cannot be seen (at least not with the naked eye). Thus, unlike the narrator of the novel who seeks to "see" her city, another voice from the novel emphasizes the arbitrary division that demarcates one city from another: "'My trip ended in a place it would be an exaggeration to call a city. By convention or convenience, its inhabitants insisted on considering it part of Brazil, which seems as arbitrary as the three or four countries within the Amazon region calling an imaginary line through an infinite horizon of trees a border'"(Hatoum 2004, 82).[1]

It is in this context that it is possible to suggest that Hatoum exposes the limits of the distinction between East and West, a theme he first takes up in *Tale of a Certain Orient* and continues exploring in his novel *Dois Irmãos (The Brothers)*. This is a distinction that figures prominently in texts that would seem to be of the very type that Edward Said would identify as Orientalist. The distinction between East and West was incorporated into our gaze, discourse, and knowledge production in relation to the immense territory that we constitute as our other and whose opposition to us is therefore the basis of our "western identity." The most comprehensive definition of Orientalism is given by Said:

> a style of thought based upon an ontological and epistemological distinction made between "the Orient" and (most of the time) "the Occident." Thus a very large mass of writers, among whom are poets, novelists, philosophers, political theorists, economists, and imperial administrators, have accepted the basic distinction between East and West as the starting point for elaborate theories, epics, novels, social descriptions, and political accounts concerning the Orient, its people, customs, "mind," destiny, and so on. (Said 1979, 2–3)

Said also refers to two other definitions of the term that will not be explored in depth here, but nevertheless deserve mention, as all three definitions are ultimately interdependent. These two definitions involve academia (as many professors and researchers of "the Orient" used to be considered Orientalists) and the institutionalization of Orientalism, the roots of which can easily be traced back to the end of the eighteenth century. In this last case, Orientalism can also be understood as a "corporate institution for dealing with the Orient ... as a Western style for dominating, restructuring, and having authority over the Orient" (Said 1979, 3).

In his article on Said's work, James Clifford argues that the last two meanings of the term cited here suggest that Orientalism refers to and preoccupies itself with an Orient which, according to its first meaning, "exists merely as the construct of a questionable mental operation" (Clifford 1988, 260). It is precisely this mental operation, as well as its radical questioning by Said, that is of interest here. This operation ultimately serves as the point of departure for any study, discourse, or fiction produced about the Orient, whether or not their authors accept it as such.

## Negotiations, Influences, and Intertextuality

Despite the fact that Hatoum takes the distinction between East and West as a point of departure in *Tale of a Certain Orient,* he neither essentializes the concept nor uses it uncritically.[2] Instead, the author plays with this distinction, demonstrating how the differences between the two are not givens and can be altered in the encounter with the other. The characters, behaviors, and customs that are present in the unique region that he constructs can neither be read reductively nor interpreted as stereotypical. The interpretation of this unique world should therefore take into account fluxes between cultures while at the same time questioning the supposed separation between them. It should also take into account the political act implicit in the choice of images to represent such a heterogeneous world. It should consider cultures, in Clifford's words, "not as organically unified or traditionally continuous but rather as negotiated" (Clifford 1988, 273).

In Hatoum's "certain Orient," Emilie, the matriarch of the Lebanese family around whom the plot centers, is a devout Christian. She is married to a Muslim, and the two are constantly bickering. But their disputes are never serious enough to shake their union; they are no more than typical lovers' quarrels. Before their wedding, the couple made "'a pact to respect the other's faith and to let their children opt for one or the other or none at all'" (Hatoum 2004, 79). The piety with which they dedicate themselves to their respective faiths does not impede their shared bedroom from containing objects from both religions. In their room, Emilie's statues of saints can be found alongside a Muslim prayer rug that is quite foreign to her.

The couple therefore fails to conform to the stereotypical image of intolerance and conflict between Christians and Muslims that is commonly associated with the Middle East in general and Lebanon more specifically. Rather, they can be seen as an ironic and critical manipulation of this stereotype, or as a reference to widespread religious tolerance in Brazil. As for the spats between the two, they can be understood as part of the aforementioned process of negotiation that constitutes the identity of people and cultures.

One specific quarrel took place many Christmases ago, when Emilie's husband become infuriated by the way in which the sheep were slaughtered—they had been made drunk and strangled. According to him, this was suffering that "'can only be the work of a Christian'" (Hatoum 2004, 35). Emilie uses two strategies to deal with her husband's rebellion. First, she acts in a conciliatory manner. Even though he has left the house on the night of an important Christian celebration and destroyed her statues of saints and the baby Jesus, she has her maid immediately go look for him the next day:

> In the midst of all her torment that night [after her husband left the house and she discovered that he had destroyed her statues], Emilie did not forget to set

aside a plate of food, a tray of sweets and dried fruit, and a bowl of guava com-
pote for him. Emilie's whispered message to Anastácia had been that the wrath
of a hot-blooded man can be tempered by affection and a few choice tidbits.
(Hatoum 2004, 48)

While the bickering continues after her husband's return home, it is no
longer as serious. Emilie's husband continues to hide her statues of saints
from her for a few days, but their eldest son diffuses the situation by revealing
their location to her each time. In this particular instance, however, Emilie
retaliates against her husband by doing something similar, which constitutes
a change in strategy for her. She patiently waits for the Muslim holy month
of Ramadan to hide the Quran from him. The strategy seems to work, as the
episode is not mentioned in the novel again. Once again, the dialogue between
the pious Christianity and Islam of these two characters can be interpreted
as a negotiation through which they disagree, provoke one another, and ultimately achieve some form of reconciliation—a temporary reconciliation, but
a peaceful one nonetheless.

As for the image of religious tolerance in Brazil, it can also be seen in the
matriarch's engagement with "superstitions" from the Amazon. Emilie carries
out a religious vow made after her brother's death that seems to stem from a
religious syncretism—or at the very least a religious tolerance. Every year, on
the anniversary of her brother's death, Emilie walks to the church where she
"'intone[s] the Responses of Saint Anthony,'" then goes to the place where Emir
committed suicide at "'the mouth of the Educandos creek, where she thr[ows]
a bouquet of flowers and a picture of her brother into the river'" (Hatoum
2004, 100–101).

The link between this "certain Orient" and the one depicted in *The Brothers*
is carefully laid out by the author himself. In the beginning of *The Brothers*, the
narrator refers to a "friend, herself nearly a hundred," of Zana, the Lebanese
mother of the twins whose bitter rivalry is the novel's main theme (Hatoum
2002, 4).[3] In the hospital right before her death, Zana speaks in Arabic to ask
her daughter and this old friend whether her two sons have reconciled. Almost
at the end of the narration—in the second-to-last chapter—the intertextual-
ity between the two novels is made explicit by the author when Emilie briefly
appears, confirming that she is in fact the friend mentioned in the beginning
of the novel.

Hatoum thus clearly links the two novels, suggesting that a reading of the
second should lead back to the first. But other links and similarities between
the two exist as well, which reinforces the idea that both deal with the same
territory "fictionalized" by the author. Even though in the second novel the

references to that Orient are less common and pointed, they continue to be attached to the sounds, aromas, and typical delicacies of the Amazon, just as in *Tale of a Certain Orient*. The family depicted in *The Brothers* is also made up of a Christian mother and Muslim father. While in this plot they do not face internal conflicts based on religious difference, they certainly face external conflicts. The Christian Maronites of the city, for example, originally do not accept Zana's marriage to a Muslim.

Zana eventually agrees to marry Halim anyway, but only after imposing her own conditions on the arrangement. She demands, for example, that they be married "at the altar of Our Lady of Lebanon, and in the presence of every Maronite and Catholic woman in Manaus" (Hatoum 2002, 40). Halim accepts these terms. But he still manages to express his disdain for those who opposed the marriage. During the ceremony at Our Lady of Remédios, while still at the altar, he passionately kisses his new wife in front of the scandalized priest and the devout women of the town.

The encounters (and exchanges) between the "Orient" and "Occident" permeate Hatoum's two novels on the lexical level as well. Both amalgamate Portuguese words from diverse origins. There are words of Arabic origin (for instance, *azáfama, alpercata, alforje, sufi,* and *açucena*);[4] words of indigenous Tupi origin (such as *curica, caboclo,* and *tucum*); and colloquialisms typical to the Amazon or the northern and northeastern regions of Brazil that are not necessarily of Tupi origin (for example, *cunhatã, chichuta, curumim,* and *maracajá*). Words of diverse origins are also used to describe different delicacies and sweets (i.e. *esfiha, tâmara, tabule,* and *cupuaçu*).[5] By mixing this varied vocabulary into one narrative,[6] Hatoum seems to highlight how the diverse origins of his characters' words makes it impossible to tie any one of them to a rigid identity. He is also suggesting that such linguistic hybridity can permeate our quotidian reality undetected. As Hatoum reminds us in an essay on Manaus in which he emphasizes the often-underestimated indigenous influence on Amazonian cities: "It is enough to pronounce the name of a fruit, of a fish, of a tree, or of a city (Manaus), in order to reignite in us the flame of that indigenous tradition, of that absence that animates us and even in its absence, makes itself both present and presence" (Hatoum 2006, 52).[7]

## Biographical Considerations

It is instructive to recall three biographical details about the author that are related to his own ties to the East and to Orientalism. It seems worthwhile to consider who is speaking, although the intention of this consideration is *not* to use biographical information as a lens through which to interpret the novels. Rather, these biographical observations are meant to scrutinize the novels' point of departure.

The first significant detail refers to Hatoum's Arab background. The author is the son of an Amazonian mother of Christian Lebanese descent, and a Muslim Lebanese father. For fifty years, his father would take his mother to church every Sunday. This did not stop him from continuing to pray in accordance with the Quran. It is impossible to forget, in this context, the characterization of the couples in the families of Hatoum's first two novels. When recalling these memories, Hatoum criticizes the prejudiced stereotype that reduces different societies to a single image of intolerance and radicalism:

> I always saw my father taking my mother to church. He would wait in the car and then they would go home together . . . My mother tells me that when she went to Beirut and wanted to see a very important church there, my father's relatives, who are Muslims, took her to see the church. There is a clichéd stereotype that Islam is intolerant and radical. This is a forged discourse. You cannot place one billion Muslims in the same basket. (DW-World 2004)

Hatoum was born and raised in Manaus. At age fifteen, he moved to Brasilia, where he remained through the politically turbulent years of 1968 and 1969. Hatoum became somewhat of a globetrotter after this period. He spent the 1970s in São Paulo, where he received his degree in architecture. He also lived in Barcelona, Madrid, and Paris. After eighteen years away, he returned to Manaus in 1984 and became a professor at the Universidade Federal do Amazonas. He left the city again in 1999 and has lived in São Paulo ever since. Throughout his travels, Hatoum ended up living in other places both inside and outside of Brazil as well. He lived in Taubaté, where he was a professor of architecture. He also lived in the United States, where he traveled as author in residence to Berkeley, Stanford, and Yale (Piza 2001; Toledo 2006; Ercilia 1990).

This biographical sketch demonstrates that the writer occupies a unique subject position, one that he can subsequently manipulate through emphasis or minimization. Depending on the perspective, Hatoum can be seen as Western, as Brazilian or Amazonian (if one wanted to emphasize the two as distinct), as an Easterner born in Brazil, or as a cosmopolitan citizen who has lived (and continues to live) in large metropolises. However, there is no reason to prioritize any one of these positions over the others. It is more likely that he has incorporated all of these influences to some degree, and that he has filtered them as well.

In accordance with this perspective, Hatoum can be located simultaneously inside and outside of the Orient. He can thus be said to constitute both a Westerner and an Easterner gazing at the Orient.[8] This is a similar position to the one occupied by Edward Said himself. Born in Jerusalem, Said studied in English-language schools and eventually received his degree in the United States, where he became a professor at Columbia University and took up the Palestinian cause. The duality of this intellectual, who can neither be identified with the Western nor the Eastern world without losing a large part of the nuance that informs his critique, is present in his very name, as he laughingly observes:

> Thus it took me about fifty years to become accustomed to, or, more exactly, to feel less uncomfortable with, "Edward," a foolishly English name yoked forcibly to the unmistakably Arabic family name Said. True my mother told me that I had been named Edward after the Prince of Wales, who cut so fine a figure in 1935 . . . and Said was the name of various uncles and cousins. . . . For years, and depending on the exact circumstances, I would rush past "Edward" and emphasize "Said"; at other times I would do the reverse or connect these two to each other so quickly that neither would be clear. The one thing I could not tolerate . . . was the disbelieving, and hence undermining, reaction: Edward? Said? (Said 1999, 2–3)

Hatoum makes a similar statement as Said in a newspaper interview with José Castello. He says, "Duality has left its mark on me: two countries, two languages, two cultures, two religions" (Castello 1998, 4). In the same way that he can place himself at the limit of the Orient, he also has the option of positioning himself simultaneously inside and outside of the Amazon, as he was born and raised there but always as the son of a foreign father and first-generation mother. In this context, the supposed separation between the East and the West is rendered problematic, or at least questionable, since the author himself is constituted by encounters, shocks, and exchanges between different cultures. This suggests that the "Orient" only exists in relation to the "Occident," and is constructed as a result of its contact with it. The border is therefore a construction, one that is constantly susceptible to change. Or, as the author himself says, "Cultures circulate and wander as much as Ibn Battuta, an eternal perambulator and the greatest travel-writer of the Arab world" (Hatoum 1996, 5).

Hatoum's position is also similar to that of the narrators he creates, specifically the unnamed narrator of *Tale of a Certain Orient*, Nael from *The Brothers*, and Lavo from *Cinzas do Norte* (*Ashes from the Amazon*). These narrators can be said to be border characters—they are situated *between* one city and another, between the house and the street. They at once belong to the family and are outside of it. This is a favorable location from which to critique the limits of our knowledge, discourses, and practices, which are often uncritically accepted as natural. It also allows the author to explore the possibility of a narration that can verticalize language and make the novel reflexive.

The second biographical detail that it is important to mention is Hatoum's strong connection to Said's work. This Amazonian author is not just an avid reader of Said—he has also played an important role in spreading the Palestinian critic's work throughout Brazil. It was Hatoum who suggested that the publisher of his own books, Companhia das Letras, should translate and publish *Orientalism* as well. After the attacks of September 11, Hatoum publicly recommended the reading of this book, which he considers "fundamental to our understanding of what we are living through" (*Jornal do Brasil* 2001, 1). According to him, the work is highly relevant after the attacks and the subsequent racist backlash against Arabs and the Islamic world. Hatoum says, "We live in intertwined worlds. To separate them is to dominate them, as the Portuguese and Spanish did in the process of colonization. The lack of understanding of that which is different is the most direct path to intolerance and racism" (*Jornal do Brasil* 2001, 1).

More recently, Hatoum selected essays from Said's *Reflections on Exile and Other Essays* for publication and translated *Representations of the Intellectual* into Portuguese. He also published an essay on *Representations* in a posthumous tribute to Edward Said. In this essay, Hatoum expresses his admiration for Said, whose intellectual work he believes could not be separated from his activity as a staunch supporter of the Palestinian cause. When speaking of the influence that Theodor Adorno's *Minima Moralia* had on Said's work, Hatoum explores the concept of exile. For Hatoum, Said's condition as an exile "nurtured" his intellectual production, including his theory of Orientalism:

> The reiteration of doubt, the absence of an absolute truth, the instability of those who do not have a homeland or nationality, all of this Said considers to be the condition not just of the exile but also of all of us who can reflect on the question of exile and, to some degree, feel or assimilate the suffering, desperation, and the affliction of those who cannot return to their home and country. (Hatoum 2005, 32)

Hatoum is familiar not only with Said's work, but also with the Orientalist texts that inform his arguments. In an article in the newspaper *O Estado de São Paulo,* Hatoum reveals that his own familiarity with Arab-Amazonian culture is the result of reading different texts about the two distinct worlds, including so-called Orientalist ones (Hatoum 1991). In this context, it is important to remember that while the author remains critical of any rigid demarcation between East and the West and of the essentialization of what are very heterogeneous worlds, he also cannot deny that the invention of this distinction played an active and fundamental role in his knowledge and being. This is reminiscent of the personal dimensions of Said's study, which he relates to his "having been constituted as, 'an Oriental'" (Said 1979, 26). Hatoum can thus perceive that the separation between the two is an artifice, and at the same time incorporate and be nurtured by the wonders and the differences that allow him to not only form new discourses and belief systems, but also to dissolve old limits of knowledge. He can thus be said to have assimilated what was of interest to him (and, of course, what was accessible to him), as if in a ritual of "literary cannibalism." In this respect, Hatoum writes:

> I appreciated certain European writers who ... wrote works that valued that "eccentric" culture, as opposed to a culture that supposes itself more complex and artificial since it is produced in the "center"—that is, Europe. In our pilgrimages to the Orient, we were often in search of another homeland, or an ideal place to dream and daydream, as people often search for the opposite of their home in foreign landscapes. For Gérard Nerval, Egypt is a country of mysteries and enigmas. ... At other moments these writers take up ethnographic projects, in which the personal glory at having made a geographic discovery is mixed with a sense of a service rendered to the homeland. The literary project can thus serve colonial expansion. ... In the face of such disparate texts, I was like a reader that takes part in a literary cannibalism, assimilating only that which gave me pleasure. However, I would like to note that Arabic literature was as important to me as orientalist texts were, and that my double interest can be explained mainly by my wonder at language, as in the stories of *1001 Nights* or Nerval's *Journey to the Orient.* (Hatoum 1991, 1)

A literary cannibal, Hatoum mixes and filters different images, references, and examples of Arab and Amazonian cultures. This creates a unique world in his first two novels, one around which the plots of the Lebanese-descendant families revolve. This universe, with all of its differences and particularities, attracts readers from other regions as well. The reader will inevitably identify with and be affected by the wonder as well as the horror that these images evoke. But as Hatoum makes clear in his work, the encounters and mutual influences that have been discussed here unfortunately do not necessarily lead to concrete realizations of equality or justice.

For despite the idyllic scenes in his novels, where Amazonian smells and spices intermingle with Arabic words and customs, Hatoum's Manaus is not the product of a peaceful process of miscegenation and assimilation, or of multicultural coexistence. Far from it: the city witnesses practices of violence and exclusion that often bear the traces of colonialism. The members of the Lebanese families around which Hatoum's novels center, for example, can use their comfortable social position to objectify their servants and exploit the Indian and *caboclo*.

In this way, although in *Relato* Emilie and Anastácia Socorro often embroider, sew, and reminisce about their distinct lands together, Anastácia—like all the other servants in the house—is never actually paid. On the other hand, Domingas and Zana's faith brings them closer together and leads Zana to confide in her servant in *The Brothers*. When Zana hears rumors from the neighbors about Indian girls being a bad influence on their children, she reminds herself that she and Domingas worship the same god. But this connection also has its limits. It does not, for example, lead Zana to treat Domingas's son with the same respect and care with which she expects her servant to treat her own children. The boy is not spared from the housework, and spends most of his time running errands around the neighborhood rather than doing his schoolwork.

In this way, Hatoum points to a fundamental characteristic of Orientalism in Latin America. Indeed, his novels demonstrate that in this region it is not necessarily the Arabs who are objectified by the dichotomous, authoritarian mental operation problematized by Said, but rather the Indian or *caboclo*. As Silvia Nagy-Zekmi explains, "Normally, in Latin America, it is not the Orient that is represented or essentialized, but the Indian, the woman, or simply, 'the latino' in relation to the European or North American" (2008, 14). In this Latin American Orientalism, the Indian is often constructed as a member of an exotic, timeless society that is linked to notions of primitivism, cannibalism, and sexual deviancy (cf. Barrueto 2008).

It is in this context that Emilie's tirade against the poor *caboclas* of the city, many of whom are pregnant with their employers' children, should be understood: "They're just a bunch of hussies that'll go off into the woods with anyone who comes along and then come here begging milk and spare change" (Hatoum 2004, 103–104). Emilie's esentialization and homogenization of the *caboclas* stands in contrast to the portrayal of Domingas in *The Brothers*. For in Domingas's case, the Indian woman cannot be understood as a timeless "product" of nature, as articulated by Barrueto's explanation of Orientalism. Instead, she is marked by a specific history of violence and transformations. Taken by force from her people after becoming an orphan, Domingas is cloistered in an orphanage in Manaus for two years. After a period of "education" and "domestication," she is "offered" to Zana and Halim by a nun.

Hatoum's construction of a "certain Orient" thus reveals the always already hybrid dimension of cultures, as well as the political act of domination that is inherent in homogenization and essentialization. But it also criticizes popular theories and images through which Brazilians imagine their country to be tolerant and devoid of racial conflict. If the meetings and exchanges among Brazil's diverse cultures, religions, and social practices require a minimum tolerance in relation to difference, such tolerance, as in Hatoum's novels, does not necessarily translate onto the social plane. Instead, it participates in negotiations, conflicts, and temporary accords that are constituted by different, unstable power relations. It is precisely because his first two novels depict vigorous intermingling and cultural miscegenation in which there is also brutal inequality and social injustice that Hatoum's critique escapes Manichean ingenuity.

**Notes**

Portions of this chapter were published in an earlier version in Portuguese as "Canibalismo literário: exotismo e orientalismo sob a ótica de Milton Hatoum," in *ALEA* 10(2): 243–255.

1. This is the voice of Emilie's husband, who remains unnamed. He and his wife raised the narrator and her brother. It should be noted that the excerpt appears in quotation marks in the novel, a common occurrence that will be indicated throughout this chapter with the use of both double and single quotation marks.

2. The recreation of this "certain Orient" stands in contrast to the images disseminated by the Western media (Said 1997), including in Brazil (Montenegro 2002; Castro 2007), where essentialized visions of Islam and its connections to fundamentalism, terrorism, and violence persist.

3. All excerpts from *Dois Irmãos* are taken from John Gleason's 2002 translation.

4. The presence of Arabic loanwords in the Portuguese and Spanish languages constitutes an important part of the legacy of Muslim Spain and the *reconquista*. These two historical moments are central to the production, interpretation, and /or distinctions among the definitions of the Orient and Hispanic and Latin American Orientalism. (For more on these Orientalisms, see, for example, Taboada 2008; Kushigian 1991; Civantos 2006).

5. Translator's note: *azáfama*: bustle; *alpercata*: sandal; *alforje*: saddlebag or wallet; *sufi*: Sufi; *açucena*: lily; *curica*: orange-winged parrot; *tucum*: palm tree native to the Amazon; *caboclo*: person of mixed Brazilian Indian and European origin; *cunhatã*: native girl; *chichuta*: hemlock; *curumim*: native boy, *maracajá*: margay; *esfiha*: Middle Eastern pastry (Arabic: *sfiha); tâmara*: date; *tabule*: tabbouleh; *cupuaçu*: a tropical fruit native to the Amazon.

6. A careful study of Hatoum's lexical choices in the two novels would be necessary to investigate the diverse origins of his words, including foreign words and proper names. Such a study falls outside the scope of this chapter. The vocabulary is mentioned here only as an indication of the richness and hybridity of the author's language.

7. Translator's note: All unattributed translations are my own.

8. It is important to note that these are both *options* for him, as he can always choose one particular identity and close himself off to all others. While it seems like this is the choice that he makes and defends publicly, it is nevertheless a choice that is undoubtedly more present in his life than in the lives of those who have always remained in the same place as their ancestors.

## References

Barrueto, Jorge J. 2008. "El indio en las tarjetas postales." *Moros en la costa,* ed. Silvia Nagy-Zekmi. Madrid: Iberoamericana.

Castello, José. 1998. "Milton Hatoum reclama a volta da indignação." *O Estado de São Paulo, Caderno 2.* São Paulo. November 14.

Castro, Isabelle Christine Somma de. 2007. *Orientalismo na imprensa brasileira.* Master's thesis, Arabic Language and Literature, School of Philosophy, Letters and Human Sciences, Universidade de São Paulo, São Paulo.

Civantos, Christina. 2006. *Between Argentines and Arabs.* Albany: State University of New York Press.

Clifford, James. 1988. "On Orientalism." *The Predicament of Culture.* Cambridge, MA: Harvard University Press.

DW-World. 2004. "O arquiteto da memória." Interview with Milton Hatoum by Soraia Vilela. October 11. http://www.dw-world.de/dw/article/0,2144,1355392,00.html. Accessed May 11, 2007.

Ercilia, Maria. 1990. "Milton Hatoum em entrevista." *Folha de São Paulo.* November 25.

Hatoum, Milton. 1989. *Relato de um certo oriente.* São Paulo: Companhia das Letras.

———. 1991. "Mil e uma noites em busca de um estilo." *O Estado de São Paulo, Cultura.* São Paulo. October 19.

———. 1996. "Diálogo entre mundos." *Folha de São Paulo, Caderno Mais!* São Paulo. March 10.

———. 2000. *Dois Irmãos.* São Paulo: Companhia das Letras.

———. 2001. "A bilbiografia básica da crise." *Jornal do Brasil, Suplemento Idéias.* January 22.

———. 2002. *The Brothers.* Trans. John Gledson. New York: Farrar, Straus and Giroux.

———. 2004. *Tale of a Certain Orient.* Trans. Ellen Watson. London: Bloomsbury.

———. 2005. "Edward Said e os intelectuais." In *Edward Said: Trabalho intellectual e crítica social,* ed. Arlene Clemesha. São Paulo: Editora Casa Amarela.

———. 2006. "Amazonas—Capital Manaus." In *Crônica de duas cidades,* ed. Benedito Nunes. Belém, Brazil: Secult.

Kushigian, Julia A. 1991. *Orientalism in the Hispanic Literary Tradition.* Albuquerque: University of New Mexico Press.

Montenegro, Silvia M. 2002. "Discursos e contradiscursos: o olhar da mídia sobre o Islã no Brasil." *Mana* 8(1).

Nagy-Zekmi, Silvia. 2008. "Buscando el Este en el Oeste: Prácticas orientalistas en la literatura latinoamericana." In *Moros en la costa,* ed. Silvia Nagy-Zekmi. Madrid: Iberoamericana.

Piza, Daniel. 2001. *"Relato de um certo Oriente." O Estado de São Paulo, Caderno 2.* São Paulo. March 26.

Said, Edward. 1979. *Orientalism.* New York: Random House.

———. 1990. *Orientalismo: O oriente como invenção do ocidente.* Trans. Tomas Rosa Bueno. São Paulo: Companhia das Letras.

———. 1994. *Representations of the Intellectual.* New York: Vintage.

———. 1997. *Covering Islam.* New York: Vintage.

———. 1999. *Out of Place: A Memoir.* New York: Alfred A. Knopf.

———. 2000. *Reflections on Exile and Other Essays.* Cambridge, MA: Harvard University Press.

———. 2003. *Reflexões sobre o exílio e outros ensaios.* Trans. Pedro Maia Soares. São Paulo: Companhia das Letras.

———. 2004. *Fora do lugar.* Trans. José Geraldo Couto. São Paulo: Companhia das Letras.

———. 2005. *Representações do intelectual: as Conferências Reith de 1993.* Trans. Milton Hatoum. São Paulo: Companhia das Letras.

Taboada, Hernán G. H. 2008. "La sombra del Oriente en la independencia americana." In *Moros en la costa,* ed. Silvia Nagy-Zekmi. Madrid: Iberoamericana.

Toledo, Marleine Paula Marcondes e Ferreira de. 2006. *Milton Hatoum: itinerário para um certo relato.* São Paulo: Ateliê Editorial.

# 17

## Arab-Brazilian Literature
### Alberto Mussa's *Mu'allaqa* and South-South Dialogue

*Waïl S. Hassan*

Hassan discusses ways in which Alberto Mussa's work has been instrumental in disseminating Arabic literature in Brazil. He also suggests that Mussa's work offers a paradigm of world literature based on South-South dialogue that does not revolve around western European or U.S. literary canons. Instead, his work contributes directly to an emerging network of relations among the cultures of the Global South that is certain to leave its mark on the twenty-first century.

~

While the last two decades have been marked by the geopolitical dominance of the United States in the aftermath of the Soviet Union's demise—dominance that was manifested militarily in the two Iraq wars, the first of which ("Operation Desert Storm" to liberate Kuwait from Saddam Hussein in 1991) spurred the rise of the postmodern phenomenon of the global terror network embodied in al-Qaeda, whose actions set the stage for the United States' second major military adventure in the Arab world in little over a decade, the 2003 invasion and occupation of Iraq. The ideological corollary of both U.S. interventionism and its militant antagonist has been Samuel Huntington's thesis on the "clash of civilizations." But there are, of course, alternatives to both models—peaceful efforts to challenge U.S. hegemony which reject Huntington's exclusionary logic. Some of those efforts have revived the idea of South-South dialogue, which reemerged several times over the past century as a way for countries of the Global South to resist imperial dominance. For example, the idea of South-South dialogue was central to the pan-Africanism of the early twentieth century, the Non-Aligned Movement that emerged in the 1950s, and most recently the Summit of South America–Arab States (ASPA) inaugurated by former Brazilian president Luiz Inácio Lula da Silva in 2005 and reconvened several times since, which aimed at intensifying diplomatic, economic, and cultural cooperation between countries of the two regions.[1]

The idea of South-South dialogue has also been the subtext of academic debates over the status of postcolonial studies in the English-speaking world, especially the charge that privileging colonial history and its vertical relations between colonizer and colonized contributes covertly to reinforcing Eurocentric historiography and theory (Ahmad 1995, 6–7). Some current articulations of world literature, such as Pascale Casanova's notion of a "world republic of letters" governed from Paris, unabashedly embody that Eurocentric logic, which an alternative paradigm of world literature based on South-South literary relations would challenge. Arab–Latin American literary relations represent a particularly rich site for that kind of exploration. In this chapter, I want briefly to outline those relations before focusing on the emblematic case of one writer, Brazilian novelist Alberto Mussa, whose work is especially pertinent in this context.

While the recent diplomatic initiative supporting Latin American–Arab cooperation has been introduced under specific geopolitical conditions, it has deep cultural roots that reach back to the eight centuries of Muslim rule in Iberia, a period that indelibly marked Spanish and Portuguese cultures, which were introduced to the New World in the wake of Columbus's voyages. Latin American cultures today are, therefore, heirs to that Arab heritage, needless to say among many other influences. As Mexican writer Verónica Murguía writes in an essay, "My Unknown Forefathers," school textbooks in her country emphasize the importance of that heritage, which has left four thousand Arabic words in the Spanish language and made contributions to architecture, mathematics, and literature, among other fields (Murguía 2006, 159–160).

There are at least four kinds of relations between Arabic and Latin American literatures, none of which has yet received the attention it deserves from critics. First is the impact of *The Thousand and One Nights* on Latin American literatures. Jorge Luis Borges's interest in the *Nights* is well known; he wrote about the work and its translators, but more importantly perhaps its world is reflected in his own works and in the works of other major writers associated with magical realism, not least of whom is Gabriel García Márquez. This is a literary history that, as far as I know, remains to be written.

The second type of relation is the impact of North and South American literatures on modern Arabic literature, particularly poetry, via the work of the *mahjar*, or immigrant writers in the early twentieth century. The important role that those poets played in the history of modern Arabic poetry is well known, but what is neglected is the role of the immigrant experience and of the specific social and cultural contexts of immigrant destinations on the formation of their poetic projects.[2] This is a difficult task because the Arabic-language work of the *mahjar* group rarely ever alludes to its American context, which is nonetheless formative.

Third, the writings of Arab immigrants and their descendants in the languages of the Americas—English, French, Portuguese, and Spanish—remains a vast and fertile field for comparative study, both within the emerging field of American hemispheric studies and also within Arabic literature. There are now several studies of U.S. Arab-American and Arab-Canadian literatures, which are gradually gaining visibility, but very little has been done on its Latin American counterparts.[3] Yet the work of writers of Arab descent in Latin America is abundant and well received within its national contexts: for instance, a recent issue of the *Hostos Review* (2010) includes nearly forty Arab-Hispanic writers, to whom we can add the names of Brazilians Gilberto Abrão, Milton Hatoum, Salim Miguel, George Medauar, Alberto Mussa, Raduan Nassar, Carlos Nejar, and Waly Salomão, among others.

Fourth, there are prominent Latin American writers with no Arab ancestry who have taken interest either in Arab culture or in Arab immigrants or both, and who can, therefore, be studied in this context. I have already mentioned Borges, García Márquez, and Murguía, to whom we can add the names of Jorge Amado, Ana Miranda, Malba Tahan (Júlio César de Mello e Souza), Angela Dutra de Menezes, and Alberto Ruy-Sánchez.[4]

Those four types of literary relations between the Arab world and Latin America represent a fertile field for the comparative study of South-South literary relations that would move us beyond Eurocentric conceptions of world literature by uncovering networks of literary relations in which Europe and North America play a secondary role. In fact, the critique of Eurocentrism has already taken root in some theoretical orientations in Europe and North America, such as in Jacques Derrida's deconstruction and in postcolonial studies, which was inaugurated by Edward Said's *Orientalism* (1978), both of which have had a tremendous impact on literary studies in the English-speaking world for the past three decades. Yet if postcolonial studies unintentionally solidified the centrality of Europe by focusing on the colonizer-colonized dialectic, a direct dialogue between the cultures of the Global South would decentralize Europe and strengthen historic cultural relations that have not yet received the attention they deserve.

## Mirrors of Identity in Alberto Mussa

Given the scope of the topic in its four dimensions just outlined, I will focus here on the work of one writer, Alberto Mussa, whose work belongs to the third category of relations mentioned above, namely the writings of the descendants of Arab immigrants in Latin America. This novelist and researcher was born in Rio de Janeiro in 1961 and has published two Africa-inspired works, *Elegbara* (1997), a short-story collection revolving around the West African deity of the same name, and *O trono da rainha Jinga* (1999), a historical novel about slavery in seventeenth-century Rio de Janeiro. These were followed by two works about pre-Islamic Arabic literature, the novel *O enigma de Qaf* (2004) and *Os poemas suspensas* (2006b), a Portuguese translation of the famous odes from that period. Next, he published a novel about triangular relationships under the title *O movimento pendular* (2006a), which reveals his interest in ancient civilizations, from Egypt to Mesopotamia, Greece, and others; an anthropological work about Brazil's original inhabitants, *Meu destino é ser onça* (2009); a history of samba, *Samba de enredo: História e arte* (2010, with Luiz Antonio Simas); and most recently a detective novel set in the early twentieth century, *O senhor do lado esquerdo* (2011).

What becomes immediately apparent from this brief account of Alberto Mussa's publications is his deep interest in the often-overlooked tributaries that combined with those of Portugal and the rest of Europe into the making of contemporary Brazilian culture. African influences on Brazilian speech, religion, folklore, art, food, and music, among other aspects of culture, are powerful and well known, but less so are those of the Tupi and the Arabs, which nonetheless have special resonance for Mussa because his ancestors include members of both ethnicities. It is not surprising, therefore, that most of his works so far have revolved around those three cultures.

In "Who Is Facing the Mirror?," Mussa relates the story of his excavation of his Arab roots, which he traces through his paternal grandfather to Lebanon. The article focuses on what he describes as the contradictory reflections of his Arab heritage in contemporary Brazil, which turned his identity into a riddle that he struggled to solve early in life. He writes:

> Since my early adolescence, when I learned that I was an Arab descendant on the paternal line, I have been trying to understand what that exactly meant, what was the character of the substance that made it different from my Brazilian portion I inherited from my mother. For it was easy to understand a certain singularity in the Arabic style of being because people who learned I was a grandchild of Arabs hoped to see something of that style in me. (Mussa 2006c, 189)

Arab identity in Brazil, then, is tied to a certain social conception of Arabness that is supposed to be discernible in certain characteristics or behaviors that are believed to be hereditary. In that sense, Mussa's preoccupation with identity was a reaction to that social conception that was manifested in the way others related to him. He adds that he began to search for his identity in "three mirrors . . . : the image the Brazilians made of the Arabs, the image my family made of itself, and the image emerging from books" (Mussa 2006c, 189).

The first of those images began to be formed with the arrival of large numbers of Syrian immigrants to Brazil in the late nineteenth century. Since those immigrants carried Ottoman passports, they were mistaken for Turks and Muslims. This misconception resulted from confusing nationality, which is a bureaucratic matter connected with the geopolitical situation in the immigrants' country of origin, and Arab identity, which is a function of language and culture (an Arab being, by definition, a speaker of Arabic). Whereas this distinction was obvious to both Arabs and Turks, it was not so in Brazil or in the other countries of the Americas that received large numbers of Arab immigrants at that time. In all of those countries, they were misidentified as Turks (in North America) and *turcos* (in Latin America). And since Turks were Muslims, those immigrants must also be of that faith. This was highly ironic, for the majority of Syrian immigrants were Christians fleeing from, among other factors, religious and sectarian strife often blamed on Ottoman authorities.

The work of many Arab immigrants in trade gave rise to another image, that of the *mascate*, or pack peddler, and the stingy merchant who has no pity for the poor. This stereotype did not fit Mussa's grandfather, who was a learned poet with a house full of books, neither did it fit the author's great-grandfather, who had founded a school in Lebanon and was reported to have possessed the largest private library there, according to the image reflected in the mirror of family. The grandfather taught young Alberto to identify the traces of Arab civilization in many aspects of Brazilian life, including Arabic words used in Portuguese. Yet even though the grandfather spoke at length of the beauty of the Arabic language, he did not try to teach it to his grandson and encouraged him instead to master Portuguese as a fundamental component of his Brazilian identity. In commenting on this attitude, which was shared by many immigrants, Alberto Mussa refers to the relatively large number of prominent Portuguese linguists of Arab descent in Brazil, such as Said Ali, Evanildo Bechara, and Antônio Houaiss, who all seem to have heeded his grandfather's advice. Yet precisely because of this advice, and despite his grandfather's great pride in Arab civilization, Alberto Mussa did not feel himself to be Arab since he did not speak Arabic, and as a result, he could not identify with the image of Arabness reflected in the mirror of family.[5]

As for the third mirror, that of books, it had, in turn, three dimensions. First is the stereotype of the *turco* merchant, which appears in Brazilian literature. Second, there is the image of Arabs that appears in *The Thousand and One Nights* and in the novels of Malba Tahan, who admired the accomplishments of Arab civilization in the fields of mathematics and algebra, and evoked them in popular novels such as *O homem que calculava* (1949) and *Salim o mágico* (1970). Yet this world, too, remained alien to the young Alberto Mussa, and he was unable to identify with it. It was in another kind of book that he could finally see himself: works written by Brazilian writers of Arab descent, such as Raduan Nassar's *Lavoura arcaica* (1975), Milton Hatoum's *Relato de um certo Oriente* (1989) and *Dois irmãos* (2000), and Salim Miguel's *Nur na escuridão* (2004), along with the work of other novelists with no Arab ancestry who have written about Syrian immigrants, such as Ana Miranda's *Amrik* (1997) and Angela Dutra de Menezes's *Mil anos menos cinquenta* (1995). Depicting the experience of immigrants and their descendants, these works reflected to him a familiar image of himself.

Yet as a writer, Alberto Mussa does not belong to this group per se; he represents yet another dimension. For while Miguel, Nassar, and Hatoum wrote about the experiences of their immigrant parents and about the generational and cultural gap separating immigrants from their Brazilian-born children (something that Nassar vividly depicts in an allegory of incest and Oedipal conflict), Mussa belongs to the third generation of the Arab-Brazilian community, the generation of the immigrants' grandchildren, and he exemplifies the maxim that the grandson tries to remember what the son wants to forget—that is, while the second generation struggles to liberate itself from the grip of its immigrant parents, who in many cases try to impose their alien customs on children born into a different society into which they want to blend, grandchildren, by contrast, try to rediscover the past and to reconnect themselves with the cultural heritage of their grandparents. It is as though the temporal distance between the first and third generations makes the cultural roots of the immigrants seem like riddles that grandchildren try to solve, whereas in the eyes of the second generation such roots seemed more like shackles to be broken.

This idea is embodied in Alberto Mussa's two Arabic-inspired works, the novel *O enigma de Qaf* and his translation of the *mu'allaqat*, the masterpieces of pre-Islamic Arabic poetry. He describes his discovery of the *mu'allaqat* during a trip to Lebanon in his mid-thirties as the most important literary event in his life. The journey itself is symbolically charged, for he traveled to Lebanon a long time after the death of his grandfather, looking for relatives he had never met before, and the search for family history in a sense led him to the discovery of the fountainhead of Arabic literature. When he read the pre-Islamic poems in their English translation, then in French and Spanish renditions, Mussa found a world with which he could identify:

> Eroticism, generosity, eloquence, nobleness, dauntlessness, pride, loyalty, abdication, wisdom, the love of pleasure, disregard for riches—all this imbedded in the most beautiful poetic language—made me see in those heroes the model of man into which I projected my identity. (Mussa 2006c, 195)

At that point, he decided to learn Arabic so as to read the poems in their original language and to devour, as he puts it, all the books he could find on pre-Islamic Arabia. Thus after fifteen years of studying Brazilian history and the languages and mythologies of Native Brazilians and West Africans, Mussa now turned to the Arabic language and to Arab history, writing a novel on pre-Islamic Arabia and eventually translating the *mu'allaqat* into Portuguese.

*O enigma de Qaf* and *Os poemas suspensos* are, therefore, companion texts that, as I argue here, are about Arabia and Brazil at the same time, about the author's favorite poets and also about the novelist-translator himself. The two texts bring alive the mythology, poetry, and culture of fifth century Arabia on the Brazilian literary scene. While the translation recreates the poems themselves, the novel amplifies the effect by presenting a fictional eighth pre-Islamic poet, added to the seven canonical greats, in a meandering quest narrative that, as the title implies, unlocks a mystery that comes to represent the author-translator's identity, which is tied in Brazilian imagination to the mystique of the East. That mystique remains somewhat pervasive in Brazilian culture today, with echoes of it resonating in popular culture (from music to *carnaval* and *telenovelas,* for example), albeit in a form of Orientalism that is non-politicized when compared to the European or North American varieties analyzed by Edward Said. Indeed, this Brazilian Orientalism, especially as elaborated in Mussa's translation and fiction, is imbued with a nostalgia that spurs his excavation of his own family's cultural roots and the hybrid mix of influences that make up modern Brazil. It is, I argue, a non-hegemonic exoticism that is not invested with the kinds of economic and geopolitical interests that have fueled British, French, and U.S. American interventions in the Middle East since the late eighteenth century.

## The Enigma of Roots

Mussa's novel is divided into fifty-five chapters that fall into three categories: twenty-eight main chapters whose titles are the letters of the Arabic alphabet, interlaced with twenty-seven chapters that, in turn, are divided into two kinds: *excursos* (excursions) and *parâmetros* (parameters). The *excursos* relate anecdotes culled from the history of pre-Islamic Arabia and present different aspects of its life, culture, language, mythology, and worldview, while the *parâmetros* contain thirteen biographies of prominent poets from the period, including, of course, the authors of the famous odes. Neither the *excursos* nor the *parâmetros* form part of the plot of the novel, but their purpose is to paint a lively picture of the Arabic cultural milieu during the two centuries before Islam, that is, the milieu within which the novel's plot unfolds in the twenty-eight main chapters. In fact, the author announces in the preface that the reader who wishes to be entertained with an adventure story can read only the twenty-eight main chapters in sequence; readers who also wish to learn something about pre-Islamic Arab culture can read the main chapters along with the *parâmetros* in any order; as for those who wish to try solving the riddle of Qaf on their own before reaching the end of the novel, they should also read the *excursos* and the epigraphs that follow each letter of the Arabic alphabet (Mussa 2004, 10).

With this unique structure, Mussa presents his novel as a love letter to the language of his ancestors, which he learned later in life, and as an attempt to approximate what to him is the lost culture of his grandfather. The enigma of the title is, therefore, a metaphor for that personal-historical quest to understand his roots via the medium of an alien language, written in an enigmatic script. As Antônio Torres states on the back cover of the novel, "O enigma é o próprio árabe: sua origem, suas tradições, seu nomadismo, seus haréns, seus algarismos, sua escrita e as múltiplas versões de uma história que por vezes soam improváveis, o que as torna ainda mais encantadoras."[6] Torres also points to the Borgesian dimension of this novelistic universe, with its riddles, labyrinths, ancient books, and strange symbols, connected in the Orientalist imaginary to the mystique of the East, all of which is intimately related to the influence of *The Thousand and One Nights* on Borges and other Latin American writers, especially those associated with magical realism. Mussa's novel, therefore, evidences the convergence of direct influences from pre-Islamic Arabic poetry and from contemporary Latin American fiction, which itself is influenced by Arabic literature. In fact, Mussa's novel closes the circle of literary influences between the Arab world and Latin America, since by focusing on the pre-Islamic period, which has rarely been the subject of a novel, he fills a lacuna in Arabic historical fiction. This ambition is replicated (and ironized) within the novel itself, which features a narrator who claims to have discovered a lost *muʿallaqa* and who hopes by that discovery to add to the canon of pre-Islamic poetry.

The narrator is a Brazilian researcher and, like Mussa, the grandson of a Lebanese immigrant. The narrator is obsessed with a strange notion, namely that an obscure Arabic poem from which his grandfather used to recite parts in Portuguese translation is, in fact, a lost *muʿallaqa* that has been omitted from the canonical compilations of pre-Islamic poetry. The poet is called al-Ghattash and belongs to the ancient tribe of Labuʾa, from which the narrator's grandfather claims descent. After the latter's death, the narrator grows up to study the Arabic language and pre-Islamic poetry, in the hopes of one day proving his theory, which becomes the subject of a postgraduate thesis that he is writing. He travels to Cairo and Beirut to discuss his findings with the authorities in the field, but those scholars reject his theory, since the poem in question, called "Qafiyyat al-Qaf" (meaning the poem whose end rhyme is the Arabic letter *qaf* and whose subject is the mythic mountain also known as Qaf), was never mentioned in any of the ancient anthologies and commentaries. Moreover, they demand that the narrator reveal his sources, forcing him to admit that he has none, save the memory of his grandfather Najib: "A essência do poema aprendi com meu avô. O resto, as lacunas que a memória do velho Najib não reteve, recuperei de lendas colhidas em minhas peregrinações pelo Oriente Médio, e de toda sorte de dados históricos dispersos que fui capaz de compilar" (Mussa 2004, 13).[7] He also explains that "aquele texto era uma reconstituação do original—tão inverídico quanto possa ser um quadro, uma escultura, um monumento recuperado pelas mãos de um restaurador" (Mussa 2004, 12–13).[8]

Predictably, the poem was deemed a forgery and denied publication, and a prominent literary historian publicly denounced the narrator as the biggest forger in the history of Semitic studies. No one concedes the validity of the narrator's claim that he did no more than restore the original poem. Yet while clearly invalid from a literary-historical standpoint, his claim is true, as far as he is concerned, insofar as the poem is true to the pre-Islamic episteme and the conventions of its poetry, as he understands them. On this view, literary truth is to be distinguished from historical truth—an old philosophical question that led Plato to charge poets with lying. The narrator alludes to that problem when he uses as an epigraph to the first chapter an apocryphal statement that he attributes to Shahrazad: "Quando conto uma mentira, não estarei restaurando ume verdade mais antiga?" (Mussa 2004, 11).[9] For him, the difference between truth and lying is anything but clear, truth being always mixed with falsehood, and vice versa. Consequently, whereas the outward form of "Qafiyyat al-Qaf" may be fabricated, its essence is true, exactly as is the case with restored monuments and artworks.

The absurdity of the narrator's project lies in his claim not only that his poem is pre-Islamic (a claim in which he mimics notorious forgers of pre-Islamic poetry like Hammad al-Rawi and Khalaf al-Ahmar), but that it is one of the great suspended odes, and that it was lost for fourteenth centuries until he discovered it in Brazil! It is literally a quixotic conviction, imbued with the madness and hallucination of a reader completely infatuated with a defunct age of romance, like the hero of Cervantes's novel. And like Don Quixote, the narrator's knowledge of his favorite genre is nothing less than encyclopedic:

> Foi o desejo de recuperar os fragmentos perdidos e dar forma escrita à *Qafiya* que me impulsionou a aprender o árabe clássico, o hebraico, o conjunto dos dialetos siríacos, até o extinto idioma epigráfico do Iêmen. Também me detive sobre a arqueologia do Oriente Médio; me debrucei sobre a geografia dos desertos da Síria e da Arábia; estudei a etnologia beduína; e praticamente guardei de cor a poesia pré-islâmica.
>
> Mas só quando me dediquei à ciência das estrelas, na forma primitiva em que surgiu entre os caldeus, pude recompor o poema original e chegar à solução do enigma de Qaf. (Mussa 2004, 21–22)[10]

As for that enigma or riddle, it involves obscure references in the poem to a mythic mountain called Qaf, a cross-eyed and half-blind jinni who travels through time, and al-Ghattash's love for Layla, whose tribe he must follow with the help of a lame old priestess who leads him to an ancient engraving that he must decipher in order to reach his destination. It is a Borgesian quest narrative that ends with the decipherment of obscure symbols belonging to a bygone age. Solving the riddle, then, means not only recovering the past, but securing his own Arabness, which is compromised by the fact of his not being a native speaker of Arabic. If he lacks what is considered the fundamental attribute of an Arab, he can more than make up for it by "restoring" (more appropriately, inventing) another lack in the canon of poetry that represents the fountainhead of that same language. Identity construction always involves an act of invention—in this case, inventing a lack in order to remedy it. In other words, by "restoring" the poem, the narrator proves himself worthy of his lineage to the mythic poet of his grandfather's tribe, and he further does so

in the manner of ancient forgers of pre-Islamic poetry who, in the early ages
of Islam, sought to gain glory for their tribes by attributing great poems to
them (Hussein [1927] 1989, 116–132; Dayf [1960] 1996, 164–175).

Since the "restored" poem has been rejected as a fabrication, it turns into a
novel, and the narrator likewise turns from poet to novelist. The subject matter
of the poem then becomes a double story: that of al-Ghattash and that of the
narrator. The riddle of Qaf, likewise, becomes two riddles: the original one
solved by al-Ghattash and that of al-Ghattash solved by the narrator. Finally,
al-Ghattash's love story becomes the occasion for recounting the story of the
narrator's love for the Arabic language. In that sense, "restoration" becomes a
creative act in its own right that, rather than returning the poem to its original,
irretrievable form, *translates* it formally, temporally, and linguistically: from
poem to novel, from the Arab past to the Brazilian present, and from Arabic
into Portuguese. The poem-turned-novel is thus a double book with two protagonists, two stories, two settings, and two cultures at one and the same time.

This doubleness bespeaks the Arab-Brazilian narrator's strong desire to connect with the Arab world, but it is a desire marked by anxiety at the possibility
of reestablishing that broken link, and fear of rejection, just as his attempt to
insert himself into the history of Arabic literature was met with rejection.
That quixotic attempt is defined by the madness of love, for his sought-after
Layla, who beckons to him and eludes him at the same time, is impossible to
reach. The impossibility of inserting himself in the Arab past leads him to
accept his place in the Brazilian present as a link between two cultures and
two histories—that is, as a translator who illuminates a forgotten aspect of the
syncretism that defines Brazilian culture.

Mussa's work has important implications not only for Brazilian literary
studies, but also for Arabic literature and for those concerned with the idea
of world literature. First, while it obviously contributes to the dissemination
of Arabic literature in Brazil, the novel also sheds a bright light on Arabic
literature for its Arab readers, for not only do we have here a rare historical
novel set in pre-Islamic Arabia, a period by and large ignored by Arab novelists, but that novel itself offers a fascinating introduction to the study of pre-
Islamic poetry, recreating and illuminating a culture that is often ignored in
discussions of that poetry. Secondly, Mussa's work offers a paradigm of world
literature based on South-South dialogue that does not concede the centrality
of western European or U.S. literary canons and articulations of global relations. Instead, his work contributes directly to an emerging network of relations among the cultures of the Global South that is certain to leave its mark
on the twenty-first century.

## Notes

A partial, earlier version of this chapter was first written in Arabic and published in *Alif: Journal of Comparative Poetics* 31 (2011): 215–229. It was translated into English by the author.

1. See the Summit website: http://www.itamaraty.gov.br/temas/mecanismos-inter
-regionais/cupula-america-do-sul-paises-arabes-aspa.

2. On the role of *mahjar* writers on modern Arabic literature, see Badawi 1993 and Jayyusi 1977.

3. On Arab-American literature, see Hassan 2011 and Salaita 2007; on Arab-Canadian literature, see Dahab 2010; on Arab-Argentine literature, see Civantos 2006.

4. In this connection, see my essay on Amado (2012).

5. In an interview with anthropologist Paulo Pinto, Mussa reports that his father experienced a great deal of harassment and discrimination when he was a child, during the 1930s and '40s, because of his Arab ancestry. As a result, he refused to speak the language of his immigrant parents or to allow them to teach it to their grandchild (Pinto 2010, 85).

6. "The enigma is the Arabic language itself: its origin, its traditions, its nomadism, its harems, its numerals, its script, and the multiple versions of a story that at times sound improbable, which makes them all the more enchanting." (This and subsequent translations from Portuguese are mine.)

7. "I learned the essence of the poem from my grandfather. The rest, those lacunas which old Najib's memory did not retain, was recuperated from legends that I collected during my peregrinations in the Middle East, and from all sorts of historical facts that I was able to compile."

8. "That text was reconstituted from the original, as inauthentic as any restored painting, sculpture, or monument."

9. "When I tell a lie, am I not [thereby] restoring an older truth?"

10. "The desire to recover the fragments and to give the *Qafiyya* a written form spurred me to learn classical Arabic, Hebrew, the various Syriac dialects, and even the dead epigraphic language of Yemen. I also lingered on the archaeology of the Middle East, pored over the geography of Syria and Arabia, studied Bedouin ethnology, and practically learned pre-Islamic poetry by heart. But it was not until I dedicated myself to the science of the stars, in the primitive form in which it appeared among the Chaldeans, that I was able to recompose the original poem and to find the solution to the enigma of Qaf."

## References

Ahmad, Aijaz. 1995. "The Politics of Literary Postcoloniality." *Race & Class* 36(3): 1–20.

Amin, Samir. 1988. *L'eurocentrisme: Critique d'une idéologie.* Paris: Anthropos.

Badawi, M. M. 1993. *A Short History of Modern Arabic Literature.* Oxford, UK: Clarendon Press.

Borges, Jorge Luis. 1974. "Los traductores de las *1001 Noches.*" In *Obras completas,* 397–413. Buenos Aires: Emecé Editores.

Casanova, Pascale. 1999. *La République mondiale des lettres*. Paris: Seuil.

Civantos, Christina. 2006. *Between Argentines and Arabs: Argentine Orientalism, Arab Immigrants, and the Writing of Identity*. Albany: State University of New York Press.

Dahab, Elizabeth. 2010. *Voices in Exile in Contemporary Canadian Francophone Literature*. Lanham, MD: Lexington Books.

Dayf, Shawqi. (1960) 1996. *Al-'asr al-jahili*. Cairo: Dar al-Ma'arif.

Ette, Ottmar, and Friederike Pannewick, eds. 2006. *Arab Americas: Literary Entanglements of the American Hemisphere and the Arab World*. Madrid: Iberoamericana; Frankfurt am Main: Verlag.

Hassan, Waïl S. 2011. *Immigrant Narratives: Orientalism and Cultural Translation in Arab American and Arab British Literature*. New York: Oxford University Press.

———. "Jorge Ahmad." 2012. Special issue on Jorge Amado. *Comparative Literature Studies* 49(3): 395–404.

Hatoum, Milton. 1989. *Relato de um certo Oriente*. São Paulo: Companhia das Letras, 1989.

———. 2000. *Dois irmãos*. São Paulo: Companhia das Letras.

Huntington, Samuel. 1996. *The Clash of Civilizations and the Remaking of World Order*. New York: Simon & Schuster.

Hussein, Taha. (1927) 1989. *Fi al-shi'r al-jahili*.Cairo: Dar al-Ma'arif.

Jayyusi, Salma Khadra. 1977. *Trends and Movements in Modern Arabic Poetry*. 2 vols. Leiden: Brill.

Menezes, Angela Dutra de. 1995. *Mil anos menos cinquenta*. Porto: Civilização Editora.

Miguel, Salim. 2004. *Nur na escuridão*. Rio de Janeiro: Topbooks.

Miranda, Ana. 1997. *Amrik*. São Paulo: Companhia das Letras.

Murguía, Verónica. 2006. "My Unknown Forefathers." *Arab Americas: Literary Entanglements of the American Hemisphere and the Arab World*, ed. Ottmar Ette and Friederike Pannewick, 159–163. Madrid: Iberoamericana; Frankfurt am Main: Verlag.

Mussa, Alberto. 1997. *Elegbara: Narrativas*. Rio de Janeiro: Editora Revan.

———. 1999. *O trono da rainha Jinga*. Rio de Janeiro: Editora Nova Fronteira.

———. 2004. *O enigma de Qaf*. Rio de Janeiro: Editora Record.

———. 2006a. *O movimento pendular*. Rio de Janeiro: Editora Record.

———, trans. 2006b. *Os poemas suspensos: Poésia árabe pré-islâmica*. Rio de Janeiro: Editora Record.

———. 2006c. "Who Is Facing the Mirror?" In *Arab Americas: Literary Entanglements of the American Hemisphere and the Arab World*, ed. Ottmar Ette and Friederike Pannewick, 189–196. Madrid: Iberoamericana; Frankfurt am Main: Verlag.

———. 2009. *Meu destino é ser onça*. Rio de Janeiro: Editora Record.

———. 2011. *O senhor do lado esquerdo*. Rio de Janeiro: Editora Record.

Mussa, Alberto, and Luiz Antonio Simas. 2010. *Samba de enredo: História e arte*. Rio de Janeiro: Editora Record.

Nassar, Raduan. 1975. *Lavoura arcaica*. São Paulo: Companhia das Letras.

Pinto, Paulo Gabriel Hilu da Rocha. 2010. *Árabes no Rio de Janeiro, uma identidade plural*. Rio de Janeiro: Cidade Viva.

Said, Edward. 1978. *Orientalism*. New York: Penguin.

Salaita, Steven. 2007. *Arab American Literary Fictions, Cultures, and Politics.* New York: Palgrave.

———. 2011. *Modern Arab-American Fiction: A Reader's Guide.* Syracuse, NY: Syracuse University Press.

Salum, Rose Mary, ed. 2010. "Almalafa y caligrafía: Literatura de origen árabe en América Latina." Special issue, *Hostos Review / Revista Hostosiana,* no. 7.

Tahan, Malba. 1949. *O homem que calculava.* Rio de Janeiro: Conquista.

———. 1970. *Salim o mágico: Romance oriental sírio-libanês.* São Paulo: Instituição Brasileira da Difusão Cultural.

# Contributors

Paul Amar, trained in the fields of political science, urban anthropology, sociology of globalization, and comparative literature, serves as Associate Professor of Global and International Studies at the University of California, Santa Barbara. He is author of *The Security Archipelago: Human-Security States, Sexuality Politics, and the End of Neoliberalism;* editor of *New Racial Missions of Policing: International Perspectives on Evolving Law-Enforcement Politics; Global South to the Rescue: Emerging Humanitarian Superpowers and Globalizing Rescue Industries; Dispatches from the Arab Spring* (with Vijay Prashad); and editor (with Diane Singerman) of *Cairo Cosmopolitan: Politics, Culture and Urban Space in the New Globalized Middle East.*

Daniela Birman is a research fellow at the Universidade Estadual de Campinas. She is the author of *Escrita e experiência do cárcere em Lima Barreto e Graciliano Ramos* and *Esaú e Jacó, Nael e Yaqub.*

José T. Cairus currently teaches in the Department of Spanish, Italian, and Portuguese at the University of Illinois at Urbana–Champaign. He is author of *Modernization, Nationalism and Elite: The Genesis of Brazilian Jiu-jitsu, 1905–1920.*

Neiva Vieira da Cunha is Adjunct Professor of Anthropology at the Universidade Estadual de Rio de Janeiro (UERJ) and a researcher for Laboratório de Etnografia Metropolitana (LeMetro) at the Universidade Federal de Rio de Janeiro (UFRJ). She is author of *Viagem, Experiência e Memória, Histórias de Favelas da Grande Tijuca,* and *História e Antropologia* (with Carlos Abrão Moura Valpassos).

Paulo Daniel Elias Farah is Professor of Arabic Literature at the Universidade de São Paulo and director of Biblioteca América do Sul–Países Árabes. His books include *Deleite do estrangeiro em tudo que é espantoso e maravilhoso: Estudo de um relato de viagem bagdali* and *Gramática da Língua Árabe para Estudantes Sul-Americanos.*

**Silvia C. Ferreira** is a PhD candidate in the Comparative Literature Program at the University of California, Santa Barbara. She is author of *Hybrid Translation: The Literature of Arab Migrations to Brazil*.

**Waïl S. Hassan** is Professor of Comparative Literature at the University of Illinois at Urbana–Champaign. He is the author of *Tayeb Salih: Ideology and the Craft of Fiction* and *Immigrant Narratives: Orientalism and Cultural Translation in Arab American and Arab British Literature;* co-editor (with Susan Muaddi Darraj) of *Approaches to Teaching the Works of Naguib Mahfouz;* and translator of Abdelfattah Kilito's *Thou Shalt Not Speak My Language* and Alberto Mussa's *O enigma de Qaf* (*Lughz al-qaf*).

**Alexandra Isfahani-Hammond** is Associate Professor of Comparative Literature and Luso-Brazilian Studies at the University of California, San Diego. She is the editor of *The Masters and the Slaves: Plantation Relations and Mestizaje in American Imaginaries* and author of *White Negritude: Race, Writing and Brazilian Cultural Identity*.

**John Tofik Karam** is Associate Professor of Latin American and Latino Studies at DePaul University. His book, *Another Arabesque: Syrian-Lebanese Ethnicity in Neoliberal Brazil*, won awards from the Arab American National Museum and the Brazilian Studies Association.

**Pedro Paulo Thiago de Mello** is a coordinator and researcher at the Laboratório de Etnografia Metropolitana at the Universidade Federal do Rio de Janiero.

**Silvia M. Montenegro** is a CONICET-affiliated researcher and Professor in the Department of Socio-Cultural Anthropology at the Universidade Nacional de Rosario. She is the author of *La Triple Frontera: Globalización y construcción social del espacio* (with Verónica Giménez Béliveau) and *Muçulmanos no Brasil: Comunidades, instituições e identidades* and editor of *A Tríplice Fronteira: Espaços nacionais e dinâmicas locais* (with Lorenzo Macagno and Verónica Giménez Béliveau).

**María del Mar Logroño Narbona** is Assistant Professor of Modern Middle Eastern History at Florida International University. She is editor (with Paulo Pinto and John Tofik Karam) of *Crescent of Another Horizon: Islam in Latin America, the Caribbean and Latino U.S.A.*

**Paulo Gabriel Hilu da Rocha Pinto** is Professor of Anthropology at the Universidade Federal Fluminense, Brazil, where he is also director of the Center for Middle East Studies. His publications include *Árabes no Rio de Janeiro: Uma Identidade Plural; Islã: Religião e Civilização*, and *Uma Abordagem Antropológica*.

**Fernando Rabossi** is Associate Professor of Cultural Anthropology at the Federal University of Rio de Janeiro. He is author of *En las calles de Ciudad del Este: Una etnografía del comercio de frontera*.

**Carlos Ribeiro Santana** is a Brazilian diplomat. A former Assistant Professor at Rio Branco Institute, he has been head of the trade office of the Brazilian embassies in Paraguay and Venezuela. His work has been published in the *Revista Brasileira de Política Internacional*. The opinions shared in this article express his personal point of view and do not reflect any official position of the Brazilian government.

**Ella Shohat** is Professor of Cultural Studies at New York University. She is author of *Memories, Diasporic Voices* and *Israeli Cinema: East/West and the Politics of Representation* and editor of *The Cultural Politics of the Middle East in the Americas* (with Evelyn Alsultany). She is co-author with Robert Stam of various publications including *Unthinking Eurocentrism: Multiculturalism and the Media; Multiculturalism, Postcoloniality and Transnational Media;* and *Race in Translation: Culture Wars around the Postcolonial Atlantic*.

**Monique Sochaczewski** teaches at the Escola Superior de Ciências Sociais e História at the Fundação Getúlio Vargas in Rio de Janeiro.

**Robert Stam** is Professor of Cinema Studies at New York University. His many publications include *François Truffaut and Friends: Modernism, Sexuality, and Film Adaptation* and *Literature through Film: Realism, Magic, and the Art of Adaptation*.

**Armando Vargas** is Assistant Professor of Arabic and Comparative Literature at Williams College. He is author of *Migration, Literature and the Nation: Mahjar Literature in Brazil*.

# Index

341

Bilac, Olavo, 303, 305
Bishara, As'ad, 204, 212n20
Bittencourt, Enio, 234, 236, 238
blackness, 171–174, 178n13
Blinder, Caio, 33
Boas, Franz, 125, 127, 128, 156n8, 169
Bonifácio, José, 186
Borelli, Silvia, 263–264
Borges, Jorge Luis, 323, 329
boycotts and oil supply, 60
Brasília Declaration, 5
Braspetro, 62, 65, 67
*Al-Brazil*, 204, 206
Brazil as psychologically female, in Freyre, 126
Brazil Mosque (Mesquita Brasil), 255n2
Brazilian Christian Church for the Arabs (Igreja Cristã Brasileira para os Árabes), 253, 256n11
Brazilian nationalism. *See* Arab identities and Brazilian nationalism
Brazil–Saudi Arabia Commission, 61
Breda dos Santos, Norma, 59
BRICS powers (Brazil, Russia, India, China, South Africa), 8, 28
Brito, José Maria de, 109n6
*Brothers, The (Dois Irmãos)* (Hatoum), 310, 312–313, 315–316, 318, 327
Browning, Barbara, 171
Burns, E. Bradford, 306n1
Bush, George W., 22–23
Butler, Judith, 300

*caboclos*, 318, 319n4
*caciquesme*, 276n3
Cameron, David, 30
Canclini, Nestor Garcia, 173
Cândido, Antônio, 299
"cannibalism," literary, 317
Cardoso, Fernando Henrique, 40, 88–89
Carneiro, Cecílio, 285–291, 293n7
Carneiro, Edison, 172
Carnival, 245, 255n5
Carpentier, Alejo, 171, 173, 178n10

*Casa-Grande e Senzala (The Masters and the Slaves)* (Freyre), 145, 125–128
Casanova, Pascale, 323
Castelo Branco, Humberto de Alencar, 63, 263–264
Castro, Araújo, 66
Catholicism: Jews and, 130, 135; Lugo and, 31; Malê revolt and, 184; Muslims and, 46–47, 147, 148; as official religion, 46, 149, 188; traditional African religions and, 151. *See also* Inquisition
Center for the Study and Dissemination of Islam, 267–268
Central Sudan, 184
Centro Cultural Árabe-Brasileira, 101, 105
Centro Cultural Beneficente Islâmico de Foz do Iguaçu, 101, 110n20
Centro Rinascenza Libano, 204
Cervantes, Miguel de, 331
Chaui, Marilena, 301, 306n3
Chimanovitch, Mario, 111n27
Chinese immigrants, 100, 232–234
Christianity: Carnival, avoidance of, 255n5; churches in Foz do Iguaçu, 253, 256n11; in Dutch Recife, 131; evangelical aim to convert Muslims, 253–254, 256n11; Freyre on, 129, 141–143; in Hatoum's fiction, 311–313; Levantine Christian immigrants, 30, 200–201, 241, 297, 326; Malê slaves and, 175–176; Maronite, 103, 107, 230, 313; Muslim Brotherhood compared to evangelicals, 4; Muslim influences on church architecture, 150–151; Orthodox, 230; repression of non-Catholic denominations, 188; ritual memory and, 129; Syria intervention and, 30; *turcos*, Christians mistaken as, 151, 326. *See also* Catholicism
Chui, Brazil, 97–98
*Cinza do Norte (Ashes from the Amazon)* (Hatoum), 315–316
Ciudad del Este, Paraguay. *See* Tri-Border Region (Argentina-Brazil-Paraguay)

history and geography of, 93–95; immigration numbers (1980s and 1990s), 102–103; in international media, 92–93; Itaipú Dam, 32, 107; Muslim identity in, 248–254; number of Muslims in,

*O trono da rainha Jinga* (Mussa), 325

"*turcos*": ambiguity and, 282; Brazilian hybridity and, 151; group formation and assimilation issues, 201; as imposed label, 201, 281–282, 326; numbers, 211n5; Orientalism and, 120, 154–155; peddler figure in Levantine-Brazilian literature, 280–285; Saara market district and, 230–232; as stigmatization, 242; Syrian and Lebanese immigrants in early twentieth century, 200–201

Turner, Victor, 256n10

*'umma* (community), 45

UN Commission on Human Rights resolution on LGBT rights, 22

UN General Assembly: Palestinian resolutions, 83–84; Rousseff's opening address to, 33; Zionism resolution, 66, 84–88

UN Human Rights Council Independent Commission of Inquiry on Syria, 30

UN Security Council, 26–29

United States: Brazil as rival to, 33; Brazilian nationalist discourse and, 242; civilizational history compared with Freyre, 176–177; comparison of Brazil to, 124; geopolitical dominance of, 322; Iran nuclear crisis and, 26–27; slave deportation to Africa and, 193–194; slavery and race relations compared to Brazil, 179n16

universalism, 64, 66, 68

University of Vega de Almeida (UVA), 267

248–249; stereotypes and transnational political engagements, 103–106; terrorist representations vs. other narratives, 92, 106–108; U.S. desire for military base in, 32

"unshadowing," 141

*Al-'Usbaal-Andalusiyya* (the Andalusian League), 209, 302–306

Valente, Mulio Gurgel, 61, 78

Velloso, Reis, 65

Vertovec, Steven, 211n3

Viana, Marcus, 152

Vianna, Hermano, 127, 178n4

*Viver a Vida* (telenovela), 153

Vizentini, Paulo, 58, 63, 66, 67

Wahhabism, 250

*Wall Street Journal,* 268

WAMY (World Assembly of Muslim Youth), 269–271

Waters, Mary, 298

weapons sales, 82

"whitening" of Arabs, 242

"Who Is Facing the Mirror" (Mussa), 325–327

witchcraft, 170–171

World Assembly of Muslim Youth (WAMY), 269–271

World Congress of Lebanese Emigrants, First, 217

World Islamic Call Society, 105

World War I, 204–205

Yom Kippur War, 59–60

Yoruba. *See* Malê revolt

Zelaya, Manuel, 31–32

Zionism and anti-Zionism, 66, 218, 223–225

www.ingramcontent.com/pod-product-compliance
Lightning Source LLC
Chambersburg PA
CBHW020334270326
41926CB00007B/171